"With world-class liturgical scholars offering creative, tradition-steeped essays on the ecological imaginaries made and possible in practices of worship, this is a milestone volume."

—Willis Jenkins
Professor of Religious Studies
University of Virginia

"Once again, the Institute of Sacred Music at Yale and Liturgical Press have provided us with a rich ecumenical collection of essays drawn from an important colloquium, this one about the manifold ways Christian liturgy locates us on our wounded planet and shapes our understanding of the cosmos. Many of the essays here will become classics, worthy of repeated reference—those on Daniel 3, on bread, on *Laudato Si'*, on environmental care in Eastern Orthodoxy, and on 'dust wisdom,' among many other examples. But the magisterial introduction by Teresa Berger, outlining the roots and the sweep of this urgent topic, is itself an important reason to read the book."

—Gordon W. Lathrop
Author of *Holy Ground: A Liturgical Cosmology*
Past-President, *Societas Liturgica*

Full of Your Glory

Liturgy, Cosmos, Creation

Papers from the 5th Yale ISM Liturgy Conference,
June 18–21, 2018

Edited by Teresa Berger

LITURGICAL PRESS
ACADEMIC

Collegeville, Minnesota
www.litpress.org

Cover design by Ann Blattner. Photo courtesy of Getty Images.

Scripture quotations are from New Revised Standard Version Bible © 1989 National Council of the Churches of Christ in the United States of America. Used by permission. All rights reserved worldwide.

Where noted, Scripture quotations are from The ESV® Bible (The Holy Bible, English Standard Version®). ESV® Text Edition: 2016. Copyright © 2001 by Crossway, a publishing ministry of Good News Publishers. The ESV® text has been reproduced in cooperation with and by permission of Good News Publishers. Unauthorized reproduction of this publication is prohibited. All rights reserved.

Excerpts from the English translation of *The Roman Missal* © 2010, International Commission on English in the Liturgy Corporation. All rights reserved.

Excerpts from *Laudato Si'* by Pope Francis © Libreria Editrice Vaticana. Used with permission.

1   2   3   4   5   6   7   8   9

Library of Congress Cataloging-in-Publication Data

Names: Yale Institute of Sacred Music. Liturgy Conference (5th : 2018), author. | Berger, Teresa, editor.
Title: Full of your glory : liturgy, cosmos, creation : papers from the 5th Yale ISM Liturgy Conference, June 18-21, 2018 / edited by Teresa Berger.
Description: Collegeville, Minnesota : Liturgical Press Academic, [2019] | Includes index. | Summary: "A collection of essays exploring the intersections between the world of liturgy and the worlds of creation and the cosmos. The essays were first presented at the 2018 Yale Institute of Sacred Music Liturgy Conference"—Provided by publisher.
Identifiers: LCCN 2019015801 (print) | LCCN 2019980318 (ebook) | ISBN 9780814664568 (pbk.) | ISBN 9780814664803 (ebook)
Subjects: LCSH: Liturgics—Congresses. | Creation—Congresses.
Classification: LCC BV169.5 .Y35 2018 (print) | LCC BV169.5 (ebook) | DDC 264—dc23
LC record available at https://lccn.loc.gov/2019015801
LC ebook record available at https://lccn.loc.gov/2019980318

Dedicated to Bryan D. Spinks

the Bishop F. Percy Goddard Professor
of Liturgical Studies and Pastoral Theology
at Yale Divinity School and the Yale Institute of Sacred Music
who in 2005 initiated and has since then shaped
all ISM Liturgy Conferences,

with profound gratitude

Contents

Part Three: REFLECTIONS ON CONTEMPORARY PRACTICES

Foreword

Fascination with the natural world has figured prominently for virtually all the world's religious traditions and as such has become infused in their corporate and individual ritual practices. Gratitude for, wonder in, concern about, and even fear of the greater world have been among the rare common issues that have knit together people of all faiths and places with the larger creation to which they are inextricably linked.

To this important subject, this collection of essays now turns. Virtually every three years since 2005, the Yale Institute of Sacred Music has convened an international gathering of scholars to consider important aspects in the ritual practices of Christian communities. These have ranged from the theological to the anthropological and sociological, and now to the crucially important ecological. This volume presents the papers first offered at the fifth ISM Liturgy Conference, convened in 2018.

The writers of these texts point us beyond the immediately ethical, although practices that attend to careful engagement with resources are not excluded. These scholars point out, however, that these practices are only symptomatic of larger networks that worship can reveal: networks that link us across time and place, through multiple levels of reality, and with every person, animal, plant, mineral, fungus, Protista, or bacteria in creation. We are in God's "network."

Allow me to honor the framers of this conference: Professors Bryan Spinks, Melanie Ross, and the editor of this volume, Teresa Berger, whose labors, along with those of our staff and others, yield the enclosed results. The volume is dedicated to Bryan Spinks. In 2010, T&T Clark published an earlier volume of essays, edited by Melanie C. Ross and Simon Jones, entitled *The Serious Business of Worship* in honor of Bryan Spinks, both to note his considerable impact on the field of liturgical studies and to indicate the importance of the act of worship itself. As such, the enactor of ritual, among other things, makes a claim on her place in the cosmos: as a child of the creator, as a co-creator, as a steward of creation. Virtually every act in the global tapestry of prayer is an ecological act that itself shapes the world around it either for good or ill. We pray that the seeds sewn here bear abundant fruit for the sake of the world.

Martin D. Jean
Director
Yale Institute of Sacred Music

Introduction

Teresa Berger

Sanctus, Sanctus, Sanctus Dominus Deus Sabaoth
Pleni sunt cæli et terra gloria tua
The Sanctus

We may think of the whole life of the Universe, seen and unseen, conscious
and unconscious, as an act of worship
Evelyn Underhill

Over the past half century, a number of developments have taken place
that converge in this volume's theme, "Liturgy, Cosmos, Creation." It is
the task of this Introduction to display these developments as well as the
contours of the—admittedly vast and amorphous—theme. The impetus
behind the initial choice of the theme was simple enough. Profound
questions have arisen in our time over the state of the natural world,
the earth system, the web of life, creation, the universe (or a possible
multiverse), and, ominously, over the very sustainability of life on planet
Earth. And this list names merely some of the most prominent markers of
the semantic terrain in question here. Other terms could easily be added:
Mother Nature, the environment, the planetary community, the cosmos,
all created reality, for example. Whatever linguistic markers one chooses
(and none of them is simply "natural," innocent, or un-marked), the field
of liturgical studies as a theological discipline is compelled to engage
with this terrain. The reason for such engagement is simple: concerns
about creation and the cosmos have come to the foreground in this era of
the Anthropocene, as it is increasingly called.[1] These concerns shape the

1. The 2018 Report by the United Nations' Intergovernmental Panel on Climate
Change states: "The 'Anthropocene' is a proposed new geological epoch resulting

lives of people of faith, in and beyond worship. And if indeed Christian faith is a way of life rather than merely a set of propositional truths and authorized rituals, then these concerns and the developments that underlie them deserve sustained theological attention today. In addition, themes of creation and cosmos are no strangers to the liturgical tradition itself. One might say, in fact, that a diversity of cosmovisions were inscribed into Christian worship practices from the very beginning.

The present collection of essays seeks to serve as one expression of attending to all these realities. More specifically, behind the key terms of the volume's subtitle, *Liturgy, Cosmos, Creation*, stands a commitment to the intersection of two spheres. On the one hand is the reality of mounting evidence for a planet now clearly in peril. To cite but one (globally respected) source: the 2018 Report by the United Nations' Intergovernmental Panel on Climate Change portrayed a dire picture of the "unprecedented rate and global scale of impact of human influence on the Earth System."[2] In particular, the report warned of rising sea levels, increasingly extreme weather, mounting food shortages, worsening wildfires, escalating biodiversity loss, the mass die-off of coral reefs, and the shrinking of arctic ecosystems. Some of these developments were identified as potentially irreversible. Intersecting with this painful reality is a second sphere, namely, the Christian faith in God's redemptive presence in and vision for the cosmos. In the present volume, this sphere is focused on Christian faith as expressed in traditions and practices of worship. The focus is well captured in the main title, which represents a fragment from the Sanctus: "Heaven and earth are full of Your glory." This biblical-liturgical text, rooted in the prophet Isaiah's vision of the celestial worship of God (Isa 6:3) has been a standard part of eucha-

---

from significant human-driven changes to the structure and functioning of the Earth System . . . The Anthropocene concept has been taken up by a diversity of disciplines and the public to denote the substantive influence humans have had on the state, dynamics and future of the Earth System" (Valérie Masson-Delmotte et al., eds., *Global warming of 1.5°C. An IPCC Special Report on the impacts of global warming of 1.5°C above pre-industrial levels and related global greenhouse gas emission pathways, in the context of strengthening the global response to the threat of climate change, sustainable development, and efforts to eradicate poverty*, 2018, rev. January 2019, https://www.ipcc.ch/sr15/, 543).

2. Ibid., 54.

ristic praying in Christian traditions of both East and West since at least the fourth century.³ Given the roots of this text in the Hebrew Bible, its presence in both Jewish and Christian liturgical traditions as well as in devotional practices,⁴ its portrayal of other-than-human worship, and its form as praise addressed to God, the phrase effortlessly presented itself as the main title of the 2018 Yale ISM Liturgy Conference. It remains eminently appropriate as the title for the volume of essays that were first presented at this conference.

The Terrain: A Planet in Peril, Scholarly Paths, Christian Signposts, and Practices of Worship

It might seem presumptuous to assert that the 2018 ISM Liturgy Conference and its companion volume mark a milestone. Yet *Full of Your Glory: Liturgy, Cosmos, Creation* does represent the first time that scholars from the field of liturgical studies and from cognate disciplines have together focused their attention on matters of liturgy, cosmos, and creation in a book-length publication in the midst of the environmental crisis of our times.⁵ The developments mentioned earlier offer evidence of the distinctive moment to which this volume responds. A closer look at those developments will make this clear. The first among them has already been identified, namely, that planet Earth stands on the precipice

3. Questions of the entrance of the Sanctus into Christian worship have been vigorously debated in recent scholarship. Maxwell E. Johnson offers a succinct overview in his "Recent Research on the Anaphoral *Sanctus*: An Update and Hypothesis," in *Issues in Eucharistic Praying in East and West: Essays in Liturgical and Theological Analysis*, ed. Maxwell E. Johnson (Collegeville, MN: Liturgical Press, 2010), 161–88. For a thoughtful engagement with questions of contemporary prayer language related to the Sanctus, see Gail Ramshaw, "Wording the Sanctus: A Case Study in Liturgical Language," *Worship* 77 (2003): 325–40.

4. For the latter, see Theodore de Bruyn, "The Use of the Sanctus in Christian Greek Papyrus Amulets," *Studia Patristica* 40 (2006): 15–20.

5. A couple of journals in the field dedicated issues to this theme prior to the present volume. The Austrian pastoral-liturgical journal *Heiliger Dienst* published an issue in 2017 titled "Liturgy and Creation" (71, no. 2). The journal *Liturgy* had published "Liturgy and Ecology" five years earlier, in 2012 (27, no. 2); see also its more recent issues, "Liturgy in Rural Settings" and "Liturgy and Food Culture," both in 2017, namely, 32, no. 2 and 32, no. 4.

of life-threatening environmental change. However one describes this reality, and with however many details, it is evident that the ecological crisis has rapidly intensified in recent years and is now at the forefront of concerns claiming worldwide attention. Movements of environmental activism have emerged around the globe as one response to this crisis. Some of these activist movements are aligned with specific faith traditions,[6] some of them are intentionally interfaith, some of them are religiously unaffiliated.[7] Within environmental-activist "green" Christianity, churches, networks, and activist groups have embraced a broad range of issues, from land conservation to fighting climate change, protecting waterways, and enhancing the lives of companion and farm animals, to name just a few.[8] Christian environmentalism has also produced its own version of a specialty Bible, the "Green Bible" whose green-tinted texts foreground themes of creation care.[9] Clearly, *Full of Your Glory: Liturgy, Cosmos, Creation* came about within this larger context and is marked by it in various ways.

If the environmental crisis and the activism it has engendered are the first development to note, a second development that undergirds this volume is represented by recent trends within the scholarly community. This community too has been marked by the environmental crisis and has advanced its own particular responses. Generally, one might say that the era of the Anthropocene has shifted or refocused contemporary scholarly energies, and mostly in non-anthropocentric directions. Across academic disciplines, there has been a surge of interest in all matters other-than-human, especially environmental, agrarian, animal, weather, and food

6. For a look at the breadth of religious engagements with environmental issues, see the website of the Yale Forum on Religion and Ecology: http://fore.yale.edu /about-us/.

7. The latter includes, for example, the National Religious Partnership for the Environment; see http://www.nrpe.org/.

8. For specifics, see, for example, the Ecumenical Water Network of the World Council of Churches, at http://water.oikoumene.org/en/about, or the Project CreatureKind, which seeks to engage Christians with farmed animal welfare, at https:// www.becreaturekind.org/.

9. Michael G. Maudlin and Marlene Baer, eds., *The Green Bible* (San Francisco, CA: HarperOne, 2008). This bible is a version of the NRSV with green-tinted text that highlights creation-themed passages. Cf. the substantial review essay by Dennis Owen Frohlich, "Let There Be Highlights: A Framing Analysis of The Green Bible," *Journal for the Study of Religion, Nature and Culture* 7, no. 2 (2013): 208–30.

related ones. Whole new transdisciplinary fields of inquiry have emerged, such as the environmental humanities, as well as new subfields within established disciplines. For the latter, there has been a burgeoning interest in a field now typically named "religion and ecology,"[10] and in new transdisciplinary lines of inquiry such as agrarian studies and animal studies. Related to this development yet offering a distinct voice within the broader scholarly community is the work of theologians who have begun to carry the Christian tradition forward into this age of ecological degradation. From notions of creation as a primordial sacrament, the world as the body of God,[11] and visions of a "deep incarnation"[12] or a "cosmocentric sacramentality,"[13] to recent creation-themed publications from such

10. Handbooks dedicated to the subject include *The Bloomsbury Handbook of Religion and Nature: The Elements*, ed. Laura Hobgood and Whitney Bauman (New York, NY: Bloomsbury Academic, 2018); *Routledge Handbook of Religion and Ecology*, ed. Willis Jenkins, Mary Evelyn Tucker, and John Grim (New York, NY: Routledge, 2017); *The Wiley Blackwell Companion to Religion and Ecology*, ed. John Hart (Hoboken, NJ: John Wiley & Sons, 2017); *Oxford Handbook of Religion and Ecology*, ed. Roger S. Gottlieb (New York, NY: Oxford Univ. Press, 2006); *The Encyclopedia of Religion and Nature*, ed. Bron R. Taylor, 2 vols. (New York, NY: Continuum, 2005). Significantly earlier, and single-authored, was Celia Deane-Drummond's *A Handbook in Theology and Ecology* (London: SCM Press, 1996).

11. See the essay by David Grumett in this volume.

12. Niels Henrik Gregersen, a Danish theologian, summarized "deep incarnation," a term he coined in 2001, succinctly as follows in 2017: "In Jesus Christ, God became part of the nexus of the entire cosmos—around us and within ourselves. . . . As a human being he was also a material being. His body was composed of material particles coming from the explosion of stars. His blood was red due to the iron running in his veins. And, like any other mammal, he was hosting a great hidden microbial world (bacteria and other microorganisms) that he carried with him, and without which he could not sustain his life as a human being. . . . Deep incarnation thus presupposes a radical embodiment of the Son of God that reaches into the roots (radices) of material and biological existence as well as into the darker aspects of creation, from the breaking down of material structures to animal and human suffering" (Niels Henrik Gregersen, "Deep Incarnation & the Cosmos," interview by Ciara Reyes, *God and Nature* [Summer 2017], https://godandnature .asa3.org/interview-deep-incarnation--the-cosmos-a-conversation-with-niels-henrik -gregersen-by-ciara-reyes--niels-henrik-gregersen.html).

13. Linda Gibler, *From the Beginning to Baptism: Scientific and Sacred Stories of Water, Oil, and Fire* (Collegeville, MN: Liturgical Press, 2010), esp. chap. 4, "Cosmocentric Sacramentality."

prominent theologians as Elizabeth Johnson and Rowan Williams, voices are increasing that seek to speak the Christian faith into the reality of a planet in peril.[14] These theological voices find echoes in statements from official ecclesial and ecumenical bodies, many of which have begun to foreground ecological concerns. In terms of ecumenical dialogues, for example, the World Council of Churches has long championed the "integrity of creation."[15] On a much smaller scale, the US Roman Catholic–United Methodist conversations produced a joint statement in 2012 entitled "The Eucharist and Stewardship of God's Creation," arguing that "Eucharistic renewal and environmental responsibility are intrinsically linked."[16] Individual churches too have embraced ecological concerns, the Orthodox Churches above all,[17] but also much smaller bodies such as the Presbyterian Church USA.[18] Most comprehensive in its treatment and far-reaching in its reception among these ecclesial statements is the 2015 encyclical of Pope Francis, *Laudato Si' on Care for our Common Home*.[19]

A third development that undergirds this volume's theme, closely related to the one just described yet also distinct, is rooted in the realm of liturgical practices. In recent years, there has been a surge of new worship materials that embrace creation care or gesture toward a planetary-cosmological vision of worship. These materials range from prayers, hymns, sermon aids, intercessions, lament, and entire rituals to a whole

14. See Elizabeth A. Johnson, *Creation and the Cross: The Mercy of God for a Planet in Peril* (Maryknoll, NY: Orbis, 2018); Rowan Williams, *Christ the Heart of Creation* (London: Bloomsbury Continuum, 2018).

15. "Justice, Peace and the Integrity of Creation" became a program priority for the World Council of Churches in 1983.

16. United States Conference of Catholic Bishops, "Heaven and Earth Are Full of your Glory: A United Methodist and Roman Catholic Statement on the Eucharist and Ecology," 13 April 2012, at http://www.usccb.org/beliefs-and-teachings/ecumenical -and-interreligious/ecumenical/methodist/upload/Heaven-and-Earth-are-Full-of -Your-Glory-Methodist-Catholic-Dialogue-Agreed-Statement-Round-Seven.pdf.

17. See the essay by Bert Groen in this volume.

18. See the 2016 "Affirmation of Creation" approved for distribution by the General Assembly of the PCUSA, available online at http://fore.yale.edu/files/Affirmation _of_Creation_2016.pdf.

19. Pope Francis, encyclical letter, *Laudato Si'* (On Care for Our Common Home), 24 May 2015, http://w2.vatican.va/content/francesco/en/encyclicals/documents /papa-francesco_20150524_enciclica-laudato-si.html.

new season in the liturgical year dedicated to creation.[20] The latter begins with 1 September, now designated as a Day of Prayer for Creation in many ecclesial traditions, and ends with 4 October, the Feast of Saint Francis of Assisi, who in 1979 was declared the patron saint of "those who promote ecology" by Pope John Paul II.[21] It is worth pondering this development in the realm of devotional and liturgical practices in somewhat more depth. The present volume's main scholarly location, after all, is the field of liturgical studies. A look at the surge of creation-attuned liturgical materials might conveniently begin with a text that is now close to a hundred years old but has garnered attention only more recently—Pierre Teilhard de Chardin's meditation *"La Messe sur le monde,"* known in English as the "Mass on the World."[22] Teilhard, a Jesuit priest and paleontologist, penned the text in 1923 on an expedition in the Mongolian Ordos, a desert plateau. His travels there had left him without eucharistic elementals: "I have neither bread, nor wine, nor altar," he noted.[23] This lack was not new to him. He had encountered it repeatedly on the frontlines of World War I, where his vision of a "Mass on the World" first emerged during his army service as a stretcher bearer. The words Teilhard penned in 1923 remained with him until the end of his life, as he prayed and re-wrote the text. Yet the key insight remained essentially stable over the years. Bereft of the eucharistic elements of bread and wine and a consecrated altar, Teilhard envisioned himself presiding on the "altar of the world," with the host to be consecrated extending into the whole universe. In this priestly presiding, the cosmos itself became the all-encompassing host, to be consecrated as the "sacrament of the world."[24] It bears emphasizing that Teilhard's text is a version of a eucharistic prayer *sans* traditional eucharistic elements and that he continued

20. One place that has gathered many of these resources is the web site of the Calvin Institute of Christian Worship, see https://worship.calvin.edu/resources/resource-library/worship-resources-for-creation-care/.

21. Pope John Paul II, *Proclaiming Saint Francis of Assisi as Patron of Ecology*, Franciscans for Ecology, 29 November 1979, https://francis35.org/english/papal-declaration-francis-patron-ecology/.

22. The text is available in English translation, for example, in Thomas M. King, SJ, *Teilhard's Mass: Approaches to "The Mass on the World"* (New York: Paulist Press, 2005), 145–58.

23. Teilhard de Chardin, "Mass on the World," in ibid., 145.

24. King, *Teilhard's Mass*, 21. This is the title of a book Teilhard envisioned but never wrote.

to pray the text regularly in situations of such lack.[25] In the initial prayer from World War I that became the "Mass on the World," Teilhard stayed closer still to the Roman Canon, identifying some parts with the canon's Latin incipits: *Te igitur, Unde et memores.*[26] Yet the opening words of the early text already heralded Teilhard's distinctive vision:

> Since today, Lord, I your Priest have neither bread nor wine nor altar, I shall spread my hands over the whole universe and take its immensity as the matter of my sacrifice. Is not the infinite circle of things the one final Host that it is your will to transmute?[27]

As extraordinary as Teilhard's insights might seem, he was not the only one to conceive of worship along cosmic lines in the first half of the twentieth century. Neither was his insight without precedent in the long history of Christian worship.[28] Moreover, it did not need a priestly or a scientific vocation to envision worship as cosmic adoration. The Anglican laywoman Evelyn Underhill (1875–1941) opened her book *Worship* in 1937 with these lines:

> WORSHIP, in all its grades and kinds, is the response of the creature to the Eternal: nor need we limit this definition to the human sphere. There is a sense in which we may think of the whole life of the Universe, seen and unseen, conscious and unconscious, as an act of worship, glorifying its Origin, Sustainer, and End.[29]

And in 1941, in the midst of World War II, a then little-known Swiss Catholic priest (and at that point in his life a Jesuit), Hans Urs von Balthasar, published his study of the Greek theologian Maximus

---

25. Ibid., XIII.

26. See the text "The Priest," in Pierre Teilhard de Chardin, *Writings in Time of War*, trans. René Hague (New York: Harper & Row, 1968), 205–24, at 205.

27. Ibid.

28. To cite but one example of this rich genealogy, the fourteenth-century German mystic Henry Suso envisioned himself, when praying the "Sursum corda," to be gathering into his heart all that God had created and conjoining himself to the praise of all living creatures, including every drop of water and each grain of sand. See Henry Suso, *The Life of the Servant*, trans. James M. Clark (1952, rept. Cambridge: Lutterworth Press, 2014), 35–36.

29. Evelyn Underhill, *Worship* (1937; London: Aeterna Press, 2015), 7.

the Confessor. Titled *Kosmische Liturgie*, the book sought to parse the cosmological-liturgical vision of Maximus, arguing—in the midst of a genocidal war!—that all "dissonances" of the world would melt into a final, cosmic harmony.[30] In a remarkable and dense sentence (not least because of its length: close to a whole page), Balthasar describes the mystical-ecstatic vision Maximus adopts from Pseudo-Dionysius in which the whole cosmos performs a "festive dance of liturgical adoration."[31] It is this trajectory which gives Balthasar's book its title, *Cosmic Liturgy*. All that is, is ordered toward the divine center of the cosmos in adoration, and worship. If this trajectory seems not too far removed from Teilhard's vision of the whole cosmos being eucharistically consecrated, it is worth noting that Balthasar and Teilhard had clear points of connection.[32]

The three twentieth-century authors mentioned here—Teilhard, Underhill, and Balthasar—shared a deep interest in and affinity with mysticism. Their mystical-cosmic visions of worship, however, remained in the background in the Liturgical Movement of their time. This movement of liturgical renewal focused on the human-divine dialogue in worship and in particular on the full, conscious, and active participation of the gathered ecclesial assembly. It is worth stressing that this ecclesial-anthropocentric focus in the Liturgical Movement was precisely that: a focus, not an exclusion. A line from Eucharistic Prayer III in the post-conciliar Roman Missal can serve as one glimpse of evidence for this. The thanksgiving proper, addressing God as Holy, acknowledges: "all you have created rightly gives you praise" (*merito te laudat omnis*

30. Hans Urs von Balthasar, *Kosmische Liturgie. Maximus der Bekenner: Höhe und Krise des griechischen Weltbilds* (Freiburg im Breisgau: Herder, 1941), 6. A second, revised edition was published in 1961. An English translation of the second edition is *Cosmic Liturgy: The Universe according to Maximus the Confessor*, trans. Brian E. Daley, Communio Books (San Francisco, CA: Ignatius Press, 2003). For an intriguing interpretation of Maximus the Confessor in Balthasar and beyond, see Willemien Otten, "Cosmos and Liturgy from Maximus to Hans Urs von Balthasar (with an excursion on H. J. Schulz)," in *Sanctifying Texts, Transforming Rituals: Encounters in Liturgical Studies*, ed. P. van Geest, M. Poorthuis, and H. E. G. Rose (Leiden: Brill, 2017), 153–69.

31. Balthasar, *Kosmische Liturgie*, 5: "Feierreigen der liturgischen Anbetung."

32. Not only were they both Jesuits at that point in time, but they also shared a connection with Fourvière, the Jesuit study house at Lyon, and with Henri de Lubac, SJ, who resided there and became a friend to both.

a te condita creatura).[33] Such glimpses notwithstanding, it was not until the second half of the twentieth century that Teilhard's cosmic insights in particular began to receive sustained attention. Teilhard's deep liturgical and devotional convictions—including the nature of his "Mass on the World" as a text of eucharistic praying (never mind the exceedingly priest-centered focus of his eucharistic vision)—have to some degree been neglected in this reception history.[34] Liturgical experimentations with a Cosmic or Planetary Mass, for example, evince this disjunction. The Planetary Mass, which garnered attention in the 1980s in England, drew on elements from contemporary club culture and involved high-intensity, multi-media staging. Such worship services were quite different from Teilhard's eucharistic lack, even if Rev. Chris Brain's vision for the Planetary Mass did sound Teilhardian themes:

> The service is an interpretive symbol for the reality of the worship already happening in creation. The whole universe is invited to an intimate event—the feasting on the cosmic Christ. In a sense, the church has no walls—we worship with and on behalf of plants, planets, animals and angels, celebrating Christ as the origin, the Alpha, the source of all creation.[35]

Similar themes mark the Cosmic Mass of Matthew Fox (who was in conversation with Chris Brain). This Mass, called the Techno Cosmic Mass when it was first launched in California in 1996, built on so-called rave celebrations, which Fox linked to ancient traditions of ecstatic, sacred dance.[36] Both the Planetary Mass and the Cosmic Mass were preceded by the Earth Mass, created by saxophonist Paul Winter and first celebrated in 1981. The Earth Mass fused traditional mass texts, contemporary music, and the sounds of animals, such as the howl of a

33. *The Roman Missal: English Translation according to the Third Typical Edition* (Collegeville, MN: Liturgical Press, 2011), 650. For more, see the essay by Joris Geldhof in this volume.

34. David Grumett argues this convincingly in his *Teilhard de Chardin: Theology, Humanity and Cosmos*, Studies in Philosophical Theology 29 (Leuven: Peeters, 2005).

35. Rev. Chris Brain, quoted in Bryan D. Spinks, *The Worship Mall: Contemporary Responses to Contemporary Culture*, Alcuin Club Collections 85 (London: SPCK, 2010), 34–35.

36. "The Cosmic Mass: Reinventing Worship for the 21st Century," at https://www.thecosmicmass.com/.

tundra wolf in the Kyrie, and the song of a humpback whale in the Sanctus. Winter's album *Missa Gaia* was released in 1982. The Earth Mass continues to be celebrated on the first Sunday in October every year at the (Episcopal) Cathedral of St. John the Divine in New York City. Earlier still than the Earth Mass, feminist liturgies were incorporating earth and eco-spiritual elements into their liturgical repertoire. Among more recent worship trends, the contemporary fascination with Celtic worship also foregrounds nature, since the Celtic tradition is thought to be deeply connected to the natural world and the earth.[37] It is worth noting that many of the liturgical materials mentioned here harken back to perceived ancient ways of creation-sensitive or cosmic ritualizing.[38] And appeals to such authorizing ancient visions are by no means limited to progressive and alternative interest groups. To cite but one prominent example: Joseph Ratzinger, in his argument for the *ad orientem* position of the priest presiding at the Eucharist, emphasized how turning to the East and the rising sun holds cosmic significance. Picking up on the contemporary importance of creation-attentiveness, he asked, rhetorically: "Is it not important, precisely today, to pray with the whole of creation?"[39] For Ratzinger, the turning *ad orientem*, toward the "cosmic symbol of the rising sun," is one fundamental expression of the fact that "liturgy . . . is and always will be cosmic."[40] One cannot help wondering how much of this harkening back to a perceived earth- and cosmos-conscious past in everything from New Age spirituality and Celtic worship to Joseph Cardinal Ratzinger is due, at least in part, to nostalgia.[41]

Others from within the field of liturgical studies have gone in quite different directions in order to strengthen the cosmic and earth-attuned orientation of eucharistic praying. I am here thinking especially of newly

37. For a perceptive analysis, see Bryan D. Spinks, "What Is Celtic about Contemporary Celtic Worship?" in Spinks, *Worship Mall*, 159–81.

38. Thomas Berry's essay "The Universe as Cosmic Liturgy" is a prime example of this, in *The Christian Future and the Fate of the Earth*, ed. Mary Evelyn Tucker and John Grim, Ecology and Justice Series (Maryknoll, NY: Orbis, 2009), 96–116.

39. Joseph Ratzinger, *The Spirit of the Liturgy*, trans. John Saward (San Francisco, CA: Ignatius Press, 2000), 82.

40. Ibid., 76, 34. It is noteworthy that Teilhard de Chardin's vision receives positive acknowledgement in this connection, see p. 28–29.

41. As Graham Ward has insisted, theological appeals to an authorizing past built on nostalgia display a form of "melancholic pathology" (Graham Ward, "Virtue and Virtuality," *Theology Today* 59 [2002]: 55–70, at 56).

composed eucharistic prayers, such as those by Gail Ramshaw, Robert J. Daly, and Catherine Vincie,[42] as well as of the labor of eco-theological critiques of existing liturgical texts.[43] Somewhat earlier, in the course of the rising interest in liturgical inculturation, elements entered eucharistic praying that highlighted other-than-human life-forms specific to particular contexts. The prominent scholar of liturgy Balthasar Fischer pointed out examples of this in a remarkable little essay in 1982. In this essay, Fischer highlighted newer Roman Catholic Mass texts from around the world that included mention of native animals.[44] One such example was a eucharistic prayer used at the 40th International Eucharistic Congress in Melbourne, Australia, in 1973, which included mention of kangaroos. Fischer saw in this feature not a contemporary oddity but echoes of what he described as the "ancient creation spirituality" of Christian eucharistic praying.[45] This ancient spirituality, he found, for example, in the anaphora of the Apostolic Constitutions and in the anaphora of Saint James. But beyond simply highlighting these mentions of animals in eucharistic prayer texts, Fischer's essay contained an additional insight. He insisted that in some prayer texts, animals are not only explicitly named

---

42. See Gail Ramshaw, "Liturgical Considerations of the Myth of Eden," *Worship* 89 (2015): 64–79, here 76–78; Robert J. Daly, "Ecological Euchology," *Worship* 89 (2015): 166–72, here 170–71; Catherine Vincie, *Worship and the New Cosmology: Liturgical and Theological Challenges* (Collegeville, MN: Liturgical Press, 2014), 105–8. An older example, now authorized as Eucharistic Prayer C in the Episcopal *Book of Common Prayer*, is the so-called "Star Trek" Prayer, written by Howard E. Galley Jr. in the early 1970s. The Preface includes the memorable line: "At your command all things came to be: the vast expanse of interstellar space, galaxies, suns, the planets in their courses, and this fragile earth, our island home." Text available online at The (Online) Book of Common Prayer, https://www.bcponline.org/.

43. Jeremy M. S. Clines offered an example of this for the Church of England's *Common Worship*, in "Earthing Common Worship: An Ecotheological Critique of the Common Worship Texts of the Church of England" (PhD diss., University of Birmingham, 2011), http://etheses.bham.ac.uk/2838/.

44. Balthasar Fischer, "Die Känguruhs im Hochgebet: zur Rolle der Tiere in den jüngsten Eucharistischen Hochgebeten der katholischen Kirche," in *Communio Sanctorum*, FS Jean-Jaques von Allmen (Geneva: Labor et fides, 1982): 173–78. I cannot but note that Fischer's descriptions of aboriginal peoples will be considered culturally insensitive today.

45. Ibid., 178: "alte Schöpfungsfrömmigkeit".

in the praise of God offered by humans, but animals themselves praise the Creator. In other words, Fischer argued that animals here "co-operate" in worship.[46] He also pointed to witnesses of such liturgical cooperation in traditional practices in rural life, where farm animals were a part of the larger liturgical life of agrarian communities. For example, major feast days such as Christmas as well as deaths in the family had to be announced to each animal on the farm individually. It is worth pointing out that Balthasar Fischer's essay predates Andrew Linzey's *Animal Rites: Liturgies of Animal Care* by close to twenty years.[47] In his book, Linzey too pointed to the Apostolic Constitutions and, encouraged by their witness, he included four "Eucharistic Prayers for All Creatures" in his collection of animal-friendly worship materials.[48] Yet disjunctions might be said to exist between scholars and practitioners in the field of liturgical studies on the one hand, and the vast and diffuse field of "creation spirituality" and its practitioners, on the other hand. In the latter, for example, rituals that mark the solstices are prominent as is the ceremonial use of the four cardinal directions of North, South, East, and West and the four cardinal elements, earth, air, fire, and water.[49] Boundaries between these practices and Christian ritualizing can be exceedingly fluid, as some of the eco-feminist rituals in the women's liturgical movement had already made clear.

The various developments sketched above reveal not only how pronounced concerns over advancing ecological devastation have become,[50]

---

46. Ibid., 177. Fischer could easily have included a classic witness to such co-operation of animals in Christian worship here, namely the labor of the bees for the Easter candle which is mentioned in the Exultet. For this, see the essay by Duco Vollebregt in this volume. For "interspecies liturgical participation" in natural burial practices, see the essay by Benjamin Stewart in this volume.

47. Andrew Linzey, *Animal Rites: Liturgies of Animal Care* (London: SCM Press, 1999).

48. See ibid., 44–56.

49. For more, see Eric Steinhart, "Practices in Religious Naturalism," in *The Routledge Handbook of Religious Naturalism* (New York, NY: Routledge 2018), 341–51, esp. 344–45.

50. Concerns are not progressing in a linear fashion, however. At the time of writing, the Trump administration has eliminated nearly eighty environmental regulations, including major policies directed at fighting climate change; for details, see Eric Lipton et al., "President Trump's Retreat on the Environment Is Affecting

but also how much has been retrieved already in terms of a Christian vision of God's redemptive purpose for the whole cosmos. The field of liturgical studies has played a part in these developments over the last few decades, in a number of different ways. For example, a seminar dedicated to "Ecology and Liturgy" was formed in the North American Academy of Liturgy in 2011.[51] As a topic of concern, the subject matter of liturgy and ecology naturally predated, and in fact led to, the establishment of this seminar. The concern was already clearly in view in 1997, when Lawrence Mick, a priest of the Archdiocese of Cincinnati and a champion of pastoral-liturgical renewal, published his little volume *Liturgy and Ecology in Dialogue.*[52] In the introduction, Mick pointed out that he had already written an article on the subject of ecology and worship in 1972. This was a quarter-century before his book appeared in print, and only four years after the historian of medieval technology Lynn White, Jr. had published his seminal essay "The Historical Roots of Our Ecological Crisis."[53] In Mick's early article, the author sought to articulate some of the connections between the liturgical renewal after Vatican II and the emerging ecological activism of the time. He pursued the same task in his 1997 book, arguing that "worship and ecology are bound together at their core," in their common recognition of the interconnectedness of all things and in their appreciation of creation as a gift to be cherished rather than abused.[54] These tenets have stood the test of time. They are carried forward and developed further in more recent

---

Communities Across America," *New York Times* (27 December 2018), https://www.nytimes.com/interactive/2018/12/26/us/politics/donald-trump-environmental-regulation.html.

51. Prior to the formation of this seminar in 2011, a first conversation about liturgy and ecology was held at the North American Academy of Liturgy in 2009, and an interest group came together in 2010. I thank Benjamin Stewart for providing this information.

52. Lawrence E. Mick, *Liturgy and Ecology in Dialogue* (Collegeville, MN: Liturgical Press, 1997).

53. See Lynn White, Jr., "The Historical Roots of Our Ecological Crisis," *Science* 155 (1967): 1203–7. White's essay appeared five years after another landmark work, Rachel Carson's *Silent Spring* (Boston, MA: Houghton Mifflin, 1962). Carson's book was published in the United States just a couple of weeks prior to the opening of Vatican II in Rome.

54. Mick, *Liturgy and Ecology*, viii–ix.

work by scholars of liturgy writing at the intersection of worship and ecology and/or cosmology.[55] Some foundational work has also been done in liturgical theology (beyond the strong emphasis on theology and ecology in Eastern churches, that is). Noteworthy here is Gordon Lathrop's *Holy Ground: A Liturgical Cosmology*.[56] In this book, the third volume of a liturgical-theological trilogy, Lathrop seeks to break open the central symbols of Christian liturgy, in order to allow them to "orient us anew in relationship to the universe."[57] Deeply theocentric, scriptural, and rooted in the experience of the liturgical celebrations of a gathered assembly, Lathrop argued that the key symbols of Christian worship—bath, table, prayer, and word—have cosmological significance because they are meant for the life of the world and therefore invite us "to keep a wider company than we had thought."[58] Five years after *Holy Ground* appeared, ecological theologian (and fellow Lutheran) H. Paul Santmire published his book *Ritualizing Nature: Renewing Christian Liturgy in a Time of Crisis*.[59] Santmire thought of liturgy as essentially a "gathering of humans," but challenged the liturgical assembly to "ritualize nature," by standing in awe and forming habits that serve and partner with nature.[60] With Benjamin Stewart's important 2011 book *A Watered Garden: Christian Worship and Earth's Ecology*, we move beyond a focus on worship as essentially a gathering of humans.[61] Stewart insists that "Christian worship has always been an act of joining the wider worship of the whole creation, a liturgy that began long before humans even existed."[62] He therefore is able to claim that "the horizon of concern in Christian worship extends outward to the entire universe."[63] With this

55. For the latter, see Vincie, *Worship and the New Cosmology*.

56. Gordon W. Lathrop, *Holy Ground: A Liturgical Cosmology* (Minneapolis, MN: Fortress Press, 2003).

57. Ibid., 15.

58. Ibid., 228.

59. H. Paul Santmire, *Ritualizing Nature: Renewing Christian Liturgy in a Time of Crisis*, Theology and the Sciences (Minneapolis, MN: Fortress Press, 2008).

60. Ibid., esp. 217 and 244.

61. Benjamin M. Stewart, *A Watered Garden: Christian Worship and Earth's Ecology*, Worship Matters (Minneapolis, MN: Fortress Press, 2011).

62. Ibid., 18.

63. Ibid., 10.

claim, we have also arrived at what motivated the choice of theme for the 2018 Yale ISM Liturgy Conference.

Mapping *Full of Your Glory: Liturgy, Cosmos, Creation*

The fifth ISM Liturgy Conference, held at Yale from 18 to 21 June 2018, sought to highlight and focus the explorations already underway, in order to deepen and further research at the intersections of liturgy, cosmos, and creation. Intentional about engaging historical as well as contemporary configurations of the theme and deeply committed as always to deliberate interdisciplinary engagement, the conference brought together scholars from the fields of Hebrew Bible, early Christian history, art history, medieval history, musicology, theology, Eastern Christian studies, and liturgical studies in all its diverse ways of attending to practices of Christian worship. Speakers had been tasked with highlighting various liturgical traditions of the past as well as addressing contemporary concerns. The broader aim of the conference was to bring insights from within the Christian tradition of liturgical practices, past and present, to the ongoing conversations around ecology, cosmology, and Christian faith.

Full of Your Glory: Liturgy, Cosmos, Creation now makes available to a broader audience the key presentations from this conference. The volume opens, appropriately, with the keynote by Rowan Williams titled "Naming the World: Liturgy and the Transformation of Time and Matter." And since the conference participants were able to engage Rowan Williams in sustained conversation after the keynote was presented, we have chosen to provide a transcription of some of the highlights from the question-and-answer exchange here, immediately following the text of the keynote itself.

The first section of the volume then gathers select biblical and historical studies. Anathea Portier-Young's chapter opens this part with a look at the Hebrew Bible's Torah and various versions of Daniel 3, a text with longstanding use in Christian liturgical traditions. In Daniel 3, three young prisoners of war worship God from amid a flaming furnace-turned-temple, addressing angels, stars, sun and moon, sky, water, wind, and fire. Portier-Young shows how in this impromptu liturgy, God's redemptive presence is not only for human beings but for the whole cosmos to acknowledge. Andrew McGowan's chapter takes us from a cosmic vision of worship to one of foundational materiality. The author investigates the ancient Mediterranean staple food of bread that becomes, for the early Christians, eucharistic food. In reconsidering references to bread and its consumption in the quotidian context not of sacred eating or even banqueting but of economy, food supply, and hunger, McGowan proposes that the Eucharist functioned among early Christians as sign of an economy of plenty and as means of establishing a distinct divine polity. The following chapter, by art historian Felicity Harley-McGowan, draws attention to the witness of Christian visual art, in particular the symbol of the globe. She shows how early Christians drew on this symbol, rooted in ancient Greek ideas about the cosmos, to develop the motif of Christ as Pantocrator, the "all-ruler." Harley-McGowan maps the development of these artistic representations of divine authority, with Jesus holding or even occupying the globe, up to the image of Christ as *Salvator Mundi*. The chapter by Duco Vollebregt, which follows, turns to natural symbols in the Easter Vigil. In particular, the author asks how evening, night, and dawn relate to each other in the liturgy of this Vigil as exemplified by the Exultet in the *Missale Gothicum*. Vollebregt concludes that the Easter Vigil not so much looks forward to dawn but rather invokes its symbolism to enhance the sacredness of the entire night of Easter, whose splendor blends evening and morning, night and day, Christ sacrificed and Christ risen, into one single "day" of festivity. In the chapter that follows, Peter Jeffery focuses his attention on the core repertoire of strophic hymns in the medieval Roman Breviary in search of an explicitly affirming theology of creation in the daily office. Analyzing in particular the hymns for Vespers, Jeffery argues that these strophic hymns, composed according to the rules of Latin poetry rather than excerpted from Scripture, offer a quite detailed, distinct view of the created order. With Nathan Ristuccia's chapter we move into the world of medieval celebrations of Rogationtide, perhaps the second most important holiday of the year at the time. Ristuccia shows how through Rogation processions, medieval Christians enacted a vision of their place within God's world, the social order, and the cosmos. He argues that contemporary liturgical attempts to restore Rogationtide are bound to fail unless they unmoor the holiday from the premodern social imaginary to which it is tied. Margot Fassler's chapter explores correspondences between views of the cosmos and of the liturgy in the work of Hildegard of Bingen (1098–1179), particularly in her *Scivias* and some of the sequences she authored. Fassler analyzes the subtly drawn parallels, made through art, liturgical commentary, poetry, and music, that Hildegard envisions. M. Jennifer Bloxam's chapter turns our attention to musical practices of the later Middle Ages, in particular the sacramental cosmology embedded in the singing of the Sanctus at the heart of the Mass. Bloxam explores a variety of musical styles and techniques employed by medieval composers to make the angelic choir sonically present in worship.

Following upon these historical investigations, the second section of the volume gathers chapters that foreground theological questions. David Grumett opens this section by identifying a lack in contemporary eucharistic theology, namely, relatively little concern for the created, material elements of bread and wine. Situating himself within the scholarly turns to the body and to materiality, Grumett argues that a concern with eucharistic materiality opens avenues for theological engagement with concrete Christian experience and wider secular culture. He outlines a theology that foregrounds eucharistic presence not as an exceptional intrusion but as exemplifying Christ's continual sustaining action upon and within the world. Joris Geldhof's chapter turns to a contemporary liturgical book for a theological reading. The author analyzes the Latin text—both euchological material as well as ritual instructions—of the most recent *editio typica* of the Roman Missal. Geldhof asks, in particular, how matter and creation are conceived in this key liturgical source of the contemporary Roman Catholic Church, what is "done" with creation, and what God is asked to do with and for creatures. Kevin Irwin's chapter, which follows, also attends to contemporary Roman Catholic life, taking its lead from Pope Francis's encyclical letter *Laudato Si.'* Based on insights from this encyclical, Irwin delineates the shape and contours of a sacramental-liturgical theology that is both creation-sensitive and tradition-rooted. Finally, we turn to the East with Nicholas Denysenko's chapter. The author explores the themes of creation and sanctification in Byzantine liturgical practices. He focuses on liturgical rites for the blessing of waters, at baptism, the great blessing of waters on Theophany, and several shorter offices throughout the year, as well as drawing attention to people's pious practices involving water.

The third and final section of the volume gathers texts that foreground contemporary developments and concerns. Bert Groen opens this section with a look at 1 September as a day dedicated to the integrity of creation and environmental protection in the Byzantine rite. He analyzes the underlying theological themes connected with this day, as well as various worship formularies composed for its celebration, including their musical settings. Groen concludes with a look at a new type of iconography dedicated to the theme of the integrity of creation. In the chapter that follows, Mary McGann turns to a particular element of both the contemporary ecological crisis and the world of liturgical symbols: water. She argues that the global water crisis is recontextualizing the symbolic use of water in Christian initiation, because the desecration, contamination, and commodification of Earth's waters threaten a foundational element for life on the planet while also shaping perceptions of water that undermine its sacredness as gift and blessing. McGann sketches an ethical-ecological-sacramental framework that might inform the teaching, practice, and theology of Christian initiation. Benjamin Stewart's chapter turns from initiatory practices to rites at the end of life. Using biblical Wisdom literature as a lens, Stewart traces this literature's earthy approach to mortality ("dust wisdom") in Ash Wednesday liturgical practices, the ritual of committal at funerals, and Eastern Orthodox funeral hymns. He then turns to the emerging natural burial movement and argues that this movement embodies some of the ecological dimensions of the Wisdom tradition. Finally, this third section and the volume as a whole are drawn to a close by something of a wild card, appropriately so, for a volume with a cosmic scope. Gerald Liu calls our attention to a 1968 avant-garde film, *Symbiopsychotaxiplasm*. Produced by the African American director and actor William Greaves, the plotless, multilayered film captured how clichéd contexts and inane conversations can nevertheless gesture toward theological implications. Liu argues that Greaves's film essentially recorded redemption and examines the film for imagining pathways of liturgical widening for ecology and the cosmos.

As will readily be apparent from the brief overview of the essays, this volume contains a wide-ranging collection of heterogeneous insights into the vast terrain that is "Liturgy, Cosmos, Creation." There is no intent here to claim a coherent, overarching view for this collection of essays. What the volume as a whole does claim, however, is that attention to this vast terrain is of utmost importance and urgency today. Maybe most importantly, the conference gestured toward a vision of liturgy that encompasses so much more than human beings at worship, namely, a vision of the redemption of the created universe at the heart of Christian worship. Within this vast vision, the gathered assembly itself comes to be situated afresh, in a larger context, planetary and cosmic. Even if one does not identify the universe itself as the primary sacred community,[64] surely the gathered assembly at worship is more than the number of human beings who breathe the same air in any given sanctuary.[65] The scholarly field of liturgical studies has only just begun its work on the implications of these insights.

In Conclusion, a World of Gratitude

If a fundamental posture of worship—not only that of human beings but of all created reality—is gratitude to the "Origin, Sustainer, and End" (Evelyn Underhill), then it is only fitting to let this Introduction draw to a close with expressions of thanksgiving.

I begin with words of deep gratitude to the presenters at the ISM Liturgy Conference who turned themselves into authors and their presentations into essays for "Cosmo" (as this volume has been known affectionately in shorthand). You are the real authors of this book, and I thank each and every one of you for your work. I am also exceedingly grateful to Rona Johnston for her outstanding editorial work on the essays. It would simply not have been possible to publish "Cosmo" without Rona's expertise and commitment. Thanks are also in order to Phoenix Gonzalez, my research assistant, and to Thomas Broughton-Willett, who provided the index for the volume.

Both the 2018 ISM Liturgy Conference and this volume were supported in a multitude of ways by the Yale Institute of Sacred Music. A special word of gratitude goes to the Director of the ISM, Martin D. Jean, who hosted the 2018 conference and generously supported the publication of these papers. I am deeply grateful also to my two colleagues in liturgical studies, Bryan D. Spinks and Melanie Ross, with whom I planned and coordinated this conference. Melissa Maier, ISM Manager of External Relations and Publications, exercised her expert planning skills

64. This is Thomas Berry's well-known claim, picked up, for example, in Gibler, *From the Beginning to Baptism*, xxiv.

65. And even these human beings can be seen anew, for example along lines sketched by Gordon Lathrop in his liturgical cosmology: "these creatures on the third rock from the sun, a relatively small star in a marginal arm of a marginal galaxy in a second-class cluster of galaxies" (Lathrop, *Holy Ground*, 19).

in overseeing the organization of the conference; she was ably assisted by Stephen Gamboa-Díaz and Sachin Ramabhadran. I continue to be grateful to the rest of the wonderful ISM staff without whose hard work the Institute's manifold activities could not flourish, especially Kristen Forman, Trisha Radil, and Liz Santamaria. Finally, in acknowledging the ISM as the institution that hosted the 2018 conference, I also wish to acknowledge the Institute's historical and bioregional context in what is now Connecticut: the land of the indigenous Quinnipiac peoples, in the Quinnipiac River watershed.

It has been a pleasure once again to work with Hans Christoffersen and his staff at Liturgical Press, which has also published the previous four volumes of papers from the Yale ISM Liturgy Conferences.

This book is dedicated to the scholar of liturgy who in 2005 first convened and since then has shaped each of the Yale ISM Liturgy Conferences: Bryan D. Spinks, the Bishop F. Percy Goddard Professor of Liturgical Studies and Pastoral Theology at Yale Divinity School and the Yale Institute of Sacred Music. "Cosmo" comes a bit too late as a gift for Bryan's seventieth birthday and a bit too early in honor of his retirement. Yet in this in-between time, it does come from the heart, and with profound gratitude. I am pleased, not least of all, to be able to dedicate a volume to my wonderful colleague with a title that invokes the Sanctus, since Bryan decisively shaped the research surrounding the Sanctus's entry into eucharistic praying.[66]

So here's to Bryan Spinks: priest, scholar, teacher, colleague, friend.

March 25, 2019

Feast of the Annunciation—Feast of God's "deep incarnation"
New Haven, Connecticut

---

66. See Bryan D. Spinks, *The Sanctus in the Eucharistic Prayer* (New York, NY: Cambridge Univ. Press, 1991).

CHAPTER ONE

Naming the World

Liturgy and the Transformation of Time and Matter

Rowan Williams

The narrative of Genesis 2:19 represents the creator inviting Adam to name his fellow creatures, as if the act of naming were from the start a necessary aspect of human presence in the world. When the items of the world are named, the environment we inhabit is mapped with a new exactitude. Not only do we learn habits of response to elements in that environment, we also create the possibility of shared memory by coding the environment in our language, in such a way that we can represent and connect different sorts of encounter with what is around us. We create the possibility of *recognizing* a regular pattern of stimulus or perception and of establishing such recognition as a shared vehicle of interaction or relation. My perception of what I encounter is shaped by the other's perception and vice versa. The concept of an "object" or "substance" emerges in our common negotiating of the world around, and our language fixes this in terms of names, nouns, words that represent areas of substantial, recognizable continuity in the environment. Maurice Merleau-Ponty's formulation is hard to improve on: language "presents or rather it *is* the subject's taking up of a position in the world of his meanings."[1] The "gesture" we make in speaking, and especially in

1. Maurice Merleau-Ponty, *Phenomenology of Perception*, trans. Colin Smith (London: Routledge & Kegan Paul, 1962), 193; see also the discussion of this and other passages in Rowan Williams, *The Edge of Words: God and the Habits of Language* (London: Bloomsbury 2014), chap. 4.

naming (Merleau-Ponty has been discussing the phenomenon of people with some sorts of amnesiac or aphasic disturbance who retain the names of colors but cannot actually distinguish them), is more than learning to associate a word with an item of the environment; it coordinates experience, it modulates the body's behavior, locating it in a specific way in relation to other speakers as well as to the environment. "The comprehension of other gestures presupposes a perceived world common to all," and the practice of language in general and naming in particular is a "behavioural style," evolving over time in inseparable relation with the agency of other speakers.[2]

Naming is thus not an imposing of labels on assorted things; it is the forming of a set of shared "policies" for interacting and relating between speakers. That is why in biblical tradition, as in folklore worldwide (all the variants of the Rumpelstiltskin story, for instance, or the Welsh legend of the child whose mother curses him by forbidding him to be named by anyone but herself and then refuses to name him), the name is bound up with issues around *power*. Knowing the name of a stranger or adversary lessens the threat; withholding a name is a refusal to submit (Gen 32:29; Judg 13:18). Names are changed when new vocations and new possibilities are given: Abram becomes Abraham (Gen 17:5), Jacob becomes Israel (Gen 32:28), kings are given divinely sanctioned royal names (2 Sam 12:24-5) or have their names changed by new political masters (2 Kgs 24:17). Christian Scripture reflects something of this in the renaming of Simon as Peter/Kephas (John 1:42). In the Revelation to John, the letters to the seven churches at the opening of the book return several times to the themes of naming and renaming. The glorified Christ promises to give the believer who endures temptation or persecution "a white stone with a new name written on it," unknown to anyone else (Rev 2:17); the name of the one who endures will be acknowledged by Christ in the presence of the Father (3:5); and Christ will inscribe on the faithful witnesses the name of God, the name of the Holy City of God and his own "new name" (3:12 and cf. 22:4). The authority of the glorified Christ in the Revelation is manifest in his freedom to redefine human beings by renaming them—though at the same time, this is presented as a gift and an enhancement, not an exercise of arbitrary power, the new name being (as we shall see later) the marker of a new liberty.

---

2. Merleau-Ponty, *Phenomenology of Perception*, 194, 403.

In the light of all this, it is not an accident that the baptismal rite, initially quite independent of any connection with naming, acquires this dimension apparently by the mid-third century[3] and certainly by the fourth. The changed relation to God that baptism celebrates and in some sense effects must be signified by a new name. For infants being baptized, this is simply a matter of a name reflecting from the start some sort of identification with the apostles or with Christian virtues and Christian mysteries (Eirene, Anastasia, Deusdedit, Adeodatus); for adults a "Christian" name will mark a clear separation from a previous pagan identity. Baptismal name changes are not universal, but the giving or acknowledging of a name does become an integral part of baptismal liturgy by the end of the patristic period. The custom persists in the Orthodox churches of addressing every communicant by their baptismal name when administering Holy Communion—a strong reinforcement of the sense that the baptismal name is bound up with a specific sacramentally defined identity. And more could be said of the later custom of taking an extra "patronal" name at confirmation (still common in parts of the Catholic world) and of assuming a new name when taking monastic vows. The point is that where personal names are concerned, so far from the name being a permanently fixed designation, it changes according to the network of relations within which the bearer is embedded or embodied; in Merleau-Ponty's terms, it reflects a bodily position, a place within a pattern of behaviors (we shall come back to the question of how this holds also with the naming of what is not "personal").

This also, though rather indirectly, connects the act(s) of naming with the passage of time: a name carries with it something of a narrative; it encodes the passing of time in a specific way, the passage of time that has brought us to *this* place. If the act of naming is bound up with what it is for us to be human and more specifically what it is for us to be language users, it is thus bound up with our awareness of ourselves as living in time. As noted earlier, names have to do with the possibilities of recognition, and so of continuity both in perception and in the exchanges of discourse; changes of name tell us that these continuities are being stretched and challenged in various ways. Our story is being retold, and so our skills of recognition need to be refined. To make sense of this, we need to explore the underlying narrative to see more fully exactly what

---

3. Eusebius, *Historia ecclesiastica* VII.25.14 seems to reflect this.

is changing. Or, to put it slightly differently, any self-conscious act of naming carries with it an implicit story of encounter and interaction, and the full meaning of the name involves that story, the story of what has led to the taking up of the position that our words imply, to use Merleau-Ponty's language again. A new name means a new "position"; a new place to speak and act from means a new set of encounters to narrate and understand. Naming the world is creating a situation, a pattern of shared behavior, and also starting to construct a narrative in which that pattern is located. And it is this basic set of human habits that gives us a foundation for understanding what is supposed to be going on in liturgy.

———————

David Jones, in his famous and very fertile essay "Art and Sacrament," described early Christianity as "a cult . . . which demanded as a condition of membership the acceptance of a belief involving certain of the arts." [4] This provocative formulation directs our attention to the way in which Christian practice can be seen as—most fundamentally—*a specific way of being human*, of exercising the basic distinctive functions of homo sapiens as a maker of names and signs. To be Christian, for Jones, is to opt for a definition of human identity in which name- and sign-making are essential, and to offer one particular narrative setting in which—it is claimed—naming takes place at the most generative level of significance, in a way that allows a maximally rich connectedness to be affirmed between speakers and their world. We could summarize the claim in something like these terms: there is a narrative of human interaction with the rest of the world that will make sense of our language in the most comprehensive way because it is aligned with the act by which the creator bestows meaning on creation. God has made a world that consists not of isolated, atomized substances but of endlessly intercommunicating systems: each crystallization of finite activity within the world represents an agency that helps to structure every other such crystallization, at every imaginable level of complexity. By virtue of their complex unity, they "inform" one another, and our naming of these complex unities and our tracing of their mutual informing is—essentially—what science amounts

4. David Jones, "Art and Sacrament" (1955), in *Epoch and Artist* (London: Faber & Faber, 1959), 143–79, quotation p. 162.

to. But the truth is that this is only a part of our naming activity: we don't only make sense of the existing patterns in our environment; we also modify them and renew them in fresh interconnections, both for practical purposes and for the sheer enrichment of interaction and understanding that is itself an aspect of language. We engage in technology and in "art" (in the widest sense), believing that the latter is at least as important as the former in building a world that humans can inhabit in a way that is lifegiving, constantly expanding and feeding back into itself so as to enhance our wonder at and our attunement with the environment we live in.

"It is not . . . outlandish," says David Bentley Hart, "to say that for Christian theology the world is 'spoken.' " The complexity of finite existence is, in Hart's account, "a kind of miraculous wordplay" overflowing from the unfathomable richness of God's presence to God's self.[5] And this in turn means that our own speech, when consciously located within this overflowing "wordplay," becomes a further stage in the unfolding of the divine self-presence to and in the finite order. I say "consciously" located, but in fact the alignment of human speech with divine self-unfolding is not dependent only on our intention, and theology has generally been fairly receptive to the idea that there may be elements of that divine indwelling that do not depend on the conscious will to be aligned with God. But the point is that conscious locating of our speech within the story of God's act in creation and God's interaction with creation states unambiguously what the narrative is within which our speech makes fullest sense, and without this dimension we should not grasp what the alignment of human language with God's self-communication entails, what is the full effect of that alignment in releasing the deepest capacities of finite agencies. We grasp the truth of the world's "spoken" character because God's self-communication, God's loving and intelligent self-presence, has been expressed as fully as it could be in a phenomenon in human history, a single human life. That narrative, we believe, is the record of how God's own action releases finite existence in general and human existence in particular from the mutual isolation which stands in the way of God's Wisdom becoming fully manifest in creation—an isolation that in the human context we call sin. The story of God's incarnate action in history tells us that the life of the incarnate Word, being both

5. David Bentley Hart, *The Beauty of the Infinite: The Aesthetics of Christian Truth* (Grand Rapids, MI: Eerdmans, 2003), 292.

human and divine, creates a new set of relations, a new set of places to occupy in relation to God and others, not limited by local or racial particularities—and so creates a new language, new practices of naming. The late Sebastian Moore in an early book with the resonant title *God is a New Language* (1967) sums this up eloquently: "When God, by a free and gracious initiative, enters into a relation with me that dissolves my illusion of being a person over-against him . . . he dissolves in principle the *derivative* lie in my relation with others . . . Thus a quite *new* sense of 'myself and others'—whose image is the Body as opposed to the confrontation of bodies—is the sign of an encounter with the self-giving God."[6] The effect of the incarnate life (a life that has demonstrated the impossibility of its being annihilated by death) is to relocate us in respect both of God and of creation, so that our naming of the world can now go beyond not only the mere identifying of substances, not only the language that establishes a culture of recognition and continuity in shared human practice, and can reach outwards toward a world of full interconnection and exchange of life. The new language of the Body, grounded in the new narrative of divine solidarity with the created world through solidarity with humanity, displays and enacts the possibility of a reconciled and fully meaningful cosmos in which the Word's presence is manifested and thus God is "glorified"—that is, God's radiant self-presence is shared and shown by finite agents.

Liturgy is the event in which the Body declares itself, the event in which the nature of the transformation entailed by the Word's life in the human world is both witnessed and intensified. To pick up a point often made, the difference between liturgy and ritual in Christian theology is simply that liturgy enacts a transition from one state or position to another: it is an event of "translation," we might say. We begin in one set of relations and end in another; we move from world to world, yet in the same place, as the same bodies in the same material environment. The new meanings that come alive in liturgy do not annihilate that materiality but fill out its capacity for meaning—that is, they fill out what it is capable of communicating, the intelligent and intelligible life that it can

6. Sebastian Moore, *God Is a New Language* (London: Darton, Longman & Todd, 1967), 43.

share. It is a mistake to see liturgy as simply a moment of "being before God" rather than a process in which our location as speakers or subjects or perceivers is shifted.[7] But to speak of liturgy as a process is also to recognize that liturgical action is not a once-for-all movement into the heavenly places: each time we embark on a liturgical act, we begin with the acknowledgement of where we actually are, as inhabitants of a world of failing and limited, not to say destructive, relations. We confess our sins—that is, we declare our need to undertake the journey that liturgy conducts us on, our need for a new language. The baptismal liturgy, as the first step in any understanding of the liturgical journey, initiates this new language by naming *us* afresh. As we have noted, this is signaled by the actual giving of a baptismal name—but this is secondary to our naming as adopted children of God. In the most basic sense, baptism "names" us as Jesus, as the one on whom the Spirit descends to activate in human life the eternal existence of the divine Logos, and because of this, we are also named as those who are free to name God as Jesus names God, *Abba*.

In the narrative of the Exodus, Moses, when confronted by God at the burning bush, asks what name he shall give to the God who has called him (Exod 3:13-14). The ancestral God of the Hebrew people has sent a message to them—but how is this God to be known or spoken to *now*? The answer is both blinding and conceptually austere: the name of this God is "I will be what I will be." The "name" of this God is the sheer statement of God's freedom to be God. And in Christian Scripture, when we are told that baptism empowers us to address God as Jesus did, the implication, in the light of the whole scriptural narrative, is that God's freedom to be God is now graspable as God's freedom to be to us what God is to Jesus, or, more correctly, God's freedom to be—for, in, and with us—what God is in eternity as Source and Word and excess of love, Father and Son and Spirit. In naming us as adopted children, God names

7. Arguably, this is a problem with the way in which Jean-Yves Lacoste treats the liturgical experience in, for example, *Experience and the Absolute: Disputed Questions on the Humanity of Man,* trans. Mark Raftery-Skehan (New York, NY: Fordham Univ. Press, 2004); see the interesting discussion of this in Christina M. Gschwandtner, "The Vigil as Exemplary Liturgical Experience: On Jean-Yves Lacoste's Phenomenology of Liturgy," and Lacoste's response to Gschwandtner in "Response to Gschwandtner, Hart, Schrijvers and Hackett," *Modern Theology* 31, no. 4 (2015): 648–57 and 676–78, respectively.

God's self as trinity. To go back to Sebastian Moore's phrase, what is "dissolved" in the baptismal waters is the over-againstness of a creature viewing God as simply "another" substance to know and negotiate with; what is overcome is a specific way of being a person as an item in the world whose identity and interests are fixed and given over against all others—and all other "items" in creation. The non-otherness of creator to creation mirrors the non-otherness of Source and Word/Father and Son, a non-otherness that still affirms a difference that is held within love, and so our relation to God and God's creation is changed when we are named God's children and learn to name God as trinity.

As baptized, we pray "in the name" of Jesus, continually renaming ourselves as Jesus and claiming an identity in him (John 16 and 17). Thus in the context of other liturgical actions we both articulate our unfinished assimilation to Jesus' filial identity and stake our claim to that identity, inviting the Spirit to bridge the gap thus opened up and confessed. The liturgical action of the Eucharist has to do with how we learn again to inhabit the Body into which we have been incorporated—and, as inhabitants of that Body, to speak that Body's (Jesus-inflected) language. We learn this by naming ourselves as the disciples and table fellows of Jesus—and thus as those who both betray him and are summoned back by him after the resurrection. As at the Last Supper, we are named as "friends" (John 15:15), but also as passive and unfaithful witnesses to Jesus "giving-up" into the hands of human power. The inexorable persistence of Jesus' self-giving, even beyond this passivity and faithlessness, is what is embodied in the giving of the signs of his flesh and blood. Our identity in him is restored and reinforced as we absorb and are absorbed by the incarnate reality figured in the bread and wine: we are addressed at the altar with the plain words "the Body of Christ," "the Blood of Christ": this is what we both receive and become.

This is the central movement of the eucharistic action, but it is not the whole story. The Eucharist is a rite whose origins lie in the Passover celebration—which is not only a commemoration of the exodus but also an offering of the firstfruits of the newly cultivated land to God (Lev 23), imagery that is sometimes used in early Christian contexts in reflection on the Eucharist.[8] The vehicle for commemorating the decisive act of liberation by God is the gift of God in harvest and vintage: the freedom

---

8. For a full study of patristic uses of the imagery of Hebrew Scripture, see, for example, Robert J. Daly, *Sacrifice Unveiled: The True Meaning of Christian Sacri-*

to be God in liberation and healing is the same freedom displayed in the regular gifts of creation; the stuff of the world is given so as to become a sign of liberating freedom. So in the eucharistic context, the naming of the stuff of the world as the flesh and blood of Jesus makes the connection between our own naming and renaming by God as baptized and liberated children of God and the renaming of the environment we inhabit as the bearer of divine meaning. The stuff of the world, the produce of its ordinary processes, becomes itself part of the new language of the Body, renamed as the carrier of the love and justice embodied in Jesus. The point is that the liturgical commemoration of the transforming work of Christ in cross and resurrection is not just a verbal rehearsing of the story but an action in which material elements are renamed in the course of the recital of that story, renamed as the present carriers of the action that is manifest in cross and resurrection; the story of what Jesus did and does is now a story about these things; and in a complementary way our story as guests at the table and consumers of the food and drink is a story about the act of God in Jesus' cross and resurrection. In the process that is the eucharistic action, we who have been renamed in baptism as God's children hear ourselves named afresh as guests and friends and as absolved betrayers; we receive again the freedom to name God as God has named God's self; and we rename the material world we inhabit as Spirit-bearing, embodying for us the transforming justice of God's work in Christ. From the central and generative moment in baptism where we receive our new names and learn the name by which we can now call God, the renewal of our language expands and feeds back into itself to produce the complex new speech and story that is the eucharistic action, the liturgical "journey" in which not only do we become again what we are named, but the world we inhabit is redefined as the bearer of God's purpose as giver and healer.

In the light of all this, we should be able to see why liturgy is more than ritual, more even than an event in which the sacred is encountered or experienced; rather, it is an event in which the sacred is experienced as uncovering itself in a movement of transition between contexts, registers,

---

fice (London: T & T Clark, 2009), Bridge 1.C, and Kenneth Stevenson, *Eucharist and Offering* (New York, NY: Pueblo, 1986), 3–37.

landscapes, however else one might put it. This is not to say that liturgical action is identical with sacramental: there may be liturgies that do not act out the fundamental transition we have been reflecting on, the transition between the language of mutual isolation and over-againstness and that of non-alienation or non-otherness. We have become rather more used in recent years to the call for "liturgical" events to mark moments of transition in personal and professional life, and while some of these bring their own problems, the demand illustrates a felt need for some way of affirming publicly that a new configuration has arisen in our world and that we are in a different place. It is easy for a traditionally minded Christian to raise an eyebrow at the idea of a "liturgy" marking the end of a marriage, say, or a transitioning to a new public gender identity, but given that such events cannot be exactly sacramental in the stricter sense, there is a strong case for recognizing that the strains and challenges of a newly named identity (perhaps not in any simple sense a chosen identity) are helped by a rite of transition. Less controversially, retirement, a new and demanding appointment, parenthood in a context where no-one is asking for infant baptism are all instances where we can see the aptness of a "renaming" occasion, and there are already models available (after all, graduation is perhaps the most easily recognizable "secular" pattern).

But what makes the sacramental context so uniquely significant, so that we rightly concentrate on this in our thinking about liturgy, is that it enacts the most basic transformation we can undergo: our alignment with the purpose and character of the creator as a result of the life, death, and resurrection of the incarnate Word. Time is transformed into the time of redemption, the time it takes for God to bring about the divine purpose or desire; matter is transformed into the vehicle of gift, nourishment, and joy. And this means that liturgy has a vital role in the communication of why Christian doctrine is the good news it claims to be. If the "stuff of the world"—through the agency of the Holy Spirit—now speaks and effects God's healing, we cannot any longer see the material world as "dead" matter. All those instincts that are attuned to the vitality and intelligence of our environment, instincts that so much of contemporary science seems to echo, are vindicated, and we understand that rather than being an isolated pocket of "meaning" in an indifferent and mechanical universe, we humans are bound into a web of life-giving and intelligent exchange. We are able to learn again how to be creatures in a finite and material world, without the arrogance of human exceptionalism or the mixture of resentment and melodrama generated by the mythical vision of a "blind" and "cruel" universe. This has obvious implications for our engagement with the rest of the material world, but also for our own use of material goods. Christian injunctions to share such goods are not just a matter of moral exhortation; they are reminders of what the material world can be as a vehicle of divine communication. Clinging to goods or ignoring the unjust distribution of goods is an implicit denial of what liturgical action displays as the potential of matter. The liturgical challenge is how we make any and all of the material things we deal in and negotiate with transparent to divine purposes in the way that the elements of the eucharistic liturgy are. These elements "act as instruments to unite the assembly. They are not possessed or deployed by anyone: they simply become the matter of a shared action."[9] There is what we could call a liturgical imperative to interrogate our understanding of wealth and possession in this light.

The title of this chapter refers to the transformation of time as well as matter; time, we have said, is transformed into the time of redemption. This means that in contrast to the time we "normally" experience, time that is to be allocated for the completion of tasks and is regularly in desperately limited supply, liturgically transformed and named time is there simply for God to act in. Our own sense of limit and pressure has to give way. The time of the liturgy is, fundamentally, the time of God's healing engagement with humanity, the time of scriptural narrative, above all the time of the paschal mystery. The time of the sacramental liturgy is the time in which this narrative is recalled, acknowledged as *present*, as the time in which we now live. Thus it is a time deliberately freed from any obligation to produce a "result" in terms that would instantly make sense to us. The story in which we find ourselves is "iterative"—that is, it is not an episode of some larger story which moves from start to finish and then gives way to another. It is something constantly re-entered, re-enacted, experienced freshly or indeed experienced routinely or boringly, a single extended story whose center, constantly approached from some new starting point, is the paschal event.[10] This is disorienting for our usual expectations, but intrinsic to the business of renaming the world.

---

9. Rowan Williams, *Liturgical Humanism: Orthodoxy and the Transformation of Culture*, Orthodoxy in America Lecture Series (New York, NY: Fordham Univ. Press, 2014), 11.

10. See Gschwandtner, "The Vigil as Exemplary Liturgical Experience," 655, on how a theology of liturgy has to take note of ordinary boredom and frustration in the experience of worship.

Our time has become not our own, our story is one we are not in control of. To return to the pregnant image of Revelation 2:17, we wait to hear at the end of time a name that we do not know; we cannot tell how our particular story will be woven in to the repeated story of God engaged with creation. But this changes our wider sense of time passing and makes another experience of our temporality possible. Instead of experiencing mortality and limit as threatening, we can learn to inhabit them as a place where the infinite resource of God is at work, in a mode and at a level beyond the simple linearity of our usual imagining. Each moment is capable of being the location of God at work in the way that the narrative of salvation defines—that is, the reality of the paschal mystery can be active whenever and wherever opportunity is given. Our own achievement of the ends we set ourselves is not what determines the freedom of God to be present and active in us (the God who names God's self in terms of the freedom to be God and the freedom to be Jesus' *Abba*). In this connection, the liturgical experience is a mode of encountering the mystery of radical unmerited grace and it is also immediately and obviously correlated with the encounter of silent contemplation. It is a serious misunderstanding to think of liturgical and contemplative prayer as somehow in tension; where such a misunderstanding prevails, we may be fairly sure that both terms have been distorted.

So the transformation effected in and celebrated in liturgy is—to make a point often underlined by liturgical theologians of the last few decades, from Aidan Kavanagh to Alexander Schmemann, and developed in a fresh direction by Jean-Yves Lacoste[11]—something that points us away from the logic of labor and output. Liturgy may be a matter of "work," as the word literally implies, but it is work designed to silence an obsessional and ego-directed form of activity. By renaming or reconfiguring the time in which we live (and die), liturgy brings us into transforming relation with the God who is free to be God and free to adopt and rename us as children; that divine liberty, the freedom simply to be what we are, is one aspect of what salvation means, and it entails a liberation in regard

11. See especially Lacoste, *Experience and the Absolute*, 77–81; cf. Gschwandt-ner, "The Vigil as Exemplary Liturgical Experience," 650.

to one another and to the entire material cosmos, as we have seen. But it is not a process we undergo all at once or even cumulatively; we must be reintroduced to it repeatedly, living as we do in a world where everything inside and outside us encourages us to go back to Egypt, where the output of labor is relentlessly measured. To quote Catherine Pickstock's still extraordinary book *After Writing*, "the resurrection is precisely that which prevents such fetishization of outcomes" because the narrative of the resurrection does not begin or end like other stories.[12] It continues to repeat itself in every particular believing life until the end of time, so that all time is a multiplicity of analogies to what it has enacted in our history. Liturgy enables the critique of modernity's myths, whether myths of the autonomous self or myths of the terrible scarcity of productive time, and so it is not too difficult to see why efforts to reconcile liturgy with unexamined modernity have been such a problematic feature of religious life in recent decades—a point that holds as much for purportedly "traditionalist" strategies as for modernizing ones, to the extent that an uncomfortable number of liturgical conservatives have been seduced by a model of liturgy as pure mystagogic performance of a fixed classic text rather than experiencing a seriously transformative immersion in a divine act that makes the world new.

These issues are explored with wit and insight by Bryan Spinks in his book *The Worship Mall*, obligatory reading for anyone seeking to understand the gravity of our liturgical challenge. He quotes Charles Davis to the effect that it is not so much specific forms of worship that are "outdated" as that the very action and idea of worship is not contemporary, either for modernity or for postmodernity.[13] But this mandates neither an abandonment of liturgy nor a self-conscious anti-modernity; rather we need to ask where the moral and imaginative deficit lies in the culture of our own age and to feel for the basic and defining forms of liturgical action in the context of theological exploration. If it is true that liturgy as such is to some degree countercultural in our time, this is the symptom of a deadening or evacuating of language itself: we have

12. Catherine Pickstock, *After Writing: On the Liturgical Consummation of Philosophy* (Oxford: Blackwell, 1998), 266.

13. Bryan D. Spinks, *The Worship Mall: Contemporary Responses to Contemporary Culture*, Alcuin Club Collections 85 (New York, NY: Church Publishing, 2010), 214.

lost certain skills of naming; we have become used to a mechanical and static view of what a name is. We have, you could say, lost some of the arts of verbal *poiesis*—using our language outside its comfort zones to unsettle prevailing habits and structures, whether of thinking or of political power. And consequently, we cannot expect most of our theology to make cultural sense. As Spinks implies, we cannot simply graft a Christian metaphysic on to a late modern idiom and expect it to sound convincing; we have to work at a different kind of anthropology.

To this extent at least, Catherine Pickstock must be correct in insisting that we cannot build a worshiping practice on a false or trivialized doctrine of the human. And it is also obvious that any theological renewal worth the name must be engaged with a serious remodeling of how our culture understands knowledge and speech. This chapter began with a discussion of one of the most creative philosophers in this area of recent times, a thinker who is crystal clear about how our speaking practice—itself an irreducibly *physical* affair—is part of our habituation to an environment in which we both stand and move, and which we learn to map reliably through a series of highly complex relations. Understanding this, understanding our speech as a "behavioural style," to quote Merleau-Ponty's phrasing again, should remind the theologian, as it reminds anyone reflecting on language, that to speak of God is to acquire a stance toward God; and since God is not an object in the world, this is going to be mediated through the stance we take toward the world as a complex system, an exchange of life and act. Christians have come to believe that certain events in the world have "addressed" them; they have discovered a new set of possibilities that they describe as having the effect of a call or invitation whose import is more than could be understood in relation to any finite agent. Thus relocated and renamed, they speak in a new way to God (and only subsequently in a new way *about* God), and in the light of this, learn new ways of recognizing meaning in the material environment. When they affirm together who they are and what they are learning, they find their way towards a "dramatic" representation of their stance—or rather their standing and their moving—that is what we call liturgy. And if any aspect of this story of discovery is missed or misapprehended, it is not only theology that is the casualty: our possibilities of relating non-destructively to one another and to the rest of the material world are damaged. We are, quite simply, in the wrong place.

When Moses asks to see God's glory (Exod 33:18), he is taken into a cleft in the rock from which he can see this glory pass before him. The image has haunted a good many Christian writers across the centuries, from Gregory of Nyssa onward. It implies that to see God's glory we need to be in a new place—and a place that is suitably secure. God manifests the divine glory and proclaims the divine name to Moses, and that name is again the declaration of God's freedom to be God, "to have mercy on whom I will have mercy": God's self-naming assures Moses that God is to be trusted, and so assures him that his human identity is indeed founded on rock. Yet there is no divine "face" to be seen. Moses must learn to see God in the passage of glory before his eyes, in something that illuminates the landscape of creation. In that light, Moses sees afresh, and is able to speak afresh. As Gregory of Nyssa interpreted it, Moses on the mountain was shown the inner life of all things. Hearing God's name, he is aware of his own newness and his security in that newness; out of that newness he names the world anew. But without the journey into the cleft in the rock, without finding that new place to stand, none of this happens. Liturgy repeats, effects, and embodies that journey, daily reappropriated: it instructs us (in one of the most memorably simple phrases of my own liturgical tradition) to "draw near with faith," and then, hearing ourselves named and remade as the Body of Christ, to move to a new place within creation itself, naming it with gratitude and delight instead of fear and the lust for power. The way in which we receive new names from God opens the way to our naming of the world in grace, naming what it most profoundly is and what it will be in God's purpose. And that is where glory becomes visible.

Some Highlights from the Question and Answer Session that Followed Rowan Williams's Keynote Address

Question: Does our customization of liturgy reflect the fact that we are more eager to be naming God than allowing God to be naming us?

RW: That's a very shrewd way of putting it. There's a sense in which if we focus too much on how we want liturgical vehicles for our story to unfold, we end up instrumentalizing the liturgical act. We start advertising: "We have a liturgy for every event!" That's why I think we have to come back to God's call to the human at the beginning of Genesis, which precedes the human activity. There is this basic *being* addressed, *being* named. The French medieval mystery play *Le Jeu d'Adam* opens simply with the *figura dei*, the representation of God, saying, "Adam," and Adam appears. That's the dimension we need to keep a hold of.

Question: I was especially taken by your discussion of "different but not other." Could you talk about how that impacts relationships that have been damaged or breached, or have somehow become toxic?

RW: Most of us, I guess, would have relationships broken in that way somewhere along the line. The best I can do, thinking of it from that point of view, is to think that the other person with whom I have a history, a friendship, intimacy isn't—and never could be—simply a stranger. That's key: the friend who has ceased to be a friend doesn't become a stranger. They're something else. That means that in my relation to them now, where I can't get to them directly, I have to try and hold them in my imagination as they are related to God, rather than to me, and see whether that abiding relation with God which I hold in my imagination ever opens a door for some renewal or healing or restoration.

I find this personally, as well as theoretically, a very big issue. I think we are so accustomed to rolling out the language of reconciliation and inclusion that we forget just how bloody difficult it is, and how regularly it just doesn't happen. So, we have to find some prayerful way—some responsible, adult, Christian way—of making sense of our failure to put together what's broken and facing the brokenness. Gail [Ramshaw] made this point briefly yesterday when we were talking about the kind of Earth-based eucharistic prayer that doesn't do justice to the brokenness or the conflict or conflictedness of the created order. That somehow has to find a place in how we praise. This question is not unconnected with that discussion.

Question: At one point as you were speaking, I was hearing Benjamin Britten's *Canticle II: Abraham and Isaac.* The tenor is cast as Abraham, the alto is Isaac, and the two voices combine—sometimes in parts, sometimes in unison—to form the voice of God. There's a sort of reconciliation taking place before our ears. Could you say a little more about how the voice of God might coalesce in ways we don't expect?

RW: That's a wonderful set of insights: the notion that, in some sense, whatever we understand about the voice of God holds together my voice and the other's or the stranger's or the enemy's voice. The holding is not in an immediate harmony, but rather the way music can sustain a very complex and risky set of discords and clashes. I'm thinking of those deliberate discords in sixteenth-century English music: the English cadence, which deliberately sort of squeezes the harmonics at the end of a phrase, as if to show that it's not just a happy ending or simple resolution. Very often we are living in the middle of a sort of English cadence. We can't quite see where it's all going to resolve. But God's address is fundamental and universal: it gives us the ability to hang out for that moment of resolution, which may be a moment that lasts a lifetime.

I think here of one of my great theological heroes, the late Elizabeth Templeton, probably not very well known on this side of the Atlantic: a theologian of the Church of Scotland, activist, feminist, contemplative poet, and a wonderful and luminous person. She wrote a book called *The Strangeness of God*, where she says that one of the things which really stays with her is the knowledge that on the Day of Judgement she will be standing before God's throne alongside, say, Ian Paisley, the great Protestant agitator from Northern Ireland. God will say, "Okay, you two, you have to find common ground, and you're not going to be sitting down until you've somehow found a table to sit at together." It really worries me when I think of all the people I might have to find a table to sit with.

Question: In the biblical story, it is humans who name the creatures. We may call them *dolphins,* but I'm sure they have their own name for themselves. How do we avoid seeing ourselves as the agents of God for the "lesser" creatures over whom we have the power of naming? How do we live with them equally, understanding that they have a story and a history to share with us?

RW: My mind immediately goes off to the question of what dolphins call us. Probably "useful idiots"!

I think that has something to do with how we imagine the naming of the beasts in the creation story. There are quite a lot of midrashic elaborations of this, but I would think the kind of theological naming we are interested in would have to be something that arises from the encounter. It's not just that there's a queue of creatures and Adam says, "You're a hippo. Next." There's some kind of engagement we can imagine that allows a self-naming of a sort, as that reality impinges on what we are.

That actually relates to a question which Teresa [Berger] suggested to me over dinner last night: does my approach privilege the articulate over the inarticulate? What about those who don't share articulacy or verbal skill? I think that's a fair question. I know that I—and I suspect I'm not the only one—am inclined to run off into the definition of human beings in terms of language use in a way that could be exclusive. That's why I'd want to talk about all the gestural, behavioral ways in which naming goes on at the pre-, post-, or para-verbal level and not imagine that to talk about naming is just to talk about simply *language,* as we often use the word.

That's part of what I was trying to feel for in using Merleau-Ponty, who is probably, for me, the most important philosophical influence in this area. Because he's so focused on the sheer physicality of language, he allows us to see that language is a very diverse, very multilevel thing, and the naming of self and other is by no means just the Adamic myth of the queue of animals. So, the person living with dementia whose memory is gone still nonetheless names themselves in relation in some way, and we lose enormously if we don't see that. The person with learning challenges and disabilities, the unborn or the newly born—we can still talk about gesture, bodily situatedness, and all the rest of it. That may help a little bit in redressing an imbalance towards that risk of the arbitrary namer who just hands out names. That's a model which reminds me of handing out slave names. We have to step back from that kind of hegemonic naming and ask, "What is it about the attentive, faithful encounter that allows a name to emerge as a shared language?"

Question: I worry about a romanticizing of this biblical account of naming. Adam names the woman in a way that is derivative of his own understanding of himself. What he recognizes of himself in her is what causes him to name her *isha*, drawn from *ish*. Similarly, the taxonomical naming of animal species is a comprehensive attempt to literally pin them down. The same idea went into the charting of the racial imagination: you could map different members of the human or "almost human" species into named and localized groups. That's an act of hegemony that persists with us today in so many ways.

RW: It's a good question, and one I don't really know how to handle. The taxonomical approach allows a degree of problem-solving. Problem-solving is not in itself a bad thing, but it becomes highly problematic when we think that the only thing that the world says to us is, "Here is a problem to be solved." I'm not sure how we manage without taxonomies, and the question I'm stuck with is how does one respond to an environment, let alone an other, or a conflict with an other, in a more than problem-solving way? It brings me straight on to the question of what are the practices that disrupt uncriticized hegemonic thinking? That's got to be one of the things which any liturgical or sacramental theology has to factor in.

PART ONE

BIBLICAL AND HISTORICAL ASPECTS

CHAPTER TWO

"Bless the Lord, Fire and Heat"

Reclaiming Daniel's Cosmic Liturgy for Contemporary Eco-Justice

Anathea Portier-Young

Bless the Lord East Rock and Mill River, bless the Lord Hanging Hills and Long Island Sound, bless the Lord moss and fern, elm and pine, bless the Lord robin, mantis, whale, and oyster. Bless the Lord, Fire and Heat.[1]

In the Old Testament, liturgy is political and the cosmos is contested domain. I argue here first that the Torah establishes an inextricable link between liturgy, cosmos, sovereignty, social justice, and ecological justice. This analysis will provide a framework for examining a text outside of Torah, namely Daniel 3, with special attention to an ancient Greek version commonly known as Theodotion. Portions of this Greek text will be well known to many in the form of the liturgical hymns or canticles *Benedicite, omnia opera Domini* and *Benedictus es Domine* and

---

1. I name here geographical features and species particular to New Haven, Connecticut, and its surrounding region, in recognition that the work of our conference was deeply rooted in place and joined its participants to the diverse lifeforms and vibrant ecosystems of this region. The fire and heat named in Daniel 3:66 take on special significance in the light of the trajectories and effects (actual and projected) of global warming documented in the report of 6 October 2018, "Global Warming of 1.5°C," by the Intergovernmental Panel on Climate Change (http://www.ipcc.ch/report/sr15/).

in readings for Easter Vigil services.[2] In Daniel 3, a furnace becomes a temple. Prisoners of war reject imperial liturgy and convoke in its stead a counter-imperial, cosmic liturgy. Improvisational worship alongside angels, celestial bodies, waters, and whales pushes back against the practices of empire and industry and declares that God's mercy and saving power are not only for human benefit, but for all the cosmos.

Genesis 1–2

Daniel 3 improvises a liturgy that rejects and counters the liturgy of an empire. A similar dynamic is found in Genesis 1. Numerous scholars have noted that the creation account of Genesis 1 provides a counternarrative to the Babylonian creation epic *Enuma elish*.[3]

Enuma elish presents creation as an act of conquest in which the body of the defeated becomes raw material that is penetrated, trampled, and

2. *Benedicite, omnia opera Domini* and *Benedictus es Domine* are excerpted from the praise hymn in Daniel 3 (Theodotion) commonly called the Song of the Three Youths or Song of the Three Young Men and are among the Canticles for Matins or Morning Prayer in the Roman Catholic Liturgy of the Hours and the Book of Common Prayer of the Church of England. For the history of the use of this hymn in early and medieval Christian liturgy, see Robert F. Taft, *The Liturgy of the Hours in East and West: The Origins of the Divine Office and Its Meaning for Today*, 2nd ed. (Collegeville, MN: Liturgical Press, 1993), 89; George Guiver, *Company of Voices: Daily Prayer and the People of God* (Eugene, OR: Wipf & Stock, 2001): 156–57; Christopher Irvine, *The Cross and Creation in Christian Liturgy and Art* (London: SPCK, 2013). The Theodotion Greek version of Daniel 3 also provides the basis for the readings for Holy Saturday Vespers in the Greek Orthodox Church and the pairing of reading and hymnody in Easter Vigil services in the Lutheran Church. In the *Lutheran Book of Worship*, the hymn *Benedicite, opera omnia* is sung after a reading of Daniel 3:1-29 and accompanies "the procession to the font for the baptisms and renewal of baptism by the assembly." See Frank C. Senn, *Introduction to Christian Liturgy* (Minneapolis, MN: Fortress Press, 2012), 138.

3. For example, Hermann Gunkel, *Creation and Chaos in the Primeval Era and the Eschaton: A Religio-Historical Study of Genesis 1 and Revelation 12* (Grand Rapids, MI: Eerdmans, 2006), originally published as *Schöpfung und Chaos in Urzeit und Endzeit: Eine religionsgeschichtliche Untersuchung über Gen. 1 und Ap. Joh. 12* (Göttingen: Vandenhoeck & Ruprecht, 1895); Bernard Frank Batto, *Slaying the Dragon: Mythmaking in the Biblical Tradition* (Louisville, KY: Westminster / John Knox Press, 1992); J. Richard Middleton, *The Liberating Image: The* Imago Dei *in Genesis 1* (Grand Rapids, MI: Brazos Press, 2005).

divided to shape a cosmos that is ordered first and foremost to provide habitations for its rulers. A form of this myth was a liturgical cornerstone of the annual Babylonian *Akitu* festival.[4] Like all creation myths, it did more work than simply tell a story of beginnings.[5] It provided a rationale and template for the creation and maintenance of the Babylonian empire through conquest, expansion, and appropriation of resources.[6] To say that Genesis 1 offers a counter-narrative is to recognize its simultaneously liturgical and political character.

The liturgical character of Genesis 1 emerges in the creative and performative repetitions of a poem that orders time and space in relation to divine making, speaking, and seeing.[7] The rhythms of divine artistry here generate and are echoed in the rhythms of the cosmos, day and night, labor and rest, seed and fruit, beating wings, creeping feet, and teeming multitudes.

The cosmos God creates in Genesis 1 bears marked structural and artistic likenesses with the tabernacle and temple described in Exodus, Kings, and elsewhere.[8] The portrayal of cosmos as sanctuary writ large foreshadows the sanctuary's role as map and symbol of the cosmos and designates the cosmos in its entirety as sacred site of worship.[9] Moreover,

---

4. For a positive reassessment of this consensus, see Benjamin Sommer, "The Babylonian Akitu Festival: Rectifying the King or Renewing the Cosmos?" *JANES* 27 (2000): 81–95.

5. On the functions of myth, see Paul Ricoeur and Richard Kearney, "Myth as the Bearer of Possible Worlds," *The Crane Bag* 2, no. 1/2 (1978): 112–18.

6. For its function in reaffirming Babylonian political and social order, see Karel van der Toorn, "The Babylonian New Year Festival: New Insights from the Cuneiform Texts and their Bearing on Old Testament Study," in *Congress Volume: Leuven, 1989*, ed. J. A. Emerton, *VTSup* 43 (Leiden: Brill, 1991), 331–44.

7. Ellen Davis writes, "As a liturgical poem, Genesis 1 is giving form to a certain way of seeing the world, and accurate perception provides an entrée to active participation in the order of creation" (Ellen F. Davis, *Scripture, Culture, and Agriculture: An Agrarian Reading of the Bible* [Cambridge: Cambridge Univ. Press, 2008], 43).

8. Jon Levenson, *Creation and the Persistence of Evil: The Jewish Drama of Divine Omnipotence* (New York, NY: Harper & Row, 1988), explores further homologies between the tabernacle and creation.

9. Levenson (ibid., 86) finds in the verbal and thematic parallels between Genesis 1–2:3 and Exodus 39–40 "the depiction of the sanctuary as a world, that is, an ordered, supportive, and obedient environment, and the depiction of the world as a sanctuary, that is, a place in which the reign of God is visible and unchallenged, and [God's] holiness is palpable, unthreatened, and pervasive." See also John Walton,

the shining of stars and black of night and the teeming and flowering of life on earth are presented as a "good" response to divine speech, will, and creativity, such that we can already begin to imagine creation's responsiveness to God's creative word and action as liturgy in itself.[10]

The narrative of divine artistry and care and the responsive rhythms, fruitfulness, and teeming of creation contradict imperial modes of "creation" through conquest, subjugation, and appropriation. This narrative instead models modes of governance that supply clean water, support diverse ecosystems, and promote biodiversity across every type of habitat and home. It also recognizes the agency and integrity of each constituent part of creation itself.[11]

As is well known, modern colonialism, industrialism, and the new imperial regimes of transnational corporations have all been fueled by the interpretive conceit that humankind is the pinnacle of creation.[12] They

---

Genesis 1 as Ancient Cosmology (Winona Lake, IN: Eisenbrauns, 2011), 101–19, 178–92. Walton concludes, "The Genesis account is distinguished from the temple theologies of its ancient Near Eastern context by virtue of the application of the temple identity to the entire cosmos" (192).

10. On liturgy as "telos of creation" see L. Michael Morales, *The Tabernacle Pre-Figured: Cosmic Mountain Ideology in Genesis and Exodus* (Leuven: Peeters, 2012), 91–111.

11. On the agency of creation, see William P. Brown, *The Ethos of the Cosmos: The Genesis of Moral Imagination in the Bible* (Grand Rapids, MI: Eerdmans, 1999), 86. Samuel Balentine argues instead that in light of the book's final, Persian period redaction and its possibly Persian-authorized dissemination, the affirmation here of an ordered and hierarchical creation and divinely ordained "cycles of work and production" supports Persian imperial rule. Samuel E. Balentine, *The Torah's Vision of Worship* (Minneapolis, MN: Fortress Press, 1999), 49–50. Balentine here draws on the work of Jon Berquist, *Judaism in Persia's Shadow: A Social and Historical Approach* (Minneapolis, MN: Fortress Press, 1995), esp. 139. Yet Balentine also argues that this liturgical text can push back against imperial hegemony and advance alternative visions of the world (215). On the relation between water, justice, and praxis of liberation see Christiana Zenner, *Just Water: Theology, Ethics, and Fresh Water Crises*, rev. ed. (Maryknoll, NY: Orbis, 2018).

12. Lynn White Jr., "The Historical Roots of our Ecologic Crisis," *Science* 155, no. 3767 (1967): 1203–7, charges that "Christianity is the most anthropocentric religion the world has seen" (1205). His claim is undergirded in part by the ways the Genesis narrative of the creation of humankind is linked with the incarnation of Christ by early interpreters such as Irenaeus and Tertullian.

are also supported by an interpretation of God's commission to human beings that understands human dominion as license to subdue and consume without concern for the welfare of creation itself.[13] Such an interpretation of Genesis 1 shares with the Babylonian creation epic *Enuma elish* an imperial ideology of exploitation and conquest. By contrast, an intertext such as Psalm 72 inflects "dominion" with custodial care, saying of the king of Israel, "May he have dominion from sea to sea, and from the River to the ends of the earth" (72:8 NRSV). The psalm partly elaborates dominion as follows: "For he delivers the needy when they call, the poor and those who have no helper. He has pity on the weak and the needy, and saves the lives of the needy. From oppression and violence he redeems their life; and precious is their blood in his sight" (72:12-14 NRSV). Dominion here opposes oppression and violence, promotes life, and restores the welfare of the disenfranchised.[14]

The commission in Genesis 1 can further be read in the context of the narrative in Genesis 2, wherein humans are charged with responsibility for serving (*la⁽ᵃbōd*) and keeping the earth (2:15).[15] Many modern translations follow cues of context to render this occurrence of the Hebrew verb *ʿābad* as "till" or "cultivate," that is, work the soil so that it produces

13. Such an interpretation is easily supported by the plain sense of Genesis 1:26-28, as argued by Norman Habel, "Is the Wild Ox Willing to Serve You? Challenging the Mandate to Dominate," in *The Earth Story in Wisdom Traditions*, ed. Norman C. Habel and Shirley Wurst, *Earth Bible* 3 (Sheffield: Sheffield Academic Press, 2001), 179–89.

14. John R. Donahue, "What Does the Lord Require? A Bibliographical Essay on the Bible and Social Justice," *Studies in the Spirituality of the Jesuits* 25, no. 2 (1993): 8, argues that when read in the light of this and other intertexts, "reverential care for God's creation rather than exploitation is the mandate given humanity in this section of Genesis."

15. Theodore Hiebert describes the contrast between the portrayal of human's role in relation to the earth in Genesis 1 and 2 this way: "for P [Gen 1:26-28] the human is the land's master, coercing it into service, while for J [Gen 2:15] the human is the land's servant, performing the duties demanded by its powers and processes" (Theodore Hiebert, *The Yahwist's Landscape: Nature and Religion in Early Israel* [Oxford: Oxford Univ. Press, 1996], 157). He adds, "The recovery of the Yahwist's modest view of the human place within the world from the very long shadow cast by the Priestly viewpoint in the history of scholarship and in modern environmental theology broadens our understanding of ancient Israelite thought" (159).

things human beings can eat. But in a linear reading of the Genesis narrative, this is not the most obvious meaning, as God has already caused the garden to produce food (2:9; cf. 2:16). A more obvious meaning, especially when paired with the verb "keep," is labor that promotes the welfare of the garden, "keeping" it in trust. The English compounds "pre-serve" and "con-serve" draw out this aspect of its meaning.

This Hebrew verb *ʿābad* ("serve") shares its root with the Hebrew noun, *ʿabōdâ* ("service" and "slavery"), including service to/for the sacred sites of tabernacle and temple (e.g., Num 3 and 4), and thus also "worship." The semantic overlap between labor or service and worship is similarly present in the Greek words *leitourgia* and *latreuō*. Following so closely on the liturgical poem in Genesis 1, the semantic connection in 2:15 between service and worship suggests that the task of serving the garden corresponds to the task of worship: it is analogous to the work of maintaining God's holy sanctuary and helps to sustain conditions in which all of creation can participate in the worship of God.

Exodus

The interrelationship between liturgy, cosmos, sovereignty, and social and ecological justice is further developed in the book of Exodus. For most, Exodus rightly conjures narratives of slavery and departure from Egypt or the giving of the law at Sinai. Equally, it is a book about worship. In Exodus, worship is the reason for and response to liberation; it is also presented as the telos of the law.[16] The instructions for and building of the tabernacle and its furnishings and the vestments, consecration, and sacred duties of the priests occupy thirteen chapters out of forty and hold a place of emphasis at the book's conclusion (Exod 25:1–31:10; 35:4–40:38).

A thematic contrast between slavery to Pharaoh and worship of God is introduced early in Exodus. The same verb, *ʿābad*, used in Genesis of humans' commission to serve the garden (Gen 2:15), names the bitter labor in brick, mortar, and soil imposed on the Israelites by their Egyptian overlords (Exod 1:13-14). The explicit contrast between this enslavement

---

16. William P. Brown offers a different interpretation, that "divine repose is the expressed goal of the exodus (29:46)" (Brown, *Ethos of the Cosmos*, 89). The verse in question states that God brings Israel out of Egypt "so that I might dwell [or "tabernacle"] in their midst." But God's dwelling amid God's people is not only for divine rest. It is also for encounter, relationship, protection, guidance, and worship.

and worship of God is first made in Moses' call narrative, when God promises: "when you have brought the people out from Egypt, you shall worship [*ta'ab'dûn*] God on this mountain" (Exod 3:12). God instructs Moses to command Pharaoh: "let my child [LXX 'my people'] go, that he may worship me [*w'ya'abdēnî*]" (4:23). God repeats the instruction at 8:1, 8:20, 9:1, and 9:13, and Moses delivers the command to Pharaoh at 7:16 and 10:3, all using a form of the verb *'ābad*. At 8:29 Moses substitutes the phrase "sacrifice to the LORD," highlighting the liturgical character of the service they will perform, while worshiping / serving and sacrificing are both named at 10:25-26.[17] Pharaoh's final dismissal of Moses and Aaron acknowledges the purpose of their departure from Egypt: "Rise up, go away from my people, both you and the Israelites! Go, worship [*'ibdû*] the LORD as you said" (12:31 NRSV).[18]

In this same narrative, a royal economy built on exploitation is shown to wreak death, destruction, and pollution throughout the land of Egypt. Pharaoh's refusal to release the people he has enslaved results in plagues upon the land, its animals, and its vegetation. The first plague afflicts the river Nile, causing its inhabitants to die and its water to become undrinkable (7:21). Subsequent plagues introduce invasive frogs (8:6), gnats (8:17), and flies (8:24), and strike animals, including humans, with disease (9:6, 10). Hail, fire, and locusts destroy crops (9:25; 10:15). The final plagues bring darkness (10:22) and death upon Egypt's firstborn (12:29). This series of plagues both echoes and undoes God's work of creation, to teach Pharaoh that God, not Pharaoh, is sovereign: "so that you may know that the earth is the LORD's" (9:29 NRSV).[19]

The linking in this narrative of cosmic and terrestrial sovereignty, economy, ecology, and service / worship finds a counterpart in the laws Israel receives and the tabernacle they build. In the laws, Sabbath observance modeled on God's work of creation and liberation countered

---

17. This verse includes livestock among those who will journey out from Egypt. While this includes animals to be sacrificed, Moses insists that "no hoof" shall be left behind: liberation from slavery in Egypt extends also to nonhuman animal life.

18. Cf. Exod 10:7-8, 11, 24, where Pharaoh's servants or Pharaoh are similarly the speakers.

19. Knowledge of God is thematized at 5:2; 6:7; 7:5, 17; 8:10, 22; 9:14, 29; 10:2; 14:4, 18; 16:6; 18:11 etc. Walter Brueggemann sees the plague cycle as a dismantling of the empire; see Walter Brueggemann, *The Prophetic Imagination*, 40th anniversary ed. (Minneapolis, MN: Fortress Press, 2018), 10.

the rhythms of slave economy with cycles of labor and rest that honored people, animals, vegetation, and soil (e.g., Exod 20:10-11; Lev 25:2, 4; Deut 5:14-15).[20] The building of the tabernacle would be equally countercultural: the silver, gold, and textiles of Egypt, luxury goods once hoarded among the wealthy, would be given as gifts to provide raw materials for the fashioning of the tabernacle (Exod 3:22; 11:2; 12:35-36; 25:3-4; 35:5-29; 38:24 etc.).[21]

In their inspired creativity the tabernacle artisans became co-creators with God, reminding God's people that in every act of worship they too would participate in and affirm God's work of creation (Exod 31:3, 6; 35:26, 31, 35; 36:1-2).[22] As Jon Levenson and others have shown, the mobile tabernacle, like the (narratively) later temple, represented the cosmos in miniature: its curtain divided (*wᵉhibdîlâ*) the holy place from the most holy (Exod 26:33), just as God established a firmament dividing (*mabdîl*) waters from waters (Gen 1:6) and lights to divide (*lᵉhabdîl*) day from night (1:14, 18).[23] Its laver or basin represented the sea (Exod 30:18; 38:8);[24] its lampstand was simultaneously a tree of life and source of light (25:31-35; 35:14; 37:17-20; 39:37).[25] The produce of the earth

20. Patrick Miller, *The Ten Commandments* (Louisville, KY: Westminster John Knox Press, 2009), 117–66, outlines the scope of a "sabbatical principle" that provides a "regularized avenue for justice and freedom" (149). He addresses the relation between release for the land and provision for the poor as well as nonhuman animals (including undomesticated animals) at pp. 135–36.

21. On the close link between the despoiling of the Egyptians and the themes of liberation and victory, see Myung Soo Suh, *The Tabernacle in the Narrative History of Israel from the Exodus to the Conquest* (New York, NY: Peter Lang, 2003), 23–42.

22. For a socio-spatial analysis of the significance of this detail, see Mark George, *Israel's Tabernacle as Social Space* (Atlanta, GA: Society of Biblical Literature, 2009), 181–89.

23. For example, Levenson, *Creation and the Persistence of Evil*; Peter Kearney, "Creation and Liturgy: The P Redaction of Ex 25–40," *Zeitschrift für die alttestamentliche Wissenschaft* 89 (1977): 375–87.

24. The analogous feature in temple narratives is called "the sea" (*hayyam* 1 Kgs 7:23-24; 2 Kgs 16:17; 25:16; Jer 52:17; etc.).

25. Carol Meyers, *The Tabernacle Menorah: A Synthetic Study of a Symbol from the Biblical Cult* (Missoula, MT: Scholars Press, 1976), 143–56, analyzes the cosmic significance of the menorah as tree of life. Among other symbolic functions, it "bring[s] the organizing principle of God's presence in the cosmos into visible focus in the midst of the people" (175).

provided bread of presence (Exod 25:30; 35:13; 39:36); seed-bearing fruit would be further represented in the pomegranates adorning the priestly vestments (28:33; 39:24-25).[26] As in Genesis, so too here homologies between cosmos and tabernacle mark all of creation as site for and participant in a life of worship that affirms the sovereignty and justice of God. Worship celebrates and reiterates God's act of liberation, rejection of exploitation, and will for the flourishing of all creation.[27]

Daniel 3

The intertwining of liturgy, cosmos, sovereignty, and justice is also at the heart of Daniel 3.[28] In the remainder of this chapter, I argue that the ancient Greek version of Daniel 3 known as Theodotion responds to the coercive liturgy of empire and industry with a voluntary, improvisational counter-liturgy that affirms the agency of all the cosmos and portrays a divine justice that is for all creation. This narrative and the counter-liturgy it portrays provide a valuable resource for a liturgical praxis that promotes contemporary ecojustice.

We have seen that the repetitive, liturgically inflected creation poem of Genesis 1 implicitly portrays the cosmos as a locus of worship of the Lord, countering a model of creation through royal conquest that was prevalent in Mesopotamia with a model of creation through performative speech, artistry, and participation. In Exodus, the narratives concerning plagues and liberation of enslaved Hebrews repudiate Pharaoh's claim to cosmic sovereignty. Worship of the Lord is there portrayed as counterpoint to slavery and the telos of liberation. The tabernacle's cosmic symbolism unites Israel's ongoing worship life to economic, social, and ecological justice that provides an alternative to Pharaoh's economy of

26. Cf. the vegetal motifs ornamenting the temple (1 Kgs 6:29, 32, 35; 7:36).

27. J. G. McConville writes, "In its synthesis of constructive work, worship and rest, Exodus offers a revolutionary antithesis to Pharaoh's degradation and enslavement of humanity" (J. G. McConville, *God and Earthly Power: An Old Testament Political Theology, Genesis–Kings* [London: T & T Clark, 2006], 54).

28. Portions of this section are adapted with permission of Civitas Dei Foundation (publishers of the journal *Chicago Studies*) from Anathea Portier-Young, "Prayer amid the Flames: Liturgy in Daniel 3, the Prayer of Azariah, and the Song of the Three Young Men," *Chicago Studies* 52, no. 3 (2013): 45–61.

exploitation. Like Genesis 1 and the book of Exodus, Daniel 3 counterposes divine cosmic rule to terrestrial, imperial sovereignty, resisting imperial practices such as conquest, enslavement, and exploitation through portrayals of worship.

Before I explain how this is so, a word is in order about the textual forms of the book of Daniel in general and of Daniel 3 in particular as they relate to the subject of liturgy within the narrative of Daniel 3 and to liturgical use of Daniel 3 among Christians. While the Masoretic Text (MT) provides the form of the book of Daniel familiar to and authoritative for Jewish and Protestant readers, a longer Greek text commonly referred to as Theodotion (Th) provides the basis for the form of Daniel familiar to and authoritative for Catholic and Orthodox readers. This longer, Greek version is also the source for narrative and hymnic material that has featured prominently in both Eastern and Western liturgical traditions, including Matins and Easter Vigil liturgies among Orthodox, Catholic, Anglican, Episcopalian, and Lutheran communities. My analysis of Daniel 3 will primarily focus on Th, as this is the version that forms the basis for most historical and contemporary Christian liturgical usage.[29] Thus, unless otherwise specified, when I refer to the text of Daniel 3 below, I refer to the form preserved in Th.

Daniel 3 portrays two liturgies, one royal, scripted, and coerced, the other cosmic, improvisational, and voluntary. The first, orchestrated by Nebuchadnezzar, king of Babylon, entails the worship of a golden statue the king has erected. At the king's command, participants from throughout his kingdom are coerced into following a responsive, liturgical script in which a musical performance cues the action and posture of worship. The story's heroes, three Judean captives named Shadrach, Meshach, and Abednego, refuse to participate in the liturgy and are punished by being thrown into a fiery furnace. The narrative portrayal of the first, royal liturgy and the fiery punishment for nonparticipation focus readers' attention on symbols of imperial exploitation and excess that illustrate the significant, negative environmental impact of imperial conquest and extraction and consumption of resources.

---

29. On the relationship among the ancient versions, see Anathea Portier-Young, "Three Books of Daniel: Plurality and Fluidity among the Ancient Versions," *Interpretation: A Journal of Bible and Theology* 7, no. 2 (2017): 143–53.

This portrayal provides a narrative foil for the second liturgy, which transforms the furnace into a space of resistance to empire and there models a form of worship that accords free agency to a vast array of living creatures, elements of nature, landscape, celestial bodies, and other features of the cosmos. The second liturgy begins the moment the three young Judean captives fall into the furnace. This second, voluntary and improvisational liturgy worships not the king's statue, but rather the Lord. In so doing it symbolically transforms the furnace, a symbol of imperial exploitation and oppression, into a temple of the Lord. Through the incorporation of two hymns, the liturgy moves from confession to praise. While its first hymn foregrounds divine justice and saving mercy, its second hymn invites all the cosmos to participate in worshiping the Lord, affirming that divine justice and saving mercy are for all creation.

In the analysis that follows, I examine first the two liturgies in sequence, beginning with Nebuchadnezzar's coercive, scripted, royal liturgy and then the Judeans' voluntary, improvised, cosmic liturgy. I conclude the essay by suggesting how this second liturgy provides a resource for contemporary eco-justice.

In the opening narrative of Daniel 3, repetitions focus readers' attention on two objects created at the command of the Babylonian king Nebuchadnezzar: a massive statue of gold and a blazing furnace. One is to be the object of worship, the other the means of enforcing it. Both are portrayed as symbols of imperial excess and exploitation. Attention is focused on the statue by means of eleven repetitions that continually link the statue to the ambitions of the king.[30] It is portrayed as impractical, constructed of soft metal, and towering a precarious sixty cubits high from atop a narrow base (Dan 3:1).[31] Its ostentatious display of imperial wealth and power simultaneously testifies to the extraction and appropriation of natural resources from subjugated lands and the coercion of labor from the people who inhabit them. Nebuchadnezzar demands that this symbol of rapine shall become an object of worship by the people he has

---

30. Dan 3:1, 2, 3 (x2), 5, 7, 10, 12, 14, 15, 18.

31. The width is six cubits in MT and Th, and twelve cubits in the Old Greek version (the Old Greek version of Daniel predates Th and translated a Hebrew text that differed in places from MT; within Christian usage Old Greek was replaced by Th). Cf. the dimensions Cyrus proposes for the rebuilt temple in Ezra 6:3: it should measure sixty cubits high and sixty cubits wide.

subjugated. The narrative will gradually shift attention from this statue to the flames of the blazing furnace, introduced in verse 6 and mentioned a total of eighteen times.[32] This shift in focus from statue to furnace will further shift the reader's attention from royal liturgy to cosmic liturgy and accentuate the transformation of a site of imperial violence into a space of worship that is oriented toward justice for creation.

Before this shift from statue to furnace occurs, however, four other sets of repeated details draw attention to the liturgical focus at the story's heart and illustrate the coercive character and universal ambition of the first, royal liturgy it depicts. These repeated details are as follows: (1) the list of summoned leaders, (2) a repeated reference to "peoples, tribes, tongues," (3) the list of musical instruments, and (4) the paired verbs fall / worship.

The first of these repetitions describes a convocation.

> He [Nebuchadnezzar] sent to assemble the high officials, generals and governors, leaders and tyrants, those in power and all the rulers of the countries, to come to the dedicatory celebration of the golden statue, which Nebuchadnezzar, the King, had erected. And they were assembled, the governors, high officials, generals, leaders, great tyrants, those in power and all the rulers of the countries, for the dedication of the statue which Nebuchadnezzar, the King, had erected, and they stood before the statue. (Dan 3:2-3)[33]

The nearly verbatim repetition of the list of officials in 3:2-3 draws attention to a summons and an assembly that will soon receive a call to worship.[34] Hector Avalos has convincingly argued that this repetition and the repeated list of instruments that follows have a subversive comedic quality.[35] Such a comedic portrayal highlights the farcical but dangerous nature of the king's ambitions and lends further substance to the contrast

---

32. Dan 3:6, 11, 15, 17, 19, 20, 21, 22, 23, 46, 47, 48, 49 (x2), 50, 51, 88, 93.

33. Unless otherwise noted, translations of Daniel are the author's own. Translations of Greek Daniel are based on Joseph Ziegler's Göttingen Septuagint text.

34. The list of gathered officials will be repeated again in part at 3:94, when these officials become witnesses to the deliverance of Shadrach, Meshach, and Abednego. The effect of this later repetition will be to mark a shift in the character of the worship and witness of the assembled congregation.

35. Hector Avalos, "The Comedic Function of the Enumerations of Officials and Instruments in Daniel 3," *Catholic Biblical Quarterly* 53, no. 4 (1991): 580–88.

between the chapter's first, royal liturgy and the subsequent, cosmic liturgy. The repetition also has a liturgical quality, and is followed by a description of the posture, location, and orientation of the assembled multitude, who "stand before the image" (3:3).

A second repetition, namely the repeated phrase "peoples, tribes, tongues," further emphasizes Nebuchadnezzar's political reach, expands the convocation's scope, and asserts the quasi-universality of Nebuchadnezzar's royal liturgy (3:4, 7). A herald first declares the universality of Nebuchadnezzar's dominion and the assembly itself by declaring to the gathered people: "to you it is said, o peoples, tribes, tongues" (3:4). The instructions to worship the statue follow. At 3:7 the narrator's repetition of the phrase "peoples, tribes, tongues" portrays a near perfect concordance between command and execution, but its assertion of universal dominion will soon be revealed to be false (see below).

A third set of repetitions introduces musical instrumentation and is closely linked to a fourth which describes the coordination of action with music. As with the list of officials and the phrase "peoples, tribes, tongues," so too with the instruments and coordinated action the repetition arises through the pairing of command and execution. The herald commands the "peoples, tribes, tongues" as follows:

> In whichever hour you hear the voice of the trumpet, both pipe and lyre, sambuca and psaltery, and every kind of musical instrument, falling, you shall worship the golden statue which Nebuchadnezzar, the King, has erected. And whoever does not fall and worship, in that same hour will be thrown into the furnace burning with fire. (3:5-6)

The proposed coordination of music, bodily disposition, and worship aims to constitute a liturgy-on-demand. In the next verse, the repeated list of instruments and repeated verb-pair fall / worship portray the obedient participation of those assembled:

> And when the peoples heard the voice of the trumpet, both pipe and lyre, sambuca and psaltery, and every kind of musical instrument, falling, all the peoples, tribes, tongues worshiped the golden statue which Nebuchadnezzar, the King, had erected. (3:7)

From assembly and address to the scripted movement of bodies in worship, each repetition sharpens the story's liturgical focus. Moreover, the first three sets of repetitions each contain a form of the word "all" or "every" (Aramaic *kol*; Greek *pas*): the king summons *all* his leaders, commands the participation of *all* nations and tongues, and orders their bodies to music from *every* kind of instrument. In short, the king aims to create a liturgy that is universal as a performance and celebration of his implicit claim to universal dominion. Yet the negative condition attached to the first repetition of the verb-pair fall / worship (3:6) reveals the possibility of royal failure: the king will not finally be able to dictate either the object and mode of worship or the range of participants. This failure undercuts his implicit claim to universal dominion.

His failure becomes manifest when a group of Chaldeans approach the king, first rehearsing his instructions, including the list of instruments, and twice repeating the now familiar pair fall / worship (3:10-11). But they do so to call attention to "Judean men . . . who do not serve your gods and do not worship the golden statue you have set up" (3:12). The nonparticipation of these Judean men falsifies the universality of this royal, coerced liturgy. Enraged (3:13) the king repeats the litany of instruments, the instruction to fall / worship, and the threat of the furnace (3:15). Shadrach, Meshach, and Abednego respond that they will never serve Nebuchadnezzar's idol or bow to his statue (3:18). Instead they invoke "our God whom we worship" (3:17); their worship and fear of God preclude worship of any other god or idol.

Their refusal incites a fast-paced action scene of stoking, binding, flinging, and falling. To punish those who will not worship his statue, Nebuchadnezzar commands the furnace be stoked "sevenfold" (3:19). A later verse adds that it was "kindled excessively" (3:22), that is, beyond what was necessary to accomplish the appointed task. Elsewhere in biblical tradition, the symbolic multiplier seven is associated with creation, liberation, and Sabbath, including rest and healing for the land (especially Lev 25:2-6). Its use here highlights the contrast between divine providential care for the cosmos, will for liberation, and the command to care for the land, on the one hand, and the destructive and exploitative practices of the empire, with harmful consequences for living creatures and land alike, on the other.

That is, like the statue, the furnace exhibits the extraction and appropriation of resources in the service of imperial ego and ambition. Unnecessary heat means proportionally unnecessary consumption of natural resources used for fuel. These fuel sources are later identified as "naphtha and pitch and tow and brushwood" (Dan 3:46). Naphtha is, according to the Oxford English Dictionary, "a volatile, flammable liquid obtained by the fractional distillation of petroleum or the destructive distillation of coal tar, shale, lignite, etc., and composed of a mixture of hydrocarbons."[36] Pitch is another hydrocarbon-containing distillate. Extraction and distilling of raw materials to create naphtha and pitch would likely have disrupted the landscape and its ecology. In a similar vein, excessive use of brushwood can contribute to deforestation and habitat removal. Burning these fuels would also have created significant air pollution. This blaze takes a great deal but gives nothing in return to the kingdom Nebuchadnezzar governs. Its function is solely to eliminate those who will not worship the statue he has made. The king ordains that they too will become fuel for the machinery of imperial exploitation. And so the three men are thrown into the furnace.

In the next moment, a second liturgy has begun: "And they were walking around in the midst of the fire, singing God's praise and blessing the Lord" (3:24). The Greek versions, including Th, here preserve sixty-seven verses not included in MT that decisively shift the chapter's focus from Nebuchadnezzar's coercive, scripted, royal liturgy to a cosmic, improvisational, and voluntary counter-liturgy. These verses have a four-part structure:

A. Narrative portrayal of worship (3:24-25)

B. Prayer of Confession (3:26-45)

C. Narrative portrayal of the furnace's transformation (3:46-51)

D. Song of Praise (3:52-90).

I argue below that the paired hymns of voluntary confession and praise in the furnace provide a template for contemporary liturgical praxis in the face of environmental exploitation, pollution, monocultural agriculture, climate change, and anthropogenic extinctions. Their incorporation within the narrative setting in Daniel 3 further reveals this liturgical praxis as a praxis of resistance, liberation, and justice for all creation.

---

36. "naphtha, n.," OED Online, June 2018, Oxford Univ. Press, http://www.oed.com/view/Entry/125022?redirectedFrom=naptha#eid.

The furnace's transformation from site of destruction and danger to site of worship and blessing models a transformation that is also possible within our world.

A. Narrative Portrayal of Worship

The immediacy of the actions of the three Judeans makes of the fiery furnace, from the moment they enter it, a place of prayer, song, praise, and worship.[37] Moreover, features of this physical setting are linked with worship elsewhere in the book of Daniel. Fire is identified with the throne of the Ancient of Days (7:9) and is the setting for angelic worship: "A river of fire breathed in before [the Ancient of Days]; thousands of thousands were serving [the Ancient of Days], and ten thousands of ten thousands were standing, attending [the Ancient of Days]" (7:10). Envisioned as a paradoxical river, the fire before the throne is liminal, holy space, like a threshold or gate. Yet it is not static, but expands and contracts like breath, suggesting a capacity to transform and be transformed. In Daniel 3, the narrator next highlights standing posture as an accompaniment to prayer, marking a contrast with the prostration commanded by Nebuchadnezzar and presaging the standing posture of angels before the blazing throne of the Ancient of Days (3:25; 7:10, 16). By

---

37. Participants at the Institute of Sacred Music, Yale, conference at which the papers in this volume were first heard noted the startling parallel between Nebuchadnezzar's command that his soldiers bind Shadrach, Meshach, and Abednego and cast them into the furnace and the burning and fatal gassing of Jews in crematoria and gas chambers at Auschwitz, Majdanek, Bełżec, Sobibór, and Treblinka by soldiers of the Third Reich. Azariah's declaration that "we have been made fewer than all other nations" (3:37) similarly foreshadows and resonates with the experience of European Jews during the Third Reich. Recognition of this parallel does not collapse ancient tale with modern atrocity nor does it suggest that the furnaces of Auschwitz and Majdanek should be construed as temple space. The narrated witness of Shadrach, Meshach, and Abednego / Hananiah, Mishael, and Azariah cannot substitute for or overwrite the witnesses of Shoah survivors and victims. Yet the witness and summons to worship by Hananiah, Azariah, and Mishael may help those who are not survivors of Nazi genocide recognize a summons to a liturgically responsive praxis of remembrance, confession, and resistance in the face of Nazi persecution as well as in the face of contemporary imperial violence. On the moral significance of poetry as a form of testimony to the Shoah, see James Hatley, *Suffering Witness: The Quandary of Responsibility after the Irreparable* (Albany: State Univ. of New York Press, 2000).

standing, singing, blessing, and praying in the flames of the furnace, the three men symbolically join in angelic liturgy before the divine throne.

The narrator now focuses attention on one individual, Azariah, who has formerly been called Abednego (3:25; see also v. 49). This transition from the quasi-Babylonian name suggestive of servitude or worship of a Babylonian god (*abed* = slave + *nego* ≈ Nabu) to a Semitic name containing a confession of Yhwh's saving help (*'azar* = has helped + *yah* ≈ Yhwh) suggests that here in the fire Azariah and his companions not only refuse to worship the gods of Babylon, they also claim and live into the very identities and confessions proclaimed by their names.

B. Prayer of Confession

The prayer that follows is the longest direct speech reported so far in the book of Daniel. Indeed, the combined prayers make Daniel 3 the longest chapter in the book, almost twice as long as the next longest chapters (2 and 11). The action slows such that the reader is drawn in to linger in the flames and join in the liturgy that unfolds in their midst.[38]

The prayer begins with a blessing anchored in the traditions of "our ancestors" (3:26, 28). This invocation establishes continuity within a tradition of faith and praxis, even as the prayer itself reflects creative, improvisational application of familiar forms to a new context. In declaring the truth of the judgments "you brought upon us" on account of "our sins" (3:28), the young men speak to God on behalf of their community, confessing not simply personal sins, but corporate ones (vv. 29-30). In this role they act as mediators who will later offer themselves as an atoning sacrifice (see below). Continual use of first-person pronouns throughout the prayer engages the reader and audience; through direct address to God, human speakers and audiences of the prayer are brought into dialogical relationship with their deity.

Confession of sin is paired with a declaration of God's intention for the well-being of God's people (3:30) and followed by an affirmation of God's just judgment (3:31). The constancy of divine justice (3:27-28, 31) is contrasted with the petty injustice of the present, earthly monarch

---

38. David deSilva notes of the two prayers in this chapter: "They may stall the forward movement of the plot, but they also transform the furnace into a place for beautiful, unhurried, ordered worship, which is, after all, the miracle of the plot" (David A. deSilva, *Introducing the Apocrypha: Message, Content, and Significance* [Grand Rapids, MI: Baker Academic, 2002], 230).

(3:32). The prayer foregrounds the struggles of the Judean people, who find themselves now fewer and low in status (3:37).

Azariah laments that there is "no leader . . . no whole burnt offering, no sacrifice, no offerings or incense, no place to bring first fruits before you and find mercy" (3:38). These conditions are consistent with exile or diaspora, as in the narrative setting of Daniel 3, and a situation in which the temple has been defiled and its worship interrupted, as in the wake of the desolating abomination foretold in Daniel 9:27, 11:31, and 12:11.

Amid such circumstances Azariah petitions God:

> But rather with a life crushed to pieces and a spirit brought low, may we be received as though among whole burnt offering of rams and bulls and as though among tens of thousands of fat lambs; so let our sacrifice become before you today. (3:39-40a)[39]

For readers today, the offering of "a life crushed to pieces and a spirit brought low" resonates with the current state of creation, exactly as depleted and debased and violated as colonial and consumerist greed has rendered it. The offering proposed by Azariah and his companions requires no further sacrifice of life, no further royal display of excess and power. Moreover, by offering human life in place of animals Azariah reverses a long pattern in which animals have substituted for and been sacrificed on behalf of humans. The vast number of animals further calls to mind the sacrificial celebrations that attended the dedication of Solomon's temple (1 Kgs 8:5, 63; 2 Chr 7:5) and the restoration of temple worship and Passover celebrations during the reigns of Hezekiah and Josiah (2 Chr 29:33; 30:24; 35:7-9). The young men offer themselves as a dedicatory sacrifice and an offering of well-being for the community, proposing to consecrate the furnace as a temple where all might worship.[40]

---

39. Cf. Psalm 51:19. Jan Joosten, "The Prayer of Azariah (DanLXX 3): Sources and Origin," in *Septuagint and Reception: Essays Prepared for the Association for the Study of the Septuagint in South Africa*, ed. Johann Cook (Leiden and Boston, MA: Brill, 2009), 5–16, at 12–13, argues that Daniel 3:39 is dependent on the Greek text of Micah 6:7; this is a key to his argument that the prayer was composed in Greek.

40. On the mediatorial role of Azariah and his companions, see Thomas Hieke, "Atonement in the Prayer of Azariah (Dan 3:40)," in *Deuterocanonical Additions of the Old Testament Books*, ed. Géza Xeravits and József Zsengellér (Berlin: Walter de Gruyter, 2010), 43–59. A parallel mediatorial role is ascribed to Daniel in the Old Greek version of Bel and the Dragon, which explicitly names Daniel "a priest" (ἱερεύς v. 2).

C. Narrative Portrayal of the Furnace's Transformation

The possibility that the furnace might become a temple is reinforced by the report of the flames' height, forty-nine cubits above the furnace (3:47). In only a few biblical texts are such precise measurements offered. Examining occurrences of the word "cubit" elsewhere in the Greek Old Testament demonstrates that within this corpus, such measurements are most commonly applied to spaces and objects designated for worship. These include the dimensions of the wilderness tabernacle and its furnishings (Exod 35–38), the temple built by Solomon and its furnishings (1 Kgs 6–7; 2 Chr 3–4), the temple envisioned in Ezekiel 40–48, and the statue at the beginning of Daniel 3.[41] With such echoes in view, the narrator's report of the flames' height does more than emphasize the danger of the furnace or the vast amount of fuel it has consumed. It counterposes statue and flames and proposes that furnace now, temporarily, take the place of temple. Its forty-nine cubits map the jubilary structure of time, known from Leviticus, onto a spatial plane, suggesting that just as seven weeks of years marked by slavery, debt, and loss culminate in the jubilee year of liberation and restoration, so this space of exile and execution will be transformed into one of life, freedom, and renewal (Lev 25:8). And contrary to Nebuchadnezzar's expectation, this fire, like the theophanic fire of Exodus 3:2, does not consume or destroy those in its midst. Rather, it signals God's attention, presence, and will to save amid suffering and trial.

The fire is further transformed when the angel of the Lord comes down, extinguishes the flame around them, and makes the middle of the furnace like a "wind of dew" (3:50). By extinguishing the flames around the young men, the angel refuses human sacrifice (cf. Gen 22).

---

41. In the Greek Old Testament, frequencies are as follows: the tabernacle and its furnishings in Exodus 25–38: 38 occurrences; Solomon's temple and its furnishings in 1 Kings 6–7: 32 occurrences; Solomon's temple and its furnishings in 2 Chronicles 3–4 and the prayer platform in 2 Chronicles 6:3: 25 occurrences; the temple envisioned in Ezekiel 40–48: 96 occurrences; the second temple envisioned in Ezra 6:3 / 1 Esdras 6:24: 2 occurrences; spoils from the temple in Jeremiah 52 and 2 Kings 25: 7 occurrences; the statue in Daniel 3: 2 occurrences. Together these constitute 202 of 239 occurrences. That is, 85 percent of all cubit measurements in the Greek Old Testament provide dimensions for spaces and objects designated for use in worship. These frequency statistics are derived from use of the lemma search tool in Bibleworks 10 and are based on the 2006 *Rahlfs-Hanhart Septuaginta*.

Instead, "wind of dew" mirrors and participates in heavenly and Edenic realities (cf. *Joseph and Aseneth* 16:14), suggesting blessing, new life, and grace (cf. Gen 27:28; Isa 26:19; Zech 8:12), a place of safety (cf. Deut 33:28), and participation in heavenly worship (cf. Dan 3:64-65). After the furnace is transformed, "the three, as from one mouth, were singing praise, glorifying, and blessing God in the furnace" (3:51). The narrator reminds the reader of this surprising location so that the reader does not forget what is possible in the furnace and remains mindful of its stunning transformation. The detail "as from one mouth" highlights their shared experience of worship. The reader will be invited into this experience through the familiar antiphons of the praise hymn that follows.

D. Song of Praise

The Song of Praise shares similarities with praise psalms known from the Psalter, especially Psalm 148.[42] Like that psalm, its repetitive language and antiphonal structure would have made it easy for a congregation to learn to pray responsively, and these characteristics have contributed to this song's longstanding use within Christian liturgical traditions, for example in the *Benedicite* and *Benedictus es Domine*. The Song of Praise's first verse (3:52) echoes the first verse of the prayer of confession (3:26), linking the two prayers, marking them as two moments in one liturgy.

The Song of Praise begins by offering praise to God in God's shrine and on God's throne, from which God looks upon the depths and sits upon the cherubim (3:53-55). Space, symbol, action, and position characterize divine sovereignty in terms of just rule, judgment, and knowledge. They also map the boundaries between order and chaos, sacred and profane, reframing an experience of suffering in relation to cosmic order. The hymn then moves from declaration to invocation, replacing the herald's command to the peoples, tribes, and tongues with imperatives that address first those in heaven, then elements, earth, nonhuman animals, and humans. This movement heavenward and back to the present situation (3:88) suggests that heaven is a starting place and eternal archetype for liturgy.[43] In this model, all blessing, praise, and worship follow from and participate in heavenly, cosmic liturgy.

---

42. See Carey A. Moore, *Daniel, Esther, and Jeremiah: The Additions* (New York, NY: Doubleday, 1977), 75–76. Moore also explores comparisons to Psalm 136.

43. The phrase "for the ages," i.e., "forever," is repeated in every verse of the hymn.

It is not only ministering angels who worship God, but also a panoply of natural phenomena. The inclusion of metereological phenomena, aspects of seasons, nights and days, light and dark, invokes categories of creation familiar from Genesis 1 and the temporal order that conditions human life (cf. Gen 8:22). In biblical and early Jewish literature, natural phenomena, elements, and properties such as wind, lightning, frost, dew, flame, cold, and heat were sometimes personified as semi-divine beings, with roles or titles including "messengers" / "angels" and "ministers."[44] By personifying these and other phenomena here, the Song of Praise amplifies and develops existing cosmologies, attributing agency to forces throughout the cosmos and animating all of creation with praise of God.[45] Moreover, it asserts that in every season, time of day, temperature, difficult weather, God is still to be praised. The inclusion of fire and heat among the addressees of the song is especially significant in light of the narrative setting: the flames of the furnace are not to be feared, for they too can be summoned to give praise. The purpose of physical realities that might otherwise be intended or interpreted as a source of danger is not ultimately injury to human life but rather worship of God.

The Song of Praise next addresses sea monsters and beasts and concludes with addresses to humans. This movement from creatures of chaos (with which the sea was symbolically associated), to wilderness animals, and finally to human life, beginning with priests, calls out religious leaders as keepers of cosmic order in a time when some had become "apostate." Corresponding to the redemption of the "many" in Daniel 11:33, 12:3, and 12:10, this exhortation opens space for conversion and renewed faithfulness on the part of leaders.[46] The Song of Praise then exhorts "the spirits and lives of the righteous" and "the holy and lowly in

44. E.g., Psalm 104:4; Zech 6:5; *1 Enoch* 14:8; *Jubilees* 2:2.

45. Martin Rösel notes a comparison between the diverse natural phenomena included here and lists in Sirach 42:15–43:33 and 4 Ezra 7:39–42. See Martin Rösel, "Enhanced and Revised: The Old Greek Edition of the Book of Daniel," in *Septuagint, Sages, and Scripture: Studies in Honour of Johann Cook*, ed. Randall X. Gauthier, Gideon Kotzé, and Gert Steyn (Leiden: Brill, 2016), 279–93, at 288.

46. In the encyclical *Laudato Si': On Care for Our Common Home* (2015), Pope Francis calls for Christians to experience an "ecological conversion," asserting, "Living our vocation to be protectors of God's handiwork is essential to a life of virtue; it is not an optional or a secondary aspect of our Christian experience" (217), http://w2.vatican.va/content/francesco/en/encyclicals/documents/papa-francesco_20150524_enciclica-laudato-si.html.

heart" (3:86-87), and finally Hananiah, Azariah, and Mishael. Humans are called to join in *last*, having first heard other voices of the cosmos, and are to join in this collective liturgy from a place of mediatorial responsibility, humility, and compassion.

Conclusion

In the inordinate heat of a summer that arrives too early and lasts too long, strange weather that swings like a pendulum, hurricanes we call by name even as we refuse to recognize our responsibilities to their victims, the growing Great Pacific garbage patch and the melting of Antarctica, the looming extinction of the northern white rhino and so many more—we must confess. We see in these news stories and in our own experience the effects of our injustice and greed. Corporations and governments are at fault, yes, and so are we. Azariah, Hananiah, and Mishael make standing and confessing a first response to finding ourselves in this blazing furnace that is also, still, by the grace of God, a temple and that may also yet be transformed by a heavenly wind of dew. Even as we confess our daily complicity in the Anthropocene extinction that Deborah Bird Rose has described as "the great unmaking of life," we also recognize the agency of all creation.[47] Thom van Dooren argues that foregrounding the lives and witness of other species in our storytelling can help us "be drawn into new connections, and with them new accountabilities and obligations."[48] I would add that joining with creation in the praise of God, in a mode that is not coercive but cohortative, affirms the agency of all creation and helps us see that our worship is not an expression of our dependency alone but of the interdependency of the cosmos God

47. Deborah Bird Rose, "Multispecies Knots of Ethical Time," *Environmental Philosophy* 9, no. 1 (2012): 127–40, at 128. This unmaking is "the irreparable loss not only of the living but of the multiplicity of forms of life and of the capacity of evolutionary processes to regenerate life" (128). Rose applies James Hatley's concept of aenocide, or the mass murder of generations that eradicates memory and future alike, to anthropogenic mass extinctions, see ibid., 127, 137–38, drawing on Hatley, *Suffering Witness*.

48. Thom van Dooren, *Flightways: Life and Loss at the Edge of Extinction* (New York, NY: Columbia Univ. Press, 2014), 10. Ken Stone applies the work of Deborah Bird Rose and Thom van Dooren to biblical interpretation in *Reading the Hebrew Bible with Animal Studies* (Stanford, CA: Stanford Univ. Press, 2018), 169–70.

has ordered. This is indeed a counter-imperial liturgy; it is political and economic, and as space travel is refashioned into a consumer commodity we remember that this cosmos remains contested domain. The liturgical creation poem of Genesis stood up to an imperial ideology of conquest. Exodus's tabernacle answered an economy of slavery with a liturgically and cosmically ordered praxis of liberation and mutual responsibility. In Daniel 3, liturgy becomes testimony that resists imperially mandated idolatry. The statue fades into the background and God emerges as the central focus. Fire elicits confession and a hymn of praise that asserts God's justice for and sovereignty over all the cosmos. The improvisational character of the second liturgy in Daniel 3 offers a supple template for liturgical praxis in this new moment of ecological crisis. With Azariah and his companions we might confess our sins against creation and join our voices to the vibrations of bacterium and virus, algae and fungus, crab and spider, fish, bear, bird, and bat, hill and mountain, stream and ocean, ice and heat, angel, star, and ravenous black hole. In this moment may we commit to a creative, improvisational praxis of restoration and liberation that recognizes with Azariah, Hananiah, and Mishael that God's mercy and justice are not only for us, but for all of creation.

CHAPTER THREE

"The Firstfruits of God's Creatures"

Bread, Eucharist, and the Ancient Economy

Andrew McGowan

Introduction: Bread and Ancient Eating

The term "cosmos" in the familiar sense of "universe" is attributed to Pythagoras.[1] This is the same philosopher many associate mainly with triangles, but his fame in antiquity was much more broadly based, encompassing geometry but also other areas of philosophy and what we would call theology too, including the pastoral, the practical, and even the liturgical. There are many stories about Pythagoras, and they are as likely to concern issues such as food and diet as astronomy or geometry. One even concerns bread: "Do not crumble bread [Pythagoras said]; it is not favorable for the judgement in Hades." The much later custodian of this curious saying, Iamblichus, struggled with this cryptic comment, as we well might. He suggests that "these precepts about what to do or not to do aim at the divine. That is the principle: all of life is so ordered as to follow the god, and that is the rationale of this philosophy." This again hints at the connection of the parts to the whole in Pythagoras's real or attributed thought. More specifically, Iamblichus offers that "to explain why one should not break bread, some say one should not separate that which unites (for in the old days friends shared one loaf, as

---

1. The traditions attributed to Pythagoras by later followers may not be particularly reliable but are certainly interesting, not least on matters of food; see Marcel Detienne, "La Cuisine de Pythagore," *Archives de Sociologie des Religions* 29 (1970): 141–62.

barbarians do), others that one should not make a bad omen by crumbling or crushing at the outset." [2] Bread for Pythagoreans was thus a symbol, of community but also of connection itself, and not just a symbol in that degraded but all-too-common sense of a mere sign of something else, but a kind of array within the greater array, one whose order and use mattered. Likewise, in calling the world itself a *kosmos*, an "array," Pythagoras or his biographers made the claim that the relations of things, local and ephemeral as well as great and astral, are themselves significant; the mundane was as much part of "cosmos" as was the transcendent, and the trivial as much as the grand. Cosmology in the ancient world may be not, as we could be tempted to imagine, about nature or about the universe, especially in opposition to the realm of the human or of culture, but rather about connection, and the relationship of parts and the whole.

The Christian eucharistic meal centers on the sharing and consumption of bread and wine, for which thanks are given to God in remembrance of Jesus Christ. While those gifts have been subject to endless analysis insofar as they are also signs of other things, bread and wine themselves have not fared so well. When interpreted, they have been seen in terms of what could be called poles of particularity and generality. In the first case, supposed essential connections with the foods of the Passover Seder are often invoked; these however tend to overread the historical connections with the Last Supper as a sole basis for eucharistic practice, connections that are in any case quite unconvincing as explanation for the use or significance of bread and wine, common rather than peculiar foods as they are. In the second, bread in particular can overloaded with vague and often romanticized universal significance, such as the common idea that it means "life." One book on the spirituality of bread suggests it means connection, calm, remembrance, peace, justice, and "meaning" itself—whatever that means—and all that just in the cover blurb. [3]

More serious attempts to consider the meaning of the eucharistic elements have tended to focus on their biological origins and hence on

2. Adapted from Iamblichus, *Pythagorean Life*, 18.86, in Gillian Clark, *Iamblichus: On the Pythagorean Life* (Liverpool: Liverpool Univ. Press, 1989), 38; note that the verbs *katagnuō* and *syntribō* used here suggest smashing or crumbling, something different from the breaking or partition discussed below.

3. Donna Sinclair and Michael J. Schwartzentruber, *The Spirituality of Bread* (Kelowna, BC: Northstone, 2007).

the natural qualities of grain and grape, perhaps allowing at least for the human dimension of agriculture.[4] Human action beyond the field and vineyard is less commonly addressed, and commentators grow more and more quiet as the process of making bread comes closer to the city. Rarely do the activities of mill, bakery, or, especially, the market make it to the conversation about the meanings of ancient eucharistic bread.

This chapter seeks to set ancient eucharistic bread in its own social and economic array, and, in particular, in the quotidian context, not of sacred eating or even banqueting per se but of economy, food supply, and hunger. These are not questions without religious significance from an ancient eater's standpoint, even if they are not always about the "cultic," or what is formal or ritualized. Bread is admittedly not often addressed directly by early Christian writers, in these ways or otherwise, although I will suggest some ancient Christian texts do look different if we consider the quest for food as a backdrop. Mostly, however, our concern will be with what Mary Douglas called "implicit meanings"—what is either assumed in the ancient setting more than discussed or, more negatively, pushed into the background by the premature quest for signs.[5] I will suggest that the eucharistic practice of the first two or three centuries would have been understood in relation to other processes by which people gained access to food, and in particular access to bread, in circumstances where hunger was an ever-present threat. This recognition has some significance for how bread would have been received in the setting of the eucharistic meals and sheds light on some early Christian texts where bread is mentioned.

Bread

The most important thing about ancient bread to its eaters was not any real or supposed meaning, but the fact that it was the staple food of the ancient Mediterranean. This may be difficult to absorb from within modern Western culture, where "baking" means making desserts, and where bread is just part of breakfast or a side dish avoided by those trying to lower "carbs." Most of the ancient world, like most of the modern, was

---

4. David Grumett, *Material Eucharist* (Oxford and New York, NY: Oxford Univ. Press, 2016), 28–29.

5. Mary Douglas, *Implicit Meanings* (London: Routledge & Kegan Paul, 1975), 4–5.

indeed concerned about carbs, but in the opposite way—they risked not having enough of them. While it seems easy to persuade contemporary Western Christians to think of the Eucharist as a kind of feast, the possibility that the starting point for understanding eucharistic meals might be poverty and necessity, rather than festivity and luxury, is difficult for many to swallow.

A Roman lamp of the imperial period offers one neat summary of diet in ancient Mediterranean cities, in words and pictures: we can see a loaf divided into sections (*quadrae*), a jug of wine, and leafy vegetables; the inscription reads, in slightly irregular Latin, "bread, wine, and greens are the dinner [*cena*] of the poor" (see Fig. 1).[6] While the ingredients here are self-consciously simple, the three-fold menu presents the typical pattern of dining in Hellenistic culture and much of the Roman Empire, the trio the Greeks referred to as *sitos, potos*, and *opson*—grain, wine, and relish or side dish—which together constituted not just food or drink but a meal, or in Latin *cena*. Since Dennis Smith's and Matthias Klinghardt's monographs in the 1990s, it has been apparent that the eucharistic gatherings of the early Christians involved a kind of *cena* also, if not in terms of luxury or decadence then in the sense of form and ritual.[7] My thesis is thus partly that the typical Eucharist was not merely a *cena*, but in particular a *cena pauperis*. The characteristic eucharistic cuisine of

Figure 1. Roman lamp of unknown provenance; from *Eranos vindobonensis* (1893).

---

6. Published by R. von Schneider as of unknown provenance in *Eranos vindobonensis* (Vienna: A. Hölder, 1893), 36, but claimed to be from Ptuj by Verena Vidrih-Perko et al., eds., *Ex oriente lux: Rimskodobna svetila in oljenke iz Slovenije* (Ptuj: Ptuj Ormož Regional Museum, 2012), 92. Paul Erdkamp however identifies it as from Aquileia; see Paul Erdkamp, *The Grain Market in the Roman Empire: A Social, Political and Economic Study* (Cambridge: Cambridge Univ. Press, 2005).

7. Dennis E. Smith, *From Symposium to Eucharist: The Banquet in the Early Christian World* (Minneapolis, MN: Fortress Press, 2003); Matthias Klinghardt, *Gemeinschaftsmahl und Mahlgemeinschaft: Soziologie und Liturgie frühchristlicher Mahlfeiern*, Texte und Arbeiten zum neutestamentlichen Zeitalter 13 (Tübingen: Francke, 1996).

bread and wine fits into this basic and typical paradigm of provision, and not into that of feasting or at least of opulence, perhaps especially given the absence of the third element—*opsa* or *pulmentarium* as the Romans referred to the side dishes.[8] As for the *pauperes*, while the Christian movement can be assumed to have been socially mixed, many eucharistic participants will certainly have been urbanites who were among what Peter Garnsey calls the "temporary poor,"[9] far larger in number than the wealthy in those ancient cities and much more exposed to general malnutrition, as well as to cycles of famine.[10] For them, the provision of bread was a daily necessity and a matter of constant effort and anxiety.

Grain Supply and Grain Dole

Christians and Bread

The typical participant in early eucharistic meals, whether wealthy or poor, did not sow or reap the grain of eucharistic bread. The Christians mostly related to the bread of their Eucharist just as to other bread, meaning that they or their ministers probably bought it[11] or perhaps received it or its constituent grain as part of a public distribution. Bread in ancient Mediterranean cities of this period was not usually made via purely domestic processes but was produced in full or in part commercially. Excavated

8. Even the limited evidence for some use of other foods beyond bread and wine in eucharistic contexts confirms this; the third century Apostolic Tradition includes cheese and olives at the rare occasion of an episcopal ordination, implying that the more typical version of the Eucharist was just that familiar pattern of bread and wine, less than the poor person's banquet rather than more; see Andrew B. McGowan, *Ascetic Eucharists: Food and Drink in Early Christian Ritual Meals*, Oxford Early Christian Studies (Oxford: Clarendon Press, 1999), 104.

9. Peter Garnsey, *Cities, Peasants and Food in Classical Antiquity: Essays in Social and Economic History*, ed. Walter Scheidel, paperback edn. (Cambridge: Cambridge Univ. Press, 2004), 227.

10. See Ramsay MacMullen, *The Second Church: Popular Christianity A.D. 200–400* (Atlanta, GA: Society of Biblical Literature, 2009), 101–2; note also the criticism of this typical view in Thomas Arthur Robinson, *Who Were the First Christians? Dismantling the Urban Thesis* (Oxford: Oxford Univ. Press, 2017).

11. See John S. Kloppenborg, "Epigraphy, Papyrology and the Interpretation of the New Testament: Member Contributions to the Eucharist," in *Epigraphik und Neues Testament*, ed. Thomas Corsten, Markus Öhler, and Joseph Verheyden, WUNT 365 (Tübingen: Mohr Siebeck, 2016).

bakery complexes across the empire include facilities for grinding grain as well as kneading, forming, and baking the loaves that were the staple food of rich and poor alike, granted that the grain and the refinement of the flour varied in keeping with the diversity of economic power and status.

Pompeii

The bakery of Modestus at Pompeii was in full swing when the staff abandoned it or were overcome during the eruption of Vesuvius in 79 CE; eighty-one carbonized loaves were found still in the oven when it was excavated. The identifying stamps on some loaves probably attest to "private" loaves being taken to ovens at bakery complexes, allowing their easy return to those who had formed and brought them for baking.[12] Such commercial and communal baking of household doughs is still known in the Middle East and North Africa. A stamp might also be a maker's mark connected with the bakery itself. Curiously the most famous instance makes the bread property or product of a slave (see Fig. 2).[13] While this baker named Celer was probably relatively well-off, and seems from other evidence in fact to have earned freedom before the destruction of the area,[14] menial slave labor including penal servitude was significant in the labor-intensive processes of Roman-era breadmaking. The processes of milling and baking can be inferred from the equipment of Modestus's and other bakeries, but are also depicted—in somewhat sanitized terms—in contexts like the reliefs on the tomb of one Eurysaces, himself a former slave who made had good through the baking and milling trade and who erected a funerary monument in Rome adorned with the apparatus and processes of his occupation in a way that depicts the scale if not the rigor of the operation (see Fig. 3).[15]

12. See Cicero, *In Pisonem* 67, where the lack of a baker at home is a matter of shame for an aristocrat.

13. The provenance of this and some other loaves is confused; some reports place this one in the House of the Stags at Herculaneum, although reports of the stamp on the Modestus loaves are widespread; see Alison E. Cooley, *The Cambridge Manual of Latin Epigraphy* (Cambridge: Cambridge Univ. Press, 2012), 318.

14. Andrew Wallace-Haddrill, *Herculaneum: Past and Future* (London: Frances Lincoln, 2011), 244.

15. Diana E. E. Kleiner, *Roman Group Portraiture: The Funerary Reliefs of the Late Republic and Early Empire* (New York, NY: Garland Publishing, 1977); Lauren Hackworth Petersen, "The Baker, His Tomb, His Wife, and Her Breadbasket: The Monument of Eurysaces in Rome," *Art Bulletin* 85, no. 2 (2003): 230–57.

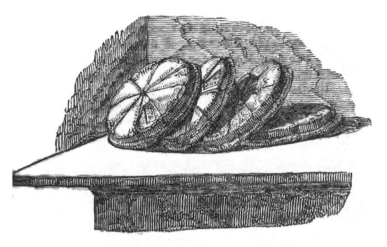

Figure 2. Pompeian bread; from G. Clarke, *Pompeii* (1832).

Condemnation to a *pistrinum* or mill-bakery complex was well-attested as criminal punishment.[16] This was part of the story of the third-century Roman bishop Callistus, he of the eponymous catacombs, formerly a slave punished for attempting to escape—from a Christian owner, by the way—by condemnation to the mill.[17] More recent uses of the term "treadmill" remind us of the cruelty as well as the tedium involved in the processes of milling for a large urban population.

In Pompeii again, a beautifully executed fresco depicts bread similar to that already seen, with the marked *quadrae* like those of the Aquileian lamp and on Celer's bread, being distributed from a platform, taking us from production to distribution (see Fig. 4). The imaginations of archaeologists and other commentators who first encountered and described this image in a Pompeian house were perhaps colored by bourgeois fantasy, since it was usually read as a baker selling bread to customers. More recently scholars have offered a quite different understanding of the image. The most obvious difficulty for the shop-keeping idea is that the

16. Fergus Millar, "Condemnation to Hard Labour in the Roman Empire, from the Julio-Claudians to Constantine," *Papers of the British School at Rome* 52 (1984): 144–45. My thanks to Matthew Larsen for this reference.

17. Hippolytus, *Refutatio omnium haeresium* 9; cf. Apuleius, *Metamorphoses* 9.

Figure 3. Reliefs from the Tomb of Eurysaces; Rostovtzeff, *Social and Economic History of the Roman Empire* (1926).

central figure distributing bread is dressed in a *toga candida*, the dress of someone running for office or perhaps of a magistrate in office. The activity being depicted is therefore not commerce, unless buying votes counts.[18] Elsewhere at Pompeii a strikingly apt graffito also related to an election urges the citizens: "I beg you to elect Gaius Julius Polybius as aedile. He brings good bread."[19] While the idea of politicians distributing largesse is of course not unknown, this has to do not just with a different diet, but with a different economic reality generally, relative to the modern American practice of "pork-barreling." The effective use of bread as an electoral incentive reminds us that the society in question is one where hunger is always close at hand and where food supply is uncertain and often manipulated or, to put it more benignly, ensured daily by the intervention of public agencies as well as the actions of private agents.

Rome

The history of such distributions of grain or bread like those of the would-be Pompeian aedile Polybius is very ancient, but the inauguration of the Roman grain dole by C. Gracchus in 123 BCE is a useful

---

18. Alison E. Cooley and M. G. L. Cooley, *Pompeii and Herculaneum: A Sourcebook* (London: Routledge, 2013), 163–64.

19. *Corpus Inscriptionum Latinarum* V 429 = *Inscriptiones Latinae Selectae* 6412e.

point of reference for this discussion. Rome was the largest city of the ancient world, its population estimated by some as close to a million through the first century of our era. Long unable to feed itself just from the traditional Latin lands or other Italian sources, Rome had been extracting grain as tribute from its expanding empire for centuries, from Sicily and then from Spain, Africa, and, not least, Egypt, after its annexation at the resolution of the Civil War between Octavian and M. Antony in 31 BCE. The need to feed far-flung legions, as well as landless citizens, was a sort of vicious circle: the expanding empire

Figure 4. Bread distribution, "House of the Baker"; Museo Archeologico Nazionale, Naples.

allowed the extraction of food from local subject populations but also created the need for armies, which required food, to subject the peoples whose food was being taken.[20]

Yet even Rome experienced food shortages and unrest over price hikes in time of dearth. Although the *cura annonae*, or general supervision of the grain supply to Rome's markets, was a much older state function, after Gracchus's law all male citizens of Rome received a dole or *frumentatio*—initially a subsidy and later a free distribution.[21] These doles, while addressing hunger and insecurity, were not directed to the needy. Eligibility was based not on need, but on citizen status, and the wealthy were as able, if they chose, to take advantage as were the poor. The need addressed was thus one of social stability more than social

20. Erdkamp, *Grain Market*; Peter Garnsey, *Famine and Food Supply in the Graeco-Roman World: Responses to Risk and Crisis* (Cambridge: Cambridge Univ. Press, 1988).

21. Initially it was not actually a free distribution but a heavily subsidized one, providing grain at close to half the market price. In the time of Julius Caesar's ascendancy, however, close to a century later and not long before the appearance of the Christian movement, the grain distribution was made absolutely free, although eligibility was also policed more rigorously. See Erdkamp, *Grain Market*, 240–44.

welfare, and the relationships emphasized were those of political and ethnic privilege—a factor that only increased over time as the Roman population grew and diversified and the fixed number of this *plebs frumentaria*—perhaps 150,000 of that unwieldy million—became a more distinct club.[22]

Other ancient cities can be imagined in partly analogous terms—all were parasitic on their agricultural hinterlands, yet most of their people had either limited or inconsistent economic power relative to their needs. Plausible estimates suggest that half or two-thirds of typical income was spent on food.[23] When grain harvests failed, or when wars took place, or when the supply was otherwise compromised, spikes in prices could be devastating. The potential to receive grain or bread in free distributions, or to be fed in civic or private banquets, was therefore a matter of huge significance for many from day to day.

Regular civic doles were not the rule, however, outside Rome, even for a minority.[24] The Pompeian and other evidence is therefore helpful precisely because it is not Roman, even though Roman practices will have been influential there. Without such civic structures, private and occasional distributions will have been more important. The urban populations of Syria, Asia, and Greece, to take the most obvious venues of the first generation or two of Christian expansion, also relied on less systematic forms of public or private distribution, based more on structures of patronage and the culture of euergetism, or benefaction, as well as on more cooperative venues like guilds, to supplement their need for food and for bread in particular.

Members of the elite—patrons—were also expected to feed their own retainers or clients from the lower orders fairly regularly, and the same elites were often expected to undertake works of philanthropy based either on food distributions or on banquets—the Pompeian electoral bread line falls somewhere between the two. Christian distributions of bread, at and outside meals, will inevitably have been perceived in some

---

22. See Garnsey, *Cities, Peasants and Food*, 236; Michele Renee Salzman, "From a Classical to a Christian City: Civic Euergetism and Charity in Late Antique Rome," *Studies in Late Antiquity* 1, no. 1 (2017): 68–69.

23. Erdkamp, *Grain Market*, 259.

24. Garnsey, *Famine and Food Supply*, 252–53.

relation to these practices and certainly as having some economic and dietary appeal as well as wider symbolic significance.

Two Contexts

Banqueting

Literature of the period makes clear the significance of invitations to dine, not merely for social advancement but also for reasons of economic necessity. The poet Juvenal (fl. 100 CE), whose life overlaps with the composition of later New Testament documents, belonged to that indistinct class of "temporary poor" and was thus constantly fishing for invitations. Jesus' own career is depicted not dissimilarly.[25] Juvenal describes the mixed blessings of being invited by patrons to banquets where the comestibles, including bread, were dispensed hierarchically like the seats:

>   scarcely
> Breakable bread, lumps of solid crust already moldy,
> That exercise your molars, while thwarting your bite.
> While that reserved for the patron is soft snowy-white
> Kneaded of finest flour. Remember to stay your hand;
> The baking-tray must be granted respect; if you show
> Presumption notwithstanding, a slave orders you stop:
> "Impertinent guest, please address the proper basket,
> Have you forgotten which bread's reserved for you?"[26]

Such distinctions were however studiously avoided in another form of banqueting, to which Christian eucharistic meals have more often been compared—the meals of associations or *collegia*. These popular guilds were based on various forms of common interest, occupational, ethnic, or religious. The bonds of solidarity among members, and the assurance of equal as well as satisfying meals, seem to have been appealing to aspirational classes, including freed slaves. The attraction of bread and

---

25. Mary Marshall, "Jesus: Glutton and Drunkard?" *Journal for the Study of the Historical Jesus* 3, no. 1 (2005): 47–60.

26. From Juvenal, *Satire* 5.66–155, trans. A. S. Kline, https://www.poetryin translation.com/PITBR/Latin/JuvenalSatires5.php (accessed 9 June 2018).

other food was not trivial among participants in these events, ranked and egalitarian alike, if we remember the reality of food insecurity.[27]

Sportulae *and* Leitourgiai

Patronage relations entailed not just shared meals but also gifts of food packages, small-scale food doles as it were, which clients might hope to receive when calling on their patron in the morning to offer a ritual greeting. This *salutatio* involved the patron holding court in their *domus* and receiving compliments and requests from retainers. An expected part of the process was the gift to clients of a *sportula*, more or less a picnic basket. Traditionally the contents would have included bread, although over time money gifts were sometimes substituted for the original in-kind version.

The *sportula* could be received independently at a *salutatio* or given in lieu of a dinner invitation or along with one. The poet Martial was, like his slightly later contemporary Juvenal, part of the class who had to seek invitations and gifts daily for practical necessity, as is reflected in the considerable number of his poems that concern regular *sportulae* as well as more specific seasonal distributions.[28] These again refer to Rome, but the practice was widespread. Pliny the Younger, who as governor of Bithynia (in central Asia Minor) famously provides the oldest contemporary account from the Roman side of the Christian movement and its "ordinary, everyday" food, describes the extent of *sportulae* in the same time and place: "It is the custom for those who assume the gown of manhood, or who marry, or enter upon office, or dedicate any public work, to invite all the senate, and even a considerable number of the common people, and distribute [*sportulae*] to each of the company."[29]

As Pliny's account indicates, the practice of such gift-giving could extend far beyond the regular circle of *clientelae* to members of a wider public, resonating with the more broadly based civic distributions we

---

27. See John S. Kloppenborg, Richard S. Ascough, and Philip A. Harland, *Greco-Roman Associations: Texts, Translations, and Commentary* (Berlin: De Gruyter, 2011).

28. George W. M. Harrison, "Martial on Sportula and the Saturnalia," *Mouseion: Journal of the Classical Association of Canada* 1, no. 3 (2001): 295–312.

29. Pliny the Younger, *Letters* 10.96, 10.116, http://www.attalus.org/old/pliny10b .html.

have noted but creating or reflecting forms of patronage somewhere between civic and private levels. Again, these distributions are not based on need at all, but are the product of notions of mutual benefit, civic identity, or other forms of solidarity.

Eucharistic Meals and Bread Distribution

Christian eucharistic practice will have been understood in some relation to these other practices of bread distribution. The connection with actual meals is the more obvious. The earliest instruction for a eucharistic meal is that of the *Didache*, from 100 CE or thereabouts. A cup is blessed first, then the bread:

> Then as regards the *klasma*: "We give you thanks, Our Father, for the life and knowledge which you made known unto us through your Son Jesus; yours is the glory for ever and ever. As this *klasma* was scattered upon the mountains and being gathered together became one, so may your Church be gathered together from the ends of the earth into your kingdom; for yours is the glory and the power through Jesus Christ for ever and ever." But let no one eat or drink of this Eucharist, unless they that have been baptized into the name of the Lord; for concerning this also the Lord has said: Do not give what is holy to the dogs. (*Didache* 9.5–12)

The Greek *klasma*, usually translated "broken bread," should be understood as the single diner's piece, a *quadra* in Latin, produced when the *panis quadratus* was broken according to its pre-shaped form. This is not a "crumb" but a meal portion. The injunction not to feed the unbaptized is a predictable application of the rules of any dining club, whose members or leaders had to provide the meal for their fellowship and expected a commitment to accompany participation. The need for the rule also implies the desirability of the meal to people who might have had no idea of its significance except as food.

The evidence for distribution of bread beyond the meal is also clear. The accounts in the Acts of the Apostles of the "breaking of the bread" (2:42), sharing of resources (2:44-47), and a daily distribution of food (6:1) seem to encompass both the "dine-in" and "take-away" versions of bread distribution neatly. Whether these pictures represent an authentic reminiscence or later projection or both, it suggests some community members received *sportulae* from the apostles or from the wealthier Christ-followers and that in this case there may have been a connection to need as well as to membership of the group. In Rome just a little later, in the 160s, the practice is clearly attested as an extension of the eucharistic meal. Justin Martyr reports that portions were being carried away from the meal for those who could not be present. Later again, in the second century, members of the church in Carthage were receiving morning *sportulae* of consecrated bread for either immediate or later consumption.[30] Clemens Leonhard has suggested that what was ultimately to become the Christian "worship service" in the morning was initially a *salutatio* wherein the bishop was patron and the members of the church were clients who received such consecrated bread at his hands.[31]

Daily Bread—Scripture and the Bread Economy

So far we have noted that bread was the staple food of the ancient Mediterranean; that poverty and hunger were daily realities in ancient cities; that the distribution of bread was associated with important institutions of political power and patronage; and that Christian eucharistic practices of sharing and distribution can be understood, and will have been understood, in this light. The fact that the earliest Christian groups emerged as sharers and givers of bread has a number of implications, including how we might read certain biblical texts.

Daily Bread

First, consider the line from the prayer from Jesus' own teaching "Give us today our daily bread" (Matt 6:11; cf. Luke 11:3. NRSV adapted, used throughout). This simple statement is famously obscure because of the Greek *hapax legomenon "epiousios"*—translated "daily" in most settings— which has often been interpreted eucharistically. While the eucharistic theology attributed to the text by various early interpreters and onward is historically implausible, it is inevitable that the prayer will from the earliest times have been interpreted in some degree of relationship with actual eucharistic eating.

---

30. Tertullian, *Soldier's Crown* 3, *To His Wife* 2.53, *On Prayer* 19.

31. Clemens Leonhard, "Morning Salutationes and the Decline of Sympotic Eucharists in the Third Century," *Zeitschrift für Antikes Christentum / Journal of Ancient Christianity* 18, no. 3 (2015): 420–42.

Ulrich Luz and others have argued that the meaning of *epiousios* is most likely to be "that which comes" rather than merely an intensification of "to be"; the more accurate translation might then be "give us today our bread for tomorrow."[32] This means, then, something like a prayer for food security, not just for the daily bread of the dole or the patron's sought-after but humiliating dinner or food parcel, which are inevitably for today, but for the promise that tomorrow's needs are also looked after, which implies an end to such dependence. God becomes the patron and the one praying is saying something akin to "your kingdom come," where current and unreliable forms of patronage are swept away by the reign of God, and by God's bread.

In any event, it is important to understand that this petition does not avoid asking the simplest question about basic human need. We need not refuse more elaborate or secondary interpretations, but they are just that. Bread does not stand for anything else here; the ancient hearer or eater could not have interpreted the prayer without immediate reference to this crucial substance and its provision.

Their Fill of the Loaves

If the Lord's Prayer relies on unavoidable issues of hunger and dependence and the place of bread in them, there are also places in Scripture where that obvious meaning is contested or presented as insufficient. Most obvious is the elaborated version of the miraculous feeding narrative in the Gospel of John. The miracle of the loaves in any version depends on the reality we have been exploring of the centrality of bread and could be elucidated further, but John characteristically enters into a critical re-interpretation of the core sign.

This is the only version of the story where the fabric of the bread is mentioned: a boy is said to have "five barley loaves" and two fish. Commentators have often noted that the reference to barley indicates the food of the poor. It could also suggest, however, domestic, and perhaps rural, food production rather than the typical product of urban industrial milling and baking. The divine economy manifested in the wilderness is marked by separation from the world of the city, and perhaps in particular from the world of Jerusalem, whose Passover festival is specifically marked

32. Ulrich Luz, *Matthew 1–7*, ed. Helmut Koester, trans. James E. Crouch (Philadelphia, PA: Fortress, 2007), 319–21.

in the text here. While barley was technically just as ritually appropriate for Passover, wheat would always have been preferred, as more desirable and festive, and the contrast is hard to avoid once this is noted.

Here as in the Synoptics the remnants are gathered after the meal, but uniquely the process is commented on by Jesus: "Gather up the pieces left over, that nothing may be lost" (John 6:12b). These elements of the story make more sense in the light of the place of bread. The leftovers are the same *klasmata* as in the *Didache*; not crumbs, that is, but meal portions. The most interesting feature, however, may be the criticism of some followers, which is expressed in the extended sequel to the miracle story itself: "Jesus answered them, 'Truly, truly, I say to you, you seek me, not because you saw signs, but because you ate your fill of the bread. Do not labor for the food which perishes, but for the food which endures to eternal life, which the Son of man will give to you; for on him has God the Father set his seal' " (6:26-27).

The observation is different when understood in terms of the bread economy and food insecurity. Jesus' popularity is a matter not of his wonder-working ability per se, but rather of his capacity to feed a hungry population, like that of the Johannine community as well as the crowd depicted in the text. Crowds did indeed gather around ancient leaders and grandees precisely for this reason, as we have seen. The author is criticizing this behavior even when applied to Jesus, but this does not mean it was irrelevant to the community; quite the contrary, it implies that behavior and seeks to press beyond it to deeper things. To say that Jesus is "the bread of life" is not merely to play with a story or symbol, as often seems to be assumed, but to produce a christological riff from a daily reality as fundamental as the other Johannine "I am" symbols such as light and life. The author says to the Johannine community, "This is not just a feeding program."[33]

These two brief case studies offer a glimpse at how texts such as these may have been generated and read in a context where the provision of daily bread was a critical and complex political and economic reality and where the Christian community had itself become a key provider for its own members.

---

33. See further Jan Heilmann, *Wein und Blut: das Ende der Eucharistie im Johannesevangelium und dessen Konsequenzen* (Stuttgart: Kohlhammer, 2014).

The Firstfruits of God's Creatures

The connections suggested here between eucharistic provision and food security did not last forever. By the third century we see a shift to apparently token eucharistic distributions of bread, closer to those familiar today. Interestingly, the third century also sees a number of significant changes in wider dole and distribution practices, with increasing evidence for grain doles in other cities during this period, a greater range of foodstuffs distributed, and a good deal of market control and other forms of public intervention to control prices and distribute food.[34]

While Christian bread distributions to members may never have been central to their diet, their significance may have shifted, both because of theological developments in the understanding of the eucharistic elements and because of more prosaic changes in the wider bread economy that made these distributions less practically important. Other forms of distribution, more obviously akin to what we could call charitable activities, do also appear more prominently in Christian circles around this time.[35] This sheds light on how Christian practice slightly later than this came to be seen as "liturgical"; *leitourgia* refers not to cultic activities, and certainly not to the popular but misleading etymology about a "work of the people," but to acts of public benefaction. Christian "liturgy," as it came to be, was described in these terms not because it was cultic but because it too had a public and benevolent character.[36]

The title of this chapter refers to the second-century bishop Irenaeus's defense of eucharistic sacrifice against the still-familiar criticism, offered in the second century by Marcion, that the offering of material things is an unworthy expression of the new Christian dispensation. All things really worth having, his opponents assert, must be spiritual. Irenaeus argues both from Scripture and from creation to the contrary, including the example of Jesus at the Last Supper: "[He gave] directions to his

34. G. E. M. De Ste. Croix, *The Class Struggle in the Ancient Greek World: From the Archaic Age to the Arab Conquests* (London: Duckworth, 1981), 195–96.

35. Salzman, "From a Classical to a Christian City," 65–85.

36. See the discussion in Susan R. Holman, *The Hungry Are Dying: Beggars and Bishops in Roman Cappadocia* (Oxford and New York, NY: Oxford Univ. Press, 2001), 48–54; thus earlier Christian texts presented in that study as "liturgical" deserve the designation not because of cultic significance but because of the philanthropic and public character of cultic service.

disciples to offer to God the firstfruits from his creatures—not as if he were in need, but so they themselves would be neither unfruitful nor ungrateful—he took that created thing, bread, and gave thanks, and said, 'this is my body.' "[37]

The Eucharist is thus a sacrifice for Irenaeus and for other second-century authors, not as first and foremost a representation of the death of Christ but as literally the offering of bread and wine.[38] In his particular case, Irenaeus emphasizes the idea of firstfruits common to Greco-Roman and Israelite cultus, where such offerings are a universal and common attribute of human life in the created order before God.

This Irenaean vision of the relationship between Eucharist and *kosmos*, not merely as arbitrary sign but as representative firstfruits, the whole represented by part, can be set next to the Pythagorean vision with which we began. To make bread the central substance in the characteristic ritual meal of the community was not to invoke a mere sign that pointed to something outside of itself; rather the bread of the Eucharist was itself an array (as the *Didache* also noted) and part of that wider reality of creation and community. The whole of the system that produces bread is invoked in the breaking of the bread: not seed and field alone, but mill and market, labor, hunger, and power.

37. Irenaeus, *Against Heresies* 4.17.5.

38. K. Suso Frank, "Maleachi 1, 10ff. in der frühen Väterdeutung: ein Beitrag zu Opferterminologie und Opferverständnis in der alten Kirche," *Theologie und Philosophie* 53 (1978): 70–78; Andrew B. McGowan, "Eucharist and Sacrifice: Cultic Tradition and Transformation in Early Christian Ritual Meals," in *Mahl und religiöse Identität im frühen Christentum*, ed. Matthias Klinghardt and Hal Taussig, Texte und Arbeiten zum neutestamentlichen Zeitalter 56 (Tübingen: Francke, 2012), 191–206.

CHAPTER FOUR

Salvator Mundi

Visualizing Divine Authority

Felicity Harley-McGowan

On the evening of 15 November 2017, the most expensive work of art ever sold at auction went under the hammer at Christie's in New York, selling for over $450 million.[1] The high-profile sale dedicated to post-war and contemporary art included one of the last works produced by Andy Warhol (1928–1987): a large silk-screen entitled *Sixty Last Suppers*,[2] comprising a series of variations on the late fifteenth-century mural by Leonardo da Vinci (1452–1519) of Christ eating his final meal with his disciples.[3] Yet it was not Warhol's response to Leonardo's own *Last*

1. "Leonardo's *Salvator Mundi* Makes Auction History," 15 November 2017, https://www.christies.com/features/Leonardo-and-Post-War-results-New-York-8729-3.aspx. The price was $450,312,500 (including buyer's premium) at Christie's Post-War & Contemporary Art Evening Sale, New York, 15 November 2017.

2. Andy Warhol, *Sixty Last Suppers*, 1986, acrylic and silkscreen ink on canvas, 294.6 x 998.2 cm. Numbered twice (PA82.020, on the overlap; PA82.020, on the stretcher). Jane D. Dillenberger, "Warhol and Leonardo in Milan," *Religion and the Arts* 1, no. 1 (1996): 50–53, figs. 12 and 13; Jane D. Dillenberger, *The Religious Art of Andy Warhol* (New York, NY: Continuum, 1998), 116–18, no. 79.

3. Refectory of the Convent of Santa Maria delle Grazie, Milan, 1490s (commissioned by Ludovico Sforza, duke of Milan, in 1495), oil and tempera on plaster, 460 cm × 880 cm. From among the vast literature, I cite: Emil Möller, *Das Abendmahl des Leonardo da Vinci* (Baden-Baden: B. Grimm, 1952), which provides a comprehensive examination of the painting, and Pinin Brambilla Barcilon and Pietro C.

Figure 1. Christ as *Salvator Mundi*.
Leonardo da Vinci and Workshop (?), after 1507,
oil on walnut wood, 65.5 x 45.1–45.6 cm.
Photo: Salvator Mundi LLC / Art Resource, NY

Supper that captured attention in the sale and received the record bid, but a painted panel of much smaller dimensions attributed to Leonardo himself (Fig. 1).[4]

Described as an "overpowering personal meditation on divinity and the cosmos," the oil painting represents Jesus according to a distinct pictorial format used in Christian art for devotional images of holy figures: a half-length, frontal depiction of the face.[5] Subscribing to this format, the artist presents a blue-robed Jesus in rigid frontality before the viewer, with head strictly symmetrical, eyes wide open, and long hair parted in the center to frame the bearded face. To present Jesus as *Salvator Mundi*, or "Savior of the World," the artist shows Jesus raising his right hand in blessing and cupping a translucent globe in his left. A number of variations on this particular *Salvator Mundi* iconography are known to have been produced by Leonardo's workshop.[6] The version offered by Christie's, purchased for Abu Dhabi's Department of Culture and Tourism, was likely painted sometime in the early sixteenth

---

Marani, *Leonardo: L'ultima cena* (Milan: Electa, 1999), which examines the history, technical features, and more recent restoration work.

4. Leonardo da Vinci and Workshop (?), *Christ as Salvator Mundi*, after 1507 (on the date see n. 7 below), oil on walnut wood, 65.5 x 45.1–45.6 cm.

5. Dianne Dwyer Modestini, "The *Salvator Mundi* by Leonardo da Vinci in the Context of Recent Research," in *Leonardo da Vinci: Salvator Mundi*, auction catalogue (New York, NY: Christie's New York, 2017), 63–91, quotation 71.

6. On these, and specifically a painting previously in the Marquis de Ganay Collection (dated ca. 1510–1513): Joanne Snow-Smith, *The Salvator Mundi of Leonardo da Vinci* (Seattle, WA: Henry Art Gallery, Univ. of Washington, 1982).

century and was sold by the auction house as an autograph work by Leonardo.[7]

In many ways, the painting was an ideal companion for Warhol's *Last Suppers*. On their own terms, both reflect on the divine and both proceed directly from a model to do so. In Warhol's case, the model was a single image that was commissioned and intended for a specific context: the north wall of the refectory of the Dominican convent of Santa Maria delle Grazie, Milan. Warhol's interaction with this image was not through study of the mural in situ however, but through reproduction.[8] In the case of the "Leonardo," the model for the representation of the *Salvator Mundi* was a well-established but fluid pictorial format, one known (according to legend) from Jesus' own lifetime and followed in countless settings and in various media across the centuries thereafter. Where Warhol has been accused of diminishing his model by repetition, of thereby transforming a "deeply religious work into a cliché," the panel attributed to Leonardo has been celebrated by some scholars as an enrichment and even perfection of his model.[9] In this process of celebration, much scholarly and

7. The scheduled display of the painting on 18 September 2018 in the Arab Emirates Museum (which, in partnership with the Musée du Louvre, is known as the Louvre Abu Dhabi) was canceled without explanation or indication of when the work will go on display. The painting appeared on the art market in 2005 and was included as an "autograph work" by Leonardo in the 2011 exhibition at the National Gallery, London: Luke Syson et al., *Leonardo da Vinci: Painter at the Court of Milan*, cat. no. 91 (London: National Gallery, 2012), 300–303, with a proposed production date of ca. 1499—the date accepted by Christie's (*Leonardo da Vinci: Salvator Mundi*, auction catalogue, 12). However, opinion about its attribution and date remain divided. For presentation of the argument that the design may be Leonardo's but the painting a product of the artist and workshop, see Frank Zöllner, *Leonardo: The Complete Paintings and Drawings*, rev. ed. (Cologne: Taschen, 2018), 6–11, with a date after 1507 proposed, 440–45.

8. For example, a line drawing from John Dennison Champlain, Jr., ed., *Encyclopedia of Painters and Paintings*, vol. 10 (New York, NY: Scribner's, 1913), 32, is among the source material located in the archives at the Andy Warhol Museum, Pittsburgh. Jessica Beck, "Andy Warhol's Sixty Last Suppers," *Gagosian Quarterly* (summer 2017): 80–88.

9. The quotation is taken from a description of the exhibition *Sixty Last Suppers* in the Museo del Novecento, Milan: "Sixty Last Suppers: Andy Warhol at Museo del Novecento, from 24 March 2017 to 18 May 2017," http://www.museodelnovecento.org/en/mostra/andy-warhol-sixty-last-suppers. Unsurprisingly, Dillenberger takes

public attention has focused specifically on technique, including in the representation of the globe.[10]

For my purposes in this chapter, the Abu Dhabi *Salvator Mundi* provides a springboard for a broader discussion about the symbol of the globe in antiquity and for its capacity to present the idea of the cosmos, on one hand, and of authority, on the other. The symbol has a long and complex history. In what follows, I focus on a small but important part of that history: the experimentation with the symbol in early Christian efforts to convey something about the divine authority of God. The publicity surrounding Christie's sale of the panel as a Leonardo occluded the extraordinary fact that the most expensive art work ever sold at auction is a painting fundamentally part of a long history of Christian devotional imagery and so indebted to the creativity of not one single artist, but of generations of anonymous artists and their theological interlocuters. In order to tease out the early development and its significance in establishing a foundation for artists in subsequent generations, let us examine the painting's iconography in more detail.

Although there is little evidence for the application of the term to this iconography before the sixteenth century, the title *Salvator Mundi* is consistently associated with a cropped, half-length image of Jesus in which he is shown striking a gesture of blessing with his right hand while holding a globe, or *orbis mundi*, in the left.[11] If we leave the globe to one side for a moment, the iconographic type stands as a fine example of the ongoing influence of an ancient portrait format, one used in Hellenistic and Roman funerary art to honor or memorialize the dead. Christians developed it as early as the fourth century to represent Jesus as universal

---

the opposite view: Leonardo's painting was the cliché and to it Warhol brought "new spiritual resonance," Dillenberger, *Religious Art of Andy Warhol*, 120.

10. Syson, "Christ as Salvator Mundi," 303; *Leonardo da Vinci: Salvator Mundi*, auction catalogue, 31.

11. Michael A. Michael, "The Bible moralisée, the Golden Legend and the Salvator Mundi: Observations on the Iconography of the Westminster Retable," *Antiquaries Journal* 94 (2014): 93–125, at 111–12 and nn. 25 and 26 concerning possible origins of the title in an antiphon.

teacher, philosopher, and lawgiver.[12] Whether displayed in a funerary or domestic context, on a coin, or in an apse mosaic, the frontal bust-image facilitated veneration of the figure depicted—be it Christ or another holy person.[13] There is no narrative context and no suggestion of specific emotion. Instead, through the tightly cropped, vertical composition, an intense encounter with the face is achieved in placing the subject in strict frontality (with shoulder-line square, the upright axis of the head parallel to the picture plane, and eyes looking forward). These key features are already present in a late fourth-century vault painting in the catacomb of Commodilla in Rome (Fig. 2), although the eyes are shown looking upward.[14] No arms or hands are depicted, and here the bearded face is encircled by a large blue nimbus, prominently bordered in red and flanked by the first and last letters of the Greek alphabet, alpha (A) and omega (Ω).[15] The juxtaposition of the portrait of Jesus with these letters specifically designates Jesus as divine and indicates that his power is infinite, extending beyond time and space: in the Revelation to John, God declares, "I am the Alpha and Omega" (Rev 1:8, 21:6), the title subsequently applied to Jesus (Rev 22:13), to whom power belonged as Word (Alpha) and at the end of days as Judge (Omega). The idea of God's authority surpassing the earthly realm is affirmed by the stars that form the background against

12. Maria Andaloro, "Dal ritratto al icona," in *Arte e iconografia a Roma: da Costantino a Cola di Rienzo*, ed. Andaloro and Serena Romano (Milan: Jaca Book, 2000), 31–67, esp. 38–48.

13. On the bust-length Christ motif see Rainer Warland, *Das Brustbild Christi: Studien zur spätantiken und frühbyzantinischen Bildgeschichte*, Römische Quartalschrift für christliche Altertumskunde und Kirchengeschichte, supplementary volume 41 (Rome: Herder, 1986); also, André Grabar, "L'imago clipeata chrétienne," *Comptes rendus des séances de l'Académie des Inscriptions et Belles-Lettres* 101, no. 2 (1957): 209–13.

14. Cubiculum N5 (Leonis), ceiling vault, last quarter fourth century. Johannes Georg Deckers et al., *Die Katakombe "Commodilla": Repertorium der Malereien* (Vatican City: Pontificio Istituto di Archeologia Cristiana, 1994), 89–104.

15. In other cases, such as the half-length portrait of a bearded man also placed in a rectangular frame in the Porta Marina house, Ostia, from the late fourth century, a nimbus and rhetorical gesture are not enough to determine the identity of the sitter—whether Christ or a late antique philosopher: Paul Zanker, *The Mask of Socrates: The Image of the Intellectual in Late Antiquity* (Berkeley: Univ. of California Press, 1995), 315–16.

Figure 2. Christ with *alpha* and *omega*. Catacomb of Commodilla, cubiculum N5 (Leonis), fresco, last quarter of the fourth century.
Photo: De Agostini Picture Library/Bridgeman Images.

which the bust is set and framed and by the nimbus, the color of which intensifies from a lighter to darker hue toward the edge to create a sense of divine aura, a technique to which we will return.[16]

In Rome two centuries later, the image is largely unchanged but has begun to draw in new features (Fig. 3). In a fresco preserved in the vault over a baptistery constructed in the sixth century inside the catacomb of Ponziano, Jesus is represented with a book tucked closely under his left arm. Without the alpha-omega, it is the golden yellow cruciform-nimbus—again boldly outlined and set against a celestial background that is simply blue rather than starry—that achieves divine identification.[17]

The portrait format observed in these paintings is more frequently found in Byzantine art from the sixth century, the most celebrated example being the sixth-century icon preserved in the monastery of Saint Catherine

16. On the symbolism of the nimbus in early Christian art and the significance of the gradient-blue colour, see Nathan Dennis, "Bodies in Motion: Visualizing Trinitarian Space in the Albenga Baptistery," in *Perceptions of the Body and Sacred Space in Late Antiquity and Byzantium*, ed. Jelena Bogdanović (New York, NY: Routledge, 2018), 124–48, esp. 133–38.

17. Joseph Wilpert, *Die Malereien der Katakomben Roms*, vol. 2 (Freiburg im Breisgau: Herdersche Verlagshandlung, 1903), plate 257. Vincenzo Fiocchi Nicolai, "Considerazioni sulla funzione del cosiddetto battistero di Ponziano sulla via Portuense," in *Il Lazio tra antichità e medioevo: studi in memoria di Jean Coste*, ed. Zaccaria Mari, Maria Teresa Petrara, and Maria Sperandio (Rome: Quasar, 1999), 323–32.

Figure 3. Christ with codex. Vault Fresco, sixth century. Baptistry in the catacomb of Ponziano, Via Portuensis, Rome.
Photo: Watercolour by Carlo Tabanelli over a photograph by Pompeo and Renato Sansaini. Published by Joseph Wilpert, *Die Malereien der Katakomben Roms*, vol. 2 (Freiburg im Breisgau: Herdersche Verlagshandlung, 1903), plate 257.

Figure 4. Christ blessing, with codex. Tempera on wood panel, first half of the sixth century. The Holy Monastery of St. Catherine, Mount Sinai, Egypt. Reconstruction of the original panel (now cut down, and measuring h. 84 cm, w. 45.5 cm).
Line drawing: George Bauer, with kind permission. Published in Kurt Weitzmann, *The Monastery of Saint Catherine at Mount Sinai: The Icons* (Princeton: Princeton Univ. Press, 1976), fig. A.

on Mount Sinai.[18] At some point in its history the icon was cut down, at the top and on both sides. However, a reconstruction of its original appearance (Fig. 4) reveals a vertical composition whose proportions compare well with the Ponziano painting. As in that version, a thick, jewel-covered codex is tucked tightly under Jesus' left arm, but the right hand is now

18. Tempera on wood panel, first half of the sixth century. Manolis Chatzidakis, "An Encaustic Icon of Christ at Sinai," *Art Bulletin* 49, no. 3 (1967): 197–208. Kurt Weitzmann, *The Monastery of Saint Catherine at Mount Sinai, The Icons* (Princeton, NJ: Princeton Univ. Press, 1976), 13–15, cat. B.1, giving the current dimensions as height 84 cm, width 45.5 cm.

shown raised, with the first and second fingers slightly bent and the third crossing the palm to touch the thumb. Originally an oratorical gesture of speech or instruction, the form is utilized here to convey a sense of divine authority.[19] This is further articulated in the nimbus (which is large, cruciform, and gold, with its shape defined with a dark border). Now the blue background used to indicate a celestial context is gradient, from dark to lighter at the top.[20] With the figure's arms held close to the body, hands placed at the front of the picture plane, the viewer is drawn directly before the subject, whose eyes look out of the image as though connecting with the viewer individually as well as with humanity collectively.

Images following this carefully formulated bust-image, with its fixed gaze, hand gesture and codex, are usually given the title *Pantocrator* (Παντοκράτωρ).[21] This epithet of God was used in the Revelation to John (4:8, for example) and was developed by the fourth century in patristic literature as "all-ruler," with additional overtones being to preserve, contain, and encompass.[22] When images carry the epithet by the twelfth century, there is a clear understanding that they represent the Father-in-the-Son, for through Christ and his human nature the divine Father

19. H. P. L'Orange, *Studies in the Iconography of Cosmic Kingship in the Ancient World* (Oslo: A schehoug, 1953), 165–68, 180, 194–97, argued that the application of the gesture to Christ derived from the speech gesture of antiquity and initially carried a philosophical-discursive significance but increasingly indicated authority.

20. Weitzmann, *Monastery of Saint Catherine*, 13–15, for a description of the original colors.

21. For the loose application of the title by art historians to a variety of images of the mature Christ in Byzantine art, and thus the difficulty of defining it as a portrait type: Klaus Wessel, "Christusbild," in *Reallexikon zur byzantinischen Kunst*, ed. K. Wessel, vol. 1 (1966): 966–1047, especially 1014; Carmelo Capizzi, *Pantocrator* (Rome: Pontifical Institutum Orientalium Studiorum, 1964), 189–203, 309–25. For the English translation of *Pantocrator*, see Jane Timken Matthews, "The Byzantine Use of the Title Pantocrator," *Orientalia Christiana Periodica* 44 (1978): 442–62, at 444–45, noting "Almighty" is incorrect.

22. Jane Timken Matthews, "The Pantocrator: Title and Image" (PhD diss., New York University, 1976), discussing the patristic literature at 21–27; also, Thomas Mathews, "The Transformation Symbolism in Byzantine Architecture and the Meaning of the Pantokrator in the Dome," in *Church and People in Byzantium*, ed. Rosemary Morris (Birmingham, AL: Centre for Byzantine, Ottoman and Modern Greek Studies, University of Birmingham, 1990), 191–214.

becomes visible.[23] Yet as we have seen in the case of the Commodilla painting, even by the fourth century images were being used to express this idea of God's continuous relationship with the world, through Christ.

For Gregory of Nyssa in the late fourth century, God could be called Pantocrator because "he occupies the orb of the earth, he holds the ends of the earth in his hand, he encloses the heavens in his palm."[24] Pictorially, God's role in sustaining, preserving, and holding the universe came to be expressed visually through the bust-format in different ways and did not immediately involve utilization of globe symbolism in the way that Gregory's definition evokes. In diverse cultural contexts and in varied viewing contexts, artists and their patrons took different approaches to the question of how to render divine authority as surpassing earthly power: Jesus could be represented as universal teacher, philosopher, emperor, priest, judge, lawgiver, and so forth. His facial structure, hair, and clothing could change according to the role chosen, as did the nature of the object he was shown holding: as a philosopher he might hold a scroll, as a priest an open book with legible text.[25] By the twelfth century, the option of replacing the book with a globe had emerged.[26] That it was an alternative option for the expression of authority, as Gregory of Nyssa had described it, is attested in a remarkable set of evidence from fourteenth-century Avignon. In the 1960s, a badly damaged fresco of the half-length

23. There is no evidence to indicate that the title was applied to images of Christ before the twelfth century: Matthews, "The Byzantine Use of the Title Pantocrator," 454, with an annotated list of labeled Pantocrator images.

24. Gregory of Nyssa, *Contra Eunomium* II, 126 (P.G. 45, 521-526, 3.4.30): ὁ κατέχων τὸν γῦρον τῆς γῆς. The English translation cited here is from Matthews, "The Pantocrator," 24. However, a more accurate translation might be "he holds fast the circle of the earth." Capizzi, *Pantocrator*, 78, notes that the Latin translation provided in the *Patrologia Graeca* expands the Greek text to "gyrum sive orbem"— apparently expressing uncertainty as to whether a two- or three-dimensional circular form was suggested.

25. While most studies of the iconic representation of Jesus have regarded the iconography as following a single archetypal model, Michele Bacci has demonstrated its diversity: Michele Bacci, *The Many Faces of Christ: Portraying the Holy in the East and West, 300 to 1300* (London: Reaktion Books, 2014).

26. One of the earliest representations survives in the *Ingeborg Psalter* (Musée Condé, Chantilly, France, Ms. 9), folio 32v. Snow-Smith, *The Salvator Mundi*, 70, fig. 73.

blessing Christ by Sienese artist Simone Martini was removed from the surface on which it was painted, above the entrance to the Cathedral of Notre Dame des Doms. In the process, conservators discovered detailed underdrawings, which revealed that Martini first represented Jesus holding a book in his left hand before replacing it with a globe.[27] The change may have been prompted by personal choice or by contemporary theological disputes and the interests of the patron.

As we seek to place the image we now label as *Salvator Mundi* in the context of different approaches to the pictorialization of God's all-encompassing authority, it is important to acknowledge the influence exerted by representations of the face of Christ known as *acheiropoieta*, or images "not made by (or with) hands." From the thirteenth century, these inspired a wealth of popular devotional imagery.[28] I will mention two examples briefly, one from Syria and the other venerated in Rome.[29]

The best-known early Christian example is the *Mandylion*, or cloth image, of King Abgar of Edessa.[30] Abgar, terminally ill, writes to Jesus requesting that he come to Edessa and heal him, but Jesus replies that he is unable to leave Jerusalem and will send a disciple in his stead. The ear-

27. Beth Williamson, "Site, Seeing and Salvation in Fourteenth-Century Avignon," *Art History* 30, no. 1 (2007): 1–25.

28. The multiple examples of *archeiropoieta* in the Christian record were examined by Ernst von Dobschütz, *Christusbilder: Untersuchungen zur christlichen Legende* (Leipzig, J.C. Hinrichs, 1899), with discussion of the relationship between the story and Byzantine iconography at 102–96. See now the essays in Herbert L. Kessler and Gerhard Wolf, eds., *The Holy Face and the Paradox of Representation* (Bologna: Nuova Alfa Editoriale, 1998), and Daniel Spanke, *Das Mandylion: Ikonographie, Legenden und Bildtheorie der "Nicht-von-Menschenhand-gemachten Christusbilder"* (Recklinghausen: Museen der Stadt, 2000).

29. Michael, "The Bible moralisée," 112, also emphasizes the connection between devotional imagery of the Holy Face and the development of the iconography we now label as *Salvator Mundi*. Syson mentions this as part of his discussion of iconographic influences on the Abu Dhabi *Salvator Mundi*: Syson, "Christ as Salvator Mundi," 303. However, for an example of the way the analysis of Byzantine sources can be more fully integrated into the analysis of a painting to determine attribution, see Joanne Snow-Smith's examination: Snow-Smith, *The Salvator Mundi*, 65–78, nn. 87–89.

30. The literature is extensive. For an essential bibliography, see Bacci, *Many Faces of Christ*, 227–28, n. 37.

liest texts that discuss this episode, including the *Ecclesiastical History* of Eusebius of Caesarea in the fourth century, focus only on the written exchange between the king and Jesus.[31] However very soon thereafter, sources describe the disciple as returning to Abgar not only with a letter from Jesus, but also with an image of him. In the Syriac *Doctrine* (or *Teaching*) *of Addai*, likely written in the first half of the fifth century,[32] the image is produced by the scribe Abgar sent to Jesus, while in the late sixth century, the Byzantine historian Evagrius Scholasticus specifies that the likeness was not made with human hands.[33] Thus while certain accounts continued to attest that Jesus' letter was an important relic,[34] in both of these texts it is the image that is powerful. That the image was created miraculously, through the impression of Jesus' face into a cloth, is first mentioned in the Greek *Acts of Thaddaeus*, probably from the sixth or seventh century—by which time the image had emerged as the

31. Eusebius of Caesarea, *Historia ecclesiastica* 1.13.5–10. Averil Cameron, "The History of the Image of Edessa: The Telling of a Story," *Harvard Ukrainian Studies* 7 (1983): 80–94, with reference to the date at which Eusebius recorded this story (ca. 290), at 81. See further on the correspondence: H. J. W. Drijvers, "The Abgar Legend," *New Testament Apocrypha* 1 (1991): 492–99; and James Corke-Webster, "A Man for the Times: Jesus and the Abgar Correspondence in Eusebius of Caesarea's Ecclesiastical History," *Harvard Theological Review* 110, no. 4 (2017): 563–87. Several later fourth-century versions of this story survive—including an account by the pilgrim Egeria, who visited Edessa (ca. 380) where the correspondence was preserved, saw the letters, and was given copies by the local bishop: *Itinerarium Egeriae*, chap. 17, English translation by Anne McGowan and Paul F. Bradshaw, *The Pilgrimage of Egeria* (Collegeville, MN: Liturgical Press, 2018), 133–34.

32. Sidney Harrison Griffith, "The Doctrina Addai as a Paradigm of Christian Thought in Edessa in the Fifth Century," *Hugoye: Journal of Syriac Studies* 6, no. 2 (2003): 269–92.

33. Evagrius Scholasticus, *Ecclesiastical History* IV, 7; English translation: Michael Witby, *The Ecclesiastical History of Evagrius Scholasticus* (Liverpool: Liverpool Univ. Press, 2000), 226.

34. The understanding that the letter was powerful such that recitation of its words would convey material benefit is attested in Procopius's sixth-century *History of the Wars*: Ernst Kitzinger, "The Cult of Images in the Age of Iconoclasm," *Dumbarton Oaks Papers* 8 (1954): 100–112, especially 103–4; see further, Derek Krueger, *Writing and Holiness: The Practice of Authorship in the Early Christian East* (Philadelphia: Univ. of Pennsylvania Press, 2004), 149–56.

"agent" of the king's healing and conversion,[35] Christ made "palpably present" through not text but image.[36]

The power of the image is equally strong in a second example of an *acheiropoieton*: the legend of Saint Veronica.[37] Many versions exist, but the earliest surviving account is that preserved in *The Cure of Tiberius' Illness*, a Latin work possibly composed in northern Italy between the fifth and eighth centuries.[38] The Roman emperor Tiberius, gravely ill, hears of the miracles of Jesus and sends an officer to find him in Jerusalem. When the officer arrives in the city and learns that Jesus has been crucified, he turns to a woman, often identified as the woman with the issue of blood from the Gospel of Matthew (9:20-22), who is known to possess an image miraculously preserved in the cloth (Fig. 5). The officer returns to Rome with the woman and the image as Christ's representative, and when Tiberius worships the likeness he is cured.[39] The story, in which the woman became known as Veronica (understood in some cases to derive from *vera icon*, that is, "true icon"), became enormously popular in Europe, and by the twelfth century pilgrims were traveling to Rome to see and venerate the cloth in Saint Peter's Basilica.[40] Yet only in the early thirteenth century was it described as bearing an image, one that apparently showed Jesus from the chest upwards.[41] In the twelfth

---

35. As Averil Cameron emphasizes, Cameron, "History of the Image of Edessa," 82.

36. Kitzinger, "Cult of Images," 104. I am grateful to Nathan Hardy for discussing the literary evidence with me.

37. Hans Belting, *Likeness and Presence: A History of the Image before the Era of Art*, trans. Edmund Jephcott (Chicago, IL: Chicago Univ. Press, 1994), 215–24, provides an overview of the extensive literature.

38. Zbigniew S. Izydorczyk, "The *Cura sanitatis Tiberii* a Century after Ernst von Dobschütz," in *The European Fortune of the Roman Veronica in the Middle Ages*, ed. Amanda Murphy et al., Convivium Supplementum (Turnhout: Brepols, 2017), 32–49.

39. John Oliver Hand, "*Salve sancta facies*: Some Thoughts on the Iconography of the *Head of Christ* by Petrus Christus," *Metropolitan Museum of Art Journal* 27 (1992): 7–18, here 10.

40. Ann van Dijk, "The Veronica, the Vultus Christi and the Veneration of Icons in Medieval Rome," in *Old Saint Peter's, Rome*, ed. Rosamond McKitterick et al. (Cambridge: Cambridge Univ. Press, 2013), 229–56. On the popularity in Europe, see the essays in Murphy et al., eds., *The European Fortune of the Roman Veronica*.

41. Kessler and Wolf, *The Holy Face*, 17–19. The earliest extant description of the object, by Gervase of Tilbury, was written sometime between 1214 and 1218:

Figure 5. Albrecht Dürer, woodcut, 6.1 x 4.1 cm. Metropolitan Museum of Art, Accession no. 31.54.30. Bequest of James Clark McGuire, 1930. Photo: Metropolitan Museum of Art, image in the public domain (CC0 1.0).

and thirteenth centuries, successive popes promoted the cloth. Innocent IV (1243–1254), for example, granted an indulgence of forty days for reciting the prayer *Ave facies praeclara* in front of the cloth, or in front of a representation of it, such that the prayer became crucial for the dissemination of both the cult and the pictorial formula of the face.[42] The earliest surviving representations of that face in Western art, extant in two English manuscripts of around 1240–1250, were likely produced by Matthew Paris, who admitted that he had not seen the cloth and its image but whose miniature depictions likely reflect descriptions he could have read and Byzantine-influenced representations he might have seen.[43]

Alexa Sand, *Vision, Devotion, and Self-Representation in Late Medieval Art* (New York, NY: Cambridge Univ. Press, 2014), 32.

42. As stressed by Hand, "*Salve sancta facies*," 14.

43. London, British Library, MS Arundel 157, folio 2, the manuscript dated around 1240. A second, slightly later version appears in the *Chronica maiora*, from before 1250 (Cambridge, Corpus Christi College Library, MS 16, folio 49v). Suzanne Lewis, *The Art of Matthew Paris in the Chronica Majora* (Berkeley: Univ. of California Press in collaboration with Corpus Christi College, Cambridge, 1987), 126–31, outlines the chronology and differences between the two miniatures (see esp. p. 129), positing a dependence on a textual source (Gervase of Tilbury) while also

In the later of the two miniatures, he included the alpha and omega on either side of the face.[44]

Legends about *acheiropoieta* and ideas about the appearance of the face stimulated a variety of devotional as well as artistic responses. Albrecht Dürer (1471–1528), who produced his own images of the "Veronica" (Fig. 5)—and as a savvy business man was cognizant of a financial benefit in doing so[45]—used the same pictorial conventions associated with the veil's image for a self-portrait executed around 1500, close to the time the Abu Dhabi *Salvator Mundi* was painted.[46] His careful following of the format included inserting his personal monogram (AD) to one side of his face and a Latin inscription on the other, in the location viewers would expect to see the alpha and omega. Dürer has been accused of manipulating the format to proclaim his own "divinity" or god-like status as an artist.[47] A more compelling reading is that the portrait arises out of piety, not hubris; that in so carefully attending to the format for the representation of divine authority, the artist is confessing and recognizing God's power, not establishing himself as a rival to it.[48]

Dürer probably knew the short treatise *The Vision of God*, written around 1453 by Nicholas of Cusa for the Benedictine monks at Tegernsee, Austria.[49] In the treatise, "vision" is deliberately ambiguous, evoking

---

suggesting that the Arundel image was inspired by the painted bust of Christ on the vault of the Chapel of the Holy Sepulchre in Winchester Cathedral, ca. 1230, which in its iconography evinces Byzantine influence. On the two images, and their reflection of a portrait type well known in Rome, see also Pächt, "Avignon," 405–9, who proposed (n. 15) that the Arundel miniature was produced "in the circle" of Paris.

44. Lewis, *Art of Matthew Paris*, 129.

45. Hans Belting, *Face and Mask: A Double History* (Princeton, NJ: Princeton Univ. Press, 2017), 126.

46. Albrecht Dürer, *Self-Portrait with Fur-Trimmed Robe*, 1500, oil on limewood panel, 67.1 cm × 48.9 cm, Munich, Alte Pinakothek, Bayerische Staatsgemäldesammlungen, inv. no. 537.

47. For a survey of interpretations in scholarship, see Margaret Sullivan, "*Alter Apelles*: Dürer's 1500 *Self-Portrait*," *Renaissance Quarterly* 68 (2015): 1161–91.

48. For example: Erwin Panofsky, *The Life and Art of Albrecht Dürer* (Princeton, NJ: Princeton Univ. Press, 2005), 43–44; Belting, *Face and Mask*, 123–26.

49. As proposed by Joseph Leo Koerner, *The Moment of Self-Portraiture in German Renaissance Art* (Chicago, IL: Univ. of Chicago Press, 1993), 127–28.

both God's vision of humanity and our human vision of God,[50] thereby uniting the concepts of God as witness and mirror.[51] Nicholas describes the nature of God as a circle and sphere, which might remind us here of Gregory of Nyssa's description of God as Pantocrator. Certainly, for an artist in late fourteenth-century France tasked with illustrating a copy of the *Roman de la Rose*, the iconography of Christ as Pantocrator furnished a means by which to portray this idea of God as witness and mirror: Jesus, with a cross-nimbus, raises a hand in blessing while glancing at his reflection in a round mirror that he holds in his left hand.[52] The kind of close looking modeled here is advocated by Nicholas, who in his treatise uses a painting to discuss the relationship a believer had with God.[53] Several early manuscripts even included a woodcut version or actual painted version of the Veronica. Nicholas insisted that readers stand in front of the image or "Vision of God" and observe it.[54] This practice is suggested in the portrait of a young man painted around 1450 by Petrus Christus (d. 1475/6), where affixed to the wall behind the sitter is a piece of parchment illuminated both with a prayer to Saint Veronica and with an image of the Holy Face (which has, positioned prominently either side of the head, the alpha and omega).[55] The prayer is a shortened version of a fourteenth-century prayer, *Salve sancta facies*, attributed to Pope John XXII (1316–1334), whose recitation before the image or the relic itself would secure an indulgence.[56] Here, the image attests to God's

50. Clyde L. Miller, "Nicolas of Cusa's *The Vision of God*," in *An Introduction to the Medieval Mystics of Europe: Fourteen Original Essays*, ed. P. E. Szarmach (Albany, NY: State Univ. of New York Press, 1984), 293–312, here 295.

51. I take this point from Walter S. Gibson, "Hieronymus Bosch and the Mirror of Man: The Authorship and Iconography of the 'Tabletop of the Seven Deadly Sins,'" *Oud Holland* 87, no. 4 (1973): 205–26.

52. *Roman de la Rose*, MS M.132, fol. 130v., Paris, ca. 1380, Pierpont Morgan Library, New York. Gibson, "Hieronymus Bosch," fig. 11.

53. See further in Miller, "Nicolas of Cusa's *The Vision of God*," including bibliography (with editions of the Latin text) at 312.

54. Koerner, *Moment of Self-Portraiture*, 127–28.

55. Petrus Christus, *Portrait of a Young Man*, ca. 1450–1460, oil on oak, 35.4 x 26 cm, Salting Bequest 1910, National Gallery, London, inv. no. NG2593. Hand, "*Salve sancta facies*," 10, figs 4, 5.

56. Hand, "*Salve sancta facies*," 14–16.

physical appearance in the world, in Jesus, but also to God's continuing divine presence.

So far, I have tried to situate the composition of the Abu Dhabi *Salvator Mundi* within the history of efforts to develop an archetypal image of the Son of God that conveyed not just his appearance, but also a clear sense of the all-encompassing power of the Christian God. In response to the interest in attribution that has otherwise dominated discussion of the painting for over a decade, I have briefly traced and so highlighted the historical development of the subject matter and function of such images. In marketing its auction of the *Salvator Mundi*, Christie's emphasized the "enduring relevance" of the painting,[57] which in the sale publicity and an associated publication was presented in terms of Leonardo's genius.

For some scholars, evidence for the "artistic genius" of Leonardo can be located in technique, particularly in the handling of the brush. The flesh tones, for instance, are built up with multiple thin layers of pigment such that, unlike in the Mount Sinai icon for example (Fig. 4), any sign of brushwork is concealed.[58] In the use of this technique in the *Salvator Mundi* painting, direct comparisons have been made to celebrated portraits by Leonardo, most notably that of Lisa del Giocondo (the so-called *Mona Lisa*),[59] where the sfumato technique, the use of smoky shadow rather than line or transition of color and light, enables a paradoxical dematerialization of the material—that is, traces of the hand of the artist disappear, such that the painted form seems to emerge from nothing.

---

57. Loïc Gouzer (Chairman, Post-War and Contemporary Art, Christie's New York), "Christie's to offer the last Leonardo da Vinci painting in private hands," press release, 10 October 2017, https://www.christies.com/about-us/press-archive/details?PressReleaseID=8839&lid=1.

58. Syson, "Christ as Salvator Mundi," 303.

59. The *Salvator Mundi* was referred to in publicity as the "male Mona Lisa": Francois de Poortere, Head of Old Master Paintings at Christies, commenting in the press release on 10 October 2017. On female portraiture in the late fifteenth century, Frank Zöllner, "From the Face to the Aura: Leonardo da Vinci's Sfumato and the History of Female Portraiture," in *Inventing Faces: Rhetorics of Portraiture between Renaissance and Modernism*, ed. Mona Körte (Berlin: Deutscher Kunstverlag, 2013), 67–83, with discussion of the technique known as sfumato and Leonardo's use of it after 1500 at 79–80.

This innovative painting technique created what Leonardo referred to as an *aria* or aura, a use of light and shadow to create a softness and draw out a sense of grace or the miraculous.[60] Works painted in this technique might be compared with *acheiropoieta*—those divine images of Christ not made by human hands.[61] The technique is not deployed for the globe however, where the skill of the artist is witnessed in different ways.

Although parts of the panel had undergone extensive conservation after the painting came onto the art market, the globe was reported to be close to its original state.[62] Its translucency affords a view directly through to the palm of the hand, which some describe the artist as having rendered "miraculously" without distortion, while at the same time depicting the surface of the globe in a detail that betrays extraordinary technical ability.[63] There is no smoky shadow here. On that surface we observe tiny flecks, painstakingly rendered in different sizes, depicting the inclusions that are characteristic of rock crystal, the purest form of quartz.[64] Luke Syson has described the representation of the globe as "marvellously modern" in that it reveals a sophisticated understanding of the way light passes through glass, the artist (who, he argues, is Leonardo) ensuring "that it would be perceived as if formed from light itself."[65] The

---

60. Zöllner, "From the Face to the Aura," 79–80.

61. So argues Alexander Nagel, "Leonardo and sfumato," *RES: Anthropology and Aesthetics* 24 (1993): 7–20, here 18.

62. *Leonardo da Vinci: Salvator Mundi*, auction catalogue, 21. See further, Dianne Dwyer Modestini, "The *Salvator Mundi* by Leonardo da Vinci Rediscovered: History, Technique and Condition," in *Leonardo da Vinci's Technical Practice: Paintings, Drawings and Influence*, ed. Michel Menu (Paris: Hermann, 2014), 139–52.

63. Syson, "Christ as Salvator Mundi," 303: "Christ's hand remains miraculously undistorted."

64. Ibid., 302.

65. Ibid., 303 at n. 9, where Syson cites two texts from the corpus of Leonardo's own writings (BN 2038, fol 22a; and R 118) as evidence to support his argument that the lack of distortion caused by the globe points to Leonardo as the artist. This chapter does not afford scope to examine the texts in more detail, but it suffices to say that in discussing shadow, on the one hand, and the transmission of light through different media, on the other, neither text brings clarity to the question of attribution. Indeed, in terms of associating the painting with Leonardo and securing an attribution to him, the absence of distortion might be identified as one of the troubling features of the work. For these comments I gratefully acknowledge Charles Hope, who discussed the texts with me.

contrasting techniques chosen for the face and globe provide insight into the function of the painting and to any supposed musing on divinity and the cosmos on the part of the artist.

A basic cosmological framework had gained currency in Greek philosophy and science by around 400 BCE and remained operative in the earliest Christian conceptions of the creation of the cosmos: it was imagined to be round, with the earth at its center.[66] On this "two-sphere" model, the symbol of the globe represented the entire cosmos, not just earth.[67] Cicero attributed the invention and construction of a celestial globe to Thales, an astronomer and philosopher from Miletus in Asia Minor;[68] and in Greek art, the globe was the attribute of Urania, the muse of astronomy.[69] As a functional object in teaching astronomy or astrology, the globe could also evoke ideas of learning and intellectual wisdom.[70] In Steven Hijmans's words, any figure bearing the globe was understood to be the "prime mover of (or in) the cosmos."[71] When Apollo is portrayed as

66. Pascal Arnaud, "L'image du globe dans le monde romain. Science, iconographie, symbolique," *Mélanges de l'Ecole française de Rome. Antiquité* 96 (1984): 53–116, gives compelling evidence that in Roman art all globes were models of the cosmos, not earth.

67. Described in more detail by Alexander Jones, "Introduction," in *Time and Cosmos in Greco-Roman Antiquity*, ed. James Evans (Princeton, NJ: Princeton Univ. Press, 2016), 19–43, esp. 24–33.

68. Cicero, *De Republica* 1.13.22; Patricia F. O'Grady, *Thales of Miletus: The Beginnings of Western Science and Philosophy* (Aldershot: Ashgate, 2002), 105–6, n. 32, contains an extended commentary.

69. Stefan Weinstock, *Divus Julius* (Oxford: Clarendon Press, 1971), 42, bibliography at n. 1. Urania is often depicted holding a stick and pointing to a globe, and sometimes holding the globe, with examples cited by R. J. A. Wilson, "Aspects of Iconography in Romano-British Mosaics: The Rudston 'Aquatic' Scene and the Brading Astronomer Revisited," *Britannia* 37 (2006): 295–336, at 316, n. 76.

70. Arnaud, "L'image du globe," 60–63; James Evans, "The Material Culture of Greek Astronomy," *Journal for the History of Astronomy* 30 (1999): 237–307, here 283. Material and literary evidence for the making of Greek globes is discussed by Elly Dekker, "Featuring the First Greek Celestial Globes," *Globe Studies* 55/56 (2009): 133–52.

71. Steven E. Hijmans, "Sol: The Sun in the Art and Religions of Rome" (PhD diss., University of Groningen, 2009), 21.

the Sun god Helios, for example, it is not the sun that he holds in his left hand, but a blue celestial globe to assert his centrality in the cosmic orbit.[72]

By the end of the Roman Republic, the idea of all-encompassing power had no doubt stimulated the use of the globe by leaders as an abstract symbol of political power.[73] Thus from the time of Caesar Augustus onward, all Roman rulers could be depicted bearing the *globus* as a sign of their authority, an equivalence thereby struck between the Roman Empire and the cosmos. This authority is underscored when deities are shown to acknowledge that power. For instance, when the goddess Venus is shown placing a large figure of Victory on top of the globe held by Augustus, the viewer is left in no doubt that his dominion is not just terrestrial; it is cosmic.[74]

With the conversion of the Roman Empire to Christianity, Christian emperors and empresses might be represented holding a globe surmounted not by the figure of Victory, but by a victorious cross—a composite symbol known as the *globus cruciger*.[75] That the cross symbolized Christ's victory over death and the devil, and the enemies of the faith, is evinced in Prokopios of Caesarea's description of the *globus cruciger* held by the emperor Justinian (527–565) on his bronze equestrian statue in Constantinople: the globe signified Justinian's rule over the earth and sea, while the cross was the "emblem by which alone he

72. For example, the painting of Apollo-Helios excavated in a house of the *Regio* VI of Pompeii: Museo Nazionale di Napoli, inv. no. 8819. Ida Bassaldare, ed., *Pompei: pitture e mosaici*, vol. 4 (Rome: Istituto della Enciclopedia italiana, 1990), 450, fig. 2.

73. On the changing significance of the globe from Greek to Roman art and its use by the Romans as "the symbol of the mastery of the world," Weinstock, *Divus Julius*, 42–45.

74. As in the representation of the emperor Augustus on one of the two silver Boscoreale cups, Musée du Louvre, BR 1 inv. no. BJ 1923. Ann L. Kuttner, *Dynasty and Empire in the Age of Augustus: The Case of the Boscoreale Cups* (Berkeley: Univ. of California Press, 1995), 15–17, figs. 1, 2, 19 (detail).

75. A fine example is the representation of a Byzantine empress (perhaps Ariadne?) on an ivory relief carved in Constantinople, ca. 500–520 (26.5 x 12.7 cm), now in the Kunsthistorisches Museum, Vienna. Diliana Angelova, "The Ivories of Ariadne and Ideas about Female Imperial Authority in Rome and Early Byzantium," *Gesta* 43, no. 1 (2004): 1–15.

has obtained both his empire and his victory in war."[76] Following this use of the composite symbol as an attribute of Christian victory and rule in depictions of imperial court ceremony, the *globus cruciger* did come to be held by Jesus himself in medieval art.[77]

Yet the placement of a plain *globus* into the left hand of Jesus, who died on a cross and secured victory in his resurrection to eternal life, was not tied to notions of the imperial court. It represented something different. The challenge of presenting a divinely authorized Christ had been encountered by Paul in the first century, long before Christian communities began to use art as a way of expressing their faith or exploring their understandings of the power and role of the Christian God. Rhetorically, when Paul had to describe Jesus to the Corinthians and to explain the concept of the cross, he had recourse to figures prominent in Graeco-Roman society at large: the philosopher, the intellectual, the lawgiver, whose wisdom Christ would challenge: "Where is the one who is wise? Where is the scribe? Where is the debater of this age? Has not God made foolish the wisdom of the world?" (1 Cor 1:20, ESV, used throughout). Christ was the power and the wisdom of God, and God's wisdom was wiser than human wisdom.[78] The challenge was how to express this power visually.

Initially, Christians seem to have been interested in roles through which Jesus' authority was made manifest. Specific stories from the four canonical gospels were represented, particularly instances of healing. Yet very quickly a new preoccupation emerged: the authority of Christ as teacher. Scenes of Jesus with the disciples were present in the Roman

76. Discussed by Angelova, "Ivories of Ariadne," 5.

77. This was not so much a real item, used in court ceremony, as an attribute of Christian rule and victory: Liz James, *Empresses and Power in Early Byzantium* (London: Leicester Univ. Press, 2001), 140. There is not space here to discuss Anglo-Saxon and Ottonian images in which Christ holds the orb, a tradition associated with post-Carolingian interest in and use of the accoutrements of kingship (as seen in Roman images of rulers) to emphasize the regality of God, on which see Michael Kauffman, *Biblical Imagery in Medieval England* (Turnhout: Brepols, 2003), 120–22.

78. 1 Cor 1:18–24, which includes a reference to Isa 29:14, "so I will again do amazing things with this people, shocking and amazing. The wisdom of their wise shall perish, and the discernment of the discerning shall be hidden."

Figure 6. Mosaic from the Villa of Titus Siminius Stephanus, Pompeii. First century BCE–first century CE, 85 cm (width) x 86cm (height). Museo Archeologico Nazionale di Napoli, inv. no. 124545. Photo: Jebulon, image in the public domain (CC0 1.0).

catacombs in the late third century,[79] but these did not illustrate a specific instance in which he is recorded as having taught, such as the Sermon on the Mount (from the Gospel of Matthew 5–7). Rather, they referred generally to his role as teacher.[80] Representations of philosophers provided an important compositional framework for the exploration of this role, and a Roman mosaic from Pompeii (believed to copy a Hellenistic Greek painting of the Seven Sages), can be used to illustrate this (Fig. 6).[81] In the mosaic, seven men gather in a circle around a celestial globe and engage in discussion, striking gestures of speech or thought as one of them (perhaps Thales, to whom Cicero attributed the celestial globe) gestures to the globe with a radius.[82] The same semi-circular arrangement, gestures of discourse, and use of scrolls as attributes of intellectual

79. Pasquale Testini, "Osservazioni sull'iconografia del Cristo in trono fra gli Apostoli," *Rivista dell'Istituto nazionale d'archeologia e storia dell'arte* 11 (1963): 230–300, here 236–37.

80. As observed by Geir Hellemo, *Adventus Domini: Eschatological Thought in 4th Century Apses and Catecheses* (Boston, MA: Brill, 1989), 20, with further discussion of the teaching theme across 21–24.

81. From the Villa of Titus Siminius Stephanus, Pompeii, first century BCE–first century CE. Museo archeologico nazionale di Napoli, inv. no. 124545.

82. Otto Brendel, "The Philosopher Mosaic in Naples," in *Symbolism of the Sphere: A Contribution to the History of Earlier Greek Philosophy*, trans. Maria W. Brendel (Leiden: E.J. Brill, 1977), 1–18. James Evans, "Images of Time and Cosmic Connection," in *Time and Cosmos*, ed. Evans, 143, fig. 1–12.

Figure 7. Christ teaching among the disciples. Painting in the lunette of an arcosolium in the Crypt of Ampliatus, ca. 340–50, Catacomb of Domitilla, Rome.
Photo: Scala / Art Resource, NY.

discussion and learning are found in early representations of Jesus and his disciples (Fig. 7): where Thales or another Sage might point to the globe, Jesus teaches directly from a book or scroll, his lap and the book being deliberately exposed to the viewer as he extends his right arm in a gesture of instruction. In this way the word, symbolized in the book and in Jesus the incarnate deity, became the center of the scene compositionally and theologically.[83]

The development of this theme in Christian art was of fundamental importance in establishing a basic iconography for the representation of Jesus as figure of authority.[84] In the mid-fourth-century fresco in the catacomb of Domitilla (Fig. 7), a shift is already apparent: adjustment of the right-hand gesture, now with open palm, creates a greater sense of Jesus' particular authority in the group and his centrality as teacher of, not in, the group.[85] Over time, different strategies were used to develop

83. On the teaching scene and philosophical influences: Hellemo, *Adventus Domini*, 19–27.

84. See further: Janet Huskinson, *Concordia Apostolorum: Christian Propaganda at Rome in the Fourth and Fifth Centuries: A Study in Early Christian Iconography and Iconology*, BAR International Series 148 (Oxford: BAR, 1982).

85. Hellemo, *Adventus Domini*, 22.

this notion of his authority, including the conceptual restructuring of the scene as a hierarchical vision of celestial space.[86] Jesus, positioned at the apex of the group and often on a larger scale, was moved backward into the scene, thereby creating a distance between the viewer and the teacher; he was enthroned, provided with a footrest, given a nimbus, and often shown with an open codex rather than a simple scroll. In the process of this restructuring and representation of the group, the viewer was no longer in the midst of the teaching circle but became an onlooker.

The image of Jesus in the catacomb of Commodilla (Fig. 2) sheds further light on this interpretation. We have seen that by the fourth century a format for the representation of Jesus as a figure of divine authority had appeared. In expressing the role of the Christian God as the summation of the cosmos, the letters in this painting are pivotal: in the Revelation to John, they refer to God (1:8) and to the divine presence seated on the heavenly throne (21:5-6), but also to Christ, who promises to return in his messianic advent, or Parousia, to judge the world at the end of time. In this way, the image preserves an early version of the Pantocrator idea. Around the same time, a different expression of this role as divine judge and summation of the cosmos was formulated—one that can be seen to impact directly on the use of globe iconography. On several marble sarcophagi produced in the second half of the fourth century, Jesus, as the focus of the decorative scheme, is shown enthroned over a personification of Caelus, the Roman god of the heavens. In some examples the arms of Caelus are raised to stretch out the heavens above his head while saints Peter and Paul stand in attendance, at Jesus' right and left.[87] In an example imported to Algeria (Fig. 8), on which seven scenes represent aspects of Jesus' divinity, his authoritative rule over

---

86. I am thinking here specifically of the vault fresco in the catacomb of Saints Marcellinus and Peter (room 3, "Cripta dei Santi"), painted in the late fourth century. Johannes Georg Deckers et al., *Die Katakombe "Santi Marcellino e Pietro": Repertorium der Malereien* (Vatican City: Pontificio Istituto di Archeologia Cristiana, 1987), 199–201, with bibliography. Huskinson, *Concordia Apostolorum*, 11, suggests that the artist copied the design from a local basilica.

87. A seven-niche single register sarcophagus found in St. Peter's (Lateran sarcophagus 174): Friedrich Wilhelm Deichmann, *Repertorium der christlich-antiken Sarkophage*, vol. 1 (Wiesbaden: F. Steiner, 1967), no. 677, 274–77, and for the same iconography, no. 680 (the sarcophagus of Junius Bassus, 359 CE).

the heavens is more pronounced: palm trees, symbols of paradise, now flank him and so displace Peter and Paul, who appear as small figures beneath the throne, one on either side of Caelus's face, gazing up to Jesus as he holds a scroll and extends his right hand with the palm open in the authoritative gesture seen earlier (Fig. 7).[88] Emperors had previously exploited Caelus in asserting their own authority, a fine example being the celebrated statue of Augustus from Prima Porta: the standing emperor, frozen in a moment of rhetorical address, wears a cuirass emblazoned with a prominent representation of Caelus.[89] In a Christian context, compressed under the feet of Jesus, Caelus not only locates the scene of Jesus enthroned between the disciples in heaven, where he is sovereign, but also simultaneously evokes the universal authority of the Christian God and his power across time.[90]

That both Christ's divinity and his representation of the Father are denoted in such images is clear in a rare catacomb mosaic from the second half of the fourth century that carries the legend *Qui filius diceris et pater inveneris* (perhaps "the one said to be the Son and found to be the Father").[91] Jesus strikes the gesture of address that is also one of power, facing the viewer in strict frontality and holding an open scroll while seated between Peter and Paul. Yet now he is seated not on a throne but on a globe.[92] To obtain a clearer understanding of this extraordinary but poorly preserved iconography we can turn to two other mosaics. The first was produced in Rome around 350, just before the production of the Caelus sarcophagus in the same city: in a vault mosaic in Santa Costanza, Jesus is represented with a gradient blue nimbus, seated on a globe while holding a scroll in his left hand and giving the keys (or a

---

88. Brigitte Christern-Briesenick, *Repertorium der christliche-antiken Sarkophage*, vol. 3 (Mainz: F. Steiner, 2003), no. 593, 274–75.

89. Although the details of the breastplate have been interpreted in different ways, the iconography is regarded as asserting the authority of Augustus. Karl Galinksy, *Augustan Culture: An Interpretative Introduction* (Princeton, NJ: Princeton Univ. Press, 1996), 158, n. 37, regarding billowing mantle as a representation of the vault of the firmament, and 24, regarding the gesture of rhetorical address, an *adlocutio*.

90. See further on the precise meaning of Caelus: Hellemo, *Adventus Domini*, 25–27.

91. Jean-Michel Spieser, "The Representation of Christ in the Apses of Early Christian Churches," *Gesta* 37, no. 1 (1998): 63–73, here 69 and fig. 4.

92. Spieser, "Representation of Christ," 68.

Figure 8. Christ enthroned over Caelus. Marble sarcophagus, Rome, 3rd quarter of fourth century, 52 x 215 x 60 cm. Musée National des Antiquités d'Alger, Algeria, inv. no. 238. Photo: Wellcome Collection (CC-BY 4.0).

codex) to Peter in his right.[93] In a different liturgical context in a different city, Jesus stands on the globe and hands an open scroll to Peter in the cupola of the baptistery of San Giovanni in Fonte, in the Duomo of Naples (Fig. 9), dating from the early fifth century.[94]

There is no question that the erection and dedication of large basilicas for Christian worship from the fourth century onward had a direct impact on the development of images asserting an authoritative role for the Christian God over the cosmos. Later in the fifth century, in the

93. The mosaic is located in the western niche of the lateral axis of the mausoleum. Hugo Brandenburg, *Ancient Churches of Rome from the Fourth to the Seventh Century* (Turnhout: Brepols, 2005), 86, fig. 41, with further discussion of the building's mosaic program at 69–85.

94. For a drawing of the mosaic program (depicting the life of Christ): Jean-Louis Maier, *Le baptistère de Naples et ses mosaïques: Étude historique et iconographique,* Paradosis: Études de littérature et de théologie anciennes 19 (Fribourg: Éditions Universitaires, 1964), plate 11. In addition to these mosaics, two poorly preserved paintings in different Roman catacombs suggest that this Christ-on-globe iconography was used elsewhere in the city: in the Catacombs of Priscilla and Via Latina. Ines Warburg, "Sobra un cubículo decorado de la Catacumba de Priscilla," *Rivista di Archeologia Cristiana* 80 (2004): 63–83, at 76–77; and Huskinson, *Concordia Apostolorum*, 9, dating the Via Latina fresco to a period after 350.

Figure 9. Christ standing on a globe.
Baptistery of San Giovanni in Fonte, Naples.
Photo: Carlo Raso, image in the public
domain (Mark 1.0).

apse mosaic in the church of Sant'Agata dei Goti on the Viminal hill in Rome, Jesus was represented seated on a blue globe and flanked by twelve standing apostles.[95] The original mosaic, created between 462 and 472, was destroyed when the apse vault collapsed in 1589. However, drawings made before the collapse indicate that a bearded Jesus, his shoulder-length hair centrally parted and lapping over his shoulders, was represented in strict frontality seated on a blue globe.[96] His right arm was close to his body with the palm raised to face the viewer while the left hand held an open codex. Inscriptions originally named each disciple and labeled Jesus *salus totius humani generis*, his authority and role as savior of all humanity thereby articulated in word as well as image. The

95. Carlo Cecchelli, "Il mosaico absidale," in Christian Hülsen et al., *S. Agata dei Goti* (Rome: P. Sansaini, 1924), 29–37. Richard Krautheimer, *Corpus basilicarum christianarum Romae* (Vatican City: Pontificio Istituto di archeologia cristiana, 1937–80), vol. 1, 2–12.

96. Colored drawings, made ca. 1590, were included by Alfonso Ciacconio (1530–1599) in a codex now in the Vatican Library (Vat. Lat. 5407, 44-72): Stephan Waetzoldt, *Die Kopien des 17. Jahrhunderts nach Mosaiken und Wandmalereien in Rom* (Vienna: Schroll, 1964), cat. nos. 1–13.

Figure 10. Sant'Apollinare in Classe, Ravenna. Sixth century apse
mosaic, and detail of the triumphal arch. Photo: author.

apse mosaic used to advertise the 2018 ISM Liturgy Conference and its
theme illustrates this articulation in more detail (Fig. 10). Consecrated
in 549, the church of Sant'Apollinare in Classe likely contained extensive mosaic imagery across its nave walls as well as the triumphal arch
and the vault of the apse, although today only those on the arch and the
apse vault survive. At the center of the arch is the bust-image of Jesus
with which we are now familiar, which looks over the vault and its extraordinary mid-sixth-century representation of the transfiguration. That
representation brings together many of the design ideas that we have
seen early Christians consider as they sought to express the concept of
God as "all-ruler."

The apse design is divided into a lower terrestrial (green) zone and an
upper celestial (gold) zone, and at the center, crossing into both zones, is
an enormous blue medallion or globe, studded with gold stars, surrounded
by a jeweled border, and containing a large jeweled cross at the center
of which is exhibited the bust-image of Jesus. In this composition Jesus
does not hold or sit upon the globe: he occupies it, in a way that Gregory
of Nyssa might have imagined. The hand of God extends from the top
of the golden sky toward the circle to indicate, according to Gospel
accounts of the transfiguration (for example, Matt 17:1-9), the words
"This is my beloved Son." Two half-length figures labeled Moses and
Elijah emerge out of the clouds to flank and gesture towards the globe in

speech, while Peter, James, and John, who witness the transfiguration, are represented as sheep in the verdant landscape below, looking upward to the medallion. Below it, facing the viewer, is the titular saint Apollinaris flanked by twelve sheep, who likely represent the congregation. Jesus, represented as the victorious cross, is the pivot point of the composition. At the center of this cross is a tiny bust-portrait bordered in pearls. It is tightly cropped as in the catacomb of Commodilla two centuries earlier such that his arms are not shown. In addition to the blue color of the medallion (seen also in the catacomb of Ponziano and on the Mount Sinai icon) and stars (seen in the catacomb of Commodilla) to denote a celestial setting, the shape of the large jeweled cross is defined by four distinct lines of tesserae in shades of dark blue to create a gradient-blue border. Flanking the cross are the alpha and omega. However, now the eschatological significance, the totality of God's power, is underscored by additional text: the words "Salus Mundi" ("salvation of the world") below, and the acrostic ICHTHYS (formed by the initials of five Greek words meaning "Jesus Christ, Son of God, the Savior") directly above.

The apse mosaic at Sant'Apollinare in Classe enables me to draw the strands of this chapter together. Ancient Greek ideas about, and visualizations of, the cosmos became fundamental in the pictorialization of divine power in early Christianity. Representations of Jesus upon, holding, or even occupying the globe appear in a myriad of cultural and material contexts leading up to the sixteenth century, when the Abu Dhabi *Salvator Mundi* was painted. Across this stretch of time, particular interests or concerns (political, theological, or liturgical) might inflect the globe with meaning, but the whole remained constant.

The artist or artists who designed and painted the Abu Dhabi *Salvator Mundi* were intensely familiar with a format for the representation of Jesus that was developed in early Christianity and was associated with miraculous images of him; they understood the power of the globe as a symbol for the articulation of divine authority. They did not need to be cognizant of the origins of the iconography of the holy face to understand the intense devotional practices with which it was connected, and like Dürer and countless artists before them, they brought to the compositional format their own skills, motivations, and painting techniques to explore their subject. As in the Mount Sinai icon, the eyes are used to manifest a sense of all-encompassing power, but there is no nimbus and no alpha and omega. In its striking surface detail and clear refraction of light, the symbol of the globe is used as the tangible mechanism of that power, while the sfumato technique is adopted for the face to create an *aria*. The two approaches, *aria* versus minute detail, juxtaposed on the one panel, bring new qualities to an ancient pictorial format. While brushwork and painting technique may hold clues about the date of the painting and the identity of the artist or workshop, the iconography and the compositional format itself betray something fundamentally important about the ongoing work of artists to evoke the eternal, and this is what is relevant about the work, as much or more than the supposed genius and attribution. The artistic interest in divinity and cosmological order is an ancient one and returns us to the earliest Christian use of art to conjure the authority of the Christian God in and over the cosmos. In this way, if "the work of Leonardo is just as influential to the art that is being created today as it was in the fifteenth and sixteenth centuries,"[97] so too is the art created by anonymous artists in the fifth and sixth centuries.[98]

97. Loic Gouzer, "Christie's to offer the last Leonardo da Vinci painting in private hands."

98. I would like to acknowledge my colleague Teresa Berger for her generosity and unfailing support of this research. I also express my deep gratitude to Charles Hope, Vasileios Marinis, Andrew McGowan, and Rona Johnston for their time and care in reading and commenting on different drafts of this chapter.

CHAPTER FIVE

Night or Dawn?

Easter Night in Light of Cosmos and Creation

Duco Vollebregt

The *Exultet*, the paschal proclamation and blessing prayer of the
paschal candle during the Easter Vigil in the Roman Catholic Church,
expresses the wish that the flame of the paschal candle "be found still
burning by the Morning Star: the one Morning Star who never sets,
Christ your Son."[1] The *Exultet* characterizes the paschal candle earlier
in the text as an "evening sacrifice" (*sacrificium vespertinum*). It situates
itself firmly in the *night* by the frequent recurrence of phrases beginning
haec nox est, nox in qua, or *O beata nox*. In this passage, nevertheless,
it invokes the morning star (*lucifer matutinus; lucifer*) as the symbol of
the risen Christ.

All these moments—evening, night, and dawn—have a great symbolic
significance in the spirituality of the early church and in the writings of the
church fathers.[2] However, how do they relate to each other in the case of
the Easter Vigil? Was the Easter Vigil, for which the *Exultet* was written,
looking forward to dawn, as the symbolic moment of the resurrection, or

1. *Flammas eius lúcifer matutínus invéniat: Ille, inquam, lúcifer, qui nescit oc-
cásum: Christus Fílius tuus*, Exultet, in *Missale Romanum. Editio Typica Tertia,
Reimpressio Emendata* (Vatican City: Typis Vaticanis, 2008), 347–49, at 349. English translation of *The Roman Missal* (International Commission on English in the
Liturgy Corporation, 2010).
2. Gregory W. Woolfenden, *Daily Liturgical Prayer: Origins and Theology*, Liturgy, Worship and Society (Aldershot: Ashgate, 2004), 9–24.

is this reference to the morning star a reminder that the paschal candle was meant to continue burning *all through the night*, and thus that the *entire night* was hallowed in the light of Christ's resurrection? To put it differently: is the night (of Easter) to be interpreted in light of the subsequent dawn (as the symbolic moment of the resurrection) or is this reference to dawn to be interpreted in light of the night (of Easter), which in its entirety is bathing in the splendor of the risen Christ? In addition, how does the evening of Passover, frequently interpreted by the church fathers as the symbolic moment of Christ's sacrifice on the cross,[3] relate to the symbolism of (Easter) night and dawn and their predominant interpretation in light of the resurrection? In other words: how do the death and resurrection of Jesus Christ, expressed in symbolic language as "evening sacrifice" (*sacrificium vespertinum*) and "morning star" (*lucifer matutinus*), relate to each other during the Easter Vigil according to the *Exultet*?

In this chapter, these questions will be explored based on the originally Gallican version of this blessing prayer of the paschal candle together with some adjacent prayers of the Easter Vigil in the *Missale Gothicum*, the oldest (Gallican) manuscript in which the *Exultet* was transmitted.[4] After a brief introduction to the *Exultet* and the Easter Vigil in the *Missale Gothicum*, three clusters of cosmic symbolism in the Gallican Easter Vigil will be discussed, that is (1) evening and night, (2) light in the night, and (3) night and dawn. It will be argued that in invoking the morning star as a symbol of the risen Christ, the epiclesis of the *Exultet* is not suggesting that the Easter Vigil is looking forward to dawn as the symbolic moment of the resurrection. It will be shown that the invocation of this symbol, through its blending with the flame of the paschal candle (designated as "evening sacrifice" earlier in the text), serves precisely to highlight the sacredness, and multifacetedness, of the entire night of Easter. The brilliance and splendor of this night, it will be argued, blend not only evening and morning, night and day, and earth and heaven but also Christ sacrificed and Christ risen into the one single reality of Easter Night. Although Easter Night is truly the night of Christ's resurrection, it will be shown that the continuing presence of the paschal candle serves as a

---

3. Anscar J. Chupungco, *The Cosmic Elements of Christian Passover*, Studia Anselmiana 72 (Rome: Pontificio Ateneo S. Anselmo, 1977), 73–79.

4. How an originally Gallican blessing prayer ended up at such a prominent position in the Roman Rite is well explained by Thomas Forrest Kelly, "Candle, Text, Ceremony: The Exultet at Rome," *Études Grégoriennes* 32 (2004): 7–68.

reminder of the unity of the entire mystery of Christ's death and resurrection, symbolically blending, as evening sacrifice and morning star, into the one light of Christ shining for the redemption of all creation.[5]

The Sources

The oldest extant manuscript that transmits the *Exultet* is the *Missale Gothicum*,[6] a sacramentary probably compiled in the vicinity of Autun, in the province of Burgundy in Merovingian Gaul (in what is now France), around 700.[7] The manuscript is a compilation of older texts, many of which, such as the *Exultet*, predate the composition of this manuscript by several centuries.[8]

---

5. My contribution to the theme of this volume concerns the ways in which cosmos and creation (and in particular the cosmic cycles of night and day and the interplay of earthly and heavenly lights) are sacramentally involved in Christ's redemptive work during Easter Night. That Christ's redemptive work actually affects the whole of the cosmos is a different (though related) matter, discussed extensively in Elizabeth A. Johnson, *Ask the Beasts: Darwin and the God of Love* (London: Bloomsbury, 2015). She observes that in the prologue of the *Exultet* (which I will not discuss in this chapter as it is not unique to the Gallican tradition) the earth is addressed as the recipient of the glory of Christ's resurrection (209).

6. The most recent edition is Els Rose, ed., *Missale Gothicum e codice Vaticano Reginensi latino 317 editum*, Corpus Christianorum. Series Latina 159D (Turnhout: Brepols, 2005). Prayer texts from this manuscript are cited henceforth as *GaG*, followed by the number of the prayer and the line number(s) in this edition. A complete English translation of the manuscript is provided by Els Rose, *The Gothic Missal: Introduction, Translation and Notes*, Corpus Christianorum in Translation 27 (Turnhout: Brepols, 2017). For discussion of and references to previous editions of the manuscript, from the seventeenth century onwards, see Rose, *Missale Gothicum*, 17–20; Rose, *The Gothic Missal*, 14–15, n. 6. A bibliography of literature on the origin and history of the manuscript is provided by Rose, *Missale Gothicum*, 12, n. 1. On the Gallican liturgy, see Rose, *Missale Gothicum*, 190–93.

7. See Rose, *Missale Gothicum*, 15–17; Rose, *The Gothic Missal*, 14–16.

8. The *Exultet* is widely considered to date from the late fourth or early fifth century. See Heinrich Zweck, *Osterlobpreis und Taufe: Studien zu Struktur und Theologie des Exsultet und anderer Osterpraeconien unter besonderer Berücksichtigung der Taufmotive*, Regensburger Studien zur Theologie 32 (Frankfurt am Main: Peter Lang, 1986), 80–82; Guido Fuchs and Hans Martin Weikmann, *Das Exsultet: Geschichte, Theologie und Gestaltung der österlichen Lichtdanksagung* (Regensburg: Pustet, 1992), 17. Kelly tends to date the preface portion of the text later, but "before the end

The formulary for the Easter Vigil in the *Missale Gothicum* consists of four parts: a paschal *lucernarium* (i.e., the rite of light including the *Exultet* as blessing prayer of the paschal candle),[9] intercessions (probably said alternately with the vigil readings),[10] rites of initiation,[11] and the Eucharist.[12] Formularies for the (probably twelve)[13] vigil readings are not included in the *Missale Gothicum*, but it is likely that they followed the paschal *lucernarium*, were read alternately with the twelve intercessory addresses and prayers provided in the *Missale Gothicum*, and preceded the rites of Christian initiation.[14]

In the paschal *lucernarium* of the *Missale Gothicum*, the part of the formulary that concerns us in this chapter, there seems to be a twofold opening: first an introductory address (*praefacio*), then a collect (*colleccio*) "at the evening of Easter."[15] These first two prayers are, in part,

---

of the sixth century," with a *terminus ante quem* of 585, when the second Council of Mâcon prescribed attendance at Masses of Easter Week. To prescribe attendance, Kelly argues, there should at least have been specific Masses, which he considers to be those preserved in the *Missale Gothicum*. Since two of these Masses, the Vigil Mass of Holy Saturday and the Mass for the Friday in Easter Week, quote the *Exultet*, he argues that the *Exultet* would have also been in existence by this year. He does date, however, the prologue beginning with *Exultet* to the fourth or fifth century. See Thomas Forrest Kelly, *The Exultet in Southern Italy* (New York, NY: Oxford Univ. Press, 1996), 53. For the distinction between prologue and preface, see the discussion that follows.

9. *GaG* 221–27: <XXX>.

10. *GaG* 228–51: <XXXI> *Oraciones paschalis* [-es] duodecim cum totidem colleccionibus.* I always give the original Latin of the *Missale Gothicum* as it is presented in the edition Rose, *Missale Gothicum.* Problematic word forms I indicate with an asterisk* followed by [the solution suggested by Rose].

11. *GaG* 252–54: <XXXII> *Ad christianum faciendum*; *GaG* 255–65: <XXXIII> *Colleccio ad fontes benedicendos* etc.

12. *GaG* 266–72: <XXXIIII> *Missa in vigiliis sanctae paschae.*

13. The Gallican lectionary of Luxeuil attests to the fact that in Gaul a vigil proper was known consisting of twelve Old Testament readings. See Pierre Salmon, *Le lectionnaire de Luxeuil*, Collectanea Biblica Latina 7 (Rome: Abbaye Saint-Jérôme, 1944), 97–116.

14. That in the Gallican tradition, as in most other traditions, the readings followed the *lucernarium* is suggested by the heading of one of the opening prayers of the *lucernarium*: *Ad inicio* [-ium] noctis sanctae paschae* (at the beginning of the Holy Night of Easter) (*GaG* 223). If the readings are to be considered part of this night, they should therefore have followed the *lucernarium*. For the alternation of vigil readings and intercessory prayers, see Baumstark, *Nocturna Laus*, 44.

15. *GaG* 221: *Praefacio in vespera paschae*; 222: *Colleccio sequitur.*

more concerned with Holy Saturday than with Easter[16] and are particularly relevant for the symbolic understanding of the evening preceding the night of Easter. Then follow an introductory address (*praefacio*) and prayer (*oratio*) "at the beginning of the holy night of Easter."[17] After the *Exultet*, ascribed by the rubric to Saint Augustine,[18] follow two more collects, "after the blessing of the candle" and "after the hymn of the candle," which will not concern us here.[19] For the symbolic understanding of the night of Easter itself, including its connection with the preceding evening and the subsequent dawn of Easter Sunday, we need to turn to the *Exultet* itself, as well as the two initial prayers "at the evening of Easter."

A last remark about the sources concerns the structure of the *Exultet* itself. The text has a tripartite structure.[20] The first part, the prologue, consists of an invitatory and apology of the deacon and begins with the famous words *Exultet iam angelica turba caelorum*, from which the text derives its name.[21] Then follows an introductory dialogue similar to the one used before the eucharistic prayer,[22] and subsequently what is commonly called the "preface,"[23] because of its similarities in structure with the preface of the eucharistic prayer. That the text derives its name from the prologue is confusing, because the prologue was much more widespread than the Gallican liturgical tradition and also preceded the prefaces for blessing the paschal candle in the Ambrosian and Beneventan liturgies.[24] In what follows, therefore, the focus will be on the actual "preface" of the text.

---

16. Cf. Rose, *The Gothic Missal*, 205, n. a.

17. *GaG* 223: *Praefacio ad inicio* [-ium] noctis sanctae paschae*; 224: *Oracio sequitur.*

18. *GaG* 225: *Benediccio caerae beati Augustini episcopi, quam adhuc diaconus cum esset, edidet* [-it] et caecinit*; the preface is subsequently introduced with *Consecracio caere* [cerae].*

19. *GaG* 226: *Colleccio post benediccione* [-em] caere* [cerae]*; *GaG* 227: *Colleccio post hymnum caere* [cerae].*

20. See A. J. MacGregor, *Fire and Light in the Western Triduum*, Alcuin Club Collection 71 (Collegeville, MN: Liturgical Press, 1992), 382.

21. *GaG* 225:1–12.

22. This part of the text is not included in the *Missale Gothicum* but is implied by the first words of the preface: *dignum et iustum est* (*GaG* 225:13).

23. *GaG* 225:13–68.

24. Zweck, *Osterlobpreis und Taufe*, 39. One often presumes that this same prologue originally also preceded two prefaces written at the beginning of the sixth

This preface begins with an expression of praise, elaborating on the preceding introductory dialogue, to God the Father and to Jesus Christ for Christ's saving deed.[25] This expression of praise for Christ's saving deed continues in the so-called "paschal proclamation," which comprises three main parts. The first part consists of a list of characterizations of Easter Night (beginning with *Haec nox est* or variants).[26] The second part begins with a citation from Ambrose but consists mostly of a series of exclamatory phrases about the paradoxes of redemption.[27] The third part is the conclusion to the paschal proclamation.[28] Then follows the so-called light-eucharistic part of the text, consisting of an offering prayer of the paschal candle,[29] an eulogy of the candle,[30] an eulogy of the bees,[31] a short reclamation of the paschal proclamation,[32] an epiclesis,[33] intercessions,[34] and a final doxology.[35]

Evening and Night

If one charts the occurrence of the Latin word forms for night (*nox, noctis*), evening or vesperal (*vespertinum*) and morning or matutinal (*matutinus*) in a table with the aforementioned structure of the Gallican preface (see Table 1), one observes that the first and only explicit reference to the evening in the *Exultet* occurs in the offering prayer of the

century by Ennodius of Pavia. See Jordi Pinell i Pons, "La benedicció del ciri pasqual i els seus textos," in *Liturgica*, part 2, Scripta et Documenta 10 (Monserrat: Abbey of Montserrat, 1958), 53; Zweck, *Osterlobpreis und Taufe*, 44, 133; MacGregor, *Fire and Light*, 383; Thomas Forrest Kelly, *The Exultet in Southern Italy* (New York, NY: Oxford Univ. Press, 1996), 52.

25. *GaG* 225:13–18: *Dignum et iustum est . . . cruore detersit.*

26. *GaG* 225:18–26: *Haec sunt enim festa paschalium* [paschalia] . . . victor ascendit.*

27. *GaG* 225:26–32: *Nihil enim nasci profuit . . . ab inferis resurrexit.*

28. *GaG* 225:32–36: *Haec nox est, de qua scriptum est . . . curvat imperia.*

29. *GaG* 225:36–39: *In huius igitur noctis gracia . . . reddit eclesia.*

30. *GaG* 225:39–43: *Sed iam columnae huius . . . apis mater eduxit.*

31. *GaG* 225:43–57: *Apis ceteris . . . virgo permansit.*

32. *GaG* 225:57–58: *O vere beata nox . . . caelestia iunguntur.*

33. *GaG* 225:58–64: *Oramus te, domine, . . . inluxit.*

34. *GaG* 225:64–67: *Praecamur ergo, domine . . . conservare digneris.*

35. *GaG* 225:67–68: *Per resurgentem a mortuis dominum nostrum filium tuum.*

paschal candle, after the text has already referred no fewer than nine times (of a total of twelve times) to the night.[36] Most of these references to the night clearly concern the present moment: *haec nox est*—*this* is the night.[37] Even the offering of the paschal candle, designated an "evening sacrifice" by the allusion to Psalm 141 (140):2, is considered to take place during the night. The text states: "In the grace *of this night*, therefore, take up, holy Father, the *evening sacrifice* of this ignited [candle]" (my emphases).[38] It is clear, therefore, that the recitation of the Gallican preface was meant to take place during the night. How, then, should this "evening sacrifice" be interpreted?

Table 1. Evening, night and morning in the preface of the *Exultet*

Section	Time indication
Praise for Christ's saving deed	/
Paschal Proclamation, part 1	3 x NIGHT
Paschal Proclamation, part 2	1 x NIGHT
Paschal Proclamation, conclusion	4 x NIGHT
Offering prayer of the paschal candle	1 x NIGHT, 1 x EVENING sacrifice
Eulogy of the candle	/
Eulogy of the bees	/
Reclaiming Paschal Proclamation	2 x NIGHT
Epiclesis	1 x NIGHT, 1 x MORNING star
Intercessions	/
Doxology	/

36. For the reference to the morning (star), see the section entitled "Night and Dawn" in this chapter.

37. *GaG* 225:21–22, 25, 32.

38. *GaG* 225:36–37: *In huius igitur noctis gracia suscipe, sancte pater, incensi huius sacrificium vespertinum.* The word *incensi* was probably originally meant to be an adjective referring to a suppressed noun *cerei* (wax-light, taper, hence candle). See Fuchs and Weikmann, *Das Exsultet*, 81. Cf. Rose, *The Gothic Missal*, 314, n. 96.

As the time of its offering had already been indicated ("in the grace of this night"), another time indication was not necessary, certainly not one that might suggest a period preceding the moment at which the paschal candle had already been said to have been offered. This reference to the "evening sacrifice," coming after nine references to the night, cannot be regarded as a precise indication of the time at which the paschal candle (in the *Exultet*) is presented to God. This notion must have another—liturgical or symbolic—significance.

Its liturgical significance must be sought in the fact that this "evening sacrifice" alludes to Psalm 141 (140):2: "Let my prayer be counted as incense before you, and the lifting up of my hands as an evening sacrifice" (NRSV, used throughout). This psalm, or this psalm verse, was typically used during the *lucernarium* service of daily Vespers, a service of lamp lighting and thanksgiving for the light in the evening that was common in the early church but later fell into disuse.[39] As the rite of the paschal candle was ultimately derived from this practice, the expression "evening sacrifice" might very well have been a remnant of this ancient practice that, having become a standing expression, had lost its literal meaning as a reference to the evening as such and had come to be used in a predominantly nocturnal context.

More important for our present purposes, however, is its symbolic significance. This significance must be sought in the connection, frequently made by the fathers of the church, between the evening of Passover and Christ's sacrifice on the cross.[40] This is part of an ancient paschal theology in which the mystery of Christ's death and resurrection had not yet been separated over several historicizing celebrations during a paschal *Triduum* (i.e., Maundy Thursday, Good Friday, Holy Saturday) but was in its entirety celebrated during the night of Easter itself.[41] It was informed by a typological interpretation of the Passover in Egypt as recounted in Exodus 12, and especially the immolation of the paschal

39. Gabriele Winkler, "Über die Kathedralvesper in den verschiedenen Riten des Ostens und Westens," *Archiv für Liturgiewissenschaft* 16 (1974): 53–102.

40. Chupungco, *The Cosmic Elements of Christian Passover*, 73–79.

41. See the insightful chapter "Why is this Night Different from the Rest of Holy Week?" in Clemens Leonhard, *The Jewish Pesach and the Origins of the Christian Easter: Open Questions in Current Research*, Studia Judaica 35 (Berlin: Walter de Gruyter, 2006), 293–314.

lamb "at twilight" (Exodus 12:6). The blood of this lamb was put on the doorposts of the houses of the Hebrews as a sign for the Lord to *pass over* their houses (hence the feast of *Passover*) when he struck down the first-born Egyptians during the night before the Hebrews were allowed to depart from Egypt.[42] The immolation of the paschal lamb was understood as a prefiguration of Christ's sacrifice on the cross, and the blood of the lamb on the doorposts as a prefiguration of the blood of Christ, which redeemed the faithful from spiritual death.[43]

The paschal proclamation of the Gallican preface alludes precisely to this event: "for these are the paschal feasts, at which he, the true Lamb, is slaughtered, and his blood is consecrated for the doorposts."[44] Together with the subsequent reference to the crossing of the Red Sea as recounted in Exodus 14,[45] this (first) statement is the only statement in the first part of the Gallican paschal proclamation that does not use a variant of the phrase *haec nox est* (this is the night), using instead the phrase *haec sunt enim festa paschalium* ("for these are the paschal feasts). Just before this opening phrase of the paschal proclamation, the preface began by stating why it is worthy and just "to praise aloud the invisible God the Father almighty and his only-begotten Son our Lord Jesus Christ," who is then characterized as the one "who paid on our behalf the debt of Adam to the eternal Father, and wiped away the obligation of the old sin-offering by his benevolent bloodshed."[46] Thus, all references to Christ's death in the

42. On the importance of Exodus 12 in the earliest Christian celebration of Easter see Leonhard, *The Jewish Pesach*, 42–55.

43. Chupungco, *The Cosmic Elements of Christian Passover*, 73.

44. GaG 225:18–19: *Haec sunt enim festa paschalium* [-ia], in quibus verus ille agnus occiditur eiusque sanguis postibus consecratur, . . .*

45. GaG 225:19–21: *. . . in qua* [quibus / Haec nox est, in qua] primum patres nostros filios Israhel educens de Aegypto rubrum mare sicco vestigio transire fecisti.* It is often suggested that the form *in qua*, which is grammatically incorrect if it refers to the *festa paschalium* [paschalia]* of the previous statement (in that case it should have been *in quibus*), in fact refers to a missing introduction *haec nox est*, as was added in later versions of the text; see Zweck, *Osterlobpreis und Taufe*, 28, n. 21; Fuchs and Weikmann, *Das Exsultet*, 134, n. 32.

46. GaG 225:13–18: *Vere quia dignum et iustum est invisibilem deum omnipotentem patrem filiumque eius unigenitum dominum nostrum Iesum Christum toto cordis ac mentis affectu et vocis ministerio personare, qui pro nobis aeterno patri Adae debitum solvit et veteris piacoli* [piaculi] caucionem pio cruore detersit.*

first sections of the Gallican preface (i.e., in the initial praising formula and the first part of the paschal proclamation) are mentioned before the list of statements about the night; statements that associate the night with "cleansing" and "illumination,"[47] with redemption and sanctification ("which restores to grace, joins to holiness"[48]), and, of course, with the resurrection of Jesus Christ ("in which, as the chains of death have been destroyed, Christ rose as victor from the dead"[49]). Interesting to note here is that in two instances the text presents the night as the active agent that "cleanses the darkness of sins by the illumination of the column"[50] and "restores to grace, joins to holiness."[51] The night (of Easter) is clearly not just a backdrop to what happens during the Easter Vigil but has an intrinsic value of its own.

A similar movement can be observed in the second part of the paschal proclamation of the Gallican preface. First, after an opening citation from Ambrose,[52] a series of exclamatory phrases rejoice in the paradoxes of redemption, including the salutary benefits of Christ's passion and death.[53] The second acclamation states, for instance, "O love of immeasurable costliness, that you handed over the Son to redeem the slave."

47. *GaG* 225:21–22: *Haec igitur nox est, quae peccatorum tenebras columnae inluminacione purgavit.*

48. *GaG* 225:22–25: *Haec nox est, quae hodie per universum mundum in Christo* [-um] credentes a viciis saeculi segregatos et caligine peccatorum reddit graciae, sociat sanctitate* [-i].*

49. *GaG* 225:25–26: *Haec nox est, in qua distructis* [destructis] vinculis mortis, Christus ab inferis victor ascendit.*

50. *GaG* 225:21–22, as at n. 47.

51. *GaG* 225:22–25, as at n. 48.

52. *GaG* 225:26–27: *Nihil enim nasci profuit, nisi redimi profuisset* (For it has profited nothing to be born, if it would not have profited to be redeemed). Cf. Ambrosius Mediolanensis, *Expositio evangelii secundum Lucam* 2.41: *Non prodesset nasci, nisi redimi profuisset*, in Ambrosius Mediolanensis, *Expositio evangelii secundum Lucam*, ed. Marc Adriaen, Corpus Christianorum Series Latina 14 (Turnhout: Brepols, 1957), 49. Fuchs and Weikmann, *Das Exsultet*, 64–65.

53. *GaG* 225:27–32: *O mira circa nos tuae pietatis dignacio. O instimabilis* [inaestimabilis] dileccio caritatis, ut servuum redimeris* [-es], filium tradidisti. O certe necessarium Adae peccatum, quo Christi morte deletum est. O filex* [felix] culpa, quae talem ac tantum meruit habere redemptorem. O beata nox, quae sola meruit scire tempus et hora* [-am], in qua Christus ab inferis resurrexit.*

And the third one states, "O surely necessary sin of Adam, which was blotted out by the death of Christ." This entire series of exclamatory phrases is without any reference to the night until the very last sentence, where the night is acclaimed as the sole witness to Christ's resurrection: "O blessed night, which alone deserved to know the time and the hour at which Christ rose from the dead." The paschal proclamation subsequently concludes with some more references to the night that concern its illumination (to which I will come back in the next section)[54] and redemption. Just as in the first part of the paschal proclamation, here too we see that the "sanctification of this night" is presented as the active agent that "chases sins away, takes guilts away, restores innocence to the fallen and to the sorrowful joy, it chases hatreds away, produces harmony and bends sceptres."[55]

It is noteworthy that in the *Exultet* the night is associated never with Christ's passion and death but solely with his resurrection. References to his passion and death precede (in the first part and in the second and concluding part of the paschal proclamation respectively) all references to the night. The night is associated with illumination and is presented as an active agent in the work of redemption and as the sole witness of Christ's resurrection. Implicitly, therefore, the text suggests that the time before the night, hence the evening, is the time associated with these preceding references to his passion and death, prefigured by the immolation of the paschal lamb on the evening of Passover as recounted in Exodus 12.

This is confirmed by the texts of the paschal *lucernarium* that precede the *Exultet* itself, particularly the introductory address and prayer "at the evening of Easter" (*GaG* 221–22). This set of texts is not only situated "at the evening of Easter," but its content is also very much related to the symbolism of the evening of Passover as we have just discussed it for the *Exultet*. In the first place, it characterizes the present moment, with a reference to the evening sacrifice similar to that we have already seen in the offering prayer of the *Exultet*, as the moment at which "the sacrifice of

---

54. *GaG* 225:32–34: *Haec nox est, de qua scriptum est: Et nox ut dies inluminabitur, et: Nox inluminacio mea in diliciis* [deliciis] meis.*

55. *GaG* 225:34–36: *Huius igitur sanctificacio noctis fugat scelera, culpas levat, reddit innocenciam lapsis et maestis laeticiam, fugat odia, concordia* [-am] parat et curvat imperia.*

evening prayer has been kindled."[56] This seems to refer, given its broader context within this text, to the kindling of fire (maybe the paschal candle) in the evening of Holy Saturday preceding the Easter Vigil. The address is situated "at the end of a period of forty weekdays, and on the Sabbath of his own buried body,"[57] a clear reference to the end of the forty-day fast of Lent and the "Sabbath" of Jesus in the tomb on Holy Saturday. As such, the content of the text is still as much related to Holy Saturday as it is already related to the beginning of the Easter Vigil.[58]

In the last part the address directs its gaze forward to the night of Easter itself: "May he also make us go forth from Egypt among the number of the true Israel."[59] The present liturgical situation is interpreted in light of Exodus 12: the ecclesial community is still considered to be in "Egypt" but is praying to be liberated "among the number of the true Israel." This moment is the evening of the Passover in Egypt, "when the doorposts of our bodies have been sprinkled by the blood of the immaculate lamb."[60] This sprinkling of blood on the doorposts of our bodies—a prefiguration of the pre-baptismal anointing[61]—is thought to protect the petitioners from spiritual death ("death being about to devastate the world"[62]). At the same time the prayer already situates itself "at the festival of this venerable night,"[63] or at least its beginning. The subsequent prayer is also associated with Holy Saturday by its reference to "sepulchers" for Christ's body.[64] It again makes clear that this event, as the antitype of Christ's sacrifice on the cross, is associated with the evening, as this prayer is brought before Jesus Christ "now the evening sacrifice has been accomplished through the cross on the evening of the world."[65] At the

---

56. *GaG* 221:4: *incensu* [-o] uespertinae praecis sacrificio.*

57. *GaG* 221:8–9: *in anni [fine] septimanae dierum quadraginta, ac sepulti corporis sui sabbato.*

58. See Rose, *The Gothic Missal*, 205, n. a.

59. *GaG* 221:9–10: *Nos quoque in numero veri Israhelis Aegypto egredi faciat.*

60. *GaG* 221:12–13: *Agni inmaculati sanguine corporum nostrorum postibus aspersis.*

61. Zweck, *Osterlobpreis und Taufe*, 326–32.

62. *GaG* 221:13–14: *vastatura mundum morte.*

63. *GaG* 221:13: *in istius noctis venerabilis sollempnitatem* [sollempnitate].*

64. *GaG* 222: *Christe Iesu, in vespera mundi vespertino sacrificio per crucem effectu* [-o] dignare nos nova corpori tuo fore sepulchra. Salvator.*

65. Ibid.

same time, it unambiguously connects the notion of evening sacrifice as we encountered it in the offering prayer of the *Exultet* with the sacrifice of Christ on the cross.

We have seen that through numerous references the *Exultet* clearly situates itself in the night, a time associated with the resurrection of Jesus Christ, with redemption and illumination. The reference to the "evening sacrifice" in the offering prayer, by contrast, coming only after most of these references to the night, was clearly neither a precise time indication nor just an allusion to Psalm 141 (140):2 or a remnant of the daily *lucernarium*. Other references to the evening sacrifice in the *Missale Gothicum*, combined with a broader current of patristic thought connecting this notion with the immolation of the paschal lamb in Egypt (Exodus 12) as a prefiguration of Christ's salutary death, make it likely that the notion of evening sacrifice in the *Exultet* was meant to connect the offering of the paschal candle to the sacrifice of Christ on the cross. Whereas in the Gallican Easter Vigil the evening seems to be associated with the salutary passion and death of Jesus Christ, the night is associated with his resurrection, with redemption, and (paradoxically) with illumination.

Light in the Night

We tend to associate the night with darkness, but this is not the logic at work in the symbolic language about Easter Night. We saw in the previous section that the paschal proclamation of the *Exultet* presented the night as an active agent in the work of redemption. If we take a closer look at the relevant passages,[66] we see that, in both instances, "cleansing," or "removing from," "darkness of sins" (*peccatorum tenebras* and *caligine peccatorum* in Latin) is used as a description of what redemption entails.[67] In the first passage the night, with "the illumination of the column" as its instrument, is actively cleansing "the darkness of sins."[68] Also in the second passage it is clearly implied that it is the work of Easter Night not only to "restore to grace, join to holiness," but also to "remove from the faults of the world and the darkness of sins."[69]

66. *GaG* 225:21–22, as at n. 47; 225:22–25, as at n. 48.
67. *GaG* 225:21–25.
68. *GaG* 225:21–22, as at n. 47.
69. *GaG* 225:22–25, as at n. 48.

That the night of Easter is associated with light rather than with darkness we clearly see in the conclusion to the paschal proclamation. Just after the exclamatory phrases of the second part of the paschal proclamation we encounter two references to Psalm 139 (138), where the night is presented as "made light like the day" (v. 12) and "my light in my delights" (v. 11).[70] In patristic exegesis these verses were frequently understood as referring to the victory of Christ over the darkness of death by the light of his resurrection, but also to the light associated with redemption and sanctification.[71] At the same time these verses referred, in a more practical sense, to the fact that during the Easter Vigil the night was actually "made light like day" through the bright illumination of the church with lamps and candles.[72]

But how does this bright illumination of the church, this night of the resurrection "made light like day," relate to the light of the paschal candle? We have seen, after all, in our discussion of evening and night, that the paschal candle was designated an evening sacrifice, a notion associated more with the salutary passion and death of Jesus Christ than with his resurrection. In this respect it is interesting to note that even before the resurrection is mentioned for the first time in the paschal proclamation, there seems to be an implicit reference to the light of the paschal candle. As part of the very first sentence referring to the night in the paschal proclamation, there is a reference to "the illumination of the column."[73] This phrase comes just after the sentence referring to the immolation of the paschal lamb according to Exodus 12—which we identified with the evening of Passover and the sacrifice of Christ on the cross—and the reference to the passage through the Red Sea.[74] The "column" of the subsequent phrase actually refers to the "column of fire" as it figures in this story about the exodus from Egypt and the passage through the Red Sea. Its connotation is that of a light guiding through the night and it is instrumental in cleansing the darkness of sins. Implicitly, however, it also seems to evoke the light of the paschal candle, which

70. *GaG* 225:32–34, as at n. 54.
71. Fuchs and Weikmann, *Das Exsultet*, 72–74.
72. Ibid., 74–75.
73. *GaG* 225:22: *columnae inluminacione*.
74. *GaG* 225:18–21.

the eulogy of the candle would later designate as "this column."[75] The paschal proclamation at this point did not yet mention the resurrection, and the context of this reference is still that of the exodus initiated by the immolation of the paschal lamb at the Passover in Egypt. If this Passover was interpreted as antitype of Christ's sacrifice on the cross, it seems that the light of the paschal candle at this point also more prominently represented the salutary light provided by Christ's passion and death than his resurrection.

Just as the paschal proclamation began with Christ's salutary passion and death, the light-eucharistic section begins in the offering prayer by designating the paschal candle an evening sacrifice. We have seen that this notion is connected with the symbolic significance of the evening as the time of Christ's sacrifice on the cross as it was prefigured in the immolation of the paschal lamb in Egypt according to Exodus 12. Although, therefore, by this time, as light was spreading and illuminating the entire church, the night had already been interpreted as the night of the resurrection, the continuing presence of the paschal candle in the midst of this dazzling light served as a reminder to keep the entire mystery of the death and resurrection of Jesus Christ together. Just as there is no night without evening and no abundance of light in the night without the initial kindling of the paschal candle, there would not have been a resurrection if not for the salutary self-sacrifice of Christ on the cross on the evening of Passover.

The remainder of the offering prayer and its continuation in the eulogy of the candle and the bees are particularly interesting in light of the theme of this volume. It states that "the most holy church" renders God this evening sacrifice, "this annual oblation of a candle," "through the hands of your ministers from the works of bees."[76] Here the paschal candle—made from beeswax—is characterized as not merely of human origin (through the hands of your ministers) but also a gift of other-than-human creation

---

75. *GaG* 225:39–40: *columnae huius.* MacGregor suggests that the resemblance of a large candle to the "column of fire" of the exodus might have been one of the reasons why, in the fourth century, a large candle replaced the lamp in the *lucernarium* of the Latin West. See MacGregor, *Fire and Light*, 303.

76. *GaG* 225:36–39: . . . *sacrificium vespertinum, quod tibi in hac caerei oblacione sollempni per ministrorum tuorum manus de operibus apum sacrosancta reddit eclesia.*

(from the works of bees). Later, at the end of the eulogy of the candle, another reference is made to "mother bee" who has drawn forth "melting waxes" "in the substance of this valuable lamp."[77] There followed in the original version of the *Missale Gothicum*—in the Roman Rite this part had already fallen away during the Middle Ages—an extensive eulogy of the bees, including praise for their "remarkable minds," for their work zeal that emerges when winter is giving way to spring, for their communal spirit and their supposed virginity.[78] A lot more can be said about the symbolic interpretation of all these elements, but for our purposes it is important to note that the paschal candle and by extension also other earthly lights in the church were apparently not considered fabrications of merely human origin. The paschal candle was truly an "earthly light," a product of the cooperation between humankind and other-than-human creation, in this case exemplified by the bees that provided the wax for the candle.

In this section we have seen that *darkness* was several times used in a negative sense ("the darkness of sins"), whereas the *night* (of Easter) was interpreted never in a negative sense, as associated with darkness, and always in a positive sense, as associated with light, redemption, and resurrection. The text even considered the night as an active agent in "cleansing" and "removing" the darkness of sins. It interprets the paschal candle, itself a product of cooperation between humankind and other-than-human creation, (implicitly) as the column of fire of the exodus, being instrumental in "cleansing" the darkness of sins, but more importantly as the "evening sacrifice" associated with the sacrifice of Christ as prefigured by the immolation of the paschal lamb as recounted in Exodus 12. In this way, the paschal candle kept together the entire mystery of Christ's death and resurrection. Its kindling as an "evening sacrifice" served as a reminder that the light of the resurrection could only begin to shine thanks to the salutary self-gift of Christ on the cross. Now, to complete the picture, we need only to return to the epiclesis, to examine the relationship between *night* and *dawn* during the Easter Vigil.

---

77. *GaG* 225:42–43: *Alitur liquantibus caeris, quam* [quas] in substancia praeciosae huius lampadis apis mater eduxit.*

78. *GaG* 225:43–57.

Night and Dawn

Just as the only reference to the evening in the *Exultet* appeared in the context of—and after—a total of nine references to the night, the final sections of the *Exultet* refer three more times to the night before finally referring to the morning star. The first of these references directly follows the eulogy of the candle and the bees and in fact resumes the paschal proclamation of the first part of the text.[79] This reference, the acclamation "O truly blessed night, which plundered the Egyptians, enriched the Hebrews," refers, again, to the book of Exodus (3:22; 11:2-3; 12:35-36).[80] Before their departure from Egypt, the Hebrews, according to this story, demanded and received "jewelry of silver and gold, and clothing" from the Egyptians, which they took with them when they departed. In this way, the book of Exodus concludes, "they plundered the Egyptians." This story was in patristic exegesis understood in a christological sense, as the night in which Christ plundered the powers of the netherworld and enriched the Christian people with eternal life and salvation.[81] Again we see the association of the night with the victory of Christ and the resulting redemption of the faithful.

More important, in light of the epiclesis that comes after it, is the second characterization of the night, as the night "on which the heavenly things are joined to the earthly."[82] This line brings the paschal proclamation of the *Exultet* to an unprecedented culmination. In this night heaven and earth, God and creation, are joined together, the apparently unbridgeable distance between God and humankind is bridged and the damage done by the fall of Adam is mended by the death and resurrection of Jesus Christ.

In the epiclesis, we see that this is not just a figure of speech: the paschal candle, as well as other lights in the church, plays a pivotal role

---

79. Cf. *O vere beata nox* (*GaG* 225:57), and the final exclamatory phrase *O beata nox* in the second part of the paschal proclamation (*GaG* 225:31). Additionally, it is connected to the conclusion of the eulogy of the bees by the parallel opening beginning with *O vere beata*, i.e., *O vere beata et mirabilis apis* (O truly blessed and wonderful bee, *GaG* 225:54) and *O vere beata nox* (O truly blessed night).

80. *GaG* 225:57–58: *O vere beata nox, quae expoliavit Aegyptios, ditavit Hebraeos.*

81. Zweck, *Osterlobpreis und Taufe*, 73.

82. *GaG* 225:58: *nox in qua terrenis caelestia iunguntur.*

in the sacramental actualization and visualization of what this sentence signifies. The first part of this section asks the Lord "that this candle, consecrated in the honor of your name to destroy the darkness of this night, may persist unfailing" and that it, "having been accepted into the fragrance of sweetness, be blended with the heavenly lights."[83] The candle has been "consecrated in the honor of your name *to destroy the darkness of this night*" (my emphasis). The paschal candle is, in the first place, instrumental in destroying darkness, something we encountered in the very first sentences of the paschal proclamation ("cleansing," or "removing from," "the darkness of sins," there accomplished by "the illumination of the column," which, as we have seen, is probably an implicit reference to the paschal candle). The *Exultet* subsequently expresses the wish that the paschal candle "may persist unfailing," that is, continue burning throughout the night, but not only that, it also asks that the paschal candle during this night "be blended with the heavenly lights." In connection with the preceding characterization of the night "on which the heavenly things are joined to the earthly," we see here a truly sacramental vision in which the paschal candle and by extension maybe other lights in the church are asked to blend with the lights of heaven. The paschal candle, an earthly light that is represented as the product not only of human endeavor but also of other-than-human creation (the bees)—as well as other lights in the church that make the night "light like day"—are asked to blend with the lights of heaven. In this way the entire cosmos, human and other-than-human creation, earthly and heavenly lights, comes together in one act of worship during Easter Night.

One heavenly light stands out, however, among all other stars and constellations in the *Exultet*—the morning star. The text asks that "the light bringer of the early morning may find its flames."[84] Strictly speaking, the adjective *matutinus* referring to *lucifer* is redundant, as Els Rose rightly remarked in her recent translation of the *Missale Gothicum*.[85] *Lucifer* in itself already signifies the morning star. As Guido Fuchs and

---

83. *GaG* 225:58–61: *Oramus te, Domine, ut caereus iste in honore nominis tui consecratus ad noctis huius caliginem distruendam* [*destruendam*] *indeficiens perseveret, in odorem suavitatis acceptus, supernis luminaribus misceatur.*

84. *GaG* 225:62: *Flammas eius lucifer matutinus inveniat.*

85. Rose, *The Gothic Missal*, 211, n. b. Hence my translation of the first *lucifer* as "light bringer" rather than "morning star."

Hans Martin Weikmann suggested, however, *lucifer matutinus* seems to serve as a parallel to *sacrificium vespertinum* in the offering prayer of the *Exultet*, suggesting the entire length of an all-night Easter Vigil, from evening to morning.[86] At the same time, this parallel suggests an important symbolic development. If the paschal candle, kindled in the evening and blessed during the night as an evening sacrifice, signifies Christ sacrificed for our salvation, the morning star "that does not know setting," with whom this light is asked to blend, signifies the risen Christ: "he who, having returned from the dead, dawned clear on behalf of the human family."[87] In the blending of evening sacrifice and morning star, therefore, evening and morning blend into the one single reality of the holy night of Easter. By invoking the morning star in the blessing prayer of the paschal candle, the *Exultet* emphasizes that during Easter Night Christ sacrificed and Christ risen are no separate realities, but two sides of the same coin, blending into the one single light of Christ shining for the redemption of all creation.

Conclusion

At the beginning of this chapter, I asked several questions about how evening, night, and dawn relate to each other in the liturgy of the Easter Vigil as exemplified by the *Exultet* in the *Missale Gothicum*. In particular I raised the question whether the significance of Easter Night must be interpreted in light of the subsequent dawn (as looking forward to dawn as the symbolic moment of the resurrection) or whether the dawn must be interpreted in light of the night (of Easter), that is, in its entirety bathing in the splendor of the risen Christ.

Although dawn, and the morning star in particular, is indeed associated with the risen Christ, it can be concluded that the Easter Vigil is not so much looking forward to dawn but rather invoking its symbolism to enhance the sacredness of the entire night of Easter. Designated an "evening sacrifice" and associated with Christ's sacrifice on the cross as prefigured by the immolation of the paschal lamb in Egypt according to Exodus 12, the paschal candle was instrumental in "cleansing"

86. Fuchs and Weikmann, *Das Exsultet*, 81.

87. *GaG* 225:62–64: *ille, inquam, lucifer qui nescit occasum, ille qui regressus ab inferis humano generi serenus inluxit.*

and "destroying" the "darkness of sins" or "the darkness of this night." Subsequently the entire night of Easter is associated, and even dazzling, with light, with redemption, with Christ's descent into hell and the victory of his resurrection. Hence, Easter Night does not derive its significance from the dawn of Easter Sunday as the symbolic moment of the resurrection. It is the night itself, dazzling with light in memory of Christ's resurrection, that is the primary symbol at stake here.

That does not mean, however, that evening and dawn have no significance in the liturgy of Easter Night. The evening sacrifice, a designation for the paschal candle, signifies Christ's sacrifice on the cross as prefigured by the immolation of the paschal lamb according to Exodus 12. In the morning Christ *is risen*, as symbolized by the "morning star that does not know setting." During Easter Night, these two realities blend into one, symbolized by the blending of the evening sacrifice and the morning star. At an unknown moment during this night, Christ *actually rose*: it is the night during which an abundance of light emerges out of the darkness of Christ's tomb and new life emerges out of his death. Easter Night is truly the night of the resurrection, but not at the expense of the importance of Christ's death. Hence, the paschal candle serves as a constant reminder of the fact that the abundant light of the resurrection could only emerge out of the darkness of the tomb, that the night dazzling with light could only emerge out of Christ's evening sacrifice. The paschal candle serves as a reminder of the unity of the entire mystery of Christ's death and resurrection. Hence, the night of the resurrection involves not only the risen Christ but also Christ sacrificed for the redemption of creation.

CHAPTER SIX

The Six Evenings of Creation in the Hymns of the Roman Breviary

Peter Jeffery

In the historic Roman Rite, the creation story was read at the beginning of the Easter Vigil, and again in the readings and responsories for the night office in Septuagesima week, when the annual cycle of nocturnal readings began with the book of Genesis. But the remarkable fact that we live in a created world was remembered all year, in the strophic office hymns that supplemented the weekly Psalter of the Divine Office. These hymns provided something not explicit in the Old Testament psalms—a Christian interpretation of the passing of time, with a designated hymn for every daily and nightly prayer time and for every day of the week.

The Hymns of the Roman Rite

The Earliest Latin Liturgical Hymns

The first person to write Christian poetry in Latin was Commodian, in the third century, but we know little about Commodian and even less about the intended purposes or contexts of his hymns. His facility with Latin meter was in any case less than expert.[1] Better poetry, by better-known authors, emerged in the fourth and fifth centuries. But the first Latin author whose poems we know to have been sung during liturgical

---

1. Roald Dijkstra, *The Apostles in Early Christian Art and Poetry* (Leiden: Brill, 2016), 67–74; Christoph Schubert, "Textphilologische Überlegungen zu Commodian, *Carmen apologeticum* 449f.," *Vigiliae Christianae* 70 (2016): 217–28.

celebrations, both during his lifetime and for many centuries afterward, is Saint Ambrose, bishop of Milan (d. 397). Medieval and Counter-Reformation breviaries contain hundreds of "Ambrosian" hymns, but only fourteen are judged likely to be his own work in the latest critical edition, the work of a team of editors headed by Jacques Fontaine.[2]

Four hymns are unquestionably by Ambrose, for they are identified as his by Saint Augustine of Hippo (353–430) and Pope Celestine I (r. 422–432), both of whom attended the liturgies in Milan at which Ambrose presided (see Table 1). Three of these four hymns are clearly about specific prayer times in a daily cycle.

Table 1. Hymns certainly by Ambrose

Hymn incipit	Subject matter	Authorship confirmed by[3]
Aeterne rerum conditor	the time of cockcrow	Augustine, *Retractionum* 1.21 Fontaine no. 1 pp. 141–45
Iam surgit hora tertia	the third hour of the day	Augustine, *De natura et gratia* 63.74 Fontaine no. 3 pp. 207–8
Deus creator omnium	the time of retiring to bed	Augustine, *De vita beata* 35; *Confessiones* 9.32, cf. 4.15, 10.52, 11.35 *De musica* 6.2, 6.57 Fontaine no. 4 p. 234
Intende qui regis Israel	the Incarnation	Celestine I in *Conflictus Arnobii* 2.13 Fontaine no. 5 pp. 269–71

A fifth hymn has a high probability of being authentic (see Table 2). It was ascribed to Ambrose by Fulgentius of Ruspe (468–533) and is apparently alluded to by Augustine also.

2. Ambroise de Milan, *Hymnes*, ed. Jacques Fontaine et al., Patrimoines christianisme (Paris: Cerf, 2008).

3. The sources cited in this column are conveniently listed in Walther Bulst, *Hymni Latini Antiquissimi LXXV, Psalmi III* (Heidelberg: F. H. Kerle, 1956): 161–62, but fully discussed in Jacque Fontaine et al., eds., Ambroise de Milan, *Hymnes* on the pages shown. See also John Moorhead, "Ambrose and Augustine on Hymns," *Downside Review* 128 (2010): 79–92.

Table 2. A hymn almost certainly by Ambrose

Hymn incipit	Subject matter	Authorship suggested by
Splendor paternae gloriae	the time of sunrise	Fulgentius, *Epistolae* 14.10, 42 Augustine, *Confessiones* 13.13.23 Fontaine no. 2 pp. 182–83

The mention by Fulgentius suggests that Ambrose's hymns were still familiar a century after his death, bridging the chronological gap between Augustine and Celestine, who worshiped with Ambrose, and the testimonies of later writers down to the Middle Ages.

About ten other extant hymns are considered seriously as works that Ambrose may have written himself. From the Maurist edition of 1686–1690 down to the 1950s, modern editors have identified between twelve and eighteen hymns as likely works by Ambrose, although with much disagreement as to which of the many possibilities should be included.[4] Arguments for authenticity have been based on manuscript transmission, matters of style and vocabulary, and both implicit allusions and explicit testimonies by authors who lived between the fifth and ninth centuries. Beyond the five hymns I have already listed, most of the remaining candidates are about the commemorations of martyrs.

What Is an Ambrosian Hymn?

In casual parlance, any strophic Latin hymn for the Divine Office can be called—and actually has been called—"Ambrosian," despite the many differences in style, structure, and content. The five hymns attested by Augustine, Celestine, and Fulgentius share common features that we can use to define the characteristics of an "Ambrosian" hymn in the strictest sense of the word. Each of these hymns has eight stanzas of four lines each. Like all classical Latin poetry, they are metrical or quantitative, based on the quantity or length of syllables. Indeed, all five authentic hymns are in the same quantitative meter: iambic dimeter. An iambic foot consists of a short syllable followed by a long syllable. Two iambic feet form a metron, and each line of iambic dimeter contains two metra, totaling four iambic feet or eight syllables. As in the best classical poetry,

---

4. Fontaine et al., *Hymnes*, 11, 114–20.

elision and hiatus are kept to a minimum. There are no acrostics and only occasional rhymes.[5]

Why are there eight stanzas? There is no evidence of numerological symbolism. In medieval times Ambrose's hymns were performed antiphonally, that is with two choirs alternating: one sang the odd-numbered stanzas, the other the even-numbered—but this type of performance is first mentioned only by the Venerable Bede (672/673–735).[6]

Many "Ambrosian" hymns are clearly not by Ambrose because their poetry is rhythmic or accentual, based on word accent, rather than metrical or quantitative, based on syllable length. Rhythmic poetry was almost unknown in classical times but became popular during the Middle Ages, when it was probably closer to the way Latin was then spoken.[7] However, some early hymns stand somewhere in between. An example would be *Ignis creator igneus*, about the paschal candle, which Alcuin attributed to Ambrose. It looks so similar to the genuine Ambrosian hymns that Cardinal Mercati was inclined to follow Alcuin's opinion, even though the hymn survives in only two manuscripts, from the Irish

5. Dag Norberg, *An Introduction to the Study of Medieval Latin Versification*, trans. Grant C. Roti and Jacqueline de La Chapelle Skubly, ed. Jan Ziolkowski (Washington, DC: Catholic University of America Press, 2004), 26–27, 181. On other aspects of Ambrose's personal style, see J. den Boeft and A. Hilhorst, eds., *Early Christian Poetry: A Collection of Essays*, Supplements to *Vigiliae Christianae* 22 (Leiden: Brill, 1993), 51–53, 77–89, 91–100; Carl P. E. Springer, "The Hymns of Ambrose," *Religions of Late Antiquity in Practice*, ed. Richard Valantasis (Princeton: Princeton Univ. Press, 2000), 347–56; Brian P. Dunkle, *Enchantment and Creed in the Hymns of Ambrose of Milan* (Oxford: Oxford Univ. Press, 2016).

6. Carin Ruff, "The Place of Metrics in Anglo-Saxon Latin Education: Aldhelm and Bede," *Journal of English and Germanic Philology* 104 (2005): 149–70, at 168. On the medieval tradition that Ambrose introduced "antiphons" at Milan, see Peter Jeffery, "The Introduction of Psalmody into the Roman Mass by Pope Celestine I: Reinterpreting a Passage in the *Liber Pontificalis*," *Archiv für Liturgiewissenschaft* 26 (1984): 147–65, and Helmut Leeb, *Die Psalmodie bei Ambrosius*, Wiener Beiträge zur Theologie 18 (Vienna: Herder, 1967). For Bede's own hymns on the days of creation, see Fidel Rädle, "Bedas Hymnus über das Sechstagewerk und die Weltalter," *Anglo-Saxonica: Beiträge zur Vor- und Frühgeschichte der englischen Sprache und zur altenglischen Literatur: Festschrift für Hans Schabram zum 65. Geburtstag*, ed. Klaus R. Grinda and Claus-Dieter Wetzel (Munich: Wilhelm Fink, 1993), 53–73.

7. The authoritative work is Norberg, *Introduction*.

monastery of Bobbio, in northern Italy.[8] More recent authorities, however, have observed that this hymn is not really in iambic dimeter, but instead in iambic tetrameter. That is to say, the poet did not rigorously follow the rules, but permitted variations in positions where a dimeter would require a strict iamb. The result is that there are four iambic feet per line, not two iambic dimeters or double feet.[9] That suggests the poem was written by an early imitator of Ambrose, which helps explain why it did not circulate more widely with Ambrose's genuine hymns. Other hymns follow the Ambrosian model more loosely or hardly at all. Thus a hymn for the hour of Sext, *Bis ternas horas*, has been described as "rhythmic verses imitating entirely the structure of the quantitative verses . . . [although] the quantity is entirely neglected."[10] However, levels of education varied so greatly across Europe that we cannot closely date poems by their quality, as if the hymn with the most metrical errors must be the latest in origin.

Early Monastic Hymnals

By the sixth century, monastic communities in different parts of Europe were using small repertories of hymns in the daily office. Ambrose's hymns served as the core of each repertory, supplemented by other similar hymns of uncertain authorship. Most notable here is the early sixth-century Benedictine Rule, which indicates that an *ambrosianum* should be sung at the major hours of Nocturns, Lauds, and Vespers, while a "hymn of the same hour" is to be sung at the little hours of Prime, Terce, Sext, None, and Compline. The original text of the rule does not name any specific hymn, but a lost manuscript, seen by Georg Cassander in

---

8. Giovanni Mercati, "Un nuovo inno pasquale di S. Ambrogio?" *II. Paralipomena Ambrosiana, con alcuni appunti sulle Benedizioni del Cereo Pasquale*, Studi e Testi 12 (Rome: Tipografia Vaticana, 1904), 17–46, at 24–36. But see Norberg, *Introduction*, 66 n. 45; A. S. Walpole, ed., *Early Latin Hymns, with Introduction and Notes*, ed. Arthur James Mason (1922; repr. Hildesheim: Georg Olms, 1966), 346–49.

9. Walther Bulst, "Hymnologica partim Hibernica," *Latin Scripts and Letters A.D. 400–900: Festschrift Presented to Ludwig Bieler on the Occasion of his 70th Birthday*, ed. John J. O'Meara and Bernd Naumann (Leiden: E. J. Brill, 1976), 83–100, at 92–93.

10. Norberg, *Introduction*, 103. For the text, see *Analecta Hymnica* 51, ed. Clemens Blume (Leipzig: O. R. Reisland, 1908), 43; Walpole, *Early Latin Hymns*, 294–98.

the sixteenth century,[11] did name sixteen hymns, ten of which are listed in Table 3.

Table 3. Hymns of the Benedictine Rule

Hour	To be sung	Incipit given by Cassander[12]	Benedictine Rule[13]
Nocturne	ambrosianum	*Aeterne rerum conditor*	RB 9.4
Lauds	ambrosianum	*Splendor paternae gloriae*	RB 12.4, 13.11
Prime	hymnum eiusdem horae	*Iam lucis orto sidere*	RB 17.3
Terce, Sext, None	hymnos earundem horarum	[Terce:] *Iam surgit hora tertia* [Sext:] *Iam sexta sensim* or *Rector potens verax* [None:] *Ter hora trina volvitur*	RB 17.5
Vespers	ambrosianum	*Deus creator omnium*	RB 17.8
Compline	hymnum eiusdem horae	*Christe qui lux es* or *Te lucis ante terminum*	RB 17.10

Of this list, *Aeterne rerum conditor*, *Iam surgit hora tertia*, and *Deus creator omnium* are among the four that are certainly by Ambrose, *Splendor paternae gloriae* is our fifth hymn, attributed by Fulgentius

11. Helmut Gneuss, "Zur Geschichte des Hymnars," *Der lateinische Hymnus im Mittelalter: Überlieferung—Ästhetik—Ausstrahlung,* ed. Andreas Haug, Christoph März, and Lorenz Welker, Monumenta Monodica Medii Aevi, Subsidia 4 (Kassel: Bärenreiter, 2004), 63–86.

12. As cited in Helmut Gneuss, "Zur Geschichte des Hymnars," 66, 82–83.

13. The passages are conveniently assembled in Bulst, *Hymni Latini Antiquissimi LXXV,* 166–67, but I give chapter and verse numberings as in *RB 1980: The Rule of St. Benedict in Latin and English with Notes,* ed. Timothy Fry (Collegeville, MN: Liturgical Press, 1981).

to Ambrose, and *Iam lucis orto sidere* appears on lists of hymns that Ambrose might have written, although it is not in the Fontaine edition.

Roughly contemporary with the Benedictine Rule are the monastic rules of Caesarius and Aurelian of Arles, which between them identify sixteen hymns by name. Many of these are different from Cassander's sixteen, and at least nine of them cannot have been by Ambrose.[14] A group of Anglo-Saxon sources that also have Benedictine connections have traces of yet another collection of sixteen hymns, similar but not identical to that of Arles.[15] In my view it is best to treat these as three distinct regional collections of hymns for monastic use—Cassander's lost manuscript, the rules of Arles, and the Anglo-Saxon sources—but many hymnologists lump them together under the designation "The Old Hymnal" (see Table 4).[16]

Table 4. The so-called Old Hymnal

Collection	Source	Number of hymns	Number of hymns likely to be by Ambrose
Cassander's lost manuscript of the Benedictine Rule	Cassander's description	16	10
Monastic rules of Caesarius and Aurelian of Arles	many	16	7–8
Anglo-Saxon sources	one lost manuscript "Vespasian Psalter" Bede	16	7–8

14. Bulst, *Hymni Latini Antiquissimi LXXV*, 89–98, 163–66, 189–91.

15. Ibid., 99–102, 167–68.

16. The three lists are identified as the "Old Hymnal" in Gneuss, "Zur Geschichte des Hymnars," 64–70, 83, but they are called "aHy" or "AHy I" in Helmut Gneuss, *Hymnar und Hymnen im englishen Mittelalter: Studien zur Überlieferung, Glossierung und Übersetzung lateinischer Hymnen in England; Mit einer Textausgabe der lateinisch-englischen Expositio Hymnorum*, Buchreihe der Anglia: Zeitschrift für englische Philologie 12 (Tübingen: Max Niemeyer, 1968), 24–25 and throughout.

Larger Early Medieval Collections

Six French manuscripts of the eighth and ninth centuries preserve a somewhat different repertory totaling thirty-four hymns, though no manuscript contains more than twenty-six of them, and one contains only three. This repertory, now known as the Frankish Hymnal, contains notably fewer of the hymns that are commonly attributed to Ambrose.[17] Yet another distinct repertory developed in Spain: the Mozarabic Hymnal. It ultimately came to contain some three hundred hymns, including most of those that are commonly ascribed to Ambrose, but the early history of this repertoire is still in many ways obscure.[18]

The hymnal that developed in Milan itself and was incorporated into the so-called "Ambrosian" Rite may tell us how Ambrose's legacy developed within his own diocese, but it is hardly attested before the tenth century, and its documented history is interwoven with the hymnal of the Cistercian Order, which imported what was assumed to be the original Ambrosian tradition in the twelfth century (see Table 5).[19]

17. Gneuss, "Zur Geschichte des Hymnars," 70–72, 82–83. The repertory of these manuscipts is called "aHy" or "AHy II" in Gneuss, *Hymnar*, 24–25 and thereafter. Clemens Blume placed both the Old Hymnal manuscripts and the Frankish Hymnal manuscripts in his group A. See Clemens Blume, *Der Cursus S. Benedicti Nursini und die liturgischen Hymnen des 6.–9. Jahrhunderts in ihrer Beziehung zu den Sonntags- und -Ferialhymnen unseres Breviers: eine hymnologisch-liturgische Studie auf Grund handschriftlichen Quellenmaterials*, Hymnologische Beiträge: Quellen und Forschungen zur Geschichte der Lateinischen Hymnendichtung; Im Anschlusse an die Analecta Hymnica (1908; repr. Hildesheim: Georg Olms, 1971), from 72 onward.

18. Ruth Ellis Messenger, "The Mozarabic Hymnal," *Transactions and Proceedings of the American Philological Association* 75 (1944): 103–26; Ruth E. Messenger, "Mozarabic Hymns in Relation to Contemporary Culture in Spain," *Traditio* 4 (1946): 149–77; Walpole, *Early Latin Hymns*, xxviii.

19. Walpole, *Early Latin Hymns*, xxvi; Chrysogonus Waddell, ed., *The Twelfth-Century Cistercian Hymnal*, vol. 1: *Introduction and Commentary*, vol. 2: *Edition*. 3 vols. in 2 (Trappist, KY: Gethsemani Abbey, 1984); A. S. Walpole, "Notes on the Text of the Hymns of St. Ambrose," *Journal of Theological Studies* 9, no. 35 (1908): 428–36.

Table 5. Larger early medieval hymnals

Conventional name	Numbers, dates, and types of manuscripts	Number of hymns	Number of hymns likely to be by Ambrose
Frankish	6 manuscripts, 8th–9th century	34	3–4
Mozarabic	6 manuscripts, 9th–11th century	eventually over 300	8
Milanese "Ambrosian" and Cistercian	Milan: 6 manuscripts, 9th–11th century Cistercian manuscripts start in 12th century	120	14
New Hymnal (standard for the medieval and Tridentine Roman Rite)	23 manuscripts, 9th–11th century	over 130	12 in Italian manuscripts 7–8 in non-Italian manuscripts

The New Hymnal

A collection of over 130 hymns that emerged in the ninth and tenth centuries is now called the New Hymnal.[20] It contained a much larger selection of hymns for feast days than any earlier hymnal. We do not know exactly where the New Hymnal originated, but it had crossed the Channel to England by the late tenth century.[21] Adopted by most medieval dioceses and religious orders, it forms the core repertory in most medieval breviaries and in the Tridentine *Breviarium Romanum* of 1568. In 1632, however, Pope Urban VIII issued a new edition of the Breviary

20. Gneuss, "Zur Geschichte des Hymnars," 72–81, 84–86. It is called "NHy" or "nHy" in Gneuss, *Hymnar*. Blume placed these hymns in his group B. See Ruth Ellis Messenger, "Whence the Ninth Century Hymnal?" *Transactions and Proceedings of the American Philological Association* 69 (1938): 446–64.

21. Gernot R. Wieland, ed., *The Canterbury Hymnal; Edited from British Library Ms. Additional 37517*, Toronto Medieval Latin Texts (Toronto: Pontifical Institute of Mediaeval Studies, 1982), 5–17; Inge B. Milfull, *The Hymns of the Anglo-Saxon Church: A Study and Edition of the "Durham Hymnal,"* Cambridge Studies in Anglo-Saxon England 17 (Cambridge: Cambridge Univ. Press, 1996), 8–9.

in which the hymn texts had been revised—some quite severely—to make their Latinity more classical and palatable to Renaissance humanists.[22] These revised texts remained in the official books of the Roman Rite and the Franciscan Order right up to the Second Vatican Council, though the Benedictines, Cistercians, Dominicans, and some other medieval religious orders managed to retain their traditional hymn texts.[23] At the Second Vatican Council, however, the Constitution on the Sacred Liturgy ordered the restoration of the medieval hymn texts,[24] a requirement fulfilled in the new Latin edition of the *Liturgia Horarum*.[25] Thus

22. Anselmo Lentini, *Te Decet Hymnus: L'Innario della "Liturgia Horarum"* (Vatican City: Typis Polyglottis Vaticanis, 1984), XVII–XVIII; Jules Baudot, *Hymnes latines et Hymnaires*, Liturgie (Paris: Bloud & Gay, 1914), 82–106; Peter Rietbergen, *Power and Religion in Baroque Rome: Barberini Cultural Policies* (Leiden: Brill, 2006), 132–35. For the hymns, with translations and commentary see Matthew Britt, ed., *The Hymns of the Breviary and Missal* (London: Burns Oates & Washbourne, 1922, with many subsequent editions).

23. For the Franciscan tradition, see *Antiphonale Romano-Seraphicum pro Horis Diurnis a Sacra Rituum Congregatione recognitum et approbatum, atque auctoritate Rmi P. Bonaventurae Marrani totius Ordinis Fratrum Minorum Ministri Generalis editum* (Tournai: Desclée 1928); for the Benedictine, see *Antiphonale Monasticum pro diurnis horis juxta vota RR. DD. Abbatum congregationum confoederatarum Ordinis Sancti Benedicti, a Solesmensibus Monachis restitutum* (Tournai: Desclée, 1934); Philip Carl Smith, "The Hymns of the Medieval Dominican Liturgy, 1250–1369" (BA Honors Thesis, University of Notre Dame, 2008); Baudot, *Hymnes latines et Hymnaires*, 59–73.

24. Vatican Council II, *Sacrosanctum Concilium* (Constitution on the Sacred Liturgy), 4 December 1963, 93, http://www.vatican.va/archive/hist_councils/ii_vatican_council /documents/vat-ii_const_19631204_sacrosanctum-concilium_en.html.

25. The restored medieval texts were officially published in Consilium ad Exsequendam Constitutionem de Sacra Liturgia, *Hymni Instaurandi Breviarii Romani*, ed. Anselmo Lentini (Vatican City: Libreria Editrice Vaticana, 1968). Lentini's more scholarly edition with extensive notes is Lentini, *Te Decet Hymnus*. The restored texts were set to medieval melodies in *Liber Hymnarius cum Invitatoriis & aliquibus Responsoriis*, Antiphonale Romanum secundum Liturgiam Horarum Ordinemque Cantus Officii Dispositum a Solesmensibus Monachis praeparatum; Tomus alter (Solesmes: Abbaye Sinat-Pierre; Paris-Tournai: Desclée, 1983). For a well-informed review, see Joseph Szövérffy, "Hymnological Notes: Some Aspects of Recent Hymnological Literature and Hymns of the New Breviary," *Traditio* 25 (1969): 457–72.

the texts of 1632 are now used only by the self-styled "traditionalists" who still follow the pre-Vatican II liturgical books.

The New Hymnal is not a mere expansion of the Old Hymnal(s), for it replaces much of the Old Hymnal content with items that are new, or at least different. Amid all this new material is an interesting series of Vespers hymns recounting six days of active creation (see Table 6).

Table 6. Vespers hymns about the creation

Hymn	Vespers on	Biblical Source	Creation of
Lucis creator optime	Sunday	Gen 1:1-5	light
Inmense caeli conditor	Monday	Gen 1:6-10	heaven separated from earth
Telluris ingens conditor	Tuesday	Gen 1:11-13	plants
Caeli deus sanctissime	Wednesday	Gen 1:14-19	sun, moon, planets
Magnae deus potentiae	Thursday	Gen 1:20-23	fish, animals
Plasmator hominis deus	Friday	Gen 1:24-31	mammals, human beings

Like the Creator himself, our unknown poet rested on the seventh day, probably because Saturday night, the vigil of Sunday, already had a Vespers hymn: Ambrose's *Deus creator omnium.* Clearly *Deus creator omnium* served as a model for the poet, who decided to complete the set by adding hymns for the other evenings of the week. The monastic rules of Arles had had only one other Vespers hymn (*Deus qui certis legibus*), used in alternation with *Deus creator omnium*; the Frankish Hymnal manuscripts each have *Deus qui certis legibus* and one of two others, none of which reappear in the New Hymnal.

Analysis of Individual Hymns

Where did this new sequence of Vespers hymns come from? Interestingly, the earliest manuscript, from the ninth century, has strong Irish connections. Its eight folia contain poetry in Irish and Latin, notes on the study of Vergil and the Greek language, and an astronomical text. In other words, it is not a liturgical book, but appears to be the academic notebook of an Irish monk who had been studying Latin and Greek: its most famous text is a delightful Irish poem known as *Messe ocus Pangur bán*, "The Cloister Brother and His White Cat," which compares its author's strenuous efforts to learn Greek with his cat's more instinctive expertise in catching mice.[26] In light of its content and because it spent most of the Middle Ages in the German abbey of Reichenau, the manuscript is known as the Reichenauer Schulheft. However, it is now preserved at the Austrian monastery of St. Paul in Lavanttal, in Carinthia.[27]

In the following discussion, the text of each hymn is presented in a new edition based on the Reichenau manuscript (designated MS), ff. 6r–8r, even though the Reichenau manuscript is not free of textual corruptions, as comparison with other modern editions makes clear. I follow the punctuation of the manuscript; italic letters represent expansions of abbreviations. Above the Latin text in the left column, other important critical editions of each hymn are cited. Significant English translations are cited above my own translation of the Reichenau text in the right column. These editions and translations are identified in Table 7.

26. Hildegard L. C. Tristram, "Die irischen Gedichte im Reichenauer Schulheft," *Studia Celtica et Indogermanica: Festschrift für Wolfgang Meid zum 70. Geburtstag*, ed. Peter Anreiter and Erzsébet Jerem, Archaeolingua 10 (Budapest: Archaeolingua, 1999), 503–29; Michael W. Herren, "Pelasgian Fountains: Learning Greek in the Early Middle Ages," *Learning Latin and Greek from Antiquity to the Present*, ed. E. Archibald, W. Brockliss, and J. Gnoza, Yale Classical Studies (Cambridge: Cambridge Univ. Press, 2015), 65–82, see 68–69.

27. St. Paul, Carinthia, MS 86b/1, olim 25.2.31b, olim XXV d 86. See Bernhard Bischoff, *Katalog der festländischen Handschriften des neunten Jahrhunderts (mit Ausnahme der wisigotischen)* 4 vols. (Wiesbaden: Harrassowitz, 1998–2017), no. 5943, vol. 3, 343. For detailed catalogues of the contents, see Karl Preisendanz, "Zeugnisse zur Bibliotheksgeschichte," in *Die Handschriften der grossherzoglich badischen Hof- und Landesbibliothek in Karlsruhe*, vol. 7: *Die Reichenauer Handschriften* 3/2, ed. Alfred Holder (Leipzig and Berlin: B. G. Teubner, 1917), 124–27, 282–83; L. Chr. Stern, "Über die irische Handschrift in St. Paul," *Zeitschrift für celtische Philologie* 6, no. 2 (1908): 546–55; Wilhelm Arndt and Michael Tangl, eds., *Schrifttafeln zur Erlernung der lateinischen Palaeographie*, 4th ed., 3 vols. (1904–7; rept. as 3 vols. in 1, Hildesheim: Georg Olms, 1976), 28–29 and Tafel 2.

Table 7. Editions and translations of the hymn texts

AH 50 = *Analecta Hymnica Medii Aevi* 50. Ed. Guido Maria Dreves. Leipzig: O. R. Reisland, 1907.
AH 51 = *Analecta Hymnica Medii Aevi* 51. Ed. Clemens Blume. Leipzig: O. R. Reisland, 1908.
F = Fontaine, Jacques et al., eds. *Ambroise de Milan: Hymnes: Texte établi, traduit et annoté.* Paris: Cerf, 2008.
L = Lentini, Anselmo. *Te decet hymnus: L'innario della "Liturgia horarum."* Vatican City: Typis Polyglottis Vaticanis, 1984.
Mil = Milfull, Inge B. *The Hymns of the Anglo-Saxon church: A Study and Edition of the "Durham Hymnal."* Cambridge Studies in Anglo-Saxon England 17. Cambridge: Cambridge University Press, 1996.
M = Mone, F. J. *Lateinische Hymnen des Mittelalters* 1: *Lieder an Gott und die Engel.* Freiburg im Breisgau: Herder, 1853.
W = Walpole, A. S., ed. *Early Latin Hymns, with Introduction and Notes.* Ed. Arthur James Mason. Cambridge: Cambridge University Press, 1922; repr. Hildesheim: Georg Olms, 1966.
Wal=Walsh, Peter G., with Christopher Husch, eds. *One Hundred Latin Hymns: Ambrose to Aquinas.* Dumbarton Oaks Medieval Library 18. Cambridge, Mass.: Harvard University Press, 2012.
Wie = Wieland, Gernot R., ed. *The Canterbury Hymnal; Edited from British Library Ms. Additional 37517.* Toronto Medieval Latin Texts. Toronto: Pontifical Institute of Mediaeval Studies, 1982.

Saturday: The Ambrosian Model

Ambrose's *Deus creator omnium* properly stands at the head of the series because Saturday Vespers was actually the First Vespers of Sunday, thus the beginning of the liturgical week. As in the Jewish calendar, each new day began at sundown (Gen 1:5). In the MS, however, the hymn was written last. As the first and oldest hymn, *Deus creator omnium* evidently modeled some of the features and content of the additional hymns. The first line addresses the Creator. The first stanza introduces the theme of light, but the last line and the entire second stanza dwell on the theme of rest, asking that rest may relieve the weariness and anxiety of the worshipers. The next two stanzas are about song itself, describing the emotional outpouring of "thanks for a completed day and prayers at the rise of night." The last three stanzas before the doxology get to the point: it is time for sleep. Light then becomes an allegory for faith, and darkness for everything that opposes faith. "Let fault [i.e., sin] sleep," while the mind and the heart, even while sleeping, somehow remain attentive to the goodness of God, protected from the nocturnal fears that can keep one awake.

MS ff. 6v–7r. Cf. F 237–39. M   Cf. Mil 113. Wal 11–13.
381–82. AH 50:13. W 46–49. Wie
53–55. L 11. Mil 111–13. Wal
10–12.

SABBATO AD VESPEROS   Saturday at Vespers
D*eus* creator omnium.   God, creator of all things
poliq*ue* rector uestiens.   and straightener of the [earth's] axis,
die*m* decoro lumine.   clothing the day with beauteous light,
noctem soporis gratia.   the night with the grace of slumber,

artus soluens[a] ut q*ui*es.   so that rest, unbinding [our] limbs,
reddat laboris usui.   may restore [them] to useful labor
mentesq*ue* fessas alleuet.   and relieve [our] wearied minds,
luctusq*ue*[b] soluat anxios.   and set free [our] worried grief.

grates p*er*acto iam die.   But now, singing a hymn, we release
et noctis exortu p*re*ces.   thanks for a completed day,
uoti reos ut adiuues. [MS uotis   and prayers at the rise of night,
hymnu*m* canentes soluimus.   that you might help those who owe a
    vow.

te cordis ima co*n*cinant.   Let the depths of the heart together
    sing you.

te uox canora concrepet.   Let the sonorous voice reverberate
    you.

te diligat castus amor. [MS deligat   Let chaste love cherish you.
te mens adoret sobria. [MS subria   Let the sober mind adore you.

ut[c] cum p*ro*funda clauserit. [MS et   So that, when the deep fog
diem caligo noctiu*m*.   of night will enclose the day
fides tenebras nesciat[.] [MS   faith will not know darkness,
    nesciat *written over erasure*   and night can illumine the faithful
et nox fideli luceat.[d]   one.

Dormire mentem ne sinas[.]	Do not allow the mind to sleep—
dormire culpa nou*er*it[.]	let fault be accustomed to sleep.
castis[e] fides refrigeret.[f]	Let faith be refreshing to the chaste;
somni uaporem temp*er*et.	let it cool the heat of slumber.
exuta sensu lubrico.	Having slipped off the fickle mind,
te cordis alta[g] somnient.	may the depths of the heart dream you.
nec hostis inuidi dolo. [f. 7r. MS ne	Nor, by the artifice of the envious foe,
pauor quietos suscitet.	may terror awaken those who are resting.
xp*istu*m rogemus[h] et p*a*trem	Let us ask Christ and the Father,
xp*is*ti p*a*trisq*ue* sp*iritu*m.	[and] the spirit of Christ and of the Father
unum potens p*er* om*n*ia.	one power through all things:
fove p*re*cantes trinitas. Amen·	enfold those who call upon [you], Trinity. Amen.

a. soluens MS I solutos F M AH W Wie L Mil Wal
b. luctusque MS F M W Wie L Mil Wal I Luxusque AH
c. ut F M W AH L Mil Wal I et MS Wie
d. fideli luceat MS I fide reluceat F M W AH L Wal I fidei luceat Wie Mil
e. castis MS F M W Wal I castos AH Wie Mil
f. refrigeret MS I refrigerans F M W AH Wie Mil Wal
g. ima W I alta MS F M AH Wie Mil Wal
h. rogemus MS M AH W Wie Mil I rogamus F L Wal

Sunday

On Sunday evening, the new series of hymns begins by invoking the Creator in the first line. Then it proceeds to the creation of light on the first day. Darkness appears in the second stanza as an allegory for sin. The mind's struggle to remain faithful takes up half the poem, the last two stanzas out of four, for these new hymns are only half the length of Ambrose's model.

MS f. 6r. Cf. M 82-83. *AH* 51:34-35. W 280-81. Wie 32. L 15. Mil 138. Wal 156.   Cf. Mil 139. Wal 157.

[f. 6r] hymnus dominico die ad
  uesp*eros*·
Lu*c*is creator optime.
luc*em* dier*um* pr*o*ferens.
primordiis lucis nouae.
mundi parans origine*m*.

q*ui* mane iunctu*m* uesp*e*ri.
die*m* uocari pr*ae*cipis.
tetru*m* chaos illabit*ur*. [MS chaus
  corr. chaos
audi p*r*eces c*um* fletib*us*.

ne mens grauata crimine. [MS
  grauat acrimine.
uitae sit exul munere.
dum nil p*e*renne cogitat.
seseq*ue* culpis illigat.

caelor*um* pulset intimu*m*.
uitale tollat pr*ae*miu*m*.
uitem*us* omne noxiu*m*.
purgem*us* omne pessimu*m*·..

hymn on Sunday at Vespers

Good creator of light,
bringing forth the light of days,
preparing the origin of the world
in the first stirrings of new light,

[you] who instruct
  morning-joined-to-evening
to be called "day"—
foul darkness descends:
Hear [our] prayers with [our]
  wailings,

Nor may the mind, weighed down by
  sin,
be an exile from the task of life,
while it gives no thought to what is
  lasting
and binds itself with faults.

Let [the mind] knock at the innermost
  of the heavens.
Let it take up the reward of life.
Let us shun all that is harmful.
Let us purge all that is worst [in us].

The poem is metrical rather than rhythmic, looking back to the classical era. But it makes use of assonance, a kind of vowel parallelism, that results in half-rhymes: *i* and *e* in *optime* and *originem* in the first stanza; *i* and *u* in *illabitur* and *fletibus* in the second stanza; *i* and *a* in *cogitat* / *illigat* in the third; *-imum* bracketing *-ium* in the fourth.[28] Assonance, which we will observe in all the hymns of this series, was not unknown in classical poetry, but was very popular in the medieval period.

The Latin word *chaos* means more than my translation conveys with the word "darkness." It implies that nighttime threatens to undo creation itself, returning to the void and empty world that existed just before God on the very first day said, "Let there be light." The word also suggested a chasm of separation, as in Luke 16:26, especially when spelled *chaus*, as

28. Lentini, *Te Decet Hymnus*, 15.

it was in our manuscript before being corrected to *chaos* in the original hand.[29] No wonder the poet fears being exiled and with prayers and wailings tells the mind (which in patristic Latin can refer to the soul) to "knock at the innermost heavens." One wonders if our poet knew that the phrase *tetrum chaos* also appears in a fifth-century north African poem about the creation.[30]

Monday

On the second evening, the main subject is the creation of a firmament to divide the waters between heaven and earth. Water becomes an allegory for grace: it can put out flames without washing away the solid ground. The poet prays that we might not be washed away by error but might instead discover the light of faith.

MS f. 6r. Cf. W 281–82. *AH*   Cf. Mil 146. Wal 159.
51:35. M 375–76. Wie 39–40.
L 19. Mil 145–46. Wal 158.

Feria·ii··	Feria II
Imme*n*se caeli conditor.	Immeasurable founder of heaven,
qui mixta ne *con*funderent.	who gave heaven a boundary,
aquae fluenta diuidens.	dividing the streams of water—
caelum dedisti limite*m*.	though mixed, they were not confused—
firmans locu*m* caelestib*us*.	making firm a place for the heavens
simulque te*rr*ae riuulis.	and at the same time for the rivulets on
ut un*da* flammas tempe*r*et.	earth,
te*rr*ae solu*m* ne dissipet.	so that flowing water could cool flames,
	[but] the soil of the land would not dissipate.

---

29. Leo Eizenhöfer, *"Taetrum Chaos Illabitur,"* *Archiv für Liturgiewissenschaft* 2 (1952): 94–95; Christopher A. Jones, "Early Medieval *Chaos*," *Verbal Encounters: Anglo-Saxon and Old Norse Studies for Roberta Frank*, ed. Antonina Harbus and Russell Poole (Toronto: Univ. of Toronto Press, 2005), 15–38.

30. Friedrich Vollmer, ed., *Fl. Merobaudis Reliquiae; Blossii Aemilii Dracontii Carmina; Eugenii Toletani Episcopi Carmina et Epistulae*, Monumenta Germaniae Historica: Auctores Antiquissimi 14 (Berlin: Weidmann, 1905), 24.

infunde n*u*nc piissime.	Pour now, most merciful one,
don*um* p*e*rennis gratiae.	the gift of lasting grace.
fraudis nouae ne casib*us*.	May the old error not wear us down
[MS nouenae	with cases of a new deceit.
nos error att*e*rat uetus..	

Lucem fides inueniat.	May faith discover light
sic luminis iubar ferat[.]	so may it carry the brightness of a lamp.
h*aec* uana cuncta t*e*rreat.	Let this [light] terrify all the vain things,
hanc falsa nulla comp*ri*mant.	may no false things hinder this [faith]

The Creator is again addressed in the first line, but the mood is more somber than in Ambrose's *Deus creator omnium*, with a stronger emphasis on nocturnal fears and anxieties about our sinfulness and nothing said about the joy and power of song. The assonance grows more frequent and rhyme-like toward the end of the poem: in this case we progress from *-ent, -ens, -em* in the first stanza, through *-et, -et* in the second, to *-at, -at, -at, -mant* in the fourth. The way assonance consistently increases toward the end of each hymn in the series suggests to me that the poet conceived each hymn as an independent unit with a specific ending, despite the absence of a doxological stanza like the one in *Deus creator omnium* (medieval hymnaries often supplied a doxology borrowed from some other hymn). Thus I am doubtful about Anselmo Lentini's suggestion that the poet may have originally written one long hymn covering all six evenings that was subsequently adapted for liturgical use by being broken up and distributed across the Vespers of the week.[31] I believe the poet fully intended his work to constitute six liturgical hymns, one to be sung each night, just as we find them in the manuscripts, expanding and extending Ambrose's classic model into every evening celebration.

Tuesday

On the third night, moving water has pushed the soil together, forming an "immovable earth" on which plants grow. The water allegorically becomes the dew of grace and the tears of repentance, washing away the deeds and crooked motivations of our wounded mind so that the mind "may conform to your commands" and "rejoice to be filled with good things" just as the earth is fertile with fruit.

31. Lentini, *Te Decet Hymnus*, 15.

MS f. 6v. Cf. M 376. *AH*
51:36. W 283-84. Wie 42.
L 23. Mil 151. Wal 160.

Cf. Mil 152. Wal 161.

[f. 6v] Fer*ia* .iii·
Telluris ingens *con*ditor.
mundi solu*m* qui eruens.
pulsis aq*u*ae molestiis.
te*rr*a*m* dedisti imobilem.

Feria III
Vast founder of the globe
who, stirring up the soil of the world
with forceful blows of water,
gave an immovable earth,

ut germ*en* aptu*m* pr*o*ferens.
fuluis decora florib*us*.
fecunda fructu sist*e*ret.
pastu*m*q*ue* gratum redderet.

so that, bringing forth the ready seedling,
adorned with bright flowers,
[the earth] would present itself fertile with
   fruit
and bestow welcome nourishment.

mentis p*e*rustae uulnera.
   [MS uulnere
mundabit rore gratiae[a]
ut facta fletu diluat.
motusq*ue* prauos att*e*rat.

The wounds of the parched mind
he will purify with the dew of grace,
so that he may wash away [our] deeds with
   weeping
and wipe away crooked motivations:

iussis tuis obtemp*e*ret.
nullis malis appr*o*ximet.
bonis repleri gaudeat.
et mortis actu*m* nesciat.·

May [the mind] conform to your commands.
May it approach no evils.
May it rejoice to be filled with good things,
and may it not know the deathly deed.

a. munda uiroris gratia M W Wal I Munda vi roris gratiae AH I munda virore
gratiae Wie L Mil

F. J. Mone's commentary on this hymn presses his opinion that Pope
Saint Gregory the Great (r. 590–604) was the author of the entire series.
He believed that the words *conditor* ("founder, creator"), *mens* ("mind,"
but meaning "soul") and *actum* (meaning "a sinful deed") were typical of
Gregory's style.[32] For our part, we cannot help noticing the alliteration of
words beginning with *f* in the second and third stanzas, or the assonant
cluster of -*at* and -*et* in the last five lines. Alliteration of consonants does

32. F. J. Mone, *Lateinische Hymnen des Mittelalters*, vol. 1: *Lieder an Gott und
die Engel* (Freiburg im Breisgau: Herder, 1853), 376. *Lucis creator* was published
as a work of Gregory in *Patrologia Latina* 78: 849.

occur in Ambrose's genuine hymns, but the same consonant six times within two stanzas is more suggestive of medieval hymnody.

Wednesday

On the fourth night, the theme of light returns as the sun and moon are created, furnishing "a boundary of separation" between night and day. The constellations are presented as courtiers who attend the moon on its monthly procession across the sky, enabling us to mark the beginnings of the months. The poet asks the Creator to "enlighten the heart of men," as if to create a boundary of separation from sin.

MS f. 6v. Cf. M 378-79, 243-44.   Cf. Mil 158. Wal 163.
AH 51:36-37. W 284-86. Wie 45.
L 27. Mil 157. Wal 162.

FER*IA*·iiii·
Caeli d*eus* s*anct*issime.
qui lucid*um* centr*um* poli.
candore pingis igneo. [MS pinguis
augens decori lumina[a]

Most holy God of heaven,
who paint the bright center of the sky
with fire of dazzling whiteness,
spreading the lamps of beauty,

quarto die q*ui* flammea*m*.
solis rota*m* co*n*stituens.
lunae ministrans ordini.[b] [MS ordine*m*.
Uagos recursus sider*um*.

who, placing the fiery disk of the sun
on the fourth day,
providing as attendants in the moon's procession
the wandering courses of the constellations,

ut noctib*us* v*e*l lumini. [MS luminis.
dire*m*ptionis ter*m*inum.
pr*i*mordiis et m*e*nsi*um*.
signum dares[c] notissim*um*. [MS daret

so that you have furnished a boundary of separation
to the nights and to daylight,
and a well-known sign
to the beginnings of the months.

illumina cor ho*minum*.

Enlighten the heart of men.

absterge[d] sordes m*e*nti*um*. [MS absterget
resolve culpae uinculu*m*.
eue*r*te moles crimin*um*.· [MS creminum.

Wipe off the dirt-marks of [our] minds.
Unfasten the bond of fault.
Overturn the heavy weights of [our] sins.

a. decori lumina MS AH | decoro lumine M W Wal | decora lumina Wie Mil
b. ministrans ordini MS AH W Wal | ministras ordinem M| ministras ordini
L | ministrans ordinem Wie Mil
c. dares M W AH L Wal | darent Wie | daret Mil
d. absterge M AH W Wie L Mil Wal

Eight of the last nine lines end in *-um*, so that the distinction between
assonance and rhyme is almost moot. The piling up of imperatives addressed to God is less subtle than in the genuine hymns of Ambrose,
who often used subjunctives to express what should be prayed for, but
it also points to something else: while some genuine hymns of Ambrose
alternate between addressing God and addressing fellow worshipers, our
hymns follow *Deus creator omnium* in being addressed entirely to God.

Thursday

The hymn of the fifth night speaks of the creation of non-mammalian
animals: the reptiles and creepy things that crawl on the ground and the
flying things that live in the air. The poet seems to imagine a process of
evolution: life began in the seas, but then diverged, with one group moving to the land and becoming the crawling things, the other going into
the air as the things that fly. Thus our poet sees a single *genus* emerging
from the water, then experiencing both a process of pushing down (onto
the land) and a process of lifting up (into the air). This contrast between
raising and lowering becomes the central allegory, itself emerging from
the allegory of water. The poet asks that "all your little servants" who
have passed through the cleansing of water and blood be neither pressed
down by sins nor puffed up with pride.

MS f. 6v. Cf. *AH* 51:37. W 286–87.   Cf. Mil 164. Wal 165.
Wie 48. L 31. Mil 163. Wal 164.

FERIA·V··	Feria V
Magnae deus potentiae.	God of great power
qui ex aq*ui*s ortu*m* genus.	who, the genus that arose out of the
partim[a] remittis gurgiti. [MS partem	waters,
partim[a] leuas in aere.[b] [MS partem	you send partly back to the abyss,
	you lift partly into the air,

dimersa lymphis imp*r*imens.
subuecta caelis irrogans.
ut stirpe una p*r*odita.
diuersa rapiant loca.

pressing down those that are
   plunged into the waters,
appointing to the heavens those that
   are lifted up,
so that, sprung from one stock,
they may snatch different places.

largire cunctis seruulis.
quos mundat unda sanguinis.
ne scire lapsum criminu*m*. [MS
   creminum.
nec ferre mortis taediu*m*.

Bestow on all your little servants
whom the water, the blood, cleanses,
not to know the failure of sins,
nor bear the weariness of death,

Ut culpa nullu*m* dep*r*imat.
nullum leuet iactantia.
elisa mens ne *con*cidat.
elata mens ne corruat..

so that fault will press no one down,
nor boasting lift anyone up.
May no broken mind tumble down.
May no proud mind fall.

a. partim AH W Wie L Mil Wal
b. MS aere | aera AH W Wie L Mil Wal

The poet—no Ambrose!—slipped in not eliding *qui ex* into a single syllable, but he correctly planned for hiatus between *a* and *e* in *aera* (MS *aere*), making it a three-syllable word.

Friday

On the sixth night, we remember the creation of mammals and human beings out of the soil. This time the soil becomes the allegory, symbolizing the uncleanness of sin, but the fact that the living beasts were created to serve humans suggests a way out of sin: by serving others, we can "dissolve the bonds of strife" in our community and "knit together treaties of peace."

MS f. 6v. Cf. M 380, 243–   Cf. Mil 171.
44. *AH* 51:38. W 287–88.
Wie 51. L 35. Mil 169–70.

FERIA ·Vi·	Feria VI
Plasmator hominis d*eus*.	Moulder of mankind, God,
qui cuncta solus ordinans.	who alone, ordaining all things,
humu*m* iubes p*r*oducere.	command the soil to produce
reptantis *et* ferae genus.	the genus of creeping thing and wild beast.

q*ui* magna rer*um* corpora.	who gave the mighty bodies of [living]
dictu iubentis uiuida.	things—
ut seruiant p*er* ordinem.	living at the bidding of [your] command—
subdens dedisti homini.	to mankind, subduing them
	so that they might serve, [each] in its place.

repelle a servis tuis. [MS	Repel from your servants
aservis	whatever, through uncleanness,
quicq*ui*d p*er* im*m*unditia*m*.	either suggests itself to [our] habits,
a*ut* morib*us* se suggerit.	or interposes itself in [our] deeds.
a*ut* actib*us* se inte*r*serit.ᵃ	

da gaudior*um* p*r*aemia.	Grant the rewards of joys
da gratiar*um* munera.	grant the gifts of grace
disolue litis uincula.	dissolve the bonds of strife
abstringe pacis foedera..	knit together treaties of peace.

a. *A marginalium reads: uel* cs *Apparently the scribe was wondering if* inter-
serit *should be* inc*e*sserit. | inserit M | interserit AH W Wie L Mil

This poem, too, reveals a weakening grasp of metrics. In the words
hominis and *homini*, the first syllable *ho-* is treated as long, although in
fact it is short. This happens because *ho-* is the accented syllable; we
are witnessing confusion between syllable length and word accent. And
homini in the eighth line is not elided with the preceding *dedisti*, as it
should be. Thus *h* is being treated as a consonant rather than a breath-
ing, as in Greek poetry, from which most of the rules of Latin metrics
are derived. There is elision on *se interserit*, but we are clearly moving toward the medieval situation in which rhythmic / accentual poetry
seemed more natural and closer to the spoken language. Even Mone felt
compelled to admit that a poet who made these mistakes could not have
been Gregory the Great.[33]

33. Mone, *Lateinische Hymnen*, 380.

Where Did These Hymns Come From?

From France?

Reichenau is one of the many continental monasteries that were founded by Irish missionary monks. But our manuscript, the Reichenauer Schulheft, was not written at Reichenau. According to the great twentieth-century paleographer Bernhard Bischoff, it is one of a handful of manuscripts and fragments that were preserved in the Reichenau library but were actually written farther west, around the year 850, in northeast France near Soissons, in some unknown center where Irish and Latin texts were written in insular script. Another manuscript of this group also contains hymns from the New Hymnal, as well as some palimpsest leaves of unidentified liturgical texts.[34] The remaining manuscripts contain works of Priscian, Bede, and Saint Augustine.[35]

From Ireland?

Could these hymns, then, be of Irish origin? Of the many other hymns that survive in Irish-connected sources, not many resemble Ambrosian hymns, with four-line stanzas in quantitative iambic dimeter. One of the few is *Ignis creator igneus* from Bobbio, regarded by many as an Irish composition.[36] But Irish evidence is at the core of a more remarkable argument made by the great early twentieth-century hymnologist Clemens Blume: namely, that our hymns were composed by Pope Gregory the Great.

34. Karlsruhe, Badische Landesbibliothek, MS. Aug. perg. 195, written in northeast France around 850. Bischoff, *Katalog*, no. 1692, vol. 1, 354. For the unidentified liturgical texts see E. A. Lowe, *Codices Latini Antiquiores* 8: *Germany: Altenburg—Leipzig* (Oxford: Clarendon Press, 1959), nos. 1088–1092, pp. 20–21.

35. For the other manuscripts in this group, see Bischoff, *Katalog*, no. 1656, vol. 1, 347; no. 1676, vol. 1, 351; no. 2046, vol. 2, 20; no. 6953, vol. 3, 458. Bernhard Bischoff, "Irische Schreiber im Karolingerreich," in *Mittelalterliche Studien: Ausgewählte Aufsätze zur Schriftkunde und Literaturgeschichte* 3 (Stuttgart: Anton Hiersemann, 1981), 39–54, at 47–50.

36. Bulst, "Hymnologica partim Hibernica," 92–93, 95; Aidan Breen, "Columban's Monastic Life and Education in Ireland," *Seanchas Ardmhacha: Journal of the Armagh Diocesan Historical Society* 23, no. 2 (2011): 1–21, at 17; Oliver Davies et al., *Celtic Spirituality*, Classics of Western Spirituality (Mahwah, NJ: Paulist Press, 1999) 49, 472 nn. 157–58, 317–18, 519–20. See David Howlett, "Insular Latin Writers' Rhythms," *Peritia* 11 (1997): 53–116.

From Gregory the Great?

According to Blume, some of the hymns in our set are attributed to Gregory by sixteenth-century authors,[37] perhaps merely echoing the tradition that Gregory established Gregorian chant. More intriguing is material that survives in a collection now known as the Irish Liber Hymnorum, preserved in two eleventh-century manuscripts. It includes the well-known hymn *Altus prosator*, which tells a very different narrative of the creation.[38] A lengthy preface in Irish gives us two incompatible stories about the hymn's origin, though both name Saint Columba (521–597) as the author. According to one account, Columba composed the entire hymn in one day, while grinding oats at a mill. But in the other, he composed it slowly over a period of seven years, in an unlighted cell where he was doing penance for the blood shed while winning a battle. According to the mill story, Columba sent the hymn to Pope Gregory in return for gifts he had received from Gregory that included something called "the Hymns of the Week." A fourteenth-century manuscript expands this expression to "the Hymn of the Week, a hymn for every night in the week."[39] Blume's case for Gregory's authorship of our set of creation hymns, then, rests largely on the supposal that our hymns can be identified with "the Hymns of the Week" that Columba received from Gregory.

There are, however, reasons to demur. First, the attribution of *Altus prosator* to Columba is "impossible as well as unlikely" according to Jane Stevenson.[40] The poem fits much better among the works of Vergilius Maro Grammaticus, who was active in the seventh century.[41] Even the Irish Liber Hymnorum gives us two conflicting accounts of the hymn's origin, with Gregory appearing in only one. What really calls for

---

37. Clemens Blume, "Gregor der Grosse als Hymnendichter," *Stimmen aus Maria-Laach: Katholische Blätter* 74 (1908): 269–78. Reviewed in A. S. Walpole, "Latin Hymnology," *Journal of Theological Studies* 10, no. 37 (1908): 143–46.

38. J. H. Bernard, and R. Atkinson, eds., *The Irish Liber Hymnorum*, 2 vols., Henry Bradshaw Society 13–14 (London: Harrison and Sons, 1898), vol. 1, 62–83. For a careful modern translation Davies et al., *Celtic Spirituality*, 405–10; commentary on 57, 475–76 nn. 184–87, 524–28.

39. Bernard and Atkinson, *The Irish Liber Hymnorum*, vol. 2, 23–24.

40. Jane Stevenson, "Altus Prosator," *Celtica* 23 (1999): 326–68, at 326.

41. D. R. Howlett, "Seven Studies in Seventh-Century Texts," *Peritia* 10 (1996): 1–70, at 54–57.

attention, but is independent of our interests here, is the curious fact that both accounts, and other material as well, connect Columba's hymnodic activity with the number seven.[42]

It is not impossible that Gregory composed hymns for the local liturgy of Rome, or (more likely) for central Italian monasteries that followed, or eventually came to follow, the Benedictine Rule. But this supposition, too, runs into difficulties. Gregory's own writings refer at times to the singing of hymns by communities of monks, but these references are not detailed enough to enable us to identify any specific hymn text.[43] Without the story from the Irish Liber Hymnorum, there is no line of transmission connecting these hymns to Gregory beyond the general belief that he was responsible for Gregorian chant. Mone was not wrong to find a few words in the hymns that were also favored in Gregory's writings, but more recent studies of Gregory's extensive oeuvre have identified more distinctive expressions for the polarities of light and darkness, day and night,[44] and especially for the idea that a Christian should be spiritually awake even while sleeping.[45] These expressions do not occur in our relatively brief hymns. Even if we did find the hymn vocabulary to be deeply Gregorian, it would be more prudent to hypothesize that our poet was not Gregory himself but a careful reader of Gregory, whose writings were extremely popular during the Middle Ages.

42. Bernard and Atkinson, *The Irish Liber Hymnorum*, vol. 1, xxi.

43. Ann Julia Kinnirey, *The Late Latin Vocabulary of the Dialogues of St. Gregory the Great*, The Catholic University of America Studies in Medieval and Renaissance Latin 4 (Washington, DC: Catholic University of America, 1935), 23, 87; Rose Marie Hauber, *The Late Latin Vocabulary of the Moralia of Saint Gregory the Great: A Morphological and Semasiological Study*, The Catholic University of America Studies in Medieval and Renaissance Latin 7 (Washington, DC: Catholic University of America, 1938), 55.

44. Cuthbert Butler, *Western Mysticism: The Teaching of SS. Augustine, Gregory and Bernard on Contemplation and the Contemplative Life*, 2nd ed. (1926; repr. Mineola, NY: Dover, 2003), 76–78; Carole Straw, *Gregory the Great: Perfection in Imperfection*, Transformation of the Classical Heritage (Berkeley and Los Angeles: Univ. of California Press, 1988), 55, 60, 113–14.

45. Bernard McGinn, *The Presence of God: A History of Western Christian Mysticism*, vol. 2: *The Growth of Mysticism* (New York: Crossroad, 1994), 61–63.

Conclusion

Our poet did know Ambrose's hymn *Deus creator omnium*, which he decided to expand into a full set of Vespers hymns for the evenings of the week. His spirituality was arguably more monastic than Ambrose's, with each evening's allegory transforming our nocturnal fear and anxiety into a reminder of our sinfulness. He ignored Ambrose's verses on the joys and power of song. His hymnic compositions are actually examples of *lectio divina*, in which, as Gregory himself explained, allegory enables the reader's mind to rise from the literal sense of Scripture to the contemplation of heavenly things, and so we come to see our true selves as if in a mirror.[46]

These poems were unknown to the sixth-century Gallican and Anglo-Saxon compilers of the monastic Old Hymnal(s) and to the compilers of the Frankish Hymnal of the eighth and ninth centuries. That suggests the poet may have lived in the very time and place in which the New Hymnal was compiled: it makes its first appearance in manuscripts of the mid-ninth century, written at an Irish monastery in northeast France near Soissons.

---

46. Mirjam Schambeck, *Contemplatio als Missio: zu einen Schlüsselphänomen bei Gregor dem Grossen*, Studien zur systematischen und spirituellen Theologie 25 (Würzburg: Echter, 1999), 208–24; Duncan Robertson, *Lectio Divina: The Medieval Experience of Reading* (Collegeville, MN: Liturgical Press, 2011), 60–63, 149–50.

CHAPTER SEVEN

Rogationtide and the Secular Imaginary

Nathan J. Ristuccia

Rogationtide—the three-day processional feast before Ascension Thursday—embodied the medieval social imaginary. At the Rogation procession, Christians acted out their relationships to God, their fellow believers, the realm, creation, and the cosmos of physical and spiritual hierarchies that enmeshed them. Over the last century, liturgical reformers from multiple denominations have attempted to restore the holiday of Rogationtide to its medieval import—the Rogation Days were once perhaps the second most prominent holiday of the year (after Easter).[1] These attempts have failed. The Rogation Days remain seldom celebrated. Modern reformers will never be able to restore Rogationtide without cutting the holiday off from its premodern imaginary—the imaginary that vitalized it in the first place.

On the Rogation Days, all the Christians of a local community were supposed to march together from one holy place to another, fasting and praying for their collective needs. Modern writers have stressed how church processions in general and Rogationtide in particular embodied

---

1. For Rogationtide in the Middle Ages, see M. Bradford Bedingfield, *The Dramatic Liturgy of Anglo-Saxon England* (Woodbridge: Boydell, 2002), 191–209; Joyce Hill, "The *Litaniae maiores* and *minores* in Rome, Francia and Anglo-Saxon England: Terminology, Texts and Traditions," *Early Medieval Europe* 9, no. 2 (2000): 211–46; Johanna Kramer, *Between Earth and Heaven: Liminality and the Ascension of Christ in Anglo-Saxon Literature* (Manchester: Manchester Univ. Press, 2014), 30–1, 147–200.

premodern social imaginaries. Philosopher Charles Taylor, for example, noted that "if we go back a few centuries . . . the only modes in which the society in all its components could display itself to itself were religious feasts, like, for instance, the Corpus Christi procession."[2] When "the whole community turns out in procession to 'beat the bounds' of the parish on rogation days"—that is, walks out to the old boundary trees or stones—such rites demonstrate that "the social bond at all these levels was intertwined in the sacred, and indeed, it was unimaginable otherwise."[3] Historian Eamon Duffy, likewise, has insisted that in the later Middle Ages, "Rogationtide observances were, with the exception of the annual Easter communion, the most explicitly parochial ritual events of the year."[4] The Rogation Days served as "rituals of demarcation, 'beating the bounds' of the community, defining its identity over against that of neighbouring parishes, and symbolizing its own unity in faith and charity."[5]

The medieval imaginary carried in the teachings and practices of Rogationtide, however, was not exclusively one of unity and neighborliness. The feast was not cheerful. At Rogationtide, Christians were vulnerable.[6] They were surrounded by threats of all kind—illness, natural disasters, wild animals, riot, warfare, demonic attack. The sole protection that they had was to throw themselves on God's mercy through collective repentance. Sin had rendered a good creation dangerous and spread strife within human communities. If the tradition of Rogationtide contributes anything to theology today, it is reminding us to fear creation again. Not to fear for it; to fear it.

2. Charles Taylor, *A Secular Age* (Cambridge, MA: Harvard Univ. Press, 2007), 1–2.

3. Taylor, *A Secular Age*, 41–43.

4. Eamon Duffy, *The Stripping of the Altars: Traditional Religion in England c. 1400–c. 1580* (New Haven, CT: Yale Univ. Press, 2005), 139.

5. Duffy, *Stripping of the Altars*, 136.

6. According to Charles Taylor, premodern rituals often express "a mode of experience . . . captured by saying we feel ourselves vulnerable . . . to benevolence or malevolence which is more than human, which resides in the cosmos or even beyond it. This sense of vulnerability is one of the principal features which have gone with disenchantment . . . Along with vulnerability to malevolence goes the need to propitiate" (Taylor, *A Secular Age*, 36–37).

Marienka's Penance

One expression of this social imaginary is the "The Golden Bread" (*le Pain d'or*), a Bohemian folktale published in 1861 by the French writer and liberal politician Édouard René Lefèbvre de Laboulaye.[7] "The Golden Bread" is a fairy tale—or perhaps more accurately a ghost story—centered around Rogationtide.[8] It illustrates the theology of the feast in narrative form.

The folktale claims that long ago a beautiful peasant girl named Marienka dreamed that she married a rich lord. In the dream, her husband clothed her in such exquisite garments and jewelry that all the people in her church thought Marienka prettier than the Virgin Mary. When Marienka awoke, her pious mother cautioned her against this proud dream and prayed the rosary on her daughter's behalf. But Marienka ignored the warnings and rejected her many local suitors as beneath her.

One day, three coaches arrived at Marienka's cottage, filled with servants and the rich lord from her dream. The lord proposed and Marienka accepted immediately, too busy putting on her expensive new wedding dress to ask questions. Marienka went to church to wed the lord without her mother's blessing. Afterwards, the carriages bore Marienka and her husband to his castle and vast estates, located within a mountain. Only then did Marienka realize that her husband was the king of the dwarves. Marienka was delighted, for she never cared if she married "a good or an evil spirit" (*bon ou mauvais génie*) as long as he was rich.[9] Hungry from the long journey, she asked the servants to bring food, but she could not eat the meats of emerald and breads of silver and gold that they brought forth. All the food in the kingdom was inedible to her. Marienka burst

---

7. Édouard Laboulaye, *Contes Bleu* (Paris: Furne et Cie, 1864), 205–16; Laboulaye had first published this tale a few years before in a newspaper: Édouard Laboulaye, "Contes Bohèmes," *Journal des débats politiques et littéraires* (31 December 1861): 3.

8. "The Golden Bread" may not be a "fairy tale," depending how you define that category—a contentious issue in folkloristics. It lacks, for instance, the sort of happy ending that fairy tales are often thought to require. Hence, I prefer to call it a ghost story. For the debate around the definition of "fairy tale," see Nathan J. Ristuccia, "The Emperor's New Sanctum: A Folktale in Jordanes' *Gothic History*," *Parergon* 35, no. 1 (2018): 8–10.

9. Laboulaye, *Contes Bleu*, 212.

into tears, but her husband just laughed—his heart was of metal, just like his kingdom. "Weep," he roared, "but it will not help. What you wished for you possess. Eat the bread that you have chosen."

Even today, the folktale asserts, rich Marienka still lives in her castle, dying of hunger and seeking in vain to eat dirty roots to allay the pain. God punished her by granting her request. But three days every year—on the three Rogation Days, when the ground opens to receive the fruitful rain that the Lord sends—Marienka returns to haunt the earth. Dressed in rags, pale and wrinkled, she begs from door to door, happy when anyone throws her a crust. Then she receives as alms from the poor what she lacks in her palace of gold—bread and a little pity.

As far as I know, "The Golden Bread" is the only nineteenth-century folktale to depict Rogationtide. But its Roman Catholic atmosphere is not uncommon. Nineteenth-century folklorists often gathered explicitly Christian tales, even if later editors tended to remove them from present-day anthologies for children.[10] The third tale in the Grimm collection, for instance, is "Mary's Child," an account of a girl adopted by the Virgin Mary who is cast out of heaven for disobedience and then restored to bliss after performing confession.[11] In the earliest extant version of Little Red Riding Hood, likewise, the girl is baptized at Pentecost and given the red cloak by her godfather—red being the liturgical color of Pentecost.[12]

As mentioned, despite its Bohemian origins, "The Golden Bread" was originally published in French by Édouard Laboulaye in 1861. Laboulaye is best remembered for the role that he played in the gift of the Statue of Liberty to the United States, but throughout his life he gathered European folktales—from Bohemia, Brittany, Naples, and elsewhere—and rewrote them in his own French style.[13] Despite his republicanism, Laboulaye

---

10. Cf. G. Ronald Murphy, *The Owl, the Raven, and the Dove: The Religious Meaning of the Grimms' Magic Fairy Tales* (Oxford: Oxford Univ. Press, 2008).

11. Jacob and Wilhelm Grimm, *Kinder– und Hausmärchen*, 7th ed. (Göttingen: Verlag der Dieterichschen Buchhandlung, 1857), vol. 1, 8–14.

12. Jan M. Ziolkowski, *Fairy Tales from before Fairy Tales: The Medieval Latin Past of Wonderful Lies* (Ann Arbor: Univ. of Michigan Press, 2009), 93–124.

13. For Laboulaye's life, see Walter Dennis Gray, *Interpreting American Democracy in France: The Career of Édouard Laboulaye, 1811–1883* (Newark: Univ. of Delaware Press, 1994); *Smack-Bam, or The Art of Governing Men: Political Fairy Tales of Édouard Laboulaye*, trans. and ed. Jack Zipes (Princeton, NJ: Princeton

was a pious Catholic who had no sympathy for the anti-clericalism intertwined with much of French liberalism.[14] "The Golden Bread" is not the only story in Laboulaye's collection set in a Catholic world; the Breton tale "Yvon and Finette," for instance, begins by comparing beautiful maidens to statues of the Madonna and concludes with a wedding Mass at the St. Malo cathedral, in Brittany.[15]

The accoutrements of Catholic peasant life abound in "The Golden Bread": parishes, rosaries, almsgiving, evil spirits, feast days, prophetic dreams, religious art depicting Mary. "The Golden Bread" is Christian, however, in more than just social setting. The narrative structure itself contrasts the Virgin Mary, the Queen of Heaven—whose cult image is at the local church and to whom the widow prays—with Marienka ("little Mary"), who seeks to become the queen of a dwarf-filled underworld. Marienka gets her wish by making a Faustian pact with an evil spirit, the dwarf king, who carries her off to a place of suffering. The veneration of the Virgin is so central to the framework of the story, that I wonder if an earlier oral version had the Virgin Mary, rather than God, as the power that punishes Marienka's sin. Miracles of the Virgin, after all, were a common genre of early modern folktale.[16]

Laboulaye claimed that he was visiting Prague sometime around 1860 when he heard Marienka's morbid tale from the grandmother of Dr. Stephan Strjbrsky, a wealthy acquaintance and Czech nationalist. The grandmother recounted several tales that she had learned as a child from her own mother—although, because Laboulaye knew no Czech, she had

---

Univ. Press, 2018). Laboulaye's tales were translated quickly into multiple languages, including English and Swedish. One recent anthology to include "The Golden Bread" is William J. Bennett, *The Moral Compass: Stories for a Life's Journey* (New York, NY: Simon & Schuster, 1995), 185–89.

14. Carol E. Harrison, "Edouard Laboulaye, Liberal and Romantic Catholic," *French History and Civilization* 6 (2015): 149–58.

15. Laboulaye, *Contes Bleu*, 17–92.

16. For this genre, see, for instance, Kati Ihnat, *Mother of Mercy, Bane of Jews: Devotion to the Virgin Mary in Anglo-Norman England* (Princeton, NJ: Princeton Univ. Press, 2016); Rachel Fulton Brown, *Mary and the Art of Prayer: The Hours of the Virgin in Medieval Christian Life and Thought* (New York, NY: Columbia Univ. Press, 2018), 356–80, 414–19.

to tell the stories in German.[17] Strikingly, a few years earlier, by 1858, the Czech novelist and folklorist Božena Němcová had discovered a Slovakian folktale about a prideful girl who starves after marrying Kovlad, the god of metal.[18] Němcová's text must share a close ancestor with "The Golden Bread," although Němcová's redaction lacks many of the Christian elements that shape Laboulaye's Czech version, such as the name "Marienka" and her annual Rogationtide haunting. Thus, even though the Strjbrsky family were from the urban professional class, the grandmother's tale evidently derives from oral traditions circulating in the Austrian Slav lands by the early years of the nineteenth century at the latest.[19]

Laboulaye, Strjbrsky, and their contemporaries were among the last generation of Christians to experience the Rogation Days in close to its full medieval pageantry. Rogation celebration had declined across France by the time of Laboulaye's book. In 1730, the Rogation procession in Paris had been restricted, the result of a centuries-old fear about immorality and disorder at the feast.[20] For a decade, the French Revolutionaries banned the Rogation Days across France, and even once it was legal

17. Laboulaye never dates his visit, but allusions to other texts (for instance, Josef Wenzig's *Westslawischer Märchenschatz*, published in 1857) indicate that it occurred between 1857 and 1861. Laboulaye does not describe the grandmother's background, but he suggests that the family was rich. For instance, Strjbrsky employed servants, owned a piano, and had studied at the University of Heidelberg. Strjbrsky was also trilingual (in Czech, German, and Latin) and his grandmother was bilingual. See Laboulaye, *Contes Bleu*, 183–97.

18. Božena Němcová, *Slovenské pohádky a pověsti* (Prague: Antonín Augusta, 1857), vol. 7, 5–11; Alexander Chodźko, *Fairy Tales of the Slav Peasants and Herdsmen*, trans. Emily J. Harding (London: George Allen, 1896), 51–59.

19. Another of Laboulaye's Bohemian stories ("Schwanda the Bagpiper": a legend about a bagpiper tricked into playing music for Satan) mirrors the plot of Josef Kajetán Tyl's popular 1847 play *Strakonický dudák*. Since the play was based on an earlier folktale, the Strjbrsky family likely knew the folktale directly. See Laboulaye, *Contes Bleu*, 221–32.

20. For instance, the use of a processional dragon—a custom dating from the twelfth century—was suppressed; Jean Delumeau, *Rassurer et protéger: Le sentiment de sécurité dans l'Occident d'autrefois* (Paris: Fayard, 1989), 70–71, 168–69; cf. Nathan J. Ristuccia, *Christianization and Commonwealth in Early Medieval Europe: A Ritual Interpretation* (Oxford: Oxford Univ. Press, 2018), 67–68, 213.

again, the holiday never returned to prominence outside Brittany and a few other areas.[21] In the mid-nineteenth century, French writers, artists, and tourists embraced the customs of the peasantry—especially of the Bretons—as "vestiges of some bygone civilization that was somehow more authentic than the artificial and polished civilization of the French national elite."[22] Thus, in 1857, for instance, the Realist painter Jules Breton produced "The Blessing of the Wheat in the Artois," a monumental depiction of a Rogation procession, the sort of which could hardly be found in France at that time.[23]

By 1870, the great French liturgist Dom Prosper Guéranger, OSB could lament that "if we compare the indifference shown by the Catholics of the present age, for the Rogation Days, with the devotion wherewith our ancestors kept them, we cannot but acknowledge that there is a great falling off in faith and piety."[24] Guéranger joked bitterly that "the faithful of those days [i.e., the Middle Ages] had not made the discovery, which was reserved for modern time, that one requisite for religious processions is that they be as short as possible." Guéranger was almost an exact contemporary of Jules Breton, Stephan Strjbrsky, and Édouard Laboulaye. Rogationtide may have fascinated these and other nineteenth-century figures because they recognized that secularizing impulses within their civilization had doomed the feast.

Folklore as Imaginary

Despite the waning of Rogationtide, "The Golden Bread" is strikingly knowledgeable about the holiday's rituals and ethos. Even in the nineteenth century, storytellers understood Rogationtide's social imaginary.

---

21. Ristuccia, *Christianization and Commonwealth*, 213–16.

22. Robert Gildea, *Children of the Revolution: The French, 1799–1914* (Cambridge, MA: Harvard Univ. Press, 2008), 66–70, 75, 128–30, 308–10.

23. Jules Breton—from Brittany as his surname implies—built his success on paintings of peasants engaged in farming or Catholic rites; Annette Bourrut Lacouture, *Jules Breton, Painter of Peasant Life* (New Haven, CT: Yale Univ. Press, 2003), 98–99.

24. Prosper Guéranger, *The Liturgical Year: Paschal Time*, vol. 3, trans. Laurence Shepherd (Dublin: James Duffy, 1871), 132–33.

The tale highlights five elements of this imaginary: penance, mandatory participation, fertility, hierarchy versus social leveling, and the demonic.

The Bohemian folktale is, first of all, a story about divine judgment. God punishes an unrepentant sinner by giving her the torment that she unwittingly desires.[25] Marienka suffers forever in a spirit-filled mountain, neither heaven nor hell. Indeed, because of her sins, the undead Marienka still haunts the area. The concept of purgatory as an inaccessible location developed slowly, so medieval ghost stories often depict the spirits of the dead coming forth to convince the living to pray for them.[26] Similarly, Marienka walks around in rags three days each year, begging people to have mercy. That is Rogationtide: three days of collective penance in which all Christians in a local area had to march together, praying for forgiveness.

According to the normal origin story, the Rogation Days were invented by Bishop Mamertus of Vienne around the year 470. Supposedly, the city of Vienne had experienced a series of omens over the year: earthquakes, wild deer coming into the middle of the forum, a fire in church during the Easter Vigil. No one was hurt. Mamertus himself, for instance, extinguished the fire right away. Nonetheless, the citizens of Vienne interpreted these events as portends signaling that far worse calamity impended, and many inhabitants fled the city as a result. Mamertus instituted a three-day fast and procession in order to propitiate God and prevent the foretold disaster.[27]

This standard origin story may be true. But all the extant sources about Mamertus's actions are years later, thirdhand, and contradictory, so I am suspicious. Regardless, medieval people knew the legend of Mamertus. Preachers frequently recounted Mamertus's feat in Rogation-

---

25. I am reminded of a quotation in *The Great Divorce*: "There are only two kinds of people in the end: those who say to God, 'Thy will be done,' and those to whom God says, in the end, 'Thy will be done.' All that are in Hell, choose it" (C. S. Lewis, *The Great Divorce* [New York, NY: HarperCollins, 2001], 75).

26. Jean-Claude Schmitt, *Ghosts in the Middle Ages: The Living and the Dead in Medieval Society*, trans. Teresa Lavender Fagan (Chicago, IL: Univ. of Chicago Press, 1998), 40, 89–91, 119–20, 142, 180–81; cf. William of Malmesbury, *Miracles of the Blessed Virgin Mary* 30.7–8, ed. and trans. R. M. Thomson and M. Winterbottom (Woodbridge: Boydell, 2015); William of Newburgh, *Historia Rerum Anglicarum* vv. 22–24, vol. 1, ed. Hans Claude Hamilton (London: Sumptibus Societatis, 1856).

27. For the origins of Rogationtide, see Ristuccia, *Christianization and Commonwealth*, 24–62.

tide sermons.[28] Churchmen often exaggerated the story. Gentle deer are not scary. So instead, medieval preachers and theologians asserted that bears, wolves, lions, boars, elephants, and even dragons overran the city of Vienne, ripping limbs off citizens, devouring babies in their cribs, and gorging on the corpses of the dead. Likewise, a fire is not impressive if no one was injured. So, later clerics claim rather that the bubonic plague had scoured Vienne for over a year and that Mamertus's procession drove off the disease. The legend of Mamertus and the penitential fast of Vienne was itself folklore, handed down orally in sermons for centuries until the narrative had altered greatly from its original version. The purpose of the Mamertus legend—like the story of Marienka—was to inspire repentance, not to chronicle history.

Secondly, "The Golden Bread" testifies to Rogationtide's role as a mandatory ritual. All Christians of a parish or baptismal church were supposed to participate in the same ceremonies.[29] By being baptized in the same place, buried in the same graveyard, confessing sins to the same priest on Ash Wednesday, processing together yearly along the same route, a local congregation constituted itself as a single ritual body.

This ethos of total communal participation appears all over medieval sermons and legislation for Rogationtide. At the First Council of Orléans in 511, for instance—the synod that originally declared the Rogation Days obligatory—the Merovingian bishops decreed "that through the three Rogation days, male and female slaves be released from all work, so that the whole people can assemble."[30] Not even a slave could be left

28. For a few of the dozens of sermons relating this story, see Ælfric, *Catholic Homilies* 1.18.5–39, in *Ælfric's Catholic Homilies: The First Series, Early English Text Society*, n.s. 17, ed. P. Clemoes (Oxford: Oxford Univ. Press, 1997); *Eleven Old English Rogationtide Homilies*, ed. Joyce Bazire and James E. Cross (Toronto: Univ. of Toronto Press, 1982), 8.1–28; *Herwagen Homiliary* 13, *Patrologia Latina* 94, col. 499C; Beverly M. Kienzle, "Cistercian Preaching against the Cathars: Hélinand's Unedited Sermon for Rogation, B.N. MS Lat. 14591," *Cîteaux: commentarii cistercienses* 39, nos. 3–4 (1988): 297–99; Thomas N. Hall and Nathan J. Ristuccia, "A Rogationtide Sermon from Eleventh-Century Salisbury," *Revue Bénédictine* 123, no. 1 (2013): 60–61.

29. Ristuccia, *Christianization and Commonwealth*, 103–5.

30. Rogationes, id est laetanias, ante ascensionem domini . . . per quod triduum serui et ancellae ab omni opere relaxentur, quo magis plebs uniuersa conueniat, *Council of Orléans* (511), 27, *Corpus Christianorum, Series Latina* 148A, ed. C. De Clercq (Turnhout: Brepols, 1973).

out. The seventh-century Frankish saint Gaugericus of Cambrai purportedly freed prisoners from the royal dungeon so that they could join the
march.[31] Churchmen exempted the sick, the very young, and the very
old from fasting during the three days, but still expected these groups
to attend, even if the sick and old had to ride horses instead of walking.
According to Caesarius of Arles, for instance, anyone who "should desert
the spiritual army camp" of the church during the Rogation Days risked
eternal perdition.[32] As a result, Caesarius advised his flock to empty their
schedules in the days leading up to the feast. Christians ought to avoid
eating too little, taking medicine, or undergoing therapeutic bleedings
before the holiday. Any of these acts might leave a congregant too ex-
hausted to endure the hours-long walk.

Marienka in the Bohemian folktale was clearly the member of a local
parish—she knew the other parishioners so well that she wanted them to
gaze at her and deem her more beautiful than the Virgin Mary. According
to medieval theology, she ought to be part of their yearly march. Thus, God
frees her from her mountain kingdom three days a year to join in. Some
Bohemian raconteur presumably invented the idea of Marienka's Rogationtide reprieve, but it draws on clear medieval precedents. Apocrypha—such
as the famous *Visio Pauli*—claim that all the humans suffering in hell
receive a one-day respite from their torment on major feasts like Easter as
well as on every Sunday.[33] These were times of rest, even for the damned.

Total Rogation participation was impossible. In practice, only a fraction of the baptized population was willing to attend. And for good reason. The Rogation Days were grueling. Christians had to walk for six
hours on three consecutive days, from the third to the ninth hour. On
the fast days, they missed not only meals (until the ninth hour), but also
their afternoon siesta. Lanfranc of Canterbury ordered his monks to sleep
longer than normal in the nights leading up to the feast so they would

31. *Vita Gaugerici* 8, *Monumenta Germaniae Historica, Monumenta Germaniae
Historica, Scriptorum rerum Merovingicarum* 3, ed. Bruno Krusch (Hanover: Hahn,
1896), 654.

32. Nullus castra spiritalia deserat, Caesarius, Serm. 207.2, *Corpus Christianorum, Series Latina* 104, ed. G. Morin (Turnhout: Brepols, 1953); cf. Caesarius,
Serm. 208.3, 209.4; *Eleven Old English Rogationtide Homilies*, 5.140–143, 8.18–28.

33. For the respite in hell, see Nathan J. Ristuccia, "The Herwagen Preacher and
his Homiliary," *Sacris Erudiri* 52 (2013): 202, 208–13.

not feel too groggy.[34] Similarly, a ninth-century hagiography of Saint Omer mentions that by the end of the Rogation procession the whole congregation was tired and one young girl left early—she skipped the concluding Mass to quench her painful thirst.[35] Saint Omer was not sympathetic to the child's plight. The girl fell into a well as punishment and nearly drowned.

Even in May, Rogation processions could be cold. According to late medieval farming lore, the last frost of the spring occurred during or around Rogationtide.[36] Moreover, marchers were supposed to wear only sackcloth and to walk barefoot across the uneven, often muddy terrain.[37] They must have traveled at a slow rate, accruing scrapes, cuts, and bruises along the way. During one Rogation march, the sixth-century bishop Gallus of Clermont stepped his bare foot on a thorn and had a deep scar there the rest of his life.[38] Fatigue bred an ill-tempered congregation. Multiple sources record fights breaking out during the procession.[39]

Proper Rogation observance required five straight days without work (counting Rogation Sunday and Ascension Thursday). That is a major time outlay, right in the middle of growing season. While a farmer was away worshiping, bad weather could kill the sprouting plants. No wonder that churchmen complain that landowners refused to let their slaves and serfs off for the feast. One hagiographer, for instance, laments that before

34. *Decreta Lanfranci monachis Cantuariensis transmissa, Corpus consuetudinum monasticarum* III, ed. David Knowles (Siegburg: F. Schmitt, 1967), 43–44.

35. *Miracula Audomari* 3, *Monumenta Germaniae Historica, Scriptorum rerum Merovingicarum* 5, ed. Bruno Krusch and Wilhelm Levison (Hanover: Hahn, 1910), 777.

36. For frosts at Rogationtide, see Ristuccia, *Christianization and Commonwealth*, 130–31.

37. For complaints about mud, see *Consuetudines Fructuarienses-Sanblasianae, Corpus consuetudinum monasticarum* XII, vol. 1, ed. Luchesius G. Spätling and Peter Dinter (Siegburg: F. Schmitt, 1985–87), 213; *Vita Procopii* 2, *Acta Sanctorum, Jul* 2, 141–42.

38. Gregory of Tours, *Historiae* 4.13, *Monumenta Germaniae Historica, Scriptorum rerum Merovingicarum* 1.1, ed. Bruno Krusch (Hanover: Hahn, 1884), 144.

39. Daniel E. Thiery, *Polluting the Sacred: Violence, Faith and the "Civilising" of Parishioners in Late Medieval England* (Leiden: Brill, 2010), 68–69, 73–74, 116–18; Duffy, *Stripping of the Altars*, 136–37; Ristuccia, *Christianization and Commonwealth*, 113, 126.

the eleventh-century papal reformer ended such abuses, the cathedral canons of Arezzo had the habit of sending their serfs and hired vicars out on errands during the Rogation Days.[40] Other hagiographers record lay people neglecting the procession due to their work: a peasant who cuts wood instead, a woman who mends clothing rather than walking.[41] Saints cursed such people for their iniquity. Absences at Rogationtide grew so widespread that by early modernity some parishes enforced attendance through head counts and fines.[42]

Thirdly, at least since the eighteenth century, many scholars have interpreted the Rogation Days as a fertility ritual—an agricultural blessing in spring. "The Golden Bread," for instance, explicitly ties the holiday to spring rain. Marienka comes with the rains; she acts much like the Greek goddess Persephone, who would return from the underworld for six months a year to bring the summer. Indeed, the whole folktale is concerned with food scarcity. Marienka's vast wealth cannot prevent her from starving when her sins offend God. Every May, she has only a three-day reprieve to gather enough food for the year. The closing picture of Marienka begging for food mirrors Rogation worshipers marching that God might bless them with good harvest. As the Victorian poet Christina Rossetti put it, in the opening lines from her poem "Rogationtide":

> Who scatters tares shall reap no wheat,
> But go hungry while others eat.
> Who sows the wind shall not reap grain;
> The sown wind whirleth back again.[43]

40. *Historia custodum Aretinorum, Monumenta Germaniae Historica, Scriptores* 30, ed. A. Hofmeister (Hanover: 1934), 1473; cf. *Eleven Old English Rogationtide Homilies*, 5.161–62.

41. Cf. *Miracula Remacli Stabulensis* 2.15, *Monumenta Germaniae Historica, Scriptores* 15.2, ed. Oswald Holder-Egger (Hanover: 1888), 442; Wolfhard of Eichstatt, *Vita Walburgis* 3.2.6, *Acta sanctorum quotquot toto orbe coluntur*, series *February*, vol. 3 (Paris: Victorem Palmé, 1865), 536.

42. For such fines in the eighteenth century, see Ruth Behar, *The Presence of the Past in a Spanish Village: Santa María del Monte* (Princeton, NJ: Princeton Univ. Press, 1986), 172, 180–82.

43. Christina Rossetti, *The Complete Poems*, ed. Rebecca W. Crump (London: Penguin, 2003), 439.

Yet the medieval evidence for this Rogationtide fertility connection is weak. Christian farmers had plentiful opportunities to get their crops blessed. As a glance at any sacramentary demonstrates, for a price, medieval churchmen were willing to bless fields, houses, boats, nets, armies, weapons, staffs, forges, ovens, beds, wells, and almost any other object that might ever be of use to anyone anywhere.[44] Rogation prayers, however, always mention sundry threats—bad weather yes, but also warfare, plague, demonic attack, wild beasts, and so on. As one scholar has noted, "the Rogation antiphon suggests that that those who sung it were not much concerned about fertility. Their most pressing concern was simply not to be dead."[45]

The first writer to describe Rogationtide—the fifth-century bishop of Clermont, Sidonius Apollinaris—differentiated the new holiday from agricultural blessings. "The earlier public prayers," he wrote in a letter to a prominent citizen in his diocese, "were uncertain, lukewarm, sporadic, and often interrupted for lunch."[46] These older supplications had "beseeched either for rain or for clear weather because the potter and the gardener could never agree." Rogationtide, though, was "a feast of bowed heads, a sigh-filled fellowship of the citizenry." As Sidonius recognized, mere weather is divisive: what is beneficial for one citizen might mean financial ruin for another. In contrast, everyone can march in the Rogation procession, because Rogationtide is penitential—not agricultural. God's wrath threatens all. Thus, the whole locality must assemble in repentance.

Later medieval churchmen also downplayed Rogationtide's weather associations. The thirteenth-century liturgist William Durandus, for

---

44. For such blessings, see Derek A. Rivard, *Blessing the World: Ritual and Lay Piety in Medieval Religion* (Washington, DC: Catholic Univ. of America Press, 2009).

45. Jeremy Harte, "Rethinking Rogationtide," *Third Stone* 42 (2002): 30.

46. Erant quidem prius . . . uagae tepentes infrequentesque utque sic dixerim oscitabundae supplicationes, quae saepe interpellantum prandiorum obicibus hebetabantur, maxime aut imbres aut serenitatem deprecaturae; ad quas, ut nil amplius dicam, figulo pariter atque hortuloni non oportuit conuenire . . . festa ceruicum humiliatarum et sternacium ciuium suspiriosa contubernia, Sidonius Apollinaris, *Ep.* 5.14.2–3, *Monumenta Germaniae Historica, Auctores Antiquissimi* 8, ed. C. Luetjohann (Berlin: Weidmann, 1887), 87.

instance, asserted that the Rogation Days are in the spring not because of the crop cycle. Rather, Durandus claimed, the holiday is in the spring because military campaigning starts then, and the church must beg God to "rescue and defend us from the enemies of Christian worship," presumably Muslims.[47] Likewise, when the church authorities discovered that many sixteenth-century Italians believed that Rogation processions would keep witches from entering their fields and cursing them with infertility, these Italians ended up before the Inquisition.[48] While folk traditions—such as "The Golden Bread"—connected Rogationtide with prosperity, churchmen stressed the diverse benefits of the feast, especially spiritual benefits, not earthly agricultural ones.

Fourth, the Bohemian tale of Marienka illustrates the tension that existed throughout the Middle Ages between the Rogation Days as a time for collective effervescence and the Rogation Days as a time for hierarchical ranking. The holiday's practices pulled in both directions. For example, Rogation marchers were supposed to progress in a single amorphous bulk, on bare feet and in sack cloth. Rogationtide was an inversion ritual. Ideally, the richest lord and lowliest peasant would look the same, so that the procession appeared as "an indiscriminate class of people" to cite one Frankish writer.[49] As Caesarius of Arles exclaimed in a Rogation sermon, "everywhere there is purity and love: peace among men, no different between the slaves and the free, one diet and one dress for rich and poor."[50] Only the clergy were visually distinct, for they walked at the front bearing crosses and reliquaries and dressed in vestments. An eleventh-century vision of the afterlife even asserts that

47. Ergo hoc tempore maxime bella emergere solent . . . ab hostibus christiane religionis nos eripiat et defendat, Guillelmus Durandus, *Rationale diuinorum officiorum* 6.102.4, *Corpus Christianorum, Continuatio Mediaevalis* 140B, ed. A. Davril and T. M. Thibodeau (Turnhout: Brepols, 2000).

48. Carlo Ginzburg, *The Night Battles: Witchcraft and Agrarian Cults in the Sixteenth and Seventeenth Centuries*, trans. John and Anne Tedeschi (Baltimore, MD: Johns Hopkins Univ. Press, 1983), 1–9, 22–24, 154–56.

49. Promiscuo populi genere, *Vita Arnulfi* 10, *Monumenta Germaniae Historica, Scriptorum rerum Merovingicarum* 2, ed. Bruno Krusch (Hanover: Hahn, 1888), 435; cf. *Vita Huberti Leodiensis prima* 6, *Monumenta Germaniae Historica, Scriptorum rerum Merovingicarum* 6, ed. Wilhelm Levison (Hanover: Hahn, 1913), 486.

50. Ubique castitas et dilectio: inter uiros pax . . . inter ancillas et liberas differentia uel nulla uel grata. Vnus diuiti uictus et pauperi, et . . . habitus erat unus in cunctis, Caesarius, Serm. 143.1.

heaven looks like a Rogation march—a throng of believers dressed alike and walking around an Elysian field—with only St. Paul in priestly attire distinguishable from everyone else.[51]

"The Golden Bread" describes at length the clothing of the lord, his servants, the peasants, and so forth. Marienka, for example, receives a beautiful golden dress as queen of the dwarves so that she can show off to her neighbors. Yet when she begs for alms on the Rogation Days, she wears rags. Almsgiving was a normal part of the Rogation Days, as were other acts of social solidary such as formal reconciliations between squabbling neighbors.[52] The Rogation liturgy leveled social ranks by forbidding conspicuous consumption—banquets, leisure, horses, fancy attire. *Communitas* reigned.

Well, at least in theory. In practice, the medieval evidence indicates that the procession was often ranked social difference on display. The oldest extant *Ordo* for Rogationtide stems from the abbey of Saint-Riquier around the year 800. According to this customary, on each of the Rogation Days, lay people from seven local villages as well as the town itself gathered at the portico of the monastery church at Saint-Riquier for prayer.[53] Each village brought its own cross and banner, displaying its unique identity within the larger community. And then the congregation would march seven abreast, ordered by rank: the ordained collegiate clergy in major orders first, then the minor orders, non-ordained monastics, and boys at the monastery school. Behind came the laity divided by gender and status: first high-born men, then high-born women and children, then a less exclusive group of "honorable men and women," and finally normal lay persons.[54] And lastly those too old or sick to march rode horses behind the marchers. Later sources for the Rogation liturgy indicate that such rigid orderings were common.[55]

51. Peter A. Stokes, "The Vision of Leofric: Manuscript Text and Content," *Review of English Studies* 63, no. 261 (2011): 548.

52. Ristuccia, *Christianization and Commonwealth*, 53, 120–22, 193.

53. *Institutio sancti Angilberti, Initia Consuetudinis Benedictinae: Consuetudines Saeculi Octavi et Noni, Corpus consuetudinum monasticarum* I, ed. Kassius Hallinger (Siegburg: F. Schmitt, 1963), 296–300.

54. Nobiles uiri . . . a proposito uel decano electi . . . feminae uero nobiliores . . . pueri et puellae . . . honorabiliores uiri et feminae . . . mixtus populus . . . equitando, *Institutio sancti Angilberti*, ed. Hallinger, 297.

55. Ristuccia, *Christianization and Commonwealth*, 108–11.

Medieval churchmen often feared that social distinctions undermined the penitential spirit of the feast. The Carolingian theologian Hrabanus Maurus, for instance, warned his congregation to not emulate those who "live more sinfully" on the Rogation Days than on normal days. For the wicked "prepare banquets and march—men and women alike—combed and ornamented as if these are days of merrymaking, not of repentance."[56] They "ride their horses through the countryside, laughing" instead of praying. "Afterwards, they return home and summon their neighbors and allies for a feast." Supposedly, these banqueters would devote the rest of the day and night to food, alcohol, and lewd singing. Hrabanus's anger targeted the knightly elites who participated in the culture of feasting and song that filled a medieval lord's hall. As much as medieval churchmen stressed the solidarity of the Rogation march, its practice was hierarchical.

Finally, the story of Marienka attests to the impact demonology had on Rogation observance. Medieval folklore is filled with tales about elves and similar supernatural beings romancing humans and stealing them away to dwell for eons with the fairies.[57] A famous example is *Sir Orfeo*, a Middle English lay—inspired by classical myths about Orpheus—concerning a king who travels to Elfland to rescue his kidnapped wife. Popular culture often presented fairy lovers positively, but churchmen usually insisted that these fairies were demonic incubi in disguise. The Marienka folktale fits the structure of a fairy abduction narrative well. At one point, Marienka even wonders whether the king of the dwarves is an "evil spirit" (*mauvais génie*), a learned Christian reinterpretation of popular belief.[58]

Throughout the Middle Ages and into early modernity, one of the main purposes of the Rogation procession was to banish demons and witches

---

56. Prae caeteris diebus turpius uiuunt, sceleratius agunt . . . instruunt sibi conuiuia, praeparant domos . . . compti et ornati in publicum uiri feminaeque procedunt, quasi dies sint laetitiae et non magis poenitentiae . . . super phaleratos resiliunt equos, discurrunt per campos, ora dissoluunt risu . . . postquam autem domum ueniunt, conuocant ad conuiuium non pauperes, uel caecos aut debiles . . . sed uicinos ac sodales suos . . . uacant epulis studentque calicibus epotandis, Hrabanus, *Homiliae ad Haistulfum* 19, *Patrologia Latina* 110, col. 38B–38C.

57. Richard Firth Green, *Elf Queens and Holy Friars: Fairy Beliefs and the Medieval Church* (Philadelphia: Univ. of Pennsylvania Press, 2016), 41, 78–81, 111–12, 163–65.

58. Laboulaye, *Contes Bleu*, 212.

out of the lands of the parish.[59] Marchers would sing and swing handbells because they believed the noise drove out terrified demons. Demons were as great a danger as famine, plague, or wild animals. The canonist Regino of Prüm, for instance, proclaims that at the time of Mamertus of Vienne, "the people of Gaul celebrated Rogation Days against the anger of visible wolves, but now we celebrate in order to escape the anger of invisible wolves—that is, of unclean spirits."[60] Medieval Christians could worry that a neighboring parish was driving devils off their own land and onto their neighbor's land. As a result, rival processions sometimes came to blows.

Exorcisms occurred at the procession. In "The Golden Bread," the power of the dwarf-king to imprison Marienka wanes during the holiday. For another example, on a Rogation Wednesday around the year 1400, a priest at Domrémy in northeastern France directed the march to a tree haunted by fairies—demons in disguise according to the clergyman.[61] There, the priest read the prologue from John's Gospel in order to exorcise the fairies. Apparently, the French priest succeeded, because no one saw fairies at the tree ever again. Such exorcisms may have been common, although premodern sources rarely mention them, probably due to the elite perspective of medieval authors.[62] Indeed, we only know of this event because Joan of Arc lived in the parish of Domrémy, so the story came up when the Inquisition later investigated her. In fact, Rogation marchers continued to make loud noises in order to protect trees from evil spirits even into the eighteenth century.[63] Many aspects of medieval Rogation practice are nonsensical apart from demonology.

What then is the vision of the world expressed in the rituals and theology of Rogationtide? First, that humans are vulnerable. Both the natural

59. Ristuccia, *Christianization and Commonwealth*, 68–69, 112, 125–26.

60. Galliarum populi luporum rabie . . . non ut uisibilium luporum rabiem euadamus, set ut inuisibilium, id est spirituum immundorum, Regino of Prüm, *De synodalibus causis* I.C.280, ed. F. W. H. Wasserschleben and Wilfried Hartmann, *Das Sendhandbuch des Regino von Prüm* (Darmstadt: Wissenschaftliche Buchgesellschaft, 2004), 148.

61. Green, *Elf Queens and Holy Friars*, 28–29, 46–47, 54, 67, 220.

62. Some hagiographers describe Rogation Day exorcisms. For instance, *Vita Arnulfi* 10, Krusch, 435; *Vita Huberti Leodiensis prima* 6, Levison, 486.

63. For such ceremonies in eighteenth-century Kent, see John Brand, *Observations on the Popular Antiquities of Great Britain*, vol. 1, rev. Henry Ellis (London: Rivington, 1813), 177.

world and the social world are filled with dangers—droughts, demons, warfare, animals, social inequalities. And second, that humans are weak. Human are unable to address their problems by their own powers. The only protections against the perils of life are divine mercy and collective repentance.

Rogationtide in a Secular Age

The Rogation Days survive here and there as a folk rural custom. Towns all over Britain, for instance, still celebrate the traditional perambulation of the parish borders—a largely secularized remnant of Rogation practice.[64] But the feast is no longer central to Christian worship. Rogationtide embodied a form of life incommensurate with modernity. The holiday declined in early modernity and then virtually disappeared over the course of the twentieth century. Liturgical Protestant churches such as the Methodists and Lutherans include "Rogation Sunday" on their official calendar, but as little more than an alternate rubric for the "Fifth Sunday after Easter."[65] In the Roman Catholic church, similarly, Rogationtide has been an optional observance since the introduction of the Mass of Paul VI in 1969. But Pope Paul VI only confirmed a change that had already occurred widely.

In 1941, for example, Monsignor Martin Hellriegel—one of the founding editors of the journal *Orate Fratres* (now *Worship*)—complained that even in a heavily Catholic area like the counties around St. Louis, he could watch Masonic parades but no longer Rogationtide. A few decades before, Hellriegel had participated in many Rogation processions. But now, "because we are afraid of half-a-dozen snickerers, we lock ourselves up" rather than marching.[66] Instead, "gentlemen . . . during the season of the holy fast, sit around the banquet table discussing the disturbed social and economic conditions." Frustrated, Hellriegel insisted, "These processions have been in prison long enough. They should be released."

64. Ronald Hutton, *Stations of the Sun: A History of the Ritual Year in Britain* (Oxford: Oxford Univ. Press, 2001), 57, 277–88.
65. Ristuccia, *Christianization and Commonwealth*, 216–17.
66. Martin Hellriegel, "Merely Suggesting," *Orate Fratres* 15, no. 7 (1941): 298–99.

As Hellriegel's article testifies, attempts to recover the Rogation Days as a Christian holiday are not new. In America, for instance, such attempts date at least to the 1920s, to the work of Bishop Edwin O'Hara of Kansas City and the National Catholic Rural Life Conference (NCRLC).[67] Founded by O'Hara in 1923, the NCRLC sought to strengthen rural Catholicism through pastoral care, economic development, and the promotion of specifically rural liturgical actions. Thus, the NCRLC published various pamphlets and manuals for the Rogation Days, including an English translation of the liturgy itself, in order to supply local parishes with the materials necessary to reinvigorate the holiday. In 1929, the NCRLC spearheaded an ecumenical effort to rebrand the fifth Sunday after Easter (i.e., Rogation Sunday) as "Rural Life Sunday": a designation accepted by Catholics and Protestants alike. By 1947, the American poet William Carlos Williams could write a moving poem for Rogation Sunday which is able never to mention God, or processions, or a church. "O let the seeds be planted," Williams exclaims. The poem—as if a new creed—promises that "we believe / in the wonder of continuous revival, / the ritual of the farm."[68] Farm had replaced church as the locus of renewal.

The last few decades have witnessed occasional attempts to revitalize the Rogation Days across denominations, this time in a manner inspired by environmentalism. Consider, for instance, a 2008 article by Michael P. Foley, a professor of patristics at Baylor University. Most of the article provides a history of the Rogation Days and describes ways in which the holiday has been and could be celebrated. The piece ends, though, with a jeremiad. Foley bemoans that "we live in an age marked by unprecedented disconnect from the land and by a growing anxiety over it. On the one hand, we fret over the barbaric or hazardous treatment of livestock, commercial pesticides, genetically modified foods, the demise of the family farm, and the rise of food cartels . . . On the other hand, at no point in American history have so many of us lived away from the farm." Foley maintains that "obligatory traditional Rogation Days are

67. For the NCRLC, see Michael J. Woods, *Cultivating Soil and Soul: Twentieth-Century Catholic Agrarians Embrace the Liturgical Movement* (Collegeville, MN: Pueblo, 2009), xix, 1–27, 61–62, 112, 119–22, 191–218, 223.

68. William Carlos Williams, *The Collected Poems of Williams Carlos Williams*, vol. 2: *1939–1962*, ed. Christopher MacGowan (New York, NY: New Direction Books, 1991), 110–11.

the religious antidote" which can "call all believers . . . to recognize
at the same time and in a shared way our common dependence on the
land and on God's mercy . . . They reconnect us to the soil . . . to the
bounds of our neighborhood, our parish, and each other."[69]

Since around the turn of the millennium, most ministers writing on
Rogationtide express sentiments of this type. Lutheran pastor Robert
Dahlen, for instance, warns that due to contemporary environmental
dangers, "it is simply wrong to wait until October or November to address
issues related to agriculture and the land"; we should lift the Rogation
Days "from the far recesses of our common Christian attic."[70] Similarly,
David Powers, a professor at the Catholic University of America, advocates restoring Rogationtide observance as one piece of a larger project of
establishing "an approach to nature . . . organistic and sustainable . . .
which suggests a symbiotic mutuality between nature and humankind."[71]

All these sentiments are decent and proper. But not, perhaps, the most
useful. As far as I can tell, the present-day revival of Rogation celebration
occurs on the pages of Christian magazines, rather than in the streets and
fields of actual parishes. Here is the basic problem. People do not want
to fast. Or to march around for hours. Or to go barefoot. As a result,
whenever modern liturgists call for Rogation renewal, they have to suggest alternative ways that the Rogation Days could be celebrated that fit
with the modern world—alternatives, that is, to celebrating the feast as
it was observed for over a millennium.

In the article just discussed, for instance, Foley envisioned Rogationtide as a private affair: individual families walking around their property
and sprinkling their houses and gardens with holy water.[72] Dahlen, likewise, advised combining Rogationtide with Arbor Day and suggested
that congregants walk around the church yard "if the weather is nice."[73]
If it is rainy, or if the church building is in a city and lacks a yard, then
Dahlen deemed it enough to just open the church windows to let in
fresh air during worship. In 2003, the Committee on Divine Worship

69. Michael P. Foley, "Rogationtide," *The Latin Mass* 17, no. 2 (2008): 39.
70. Robert W. Dahlen, "Prayer on the Prairies: Rogation Days in Changing Times," *Word and World* 20, no. 2 (2000): 195.
71. David N. Powers, "Worship and Ecology," *Worship* 84, no. 4 (2010): 290.
72. Foley, "Rogationtide," 38–39.
73. Dahlen, "Prayer on the Prairies," 200.

of the United States Conference of Catholic Bishops allowed dioceses to treat civic holidays like Independence Day, Labor Day, and Thanksgiving as "equivalents to Rogation Days."[74] Ironically, a once-vibrant medieval Christian feast is now observed on days established by the secular American government—none of them in the springtime.

Conclusion

This form of Rogationtide is alien to the medieval world. I cannot blame liturgists for these milquetoast proposals. Not many present-day congregants would agree to attend multiple weekday masses, march outside for six hours even in the worst weather, go shoeless and in sackcloth, or fast until 3 p.m. each day. Yet, during the Middle Ages, these were the standard actions of the feast.

Busyness is part of the problem. Lifecycles today turn upon the calendar of schools, corporations, and tax offices, more than upon the liturgical year. More deeply, though, Rogationtide in anything like its traditional form is impossible in the contemporary West because the Rogation procession embodied a premodern social imaginary. Secularism too is a form of life, and a form of life that has little in common with the Rogation Days. Medieval Christians did not march because they wished to reconnect with the soil or to restore their symbiotic mutuality with nature. They marched because perils surrounded them at all times. In the modern developed world, humans are safe, at least the kinds of humans who are wealthy and educated enough to write position papers on Christian liturgy. We do not fear as we once did. Most contemporary people no longer envision a world of saints and demons, of ranked hierarchies and festal inversion, of storms of divine punishment and rains of divine mercy. Most of us do not think of humans as fundamentally impotent. Modern attempts to revive the Rogation Days will fail unless this entire social imaginary revives alongside the feast.

74. Committee on Divine Worship of the United States Conference of Catholic Bishops, *Newsletter, Committee on Divine Worship* 39 (December 2003): 1–4.

CHAPTER EIGHT

The Cosmos and the Altar in Hildegard's *Scivias* and Select Sequence Texts

Margot E. Fassler

The chapters contained in this volume dedicated to our friend and colleague Bryan Spinks explore correspondences between the cosmos and liturgy, and these correspondences are of many types. Hildegard of Bingen (1098–1179) is a worthy subject for this exploration of liturgy and cosmos because her works provide an opportunity to look at a series of subtly drawn parallels made through art, liturgical commentary, poetry, and music, all four, an approach that is unique in the history of the interrelationship of cosmos and liturgical understanding. The parallels created by Hildegard were made for communities of religious, in her case especially of Benedictine nuns. They were of a type that could provide artistic and theological nurturing throughout a lifetime of discovery, which accounts for her particular "slow burn" aesthetic, here described through discussion of the digital model of the cosmos Christian Jara and I have been constructing in accordance with Hildegard's thought, music, drama, and art.[1] In order to discuss our work, which seeks to make the complexities of Hildegard's ideas concerning cosmos and liturgy available for a broader constituency, I begin with an overview of how our digital model fits in with recent ideas concerning creation, cosmos, and the study of

---

1. See Margot Fassler, "Images and Chants for a Digital Model of the Cosmos," *Journal of the Alamire Foundation* 9, no. 1 (2017): 161–78.

theology, which is followed by a short introduction to the classical and Christian underpinnings of Hildegard's cosmic map. The second part of the chapter unpacks the map itself and demonstrates the ways in which Hildegard's thoughts about the cosmos and its workings are couched in liturgical understanding, especially within her eucharistic hermeneutic.

Just a few years ago, the average educated citizen in North America and Europe was familiar with a commonly held picture of the universe and its creation. In an article published in 1999, astrophysicist Michael Turner of the University of Chicago asked if the nature-of-the-universe debate was really about to be solved, and his answer was "quite possibly." He wrote that the hot big bang cosmological model developed in the late twentieth century "describes accurately the evolution of the universe from a fraction of a second after the bang (about 13.8 billion years ago) until today."[2] In paraphrasing Turner's summation we can note that the model has three pillars: (1) the observed expansion of the universe, (2) the existence of cosmic microwave background radiation, and (3) the pattern of light elements produced immediately after the bang in "a sequence of nuclear reactions." On the simplest level, then, it seems the universe has left a kind of picture of the big bang in light waves.

But since Turner wrote in 1999, several problems with this standard cosmological model have arisen, and each requires new calculations and opens up aspects of the debate.[3] Most dramatically, in 2013 universal celebration followed reports that the big bang theory had been proven through new measurements of light and radiation, but these proofs were soon questioned, however, by several other teams of astronomers. At present, scientists using the Large Hadron Collider near Geneva, Switzerland, are testing ideas about parallel universes that would cause reevaluation of the big bang.[4] The idea that small black holes in our universe

2. Michael Turner, "Cosmology Solved? Quite Possibly!" *Publications of the Astronomical Society of the Pacific* 111, no. 757 (1999): 264–73.

3. For example, scientists have been questioning the rate at which the universe is expanding. See Tom Siegfried, "Cosmic Question Mark: The Planck Mission's Data Put a Kink in Precision Cosmology," *Science News* 185, no. 7 (2014): 18–21.

4. See Sarah Knapton, "Big Bang Theory Could Be Debunked by Large Hadron Collider," *The Telegraph*, 23 March 2015, http://www.telegraph.co.uk/news/science /large-hadron-collider/11489442/Big-Bang-theory-could-be-debunked-by-Large -Hadron-Collider.html.

"leak" gravity is now a thesis to be explored as well. The properties of black holes in space have captured the imagination of cosmologists and persons on the street alike. Ideas about dark matter and dark energy are crucial to theorizing about them. Timothy Ferris, author of many books of popular science, writes:

> In the nearer future, making sense of dark energy may require radical improvements in the way we conceive of space itself. The voids between the planets and stars were long thought to be sheer nothingness . . . quantum field theory. . . [demonstrated] that space is never really empty but instead is suffused with quantum fields, which are literally everywhere.[5]

Scientists now study what the human eye can see just by looking upward: there is far more sky than star. What dark matter and dark energy are, how to measure them, and what their existence reveals about the universe and its formation remain to be determined. Ferris says of cosmologists, "Nowadays they're less often in error, but their doubts have grown as big as all outdoors."[6]

As the doubts about accepted theories have magnified, so too have new ways of thinking about astronomy.[7] The study of Hildegard's cosmology in its religious contexts speaks in several ways to contemporary concerns. Comparative cosmology is a fairly recent field of endeavor, one requiring examination of ideas about cosmology and their representations by specialists in a broad array of disciplines and with concentration upon many time periods and cultures. Nicholas Campion describes some of the issues related to this mode of study in the introduction to a collection of essays from the perspectives of several world religions. He mentions a shift from universalism to localism, that is, from all-pervasive archetypes to the distinctiveness of each system, warning, however, that the result can be a failure to discuss or even recognize apparent commonalities.

5. Timothy Ferris, "Dark Matter," *National Geographic*, January 2015, http://ngm.nationalgeographic.com/2015/01/hidden-cosmos/ferris-text; Devin Powell, "In Pursuit of Dark Matter," *Proceedings of the National Academy of Sciences of the United States of America* 110, no. 35 (2013): 14113–15.

6. Ferris, "Dark Matter," opening sentence.

7. Adam Frank, *About Time: Cosmology and Culture at the Twilight of the Big Bang* (New York, NY: Free Press, 2011).

The place of religion in the study of comparative cosmology and also the truth claims that various groups make are other important topics. "Worldview" seems to be a term that encompasses many kinds of belief systems, and Campion endorses it, while acknowledging that "beliefs about the cosmos go to the heart of most religious traditions."[8]

While a host of arguments remain about whether the study of the cosmos should have a theological dimension today, in the past it did for many cultures and today still does.[9] The study of cosmological systems from the past or from contemporary cultures, then, will surely involve religious perspectives, at least for some of the scholars involved, especially in the case of ritual action. A galaxy of scientists and powerful new tools for measurement have made the study of the cosmos more dynamic than it has ever been, and the subject has a renewed speculative strain that is philosophical and sometimes even theological in nature.[10] Astro-theology was recently welcomed as an area of investigation for a special issue of the *Journal of Cosmology* with the following announcement:

> Because the refereed *Journal of Cosmology* is abstracted and indexed with traditional mathematical and highly technical literature, we require constraint in use of those terms laden with religious baggage, like "faith" and G**; and we particularly request that such words be avoided in titles and abstracts, which will be indexed and reproduced alongside papers on scientific results from NASA programs, and mathematical formulations of black hole theory, etc. We hope you will see this as an opportunity to express ideas about connections between theology and scientific cosmology.[11]

Because the immensity of the universe is a subject broached by contemporary astrophysicists who bring their work to all through popular

---

8. Nicolas Campion, *Astrology and Cosmology in the World's Religions* (New York: New York Univ. Press, 2012), 10.

9. For a popular book laying out two sides of the argument over whether religious perspectives belong in the study of the cosmos and how they might be included, see *God and Cosmology: William Lane Craig and Sean Carroll in Dialogue*, ed. Robert B. Stewart (Minneapolis, MN: Fortress Press, 2016).

10. John Edward Huth, "Stars," in *The Lost Art of Finding Our Way* (Cambridge, MA: Belknap Press, 2013), 125–60.

11. "Commentary: Introduction to Astro-Theology," *Journal of Cosmology*, June 2012, http://journalofcosmology.com/JOC19/commentary.pdf.

science, the theories of scientists can offer comfort to humans who wish to understand when and how the universe was born. But the answers provided by the scientific community are presently in flux and approaches to studying the cosmos and its origins are many, and include the use of digital tools for exploration, representation, and pedagogy. The Ordered Universe Project, which comes out of the University of Durham and Oxford University, provides an example of the several ways in which even small-scale digital models are useful for teaching about contemporary views of the universe and time.[12] Views formed of the cosmos in the past can be not only educational but also comforting. They demonstrate a commonality of wonder that joins humans across time and location. Robert Grosseteste (ca. 1168–1253), scientist, theologian, and bishop of Lincoln, is the focus of the Ordered Universe Project, which seeks to explore cosmology in Grosseteste's age through a variety of means, including digital modeling of the cosmos as understood during his lifetime in a part of the project called "The Medieval Cosmos." Now and then the cosmos remains a seat of speculation that pushes humans to engage with all-encompassing questions of existence. The Medieval Cosmos is the first public version of a complete visualization of the themes and subjects explored by Grosseteste in his scientific works. It will take shape in two-dimensional and three-dimensional versions, to lead the viewer on a guided tour of the birth and creation of the medieval universe, meteorological phenomena from the rainbow to climactic conditions, the nature of the elements, the relation between the heavens and the Earth, comets, the notion of place, and geometrical phenomena. The project's website records, "Grosseteste's powerful ability to conjure examples for the complex subjects he sought to explain is the inspiration for the visualization. His examples are consistently explained precisely and succinctly, allowing us, even eight hundred years apart, to follow his thought processes and, with our own interpretative toolkits, draw out a representation of the concepts and phenomena that so fascinated him."[13]

Our project "Cosmos and Creation in Hildegard of Bingen's *Scivias*" is a digitized model of the cosmos and its stages of creation as Hildegard

12. See, for example, a presentation by Richard Bower: https://ordered-universe .com/ou-team-on-time-2016/.

13. For further information, see https://ordered-universe.com/the-medieval -cosmos/.

depicted them and wrote about them. The model includes appropriate music, and the visuals are based completely upon paintings accompanying a twelfth-century copy of her treatise *Scivias*, which she wrote in the 1140s.[14] The treatise includes at its close a version of Hildegard's play *Ordo Virtutum*.[15] Our model proceeds through the stages of creation, the hexameron, as Hildegard envisioned it, beginning with her understanding of time before time and matter before matter. It then explores the model she created of the cosmos, depicted most graphically in *Scivias* book I, vision iii, the cosmic egg. This model had many meanings for her, beyond the traditional understanding of the universe as scientists in the early twelfth century in northern Europe knew it. The model Hildegard drew relates the cosmos to the church and its sacraments (in heaven and on earth); to her play *Ordo Virtutum*; to her views on the purpose of the cosmos, its beginnings, its inevitable end, and on the nature of time; and to the place of human beings within the cosmos. Our digital model

14. The critical edition of *Scivias*, by Adelgundis Führkötter with Angela Carlevaris, is in Corpus Christianorum, Continuatio Mediaevalis 42 (Turnhout: Brepols, 1978). The other two major treatises constituting her trilogy are *Liber Vitae Meritorum* (*Book of Life's Merits*, ed. Angela Carlevaris, Corpus Christianorum, Continuatio Mediaevalis 90 [Turnhout: Brepols, 1995]), composed from ca. 1158–1163, and *Liber Divinorum Operum* (*Book of Divine Works*, ed. Albert Derolez and Peter Dronke, Corpus Christianorum, Continuatio Mediaevalis 92 [Turnhout: Brepols, 1996]), composed ca. 1163–1174. All references to *Scivias* are to this edition and to the English translation of *Scivias* (sometimes with modifications) by Mother Columba Hart and Jane Bishop (New York, NY: Paulist Press, 1990); the Latin line numbers are given first, followed by the page of the Latin and then the page of the English translation.

15. The play *Ordo Virtutum* exists in two versions; the one referenced here is a shorter version included at the end of *Scivias*. The text of the longer version of the *Ordo Virtutum* is the one that has music. It has been edited and translated into English by Peter Dronke in his *Nine Medieval Latin Plays* (Cambridge: Cambridge Univ. Press, 1994), pp. 147–84, with notes and introduction, and has also appeared in a critical edition that takes into account the copy commissioned by Trithemius in the fifteenth century: Dronke in *Hildegardis Bingensis Opera minora*, ed. Peter Dronke, Christopher P. Evans, Hugh Feiss, Beverly Mayne Kienzle, Carolyn A. Muessig, and Barbara Newman, Corpus Christianorum, Continuatio Medievalis 226 (Turnhout: Brepols, 2007), pp. 481–521. A critical edition of the music is Hildegard of Bingen, *Ordo Virtutum: A Critical Edition*, ed. Vincent Corrigan (Lions Bay: Institute of Medieval Music, 2013).

of the cosmos as Hildegard envisioned it moves and is zoomable, and it sounds as well, for the songs associated with the treatise *Scivias* have poetic texts that relate to her postlapsarian, post-incarnational universe. The cosmos is a backdrop for human struggle and revelation, a vast stage set on which the mysteries of the sacraments unfold and the place of human beings within them is told and foretold.

This discussion of our digital model and its workings relates to the ways in which Christian theologians and scientists in the first half of the twelfth century thought about the universe, and not only in their tractates and scientific calculations but also in their ecclesiology, the visual arts, music, poetry, and drama.[16] Only by accounting for several dimensions of understanding can a sense of the whole be achieved. And for this work, Hildegard is a unique and skillful guide. The system she designed is far removed from our modern-day understandings, rooted as it is in her time and place, but it is dynamic and systematic, and to comprehend it is to gain otherwise unattainable knowledge about the past and about medieval cosmological investigations in their multidisciplinary splendor. To create our model, we have studied Hildegard's cosmography and her reading of the cosmos as reflecting the liturgical practices she knew and wished to make part of the workings of the universe; hers is a holistic vision, one that binds the natural world to the sacraments and to liturgical song and ritual action.

The model of the cosmos that informed most scholars and theologians in the first half of the twelfth century, when Hildegard wrote *Scivias*, her first treatise, was geocentric, with the Earth a sphere. The whole was believed to be surrounded by an outermost shell, the empyrean, which contained the signs of the zodiac in some views and was depicted as a circle of fire in others.[17] Between the Earth and the outer empyrean were

16. Of special relevance to my study are two books that deal with Hildegard's contemporaries: Conrad Rudolph, *The Mystic Ark: Hugh of St. Victor, Art, and Thought in the Twelfth Century* (Cambridge: Cambridge Univ. Press, 2014); and Danielle B. Joyner, *Painting the Hortus deliciarum: Medieval Women, Wisdom, and Time* (University Park: Pennsylvania State Univ. Press, 2016).

17. Alexander A. Gurshtein, "The Origins of the Constellations: Some Provocative Hypotheses Link the Origins of the Constellations to the Precession of the Earth's Axis and the Symbolic Imagery of Ancient Peoples," *American Scientist* 85, no. 3 (1997): 264–73.

seven planets in circular orbits and in a particular order, which most commonly ran, after Earth: Moon, Mercury, Venus, the Sun, Mars, Jupiter, Saturn. Sometimes the distances between the planets were represented by particular musical tones.[18] The planets were located in a shimmering area of the whole, the aether, that did not interact with the subluminary zone immediately surrounding the Earth, a mutable area. This view of the cosmos was sustained by a long tradition of writings from late antiquity that informed medieval understandings of cosmology until the coming of much new knowledge, which began in the second half of the twelfth century.

The ancient astronomers most significant for the western European tradition were the Greeks, especially Plato (428/427 or 424/423–348/347 BC) and his pupils Eudoxos of Cnidus (ca. 408–355 BC) and Aristotle (384–322 BC). For Plato, the cosmos had been created by a divine craftsman, and the work was an image, a construct. As the physical world was an image, so too were descriptions of it, but both contained information about the nature of the divine and were a product of design.[19] Aratus of Soli (ca. 310–240 BC) preserved in verse form a version of Eudoxos's now lost *Phaenomena*; this Latin translation of Aratus was known in the medieval West. From the school of thought centered in Athens came the idea of the universe as a series of concentric circles with the Earth in the center, and with the Earth as changing but the universe as eternal. After the time of Eudoxos, most Greeks believed in a geocentric universe.[20]

18. Pliny the Elder, *Natural History*, vol. 1: *Books 1–2,* trans. H. Rackham, Loeb Classical Library 330 (Cambridge, MA: Harvard Univ. Press, 1938), book II, xx, 227–29. For discussion of other systems regarding tonal space and distances between the planets, see Gabriela Ilnitchi, " 'Musica Mundana,' Aristotelian Natural Philosophy, and Ptolemaic Astronomy," *Early Music History* 21 (2002): 37–74; and Susan Rankin, " 'Naturalis concordia vocum cum planetis': Conceptualizing the Harmony of the Spheres in the Early Middle Ages," in *Citation and Authority in Medieval and Renaissance Musical Culture: Learning from the Learned,* ed. Suzannah Clark and Elizabeth Eva Leach (Woodbridge: Boydell & Brewer, 2006), 3–19.

19. A. Freire Ashbaugh, *Plato's Theory of Explanation: A Study of the Cosmological Account in the Timaeus* (Albany: State Univ. of New York Press, 1988), 7. For an overview, see G. E. R. Lloyd, "Greek Cosmologies," in *Ancient Cosmologies,* ed. Carmen Blacker and Michael Loewe (London: Allen & Unwin, 1975), 198–224.

20. Heliocentricity was known but rejected for a variety of reasons. In his *Sand Reckoner,* Archimedes (d. 212 BC) spoke of the theories of Aristarchus of Samos,

Eudoxos's work was important too for explaining how the Greek model of the universe worked mathematically: he claimed that the fixed stars "were attached to a single sphere that revolves around the Earth at its center."[21] Each planet moved relative to this sphere in a system of three or four Earth-centered rotational spheres. Gad Freudenthal records, "This was an ingenious theory that afforded for the first time a mathematical (geometrical) representation of the cosmos."[22] Aristotle's view of time and eternity would be especially significant in the debates of scholastics in the thirteenth century: his belief that the universe was eternal contradicted Jewish, Christian, and Muslim understandings of creation based on the book of Genesis. Complexities abound, for Aristotle argues for two infinities, small and large, actual and potential.[23]

The most influential of the fundamental classical Roman works were Pliny the Elder's *Natural History*, Macrobius's commentary on Cicero's *Dream of Scipio*, Martianus Capella's *Marriage of Philology and Mercury*, and Calcidius's commentary on the *Timaeus* of Plato. All four of these texts had rich manuscript traditions that included planetary diagrams, especially from the Carolingian period forward.[24] Augustine, like so many Christian writers on creation and the cosmos from the patristic and medieval periods, turned to the Bible as a source for his speculation, as is nowhere more apparent than in his five commentaries on the book

---

saying "he supposes that the fixed stars and the sun do not move, but that the Earth revolves in the circumference of a circle about the sun." As found in E. J. Dijksterhuis, *Archimedes* (1938), trans. C. Dikshoorn (Princeton, NJ: Princeton Univ. Press, 1987), 362–63.

21. Gad Freudenthal, "Cosmology: The Heavenly Bodies," in *The Cambridge History of Jewish Philosophy*, ed. S. Nadler and T. M. Rudavsky (Cambridge: Cambridge Univ. Press, 2009), 302–361, at 304.

22. Ibid.

23. An introduction to Aristotle's views on infinity can be found in the preface by Roger Ariew to his translation of excerpts from Pierre Duhem's writings on medieval cosmology, *Medieval Cosmology: Theories of Infinity, Place, Time, Void, and the Plurality of Worlds* (Chicago, IL: Univ. of Chicago Press, 1985); and in Norman Kretzman, ed., *Infinity and Continuity in Ancient and Medieval Thought* (Ithaca, NY: Cornell Univ. Press, 1982).

24. Bruce Eastwood and Gerd Graßhoff, "Planetary Diagrams for Roman Astronomy in Medieval Europe, ca. 800–1500," *Transactions of the American Philosophical Society* 94, no. 3 (2004): 1–158.

of Genesis, of especial interest here when he discusses Genesis 1 and 2, which contain descriptions of the stages of creation.[25]

These and other authors were summarized and transmitted to the Middle Ages by two figures whose works formed the backbone of medieval cosmology for centuries. Isidore of Seville, in his "On the Nature of Things," written in the early seventh century, not only incorporated the writings of pagan authors but also submitted them to Christian allegory. Bruce Eastwood says of him: "Isidore believed that just as we can find moral and mystical meanings in the Bible, so we can 'read' the visible book of nature, exposed through the accounts of classical writers."[26] In the eighth century, the Venerable Bede penned a treatise also called *De Natura Rerum*, on the nature of things. His treatise forms a departure from the work of Isidore in that it does not allegorize. Rather, Bede offered a model that provided greater detail about the physical nature of the universe as he knew it, with more attention to time reckoning, a subject on which he also wrote a treatise.[27] As it was designed as a textbook for teaching science in the monastery, Bede's work became even more popular than Isidore's.

Through these authors and their many classical sources and through the treatises of Augustine whose writings on Genesis led the way, what was known of science and of theology were joined, and in a fascinating array of possibilities, including medieval maps and diagrams such as those referenced above. The twelfth century was a time when new scientific knowledge was entering northern Europe from translations of previously unknown or untranslated works from Arabic, Hebrew, and Greek sources, but it was also a time when Christian theologians were

25. These writings by Augustine are, in chronological order: *On Genesis: Against the Manicheans* (ca. 388–389); his *Unfinished Literal Commentary on Genesis* (393–395); the last three books of his *Confessions* (397–401); *The Literal Meaning of Genesis* (401–416); and his commentary on angels in *City of God* book IX (ca. 416).

26. Bruce S. Eastwood, "Early Medieval Cosmology, Astronomy, and Mathematics," chap. 12 of *The Cambridge History of Science*, vol. 2: *Medieval Science*, ed. David C. Lindberg and Michael H. Shank (Cambridge: Cambridge Univ. Press, 2013), 302–22, at 306; and see also, in the same volume, Stephen C. McCluskey, "Natural Knowledge in the Early Middle Ages," chap. 11, at 287–89.

27. See Bede, *On the Nature of Things and On Times*, in the series *Translated Texts for Historians*, vol. 56, trans. Calvin B. Kendall and Faith Wallis (Liverpool: Liverpool Univ. Press, 2010); chapters 13–15 relate to calculating the date of Easter.

looking intensely at the cosmos as a divine work for human instruction, a point of view with roots in Augustine and Isidore. To quote Barbara Obrist, "there was a growing interest in theorizing about the relation of nature to the Godhead," and this development included the Christianization of the kinds of maps and diagrams that had long accompanied cosmological treatises.[28]

In their study of planetary diagrams accompanying medieval copies of the Roman astronomers cited above, Bruce Eastwood and Gerd Graßhoff provide a list of medieval cosmological treatises with diagrams. It includes works by Pliny, Macrobius, Martianus, and Calcidius, the main subjects of their study, but also, as many instances are compendia, works by Isidore and Bede. The list is long. Many of the sources date from the eleventh and twelfth centuries and they come from every region of Europe. We can imagine that Hildegard was exposed to such illustrated treatises and that they informed her own cosmographical diagram. The relationships between the planets as described in Macrobius's commentary on Cicero's *Dream of Scipio*, a text seemingly known in one way or another to Hildegard, is of special relevance here, for it recorded that the Sun and the three planets "above" were located in the purest aether in which everything is light; the Moon is in the lowest aetherial zone, "next to the nonluminous realm of transitory things" in which the Earth is found. The Moon, indeed, "could have no light if not for the Sun above it, to which it shines back."[29]

A different kind of cosmographical diagram was provided by the wind chart, a subject studied by Barbara Obrist.[30] Obrist divides understanding of the winds into two chronological periods. Beginning with Isidore, who, as we have seen, relied on the Greco-Roman tradition, the winds were studied as subluminary phenomena, but especially in the twelfth century this view shifted to sometimes placing them in the celestial sphere, thereby relating them and their powers to the Godhead. When this transformation took place, the power of the winds as forces that sustained the whole became apparent, as will be seen in Hildegard's map of the cosmos from her *Scivias*.

28. Barbara Obrist, "Wind Diagrams and Medieval Cosmology," *Speculum* 72, no. 1 (1997): 33–84, at 75–76.

29. As quoted in Eastwood and Graßhoff, "Planetary Diagrams," 60.

30. Obrist, "Wind Diagrams," 33–84.

Figure 1. *Scivias* I.iii: The Cosmic Egg, Wiesbaden, Hochschul- und Landesbibliothek, Hs 1, fol. 14r (manuscript has been missing since 1945); black and white photo, courtesy of the Abbey of St. Hildegard, Eibingen.

This map of the universe, shown in Figure 1 in an early twentieth-century copy of the now-lost twelfth-century manuscript that contained it, was surely designed under Hildegard's influence.[31] The painting of the cosmos is one of thirty-five illuminations found in the treatise *Scivias*, a work copied in Hildegard's scriptorium on the Rupertsberg and by at

31. The manuscript of the illuminated *Scivias*, the former Wiesbaden, Hochschul- und Landesbibliothek RheinMain, 1, has been lost since World War II, destroyed in the bombing of Dresden, where it had been taken for safekeeping. A manuscript that was apparently with it, Wiesbaden, Hochschul- und Landesbibliothek RheinMain, 2, the so-called Riesencodex, which contains the only complete copy of Hildegard's music, survived, as is described in an essay by Jennifer Bain: "History of a Book: Hildegard of Bingen's 'Riesencodex' and World War II," *Plainsong and Medieval Music* 27, no. 2 (2018): 143–70 (a link to the digitized Riesencodex is provided in n. 37). Fortunately, in addition to black-and-white photos of Wiesbaden 1 that survive, in the late 1920s the nuns of Eibingen, under the supervision of Sr. Josepha Knipps, made an exact copy on parchment of the original, preserving a sense of the vibrant colors in the original manuscript. The Riesencodex is digitized and available on line: Wiesbaden, Hochschul- und Landesbibliothek RheinMain. The black-and-white photos of the manuscript copied in this essay belong to the abbey of St. Hildegard, Eibingen, and are used with permission.

least one scribe whose pen was responsible for other treatises as well. It was closely related to scientific diagrams Hildegard would have known from her vantage point as an extremely well-read person. This plan of the cosmos (the so-called "cosmic egg") has been much studied, but rarely for its relationship to Hildegard's liturgical sensibilities. The manuscript Walters Art Gallery, MS 73, a cosmographical study copied in the later twelfth century, contains maps of the cosmos showing the concentric circles that were typical of cosmographical maps in Hildegard's age.[32] The extraordinary differences between the contemporary images found in the English treatise in the Walters and Hildegard's plan are immediately apparent.[33] Strikingly unusual, this map of the cosmos from *Scivias* book I can be contextualized, however, as a product of mid twelfth-century times. Hildegard's cosmic egg is an amalgamation of a Macrobian set of concentric circles depicting the Earth and its planets and a wind chart, which are overlain by a visionary Christian exegesis explaining the whole, and so related also to the Augustinian and Isidorian traditions, which she surely would have known. Hildegard was far from alone in seeing the cosmos as a kind of egg: her older contemporaries Rupert of Deutz (ca. 1075–1129) and Peter Abelard (1079–1142) saw the cosmos as an egg over which the Holy Spirit broods.[34]

32. See "The Digital Walters," http://www.thedigitalwalters.org/Data/Walters Manuscripts/W73/data/W.73/sap/W73_000006_sap.jpg.

33. Lieselotte Saurma-Jeltsch,"Introduction," in Hiltrud Gutjahr and Maura Zátonyi, *Geschaut im Lebendigen Licht: die Miniaturen des Liber Scivias der Hildegard von Bingen* (Beuron: Beuroner Kunstverlag, 2011), 7–22, and Lieselotte Saurma-Jeltsch, *Die Miniaturen im Liber Scivias der Hildegard von Bingen: die Wucht der Vision und die Ordnung der Bilder* (Wiesbaden: Reichert, 1998), the latter of which provides many examples of the visual contexts for the paintings, which I believe Hildegard designed. An excellent early study is Louis Baillet, "Les miniatures du *Scivias* de Sainte Hildegarde conservé à la bibliothèque de Wiesbaden," *Mémoires publiés par l'Academie des Inscriptions et Belles-Lettres* 19 (1911): 49–149.

34. Useful discussions of the egg as a cosmological model are found in Wanda Ciezewski, "The Doctrine of Creation in the First Half of the Twelfth Century: Select Authors (Rupert of Deutz, Honorius Augustodunensis, Peter Abelard, and Hugh of St. Victor)," (PhD thesis, University of Toronto, 1983), and Peter Dronke, "Fables of the Cosmic Egg," with an appendix, in his *Fabula—Explorations into the Uses of Myth in Medieval Platonism* (Leiden: E.J. Brill, 1974), 78–89, 154–66. Andrew Hicks, *Composing the World: Harmony in the Medieval Platonic Universe* (Oxford: Oxford Univ. Press, 2017), offers a detailed study of the ways in which

But in the process of designing her version of the egg, Hildegard created something new, quite different from any other such schemata: she added to the designs and vibrant colors unique features that relate to her theology and to her interpretation of the liturgy. This is a cosmography created by a liturgical commentator. It was meant to instruct members of her community in the ways in which the sacraments they knew reflected the workings of the universe. The planets line up here as they would in a common cosmography from the early twelfth century: Earth, Moon, and then Mercury and Venus, followed by the Sun, Mars, Jupiter, and Saturn. Hildegard does not address this feature specifically in her explanations, although she does name Sun, Moon, and Earth—for her the entire structure was an allegory.

In Hildegard's model, the cosmic empyrean is a ring of fire and within it is the Sun, which she calls "a globe of sparkling flame, so great that the whole instrument is illuminated by it," noting "every creature is illumined by the brightness of this light." Also within the ring of flaming brightness are three "torches," representing the Trinity, "arranged in such a way that by their fire they hold up the globe lest it fall." In a cosmographical map, these four would be the Sun, Mars, Jupiter, and Saturn, but here they have become representative of the Son and of the Trinity, three and one. Hildegard says this arrangement shows that the Son of God, "leaving the angels in the heavenly places, descended to earth, and showed humans . . . heavenly things." The Sun rises and falls, and this is because the Son became gloriously incarnate in the Blessed Virgin, and so through this brought forth celestial mysteries, but it falls too, because he incurred many miseries and sustained great anguish before he returned to the father. The "rising and falling" of the source of light and life is one with the heavenly and earthly existence of Christ. The arrangement of the cosmos is a testament to this fundamental relationship in Hildegard's view.[35]

Hildegard's cosmographical map includes a wind chart, but an idiosyncratic one. Each of the four tripartite windheads stirs one of the particular

---

the Platonists of the twelfth century designed a cosmos that was dependent upon musical understanding. Hildegard produced a musical hermeneutic that was quite different from, although related to, the work of the Platonists.

35. For quotations taken from Hildegard's initial description of the cosmos, see *Scivias* I. iii. pref., 40–105, 40–41/93–94. In subsequent chapters, there is exegesis on each of the elements comprising the cosmos.

zones. These too can be located on the map, and Hildegard provided greater detail in her exegetical allegories. The fiery zone issues a blast with whirlwinds, which "shows the truth rushes forth and spreads with words of justice" (*Scivias* I.iii.8, 96). Beneath this fiery zone, however, is another set of "whirlwinds that diffuse themselves hither and thither throughout the instrument . . . spreading dishonor and most evil utterances" (I.iii.9, 96). Here there is dark fire, "whose force shakes the whole zone . . . full of thunder, tempest, and exceedingly sharp stones . . ." (I.iii.10, 96). This is the realm of Satan, the fallen angel, and his minions, and he himself excretes the piles of vices, which are the sharp stones found in this zone. Beneath these two is a zone of "purest ether." "In it you see a globe of white fire of great magnitude," and this is "a true symbol of the unconquered Church" (I.iii.11, 96). Over it are two little torches, the two testaments given from heaven. These "connect it to the divine rules of the celestial mysteries" and keep the Moon in check (I.iii.11, 96–97). In the aether too are many "bright spheres, into which the white globe pours itself out and emits its brightness." To do this, the white globe "moves back under the globe of red fire and renews its flames from it, and then sends them out into those spheres" (for these two lines with their exegesis, see I.iii.12, 97). The third wind makes "a strong tradition of true and perfect statements" (ibid.). "Beneath that ether you see watery air with a white zone beneath it, which diffuses itself here and there and imparts moisture to the whole instrument . . . when this zone suddenly contracts it sends forth rain with great noise . . . sometimes it contracts gently" (these words exist twice, once in the preface and then again in I.iii.14).

Hildegard relates this action in the cosmos to the sacrament of baptism, which is sometimes quickly inspired and sometimes moves with sweet moderation. The waters of baptism, which surround the Earth, are stirred by the fourth wind and its whirlwinds. They blow here and send news forth, since after baptism a true report goes forth and pervades the whole world with its manifest blessedness (I.iii.15, 280–89, 48/98). As can be seen from the cosmic map, a deliberate balance between the windheads exists, with one in each corner as it were: the eastern-most is just below the Moon; the southern windhead stirs the fiery outer shell; the northern windhead blows out violence in the dark zone; and the western winds blow through the lower layer of aether, which contains the Moon, the stars, Mercury, and Venus.

In her exegesis on the motions of the various elements that constitute the cosmos, Hildegard describes baptism in ways that resemble the squeezing out of souls that have been regenerated and purified by the waters surrounding the Earth. The many actions of preaching are allegorized in all of the windheads, three for good and one for ill. The most dramatic cosmic action is that expressed in the relationship between Sun and Moon, allegorized as Christ and the church (see Fig. 2). The white globe moves beneath the Sun, receives light from it, and then sends this light out, transmitting its powers. Both the Moon and the two testaments

are found in the pure aether that surrounds the Earth and is distinct from it, and relate the church represented by the Moon to the divine mysteries found in the two testaments, represented by Venus and Mercury. This pure aether, which bathes the Moon and sustains its relationship to the Sun and to the planets Venus and Mercury, shines with a pure and innocent faith (I.iii.11, 46/96):

therefore, it [the Moon] moves back under the globe of red fire and renews its flames from it, and then again sends them out into the spheres; for moving in contrition back under the protection of the Only-Begotten of God, and receiving from Him the pardon of divine consolation, it again shows the love of heavenly things in blessed works. (I.iii.12, 248–51, 46/97)

Figure 2. Detail of the Cosmic Egg. From the copy made by the nuns of Eibingen of Wiesbaden, Hochschul- und Landesbibliothek, Hs 1, fol. 14r; this detail courtesy of the Abbey of St. Hildegard, Eibingen.

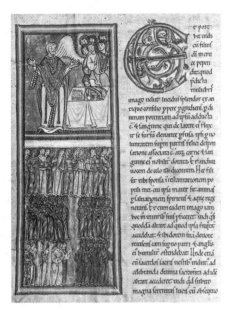

Figure 3. *Scivias* II.vi: The Sacrament
of the Altar, Wiesbaden, Hochschul- und
Landesbibliothek, Hs 1, fol. 86r (manuscript
has been missing since 1945); black and
white photo, courtesy of the Abbey of
St. Hildegard, Eibingen.

The mystery-filled irradiation of the aether bathing the Moon/church
and the Venus/Mercury Scriptures relates to the actions of the altar described by Hildegard in another part of the treatise (II.6), the painting for
which is given here as Figure 3, in a black-and-white photo. The basic
action is cosmic: just as the Moon receives light from the Sun and then,
in Hildegard's cosmology, sends this light out to form the stars, so the
elements of the eucharistic sacrifice are instantly radiated from on high
during the Mass liturgy and then given to the people to be transformed
through their faithful consumption of them (II.vi.pref). From this general
understanding of cosmic action as reflected in the liturgical events of the
altar comes a more specific exploration of the Eucharist. Five aspects of
this liturgical commentary are tied to the discussion of the action of the
cosmos earlier in the treatise, relating the macrocosm of the universe to
the microcosm of the altar.

1. When a priest "clad in sacred vestments" and served by a figure of the
   church approaches the altar, a heavenly light is brought so it "completely illumines the plan of sanctification." This "calm light shines
   around the altar until the sacred rite is ended and the priest has with-
   drawn from it" (II.vi.pref., 206–14, 230/237–38). The church here is
   proclaimed to be the spouse of the crucified redeemer. The relationship

is complex, for she is both consecrated by him and is engaged in offering him on the altar of salvation. The banner running along the right side of the painting reads: "This woman is a spouse for you, my son, in restoring of my people for whom she is a mother, regenerating souls through the saving powers of the spirit and the water."[36]

2. This general illumination is not the only irradiation, for the moment of consecration calls down light too, but a more intense light. Hildegard says: "And when the Gospel of peace has been recited and the offering to be consecrated has been placed upon the altar . . . holy, holy, holy begins the mystery of the sacred rites . . . and heaven is suddenly opened and a fiery and inestimable brilliance descends over that offering . . . and irradiates it completely with light, as the sun illumines anything its rays shine through" (II.vi.pref., 212–33, 230/237).

3. This offering and the heat and light of the moment are meant to remind that perpetually, "in the secret places of heaven, are seen the sufferings of the Only-Begotten." The oblation is united to the son in ardent heat in a profoundly miraculous way and "becomes most truly His body and blood. And thence the Church is quickened with blessed strength" (II.vi.pref., 226–29, 230–31/237).

4. The illumination bears the oblation on high and makes it flesh and blood. "*For thus illuminating it [the elements], as was said, the brilliance invisibly bears it on high into the secret places of heaven*; for that fiery brilliance, which streams through and illumines the sacrament, and bears it upward with invisible power to those places mortal eye cannot see. *And then replaces it on the altar . . .* as a person draws in a breath and lets it out again" (II.vi.12, 555–65, 241/244).[37]

5. The taking in of the irradiated elements by communicants makes them glow with this living light and offers the potential for sanctity. The bread is pure, made from virginal flesh without human seed, and rises like a great branch with many shoots from which is built the heavenly Jerusalem. This body and blood "must be worshipped in the Church in

---

36. Haec sit tibi, Fili, sponsa in restaurationem / populi mei cui ipsa mater sit, animas / per salvationem Spiritus et aquae / regenerans.

37. As here, when the text of the vision was quoted later in Hildegard's exegesis of the vision, the vision text was placed in italics.

a true service, until the last person to be saved by the mystery appears at the end of the world" (II.vi.24, 979–80, 254/252).

The way in which the Moon moves beneath the Sun in Hildegard's cosmographical plan is directly mirrored in the way the heavenly light irradiates the elements on the altar and transforms them. This transformation is incarnational, an action that makes something living on the altar of sacrifice. In this work, the church, gendered female in Hildegard's depiction, serves at the altar, catching the blood from the side of Christ as she is also anointed by it and presenting the elements as her dowry, which makes salvation possible as the mysteries of Christ's action are revealed, as can be seen here in the painting. These mysteries shine brightly in the sacrament of the altar and remind the knowing viewer that in Hildegard's description of the cosmos, the two torches in the aether, the Old and New Testaments, connect the church, the Moon, to the celestial mysteries.

Yet another parallel between the cosmic action of Sun and Moon and stars is found in the ways that the heavenly light of the elements can be consumed by humans who partake of them correctly. Likewise, the irradiated Moon transfers (pours out) light to the stars, which are replicas of the saints. There is a transferal of energy in the cosmos as Hildegard understood it, from Sun to Moon to stars, that is like the action of the altar, with irradiated and transformed elements being distributed to those who receive rightly. The transformed people are in turn light-filled gems to ornament the walls of the heavenly Jerusalem, which is the church. Hildegard says: "let there be no doubt about this most sacred flesh; for He Who formed the first man neither from flesh nor from bone is certainly able to produce sacrament in this way. Therefore, O virginal Origin, you arise, grow, spread out and produce a great branch with many shoots from which to build the Heavenly Jerusalem" (II.vi.24, 969–73, 253/252).

Hildegard uses her cosmology and its theological meanings in many of her writings, including her letters. But for our purposes as students of the liturgy, we must understand this interlocking set of themes if we are to better comprehend the music Hildegard created for the Mass.[38]

---

38. The two major sources for Hildegard's chants are both found in facsimile editions: Hildegard von Bingen, *Lieder: Faksimile Riesencodex*, also available online at http://www.hs-rm.de/de/service/hochschul-und-landesbibliothek/suchen-finden /sondersammlungen/the-wiesbaden-giant-codex/; *Symphonia harmoniae caelestium*

Most of Hildegard's chants were written for the Divine Office, but she did write a significant body of Mass music as well, her eight sequences.[39] Sequences are long chants, sung before the reading of the gospel at Mass and related to the meanings of particular feasts, seasons, categories of saints, and individual saints,[40] in Hildegard's case for the Virgin Mary, for the Holy Spirit, and for the saints Disibod, Rupert, Eucharius, Maximinus, Mathias, and Ursula. As a form, sequences are through composed, with new music for each poetic unit. In all of these chants, to one degree or

---

revelationum: Dendermonde, St.-Pieters & Paulusabdij, ms. Cod. 9, introduction by Peter van Poucke (Peer [Belgium]: Alamire, 1991). The music of both manuscripts has been transcribed and made available on the CANTUS database: a transcription generally following the Riesencodex is *Lieder: Hildegard von Bingen; nach den Handschriften*, ed. Pudentiana Barth, M. Immaculata Ritscher, and Joseph Schmidt-Görg (Salzburg: O. Müller Verlag, 1969). The texts of Hildegard's chants are edited by Barbara Newman in *Hildegardis Bingensis Opera minora*, ed. Peter Dronke, Christopher P. Evans, Hugh Feiss, Beverly Mayne Kienzle, Carolyn A. Muessig, and Barbara Newman, Corpus Christianorum, Continuatio Medievalis 226 (Turnhout: Brepols, 2007), 337–477. For the chant texts translated into English, see Barbara Newman, ed. and trans., *Symphonia*, 2nd ed. (Ithaca, NY: Cornell Univ. Press, 1998); this edition also includes valuable commentary on the texts and an essay by Marianne Richert Pfau on Hildegard's antiphons (74–94).

39. Hildegard's sequences have been selectively studied. See for example, Hildegard von Bingen, *Lieder. Faksimile Riesencodex (Hs. 2) der Hessischen Landesbibliothek Wiesbaden fol. 466–481v*, ed. Lorenz Welker, commentary by Michael Klaper (Wiesbaden: Ludwig Reichert Verlag, 1998); Margot Fassler, "Volmar, Hildegard, and St. Matthias," in *Medieval Music in Practice, Studies in Honor of Richard Crocker*, ed. Judith A. Peraino, Miscellanea 7 (Middleton, WI and Münster: American Institute of Musicology, 2013), 85–109; and Jennifer Bain, "Hildegard of Bingen, 'O Jerusalem aurea civitas' (ca. 1150–1170)," in *Analytical Essays on Music by Women Composers: Secular and Sacred Music to 1900*, ed. Laurel Parsons and Brenda Ravenscroft (New York, NY: Oxford Univ, Press, 2018), 11–46.

40. Margot Fassler, *Gothic Song: Victorine Sequences and Augustinian Reform in Twelfth-Century Paris*, 2nd ed. (Notre Dame, IN: Univ. of Notre Dame Press, 2011), reviews the scholarship on the later sequence in the decades since the first edition of this book in 1993. Other overviews are found in Lori Kruckenberg and Andreas Haug, eds., *The Sequences of Nidaros: A Nordic Repertory and Its European Context* (Trondheim: Tapir Academic Press, 2006); my textbook, Margot Fassler, *Music in the Medieval West* (New York, NY: W.W. Norton, 2014) and its accompanying *Anthology*; and Lori Kruckenberg, "Sequence," in *The Cambridge History of Medieval Music*, ed. Mark Everest and Thomas Forrest Kelly, vol. 1 (Cambridge: Cambridge Univ. Press, 2018), 300–56.

another, Hildegard incorporates both her understanding of the cosmos and her exegesis on the eucharistic meal, which would take place later in the liturgy, after the singing of the work. Three very different types of exegetical themes are encountered in the works, and in this overview I take each of them in turn, from the simpler to the more complex.

Many of the subjects chosen for Hildegard's sequences are priests or proto-priests, and Hildegard used the genre to offer a sung commentary on the liturgy, rendered as praise in anticipation of communion to come. One such work is that for Saint Maximinus, a patron saint of nearby Trier.[41] The ideal of the church as heavenly Jerusalem shining with gems that are the saints is basic to this poem; so too are the allusions to the priestly actions of the Old Testament. Maximinus in the first strophe is *lucidus*, shining, as the Holy Spirit in the form of a dove observes him, in language from the Song of Songs. The heat of the Sun then makes him a gem for the glistening wall of the heavenly Jerusalem. The priestly saint is seen both as a stone in the church in heaven and as an architect for its building through his actions at the altar. He stands in the shimmer of the altar, which is present in the heavenly light that bathes it as the Sun bathes the Moon, and then leads the people through intercession to the mirror of light they seek, which is Christ. The actions of the altar are contextualized through Hildegard's writings both about the cosmos and about the sacrament of Eucharist in this work, and other priestly subjects are also found offering at the altar of praise and sacrifice in this group of chants.

Quite different in nature, however, is the sequence Hildegard penned for the Holy Spirit: "O ignis Spiritus Paracliti."[42] In this sequence, the poet makes a strong connection between the winds that stream through the natural world and the power of the spirit to flow, wind-like, through all living creatures and make them part of a single thing:

Strophe 4a: O mighty course that penetrated all, in the heights, upon the earth, and in all abysses: you bind and gather all people together.

Strophe 4b: From you clouds overflow, winds take wing, stones store up moisture, waters well forth in streams and earth swells with living green.[43]

41. Newman, *Symphonia*, 212–15, and commentary, 302–3.
42. Ibid., 148–51, and commentary, 281–82.
43. O iter fortissimum, quod penetravit omnia in altissimis et in terrenis et in omnibus abyssis, tu omnes componis et colligis. This text is sung during the part of our digital model of the cosmos that depicts the days of creation.

In the opening of this sequence, Hildegard invokes the Sanctus of the Mass, the chant that prefaces the irradiation of the elements in her Mass commentary found in *Scivias*. Of the fire of the Spirit she says: "Holy are you giving life to the forms, Holy are you anointing the dangerously broken, Holy are you cleansing the fetid wounds."[44] Most important here is the life the fire gives to the forms about to be transformed, in this case a probable allusion to the elements of bread and wine on the altar.[45]

Hildegard's sequence for the Virgin Mary, "O virga ac diadema," is also concerned with the power of the church to heal and transform. Mary comes as a new dawn, bearing the sun of Christ. "From your womb oh dawn has come forth a new sun . . . the woman who bore the new light . . . gathers the members of the son," as church, "into heavenly harmony."[46] The action of the personified church at the altar is more dramatically described in the sequence "O ecclesia," for the martyr Saint Ursula, who was killed as a result of refusing sexual favors to her pagan captors and who, Hildegard proclaims at the opening of the sequence, is a model of the church. She says of Ursula, in imagery from the Song of Songs but related to the sacraments:

> O Church, your eyes are like sapphire,
> and your ears like Mount Bethel,
> your nose is like a mountain of myrrh and incense,
> your mouth the sound of many waters.[47]

When the martyr Ursula is slaughtered by her pagan captives, the whole cosmos resounds:

> 8. And all the elements heard this with a loud cry
>   and they shouted before the throne of God:
> 9. "Wach, the red of the Lamb's innocent blood has flowed at this
>   betrothal."[48]

44. Newman, *Symphonia*, 151.
45. Ibid.,148–49.
46. Ibid., 128–29, strophe 6a and 6b: "Sed, o aurora, de ventre tuo novus sol processit . . . unde, o salvatrix, que novum lumen humano generi protulisti: collige membra Filii tui ad celestem armoniam."
47. Ibid., 238–39, strophe 1.
48. The Latin reads, "Wach! rubicundus sanguis innocentis agni in desponsatione sua effusus est."

10. May all the heavens hear, may they praise the Lamb of God in highest
      harmony,
   because the ancient serpent's throat has been choked with this necklace
      of pearls
   made of the material of the Word of God.[49]

The church runs red with the blood of martyrs, who are joined with the
blood of Christ on the altar. Those who take communion join with him
and with his saints as the elements are vivified—wine is blood, bread
is flesh. Ecclesia serves the altar; Ursula lies upon it—the imagery is
clearly wedded to Hildegard's description of the cosmos and the Eucharist in *Scivias*.

The penitent sinner who receives communion rightly completes the
action of the sacrament and its purpose; accordingly the building of the
church, which is the body of Christ, is slowly constructed by those who
receive, and the completion of the epic journey of humankind and individuals who chose to move toward redemption is initiated and sustained by
the action of the altar. Those who knew the treatise and the illuminations
and sang the chants could contemplate this commentary in its several
voices within the imagination and might bring it to every Eucharist. Effective liturgical commentary instructs; it offers understanding for the
intellect. But it can also offer multi-sensual ways of experiencing the
inner meanings of things—the unguent in the bread, the sapphire in the
wine, the rising of the Moon, the daily cyclical motions of the Earth—and
make them part of one magnificent rhythm of action. This role is particularly significant for commentary on the Eucharist, where the outer
elements of bread and wine can symbolize a great number of meanings
beneath the veil of materiality, revealing a mystery that can be known
and cannot be known.

Hildegard's sequences are replicas of light-filled praise of saints and
angels, constructed from melodies that Hildegard heard without words,
recalled, and later set to words for singing in church. They are not made
like any other known songs of this genre, although they loosely follow its
form. The poetry does not rhyme like a twelfth-century sequence would,
but it also has not been set up like a Notkerian sequence, in that the repetitions built into the paired half strophes are not exact. In every example,
Hildegard proclaims the radiant character of the music, a radiance from

---

49. Newman, *Symphonia*, 242–43, strophes 8–10.

the heavenly realms that exists in a musical parallel with the shimmer of the altar and that is contextualized variously through Hildegard's exegesis on the cosmos.

In conclusion, Hildegard's liturgical commentary *Scivias* explicates sacramental action, relating it not only to the interaction of human beings on earth but also to the very workings of the cosmos. The actions of people within the church, in baptism, and at the altar achieve a dramatic importance related to communal celebration and to the individual lives of believers.

CHAPTER NINE

Cum angelis et archangelis

Singing a Sacramental Cosmology in the Medieval Christian West

M. Jennifer Bloxam

Full of Your Glory: Liturgy, Cosmos, Creation.[1] The pithy title of this essay collection, though experienced initially as silent words on a page, resounds with unheard music, conjuring the music of the spheres with the word "cosmos" and the angelic choir with the phrase so familiar from the Sanctus, "Heaven and earth are *full of Your glory.*" These combined resonances encapsulate the idea of cosmic music that has been at the heart of humankind's efforts to understand and honor the mysteries of God's creation since well before the birth of Christ. How did people from long ago upon contemplating the heavens conceptualize and attempt to realize its song? What continuities and contrasts emerge over time, from the ancient Greek to the medieval Christian world? This essay engages these large questions by traversing a small sampling of music inspired by the idea of "cosmos" and, in particular, "full of Your glory." A consideration of the audible sounds of the cosmos recently captured by NASA scientists begins my exploration.

1. I am grateful to Teresa Berger, Melanie Ross, and Bryan Spinks for inviting me to contribute to the 2018 Yale Liturgy Conference from which this essay collection stems, and to Jessie Ann Owens for providing invaluable suggestions for improvement. My title pays serendipitous homage to Bryan, whose classic study *The Sanctus in the Eucharistic Prayer* (Cambridge: Cambridge Univ. Press, 1991) inspired my topic; I discovered only after deciding on my title that the dissertation on which he based this book was entitled "With Angels and Archangels: The Background, Form, and Function of the Sanctus in the Eucharistic Prayer"!

From Space Probe to Pythagoras

On 5 September 1977, NASA launched the Voyager 1 space probe from Cape Canaveral. Three years later, after completing flybys of Jupiter and Saturn, Voyager escaped our solar system, and it is now over 13 billion miles from the sun, in interstellar space. Among the scientific instruments it carries are two plasma wave antennae that collect data on the electromagnetic vibrations occurring in the ionized gas, or plasma, of space. No human ear can hear these plasma waves in space because there is no air to transmit them. Nonetheless, as explained by Don Burnett, the University of Iowa astrophysicist and principal investigator for the Plasma Wave Science instrument on Voyager since its launch, because these occur at frequencies that humans can detect, "we can play the data through a loudspeaker and listen. The pitch and frequency tell us about the density of gas surrounding the spacecraft."[2]

When Voyager 1 was inside our sun's vast magnetic bubble, known as the heliosphere, the tones were low, around 300 hertz (a pitch slightly higher than the D above middle C), typical of plasma waves coursing through the rarified solar wind. But beginning in August 2012, when the space probe was about 12 billion miles from the sun, the frequency began to climb to a higher pitch, between two and three kilohertz (pitches roughly between C and G three octaves above middle C), indicating that the probe had entered the denser gas in the interstellar medium. This can be observed in a spectrogram animation, created from raw uncompressed audio, which shows the change in the spectrum of sounds as a function of time by compressing 225 days (from early October 2012 into May 2013) of audio frequency data into just twelve seconds.[3] Simply put, the farther Voyager 1 travelled away from our solar system, the higher the frequency of the plasma waves it encountered.

This, then, is the current empirical evidence for the sounds of the cosmos. They seem at first quite far removed (light years away!) from the mathematically ordered and musically harmonious universe theorized

2. Tony Phillips, "The Sounds of Interstellar Space," *NASA Science: Share the Science*, 1 November 2013, https://science.nasa.gov/science-news/science-at-nasa/2013/01nov_ismsounds.

3. Radio and Plasma Wave Group, Department of Physics & Astronomy, College of Liberal Arts & Sciences, "Voyager-1 PWS: electron plasma oscillations beyond the heliopause," The University of Iowa, 2013, http://www-pw.physics.uiowa.edu/voyager/v1pws_interstellar_epo.html.

as the *musica mundana* or "music of the spheres" some five centuries before the birth of Christ by the Pythagoreans, back to whom etymologists trace the very word "kosmos" (κόσμος).[4] But just as the Voyager scientists' quest to understand the universe depends on the analysis of quantifiable data (that is, numbers) expressed as frequency (that is, pitch), so too did the ancient Greek philosophers' efforts to grasp creation's mystery rely on number and pitch. They postulated harmonious relationships among the celestial bodies according to their proportionate speed of revolution and distance from the earth, which they understood to be the center of the universe, and expressed these relationships using the numerical proportions that produce the most pleasing musical harmonies, ratios whose discovery was attributed to Pythagoras himself. Thus each heavenly body was understood to produce a distinctive sound in its revolution, and these sounds combined to generate a musical scale whose underlying structure rested on the fundamental frequency ratios of the most consonant intervals: the *diapason* or octave (2:1), the *diapente* or perfect fifth (3:2), and the *tetrachord* or perfect fourth (4:3).[5] In the fourth century BCE, Aristotle summarized the Pythagorean worldview with the observation that "they saw that the attributes and the ratios of the musical scales were expressible in numbers; since, then, all other things seemed in their whole nature to be modelled after numbers, and numbers seemed to be the first things in the whole of nature, they supposed the elements of numbers to be the elements of all things, and the whole heaven to be a musical scale and a number."[6]

Over the past two millennia there have been as many cosmic scales proposed as there have been philosophers inclined to imagine them, but the scale described by Pliny the Elder in the first century CE as that conceived by Pythagoras himself captures the essentials of the planetary

---

4. "cosmos, n.1," OED Online, December 2018, Oxford Univ. Press, http://www.oed.com/view/Entry/42270?isAdvanced=false&result=2&rskey=pEJrC1&.

5. Before the development of wave theory in the eighteenth century, monochord string lengths provided a means of discovering wavelength ratios; thus the octave, in which the frequency of the upper note is twice that of the lower note, can be realized by plucking the taut string and then stopping it at half its length to sound the octave above.

6. Aristotle, *Metaphysics* 1.5, trans. William David Ross, in *The Complete Works of Aristotle: The Revised Oxford Translation*, ed. Jonathan Barnes, Bollingen Series 71 (Princeton, NJ: Princeton Univ. Press, 1984), vol. 2, 1559.

scale concept (see Fig. 1).[7] The earth, as the center, emits the lowest tone, and those celestial bodies in orbit around it rise in pitch as their distance from earth grows, with the fixed stars producing the highest tone. Fundamental ratios knit this cosmic fabric together: conjunct perfect fifths join earth to sun and sun to stars, and the moon is connected to stars by an octave formed of two disjunct perfect fourths. The basic premise of the ancients' notion regarding the general trajectory of the planetary scales, which ascend in pitch toward the stars, thus accords with what Voyager's plasma antennae revealed about the rising frequency of plasma waves as an object travels from our solar system into interstellar space.

The Early Sanctus Imagined and Expressed

Early Christian theologians inherited and profoundly transformed the ancient Greek musical cosmology by wedding it to the Judaic musical cosmology of the Old Testament. One of the earliest Christians to unite these worldviews was the fourth-century Cappadocian bishop Saint Gregory of Nyssa (ca. 335–ca. 395). In his treatise *On the Inscriptions of the Psalms*, written around 375 CE, he connects the Pythagorean concept of cosmic harmony to the cosmic liturgy articulated in the psalms, the bedrock of Christian liturgy on earth. Gregory writes:

> I once heard a wise man expound a theory about our nature. He said that man is a miniature cosmos and contains all the elements of the great cosmos. And the orderly arrangement of the universe, he said, is a diverse and variegated musical harmony which has been tuned in relation to itself . . . It is this tune which the mind hears without the use of our sense of hearing. It listens to the singing of the heavens by transcending and being above the faculties of sense-perception that belong to our flesh. This, it seems to me, is also how the great David was listening when he heard the heavens describing the glory of the God who effects these things in them by observing their systematic and all-wise movement. For the concord of

7. On planetary scales, see Joscelyn Godwin, *Harmonies of Heaven and Earth: The Spiritual Dimension of Music from Antiquity to the Avant-Garde* (Rochester, VT: Inner Traditions International, 1987), 124–93; on Pliny's scale and others like it, see 125–26. See also *The Harmony of the Spheres: A Sourcebook of the Pythagorean Tradition in Music*, ed. Joscelyn Godwin (Rochester, VT: Inner Traditions International, 1993), 7–8.

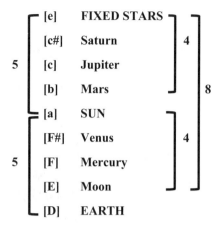

Figure 1. Planetary Scale of Pliny the Elder (23–79 CE). After Gabriela Ilnitchi, "*Musica mundana*, Aristotelian Natural Philosophy, and Ptolemaic Astronomy," *Early Music History* 21 (2002): 57.

all creation with itself . . . is truly a hymn of the glory of the inaccessible and inexpressible God.[8]

Gregory later elaborates a complementary vision of celestial music indebted to the Judaic cosmology rooted in the psalms themselves. In his gloss on Psalm 150:5 ("Praise him on high-sounding cymbals, praise him on cymbals of jubilation"), Gregory imagines redeemed humanity joining with the angelic choir to make music in God's praise. The psalmist's focus on the cymbals inspires the bishop-saint, who writes:

> I take this to mean the union of our nature with the angels, because he says "Praise the Lord with euphonious cymbals." For such a combination, I mean of the angelic with the human, when human nature is again exalted to its original condition, will produce that sweet sound of thanksgiving through their meeting with one another . . . For the coming together of cymbal with cymbal shows this. The supernatural nature of the angels is one cymbal; the rational creation consisting of mankind is the other. But sin separated the one from the other. Whenever, then, the mercy of God again unites the two with one another, then what comes about from the two with one another will cause that praise to resound.[9]

8. Ronald E. Heine, *Gregory of Nyssa's Treatise on the Inscriptions of the Psalms: Introduction, Translation, and Notes* (Oxford: Clarendon Press, 1995), 88–89.

9. Ibid., 121.

Gregory's vision of the angelic hosts and humankind uniting, like cymbals, to create music in praise of God resonates powerfully with the final segment of the ancient preface prayers at the beginning of the eucharistic liturgy of the Mass. These prayers invoke the angelic choir and join our voices with theirs, employing formulations such as "And therefore, with angels and archangels, with thrones and dominions, and with the whole host of the heavenly army, we sing the hymn of your glory endlessly, saying . . ."

The "hymn of your Glory" prepared by the preface prayer is of course the Sanctus, whose text begins with an adaptation of Isaiah's vision of the seraphim's jubilant cry before the throne of God (Isa 6:1-3) and concludes with an adaptation of Matthew's account of the people's praise as Christ enters Jerusalem (Matt 21:9). Bryan Spinks traces the use of Isaiah's text within the anaphora back to Christian communities in third-century East Syria and charts the inclusion of the Benedictus some centuries later.[10] How, then, did these early Christians capture the sound of heaven and earth united in song, anticipating Christ's Real Presence in the Eucharist?

We can only speculate. Musical notation in the West did not develop until the eighth century, and no melodies for the Sanctus were written down until the tenth century. We must therefore extrapolate backwards from later sources. Two trailblazing scholars of Christian chant, Michel Huglo and Kenneth Levy, considered one of the strongest candidates for inclusion in the earliest layer of Sanctus melodies to be the Greek *Agyos*, preserved in tenth- and eleventh-century sources from Aquitaine and Italy but likely originating many centuries earlier.[11] The first three lines, through the end of the Pleni segment, exemplify its ancient recitational style, characterized by a narrow range and a repetitive, formulaic quality (see Example 1).[12]

---

10. Spinks, *The Sanctus in the Eucharistic Prayer*, 57–61 (on the East Syrian anaphora) and 120–21 (on the Benedictus). Details of the entrance of the *Sanctus* into Christian worship continue to be debated. Maxwell E. Johnson offers a succinct overview in his "Recent Research on the Anaphoral *Sanctus*: An Update and Hypothesis," in *Issues in Eucharistic Praying in East and West: Essays in Liturgical and Theological Analysis*, ed. Maxwell E. Johnson (Collegeville, MN: Liturgical Press, 2010), 161–88.

11. Transcription from Kenneth Levy, "The Byzantine Sanctus and its Modal Tradition in East and West," *Annales musicologiques, Moyen-âge et renaissance* 6 (1958–62), 11. See also David Hiley's discussion of the oldest Sanctus melodies in *Western Plainchant: A Handbook* (Oxford: Clarendon Press, 1993), 161–62, which also includes a transcription of the Greek *Agyos* on 163.

12. The musical structure can be clearly heard on a recording by Schola Hungarica, directed by Lázló Dobszay and Janka Szendrei, entitled "Ravenna the City

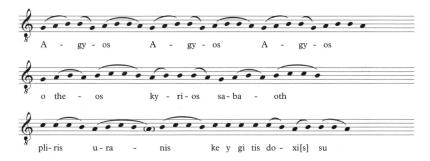

Example 1. The Greek *Agyos*, opening phrases

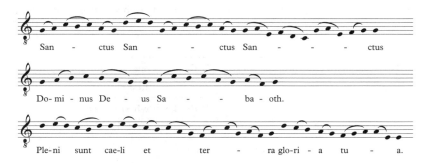

Example 2. Sanctus VII from Mass VII (*Kyrie Rex splendens*), opening phrases transcribed from the *Liber usualis*

This simple version opens a sonic window back to the early centuries of the faith, when the Sanctus was a communal song; it captures a sense of saying rather than singing, in agreement with the verb *dicentes*, used at the close of most preface prayers, rather than *clamantes*, found in some. However, most Sanctus melodies from later centuries are longer and more ornate, with wider ranges and melismatic flourishes, suggesting performance by trained choir singers. Sanctus VII from Mass VII in the *Liber usualis* (*Kyrie Rex splendens*), is typical: this eleventh-century melody spans a range of a tenth and boasts melismas stretching to as many as twelve notes (see Example 2).[13]

---

of Mosaics: Liturgical Chant" (Hungaroton Records Ltd., 2001).

13. This melody, sung by Matthew J. Curtis, can be heard at AntoineDanielMass, "Sanctus VII from Mass VII, Gregorian Chant," 30 December 2009, https://www .youtube.com/watch?v=374R_mQJ8GU.

Sounding Angel Voices in the Medieval Sanctus

Beginning in the eleventh century, two new creative approaches to embellishing liturgical music further magnified the length, complexity, and dramatic nature of the Sanctus: tropes and polyphony. Sanctus tropes are lines of newly composed text and melody interpolated into an existing plainsong; many of these insertions dwell on the singing of the angelic choir, palpably evoking their voices. Loud verbs abound: to clang, proclaim, chant, sing psalms, resound, harmonize, cry out, sing (*clangere, proclamare, decantare, psallere, resonare, concinere, clamare, cantare*). An eleventh-century troped Sanctus from Italy, for example, incorporates phrases that conjure a noisy dramatic scene set in cosmic and Biblical time (the first section referencing Isaiah's vision, the second Christ's entry into Jerusalem):

Sanctus, Quem Cherubin atque Seraphin incessanter proclamant:	*Holy* is the one whom the Cherubim and Seraphim continually proclaim:
Sanctus. Qui senas alas habent quotidie decantant:	*Holy.* They who have each six wings, day after day they chant:
Sanctus, Domine Deus Sabaoth. Pater, proles cum flamineo almo qui es ante saecula, nunc et in aevum:	*Holy, Lord God of hosts.* Father, offspring together with the nurturing breath, you who exist before the ages, now and forever:
Pleni sunt caeli et terra gloria tua. Hosanna in excelsis. Cui pueri Hebraeorum obviantes clamabant:	*Heaven and earth are full of your glory.* *Hosanna in the highest.* Running to meet you, the children of the Hebrews cry out:
Benedictus qui venit in nomine Domini. Ex plebs Hebraea, vociferantes, vaticinantes dicebant:	*Blessed is he who comes in the name of the Lord.* And the Hebrew people, shouting out and prophesying, said:
Hosanna in excelsis.	*Hosanna in the highest.*[14]

14. Adapted from Gunilla Iversen, *Laus angelica: Poetry in the Medieval Mass*, ed. Jane Flynn, trans. William Flynn, Medieval Church Studies 5 (Turnhout: Brepols, 2010), 203–5; the text is found in Pistoia, Biblioteca Capitolare, MS C 121, f.79r. See also John Boe, ed., *Beneventanum Troporum Corpus II: Ordinary Chants and Tropes for the Mass from Southern Italy, A.D. 1000–1250*, part 3: *Preface Chants*

The qualities of angelic song are sometimes characterized in the long, rhymed trope verses known as *prosulae* that are a special feature of the final Hosanna. Adjectives such as "sweet," "sweet as honey," "melliflu-ous," and "harmonious" are typical, as captured in the opening of three such insertions:

1a. *Hosanna* dulcis et cantica,	1a. *Hosanna* is a sweet canticle,
1b. nimisque laudabilis, organica.	1b. smooth as honey, and laudable beyond measure and harmonious.[15]

1a. *Hosanna* Rex gubernans omnia,	1a. *Hosanna* O King, governing all,
1b. quem virtus uranica laude celebrat organica.	1b. to whom the heavenly power celebrates with harmonious praise.[16]

1a. *Hosanna* dulciflua Deo resonant cuncta.	1a. *Hosanna* sweet as honey, resound to God.
1b. Agmina angelica psallant tibi in astra.	1b. The angelic host sing psalms to you in the stars.[17]

The Pythagorean idea of the harmonious cosmos underlies the heav-enly clangor of the angelic choir conjured in these Sanctus tropes, but it comes most dramatically to the fore in a long poetic insertion to the final Hosanna first found within two French Sanctus chants during the latter half of the eleventh century, one from Moissac Abbey and one from the

---

and Sanctus, Recent Researches in the Music of the Middle Ages and Early Renais-sance 25 (Madison, WI: A-R Editions, 1996), 98–103 (commentary), and vol. 26 (Madison, WI: A-R Editions, 1996), 98–101 (edition).

15. Iversen, *Laus angelica*, 210–11; the text is from Paris, Bibliothèque nationale de France, MS lat. 903, f.178v. See also Charles M. Atkinson, "Text, Music, and the Persistence of Memory in *Dulcis est cantica*," in *Recherches nouvelles sur les tropes liturgiques*, ed. Gunilla Björkvall and Wulf Arlt (Stockholm: Almqvist & Wiksell, 1993), 95–117.

16. Adapted from Iversen, *Laus angelica*, 210–11; the text is found in Paris, Bibliothèque nationale de France, MS lat. 778, ff.214v–215r.

17. Adapted from Iversen, *Laus angelica*, 212–13; the text is from Paris, Biblio-thèque nationale de France, MS lat. 1139, f.74r–v.

abbey of Saint Martial, Limoges.[18] Musicologist Charles Atkinson has
drawn attention to the fact that this trope, *Clangat hodie*, is replete with
musical terms drawn largely from the Pythagorean vocabulary associated
with the music of the cosmos, as shown in boldface below:

Benedictus qui venit in nomine Domini. Hosanna	*Blessed is he who comes in the name of the Lord. Hosanna*
1a. Clangat hodie vox nostra melodum **simphonia**,	1a. May our voices ring out today in a **concord** of melodies,
1b. Instant annua iam quia praeclara sollemnia.	1b. for the brilliant annual feast is now here.
2a. Personet nunc tinnula **harmoniae organa** musicorum chorea!	2a. May the ring of musicians now loudly make the clangorous **instruments of *harmonia***
2b. **Tonorum** quam dulcia alternatim concrepet necne **modulamina**!	2b. and in alternation make resound the **modulations**, so sweet, of the **tones**.
3a. **Diapason** altisona per **vocum discrimina tetracordis** figuratum alta conscendens culmina,	3a. High-sounding at the **octave**, ascending in **tetrachords** through **discrete pitches** to the high summits of its contours,
3b. Sustollat nostra **carmina** ad caeli fastigia, **hymnis** angelicis coherenda patri melodia,	3b. may the **melody** lift our verses to heaven's pinnacles to join the angelic **hymns** for the Father,
4a. Quo nos mereamur ampla capere promissa,	4a. So that we may merit to reach the rich promises,
4b. Sine fruituri meta sanctorum gloria,	4b. to enjoy without end the glory of the saints.
5. Ad quorum collegia pia nos ducant merita.	5. May our good works lead us to their community.
in excelsis.	*in the highest.*[19]

18. The fifteen extant manuscript sources of *Clangat hodie* are listed in Charles
M. Atkinson, "Music and Meaning in *Clangat hodie*," *Revista de Musicologia* 16,
no. 2 (1993): 794.

19. Adapted from ibid., 791.

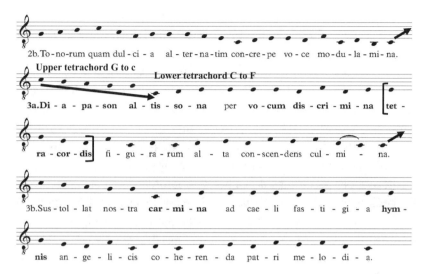

Example 3. The monophonic Sanctus trope *Clangat hodie*, excerpt

Moreover, Atkinson has discerned that the music of one of the two Sanctus melodies associated with this textual trope (the version whose earliest source comes from Limoges) vividly paints the Greek musical terms in sound. For example, in verse 3a, the word *diapason* is introduced with an octave leap up from the close of the previous verse to the topmost range of the chant followed by a quick octave descent, and the melody for lines 3a and 3b is built of two disjunct tetrachords (G-c, C-F) linked appropriately by the four-note figure on the word *tetracordis* (see Example 3).[20]

The Pythagorean notion of cosmic harmony evident in verse 3a then gives way in verse 3b to the Old Testament vision of humankind and angels singing in praise of God the Father. As shown in Example 3, the verb *sustollat* (lift) is here depicted with another octave leap that captures the idea of lifting song to heaven. The unknown poet of this prosula thus offers a musical analog to Gregory of Nyssa's embrace of both cosmologies in his treatise written 800 years earlier.

---

20. For additional analytic details and the larger context for the musical depiction of ancient Greek harmonic theory in *Clangat hodie*, see ibid., 799–806. See also Gunilla Iversen, "The Mirror of Music: Symbol and Reality in the Text of *Clangat hodie*," *Revista de Musicologia* 16/2 (1993), 771–89.

More than a century later, this version of the Hosanna trope *Clangat hodie* served as the basis of a piece of two-part polyphony in a manuscript copied around 1300 for the royal convent of Santa Maria la Real de las Huelgas in the Castilian city of Burgos.[21] As shown in Example 4, the plainsong melody just examined is rhythmicized in the lower voice and a new melodic line placed above it, creating a succession of vertical harmonic intervals.[22] The composer of this upper line uses this vertical dimension to amplify the sonorous cosmic harmony described in the text: when the original chant melody in the lower part leaps up an octave, the new upper part jumps down below it in order to create an octave at the beginning of the word *diapason*. Pure consonances follow, with two perfect fifths followed by a perfect fourth, the word closing on a unison (mm. 20–21). On *altisona* (highest sounding) the added voice extends to the top of its range, as though reaching to the heavens (mm. 22–23). At the beginning of m. 29, the word *tetracordis* closes on a perfect fourth, the only use of this interval in this strong metric position in the entire composition. Musical harmony is here harnessed to sound the perfect intervals of the cosmic harmony theorized by the ancients even as it decorates a composition made to sing Christ's praise during the Mass.

Cosmos and Creation in a Late Medieval Sanctus

This technique of polyphony greatly enriched composers' ability to capture concepts and images in sound, and polyphonic settings of the Sanctus became a special site for such efforts to amplify and elaborate the sacramental heart of the Mass. An especially illustrative final example by the preeminent composer of the fifteenth century, the French priest Guillaume Du Fay, presents a fusion of the concepts of cosmic music and angelic song designed to convey the idea of Christ present on earth.

In the 1460s, Du Fay composed a four-voice setting of the Mass Ordinary intended to celebrate the Annunciation, the *Missa Ecce ancilla*

---

21. Burgos, Monasterio de Las Huelgas, Ms. s/n, "Codex Las Huelgas," ff.15r–16r.

22. A complete modern edition is found in *The Las Huelgas Manuscript: Burgos, Monasterio de Las Huelgas*, ed. Gordon A. Anderson, Corpus Mensurabilis Musicae 79 (Neuhausen-Stuttgart: American Institute of Musicology: Hänssler-Verlag, 1982), vol. 1, 24–25.

Example 4. The polyphonic Sanctus trope *Clangat hodie*, excerpt

Domini/Beata es Maria.[23] He signals his purpose by embedding the melodies and texts of two Annunciation chants in the tenor voice; these are sung simultaneously with the words of the Mass and function essentially as do tropes in plainsong, enriching the surrounding textual and musical content. This is apparent at the outset of the Kyrie, shown in Example 5: the arrow marks the entrance of the tenor, singing the melody and words of the antiphon *Ecce ancilla Domini* ("Behold the handmaid of the Lord, be it done unto me according to Your Word"). Drawn from the close of Luke's Annunciation narrative (Luke 1:38), this is the Virgin's mighty reply to the angel Gabriel: by recognizing

23. For a full discussion of this Mass, see Alejandro Enrique Planchart, *Guillaume Du Fay: The Life and Works*, vol. 2: *The Works* (Cambridge: Cambridge Univ. Press, 2018), 603–10. For a complete modern edition, see Guillaume Du Fay, *Opera omnia 03/06, Missa Ecce ancilla Domini/Beata es Maria*, ed. Alejandro Enrique Planchart (Santa Barbara, CA: Marisol Press, 2011), 1–35, https://www.diamm .ac.uk/resources/music-editions/du-fay-opera-omnia/. A particularly fine recording is that by the Ensemble Gilles Binchois, dir. Dominique Vellard, *Missa Ecce ancilla Domini Proprium de angelis Dei officium: A 15th-century Mass from the Cathedral of Cambrai* (London: Virgin Classics, 1994).

Example 5. Du Fay, *Missa Ecce ancilla Domini/Beata es Maria*, Kyrie opening

and accepting the Word responsible for all creation, Mary with her *fiat* precipitated Christ's incarnation.[24]

24. This understanding is forthrightly declared, for example, in the enormously popular *Legenda aurea* (*Golden Legend*), a collection of saints' lives compiled by the Dominican Jacobus da Voragine in the thirteenth century and copied and printed many times over. In the entry devoted to the Annunciation, Jacobus glosses the phrase *fiat mihi secundun verbum tuum* with the assertion "and in an instant the Son of God was conceived in her womb, perfect God and perfect man" (Jacobus de Voragine, *The Golden Legend: Readings on the Saints*, trans. William Granger Ryan [Princeton: Princeton Univ. Press, 1993], vol. 1, 200). Du Fay himself owned a copy valued at six *livres*, making it the fourth most valuable book in his library of 34 volumes; see Craig Wright, "Dufay at Cambrai: Discoveries and Revisions," *Journal of the American Musicological Society* 28 (1975): 215.

Sanctus (à4) – triple meter
Holy, holy, holy, Lord God of Hosts,
T. *Behold the handmaid of the Lord:*

Pleni (à2) – triple meter
Heaven and earth are full of your glory,

Hosanna I (à4) – triple meter
Hosanna in the highest!
T. *Be it done unto me according to Your Word.*

CONSECRATION - ELEVATION

Benedictus (à2) – duple meter
Blessed is He who comes in the name of the Lord.

Hosanna II (à4) – duple meter
Hosanna in the highest!
T. *Blessed are you, Mary, for you believed that in you would be perfected those things said to you by the Lord. Alleluia.*

Figure 2. Du Fay, *Missa Ecce ancilla Domini/Beata es Maria*, bi-partite Sanctus design

In the Sanctus of his *Missa Ecce ancilla Domini/Beata es Maria*, Du Fay creates a dramatic and complex musical evocation of cosmos and creation by shining a spotlight on the Word that was in the beginning, that made Christ incarnate in the Virgin's womb, and that makes Christ present in the bread and wine. He divides the Sanctus into two musically distinct parts: first, the Sanctus-Pleni-Hosanna I in triple meter and based on the *Ecce ancilla Domini* antiphon, and second, the Benedictus-Hosanna II in duple meter and based on the second antiphon, *Beata es Maria* ("Blessed are you, Mary"). He splits the Sanctus in this way in order to construct a sonic frame for the words of consecration and the Elevation of the Host (see Fig. 2). This organization of the Sanctus into two discrete halves reflects a late medieval practice that allowed the celebrant to begin the silent prayers of the Canon when the choir began to sing a polyphonic Sanctus.[25] The consecration and elevation thus occurred

25. Joseph A. Jungmann, SJ, *The Mass of the Roman Rite: Its Origins and Development (Missarum Sollemnia)*, trans. Francis A. Brunner (New York: Benziger, 1951–55; repr. Notre Dame: Ave Maria Press, 2012), vol. 2, 137. A useful overview

at the close of the first Hosanna, allowing the words of the Benedictus ("Blessed is He who comes in the name of the Lord") to greet Christ present in the Host.[26]

A close examination of Du Fay's compositional strategy in the first half of this musical frame, the Sanctus-Pleni-Hosanna I segment that anticipates the Real Presence, reveals the composer engaged in a dramatic dual exegesis of incarnation and transubstantiation. As seen in Figure 2, Du Fay separates the two clauses of Mary's declaration: her initial exclamation, "Ecce ancilla Domini," combines with the angelic choir for the Sanctus acclamation, but the activating phrase "fiat mihi secundum verbum tuum" is delayed until Hosanna I (the tenor remains silent in the Pleni). As shown in Example 6, the melody and text of the antiphon's *fiat mihi* phrase appear in the tenor at the outset of Hosanna I (the tones of the chant melody are circled; note in particular the four-note motive, g-e-f-g, to which the word *fiat* is set). Something extraordinary happens just six measures into this section—for the first and only time in the entire Mass, Du Fay allows a melodic motive from Mary's musical speech (the stepwise ascent of the chant melody that begins with the word *secundum*) to infuse other voice parts (note the circled notes of the chant melody appearing in the upper voices). The contratenor picks it up first in m. 69, a fifth above the tenor, and the cantus next sounds the motive an octave above the tenor (all perfect consonances). All three voices then climb upward by step; the bass falls away as her reply rises heavenward to reach a momentary cadence at m. 73 (marked by the star). The textual spark for these lovely and very audible details is the generative phrase *secundum verbum tuum* ("according to Your Word"). Mary's voice in the tenor then falls silent as the motive is reversed, cascading down from the top to the lowest register of the bass. Du Fay thus creates a sounding

---

of evidence for this practice is found in Andrew Kirkman, *The Cultural Life of the Early Polyphonic Mass: Medieval Context to Modern Revival* (Cambridge: Cambridge Univ. Press, 2010), 196–200.

26. The exegesis of the Sanctus contained in the *expositiones missae* treatises generally follows Amalar's lead in interpreting the beginning (*Sanctus sanctus sanctus Dominus Deus Sabaoth*) as expressing "praise of the divine majesty offered by the angels" and that the end (*Benedictus qui venit in nomine Domine, Hosanna in excelsis*) is "the song of the earthly host announcing the Incarnation of the Lord" (Iversen, *Laus angelica*, 187–88).

Example 6. Du Fay, *Missa Ecce ancilla Domini/Beata es Maria*, Hosanna I

Example 6, cont.

image of the Annunciation: hearing the Word of God, the Virgin raises
her voice in consent, whereupon the Holy Spirit descends to overshadow
her and Christ becomes incarnate in her womb.

Most extraordinary is the final measure of this first Hosanna, the last
bit of music sung before the consecration and elevation. After a long
silence, the tenor re-enters at the sounding of the final cadence with a
short four-note motive (m. 80). The two extant manuscript sources of
Du Fay's Sanctus setting provide no text underlay for this kernel, but the
melodic source is unmistakable—this is the motive to which the word *fiat*
is set every time it is sung in this Mass. Du Fay thus creates an audible
punctuation that proclaims incarnation: Christ incarnate both in the Virgin's womb and in the Host, both by the power of the Word and through
the Holy Spirit. A more harmonious sonic synthesis of the Pythagorean

idea of the cosmic scale ascending from earth to the stars with the idea of the angelic choir uniting with human song is hard to imagine.

The Sanctus as Aspirational Aurality

In his far-ranging and thought-provoking study of the speculative philosophies of musical harmony in the medieval West, at the outset of a chapter entitled "Composing the Cosmic: Harmonies of the Macrocosm," Andrew Hicks observes, "The music of the spheres is sight unheard. It demands an aspirational aurality that is itself the product of an anxious desire to know and to hear."[27] Although his felicitous formulation of "aspirational aurality" is intended to make the point that the concept of a cosmic musical harmony belongs ultimately to the realm of intellect and imagination (a fact that the musically unharmonious data from Voyager 1 seems to confirm), it might also serve to describe the project of medieval Christian musicians who aspired to make music that reflected and contributed to an inaudible heavenly harmony. The Sanctus presented a most potent site for such an aspiration, being the faithful's response to the celebrant's invitation to join their voices with those of the angelic choir in celebration of the Creator's imminent presence in the sacrament of the Eucharist.

The Sanctus settings explored here stand as sounding evidence of Christians' longing to bridge the terrestrial/celestial divide, a longing also expressed visually in the sacred spaces in which humankind sang "Holy, holy, holy!" with angels and archangels. Churches throughout medieval Christendom were frequently decorated with angels sculpted and painted, and ceiling vaults were often painted to represent the night sky. Indeed, a manuscript illumination from Du Fay's very time and place depicts just such a setting.[28] Executed in northern France around 1455,

27. Andrew Hicks, *Composing the World: Harmony in the Medieval Platonic Cosmos* (Oxford: Oxford Univ. Press, 2017), 190.

28. Brussels, Bibliothèque royale, Ms. 9232, f.269r. See the catalogue entry by Lisa Deam in *La Librairie des ducs de Bourgogne: Manuscrits conservés à la Bibliothèque royale de Belgique*, vol. 5: *Textes historiques*, dir. Bernard Bousmanne, Tania Van Hemelryck, and Céline Van Hoorebeeck (Turnhout: Brepols, 2015), 141–46, http://www.koregos.org/fr/brigitte-d-hainaut-zveny-les-retables-sculptes -dans-les-anciens-pays-bas-xve-xvie-siecles/1574/.

it is found within a copy of Jean Mansel's *Fleur des histoires* made for Du Fay's patron, Philip the Good, duke of Burgundy. Choirmen stand singing before a large music stand as Philip kneels in prayer and the people assemble for Mass. On either side of the crucifix are statues of angels; a profusion of gold stars adorns the ceiling vault above the altar. With these painstakingly and beautifully rendered details, the artist confirms that when Christians make music at the Lord's Supper, they are as one of Gregory of Nyssa's cymbals, uniting with the celestial choir in an eternal cosmic liturgy.

PART TWO

THEOLOGICAL-
LITURGICAL
PERSPECTIVES

CHAPTER TEN

The World as Christ's Body

Problems and Possibilities

David Grumett

In much current eucharistic theology, there is curiously little concern for the created, material elements of bread and wine. Worship is viewed, following Henri de Lubac, as building the church community, and the original subtitle of his programmatic study of ecclesiology indeed privileges these "social aspects" of dogma.[1] The primary goal of this community is often identified, for example by theologians such as William Cavanaugh, as the pursuit of political and economic justice.[2] These are important perspectives, and a view of the Eucharist as social—whether because of its action in the society of the church or in wider secular society—has a great deal to commend it. As de Lubac rightly saw in his groundbreaking *Corpus Mysticum*, the relation between the material elements and the human relationships configured around them is reciprocal, and neither can be conceived without the other.[3]

However, in theological thinking about the Eucharist, and maybe even more so in practical church life, the material elements, although

1. Henri de Lubac, *Catholicisme: les aspects sociaux du dogme* (Paris: Cerf, 1938); translated as *Catholicism: Christ and the Common Destiny of Man* (San Francisco, CA: Ignatius Press, 1988).

2. William T. Cavanaugh, *Torture and Eucharist: Theology, Politics and the Body of Christ* (Oxford: Wiley-Blackwell, 1998).

3. Henri de Lubac, *Corpus Mysticum*, trans. Gemma Simmonds (London: SCM, 2006), 75–119.

liturgically central, receive little theological reflection. The past seventy years have seen an explosion in the number of individual acts of communion worldwide: frequent lay reception of the Host is now normal for Roman Catholics, parish communion has become typical in Anglican churches, and Lutheran worship has enjoyed a eucharistic revival. However, while the number of acts of Communion has risen steeply, just one East Coast corporation has come to dominate the wafer Host market in the English-speaking world. This company produces a large majority of the Hosts used across North America, the United Kingdom, and Australia. Many of the small production plants previously located in convents are closed or have become mere distribution centers for the wafers made elsewhere.[4] Although churches and theologians congratulate themselves, and rightly so, for promoting wide Eucharist participation, they have become unwitting promoters of a secular model of mass consumption and exchange, even while claiming that in worship a new, relational form of consumption is being modeled, based on local community.

So much, then, for social eucharistic theologies and their material, societal, and political engagements. A converse emphasis, however, which may be termed spiritual eucharistic theology, stresses the risks of excessive focus on the material elements or, it sometimes seems, the risks of even limited focus on them. This theology comes out of a long Platonic-Calvinist tradition in which the elements are means for the worshiper's spiritual elevation to God, who raises the worshiper up through the elements rather than descending to them within, or in the shape of, the elements. In the 1560 Scots Confession, this spiritual ascent is accomplished by the Holy Ghost, "who by true faith carries above all things that are visible, carnal, and earthly, and makes us feed upon the body and blood of Christ Jesus . . . in heaven."[5] This is powerful language, and the significance of the Calvinist focus on the ascended Christ and his reception of worshipers, rather than on the incarnate Christ and worshipers' reception of him, should not be underestimated. Spiritual understandings of the Eucharist are also frequent in Anglican theology, and are put to good use by Rowan Williams, who when writing about the Eucharist

4. Ben Humphris, "Has the Body of Christ Been Made into a Commodity?" *The Expository Times* 127 (2016): 225–29.
5. The Scottish Confession of Faith, chap. 21, in *Reformed Confessions of the 16th Century*, ed. Arthur C. Cochrane (London: SCM, 1966), 179.

is at pains to warn against the fetishization of the elements, reminding his readers that the Eucharist is not primarily about material presence or change but concerns spiritual participation and transformation.[6] In far less theologically sophisticated Anglican and Protestant thought and practice, a polemical disregard for the material elements contests what is misunderstood as Roman Catholic superstition or idolatry.

Both social and spiritual eucharistic theologies need to take eucharistic materiality seriously. The cross-disciplinary turns to the body and more recently to materiality are based on the acknowledgement that embodiment is a condition shared by all humans, while materiality is common not only to all humans but also to the whole visible created order.[7] Faced by these developments, theologians need to recognize that a concern with eucharistic materiality, far from signaling a drift into social irresponsibility and even idolatry, opens avenues for theological engagement with concrete Christian experience and wider secular culture. The same may be said for eucharistic embodiment—although the Johannine notion of enfleshment may be preferable, because the Pauline language of *soma* is too easily and too quickly transposed into communitarian contexts in ways that bypass the mystery of Christ in the sacrament.

Materiality has certainly been taken seriously within the historical theology and liturgy of the Roman Catholic Church, with the doctrine of transubstantiation reaffirmed by papal encyclical during the final months of the Second Vatican Council.[8] However, in the context of the cross-disciplinary turns to materiality just identified, theologians and liturgists need to do more to explore the constructive possibilities that this doctrine offers. This is especially true in ecumenical dialogues, where questions around the status of the material elements are typically avoided, seeming at best unconstructive and at worst contentious. Yet

6. Rowan Williams, *Resurrection: Interpreting the Easter Gospel* (Cleveland, OH: Pilgrim Press, 1985), 51; Rowan Williams, *On Christian Theology* (Oxford: Wiley-Blackwell, 2000), 200–201, 210; Rowan Williams, *Anglican Identities* (London: Darton, Longman & Todd, 2004), 28–29 (on Richard Hooker and George Herbert), 131 (on St John).

7. Caroline Walker Bynum, *Christian Materiality: An Essay on Religion in Late Medieval Europe* (Brooklyn, NY: Zone, 2011), 31–33.

8. Pope Paul VI, *Mysterium fidei* 11, 46, 54, in *The Papal Encyclicals*, ed. Claudia Carlen, 5 vols. (Ann Arbor, MI: Pierian, 1990), vol. 5, 165–77.

the ecumenical problem seems to be a consequence of the historic tendency to try to conceive Christ's eucharistic presence in abstraction from Christ's presence in the wider created order. I wish to offer a different approach by beginning not with the Eucharist but with the created order and by considering how Christ's presence in the created order provides the necessary backdrop to his presence in the Eucharist. I thereby regard eucharistic presence not as an exceptional intrusion into normal, unproblematic ontology, but as exemplifying Christ's continual sustaining action upon and within the world.

At this point, the work of Grace Jantzen, Matthew Fox, and John Keenan should be briefly acknowledged. In different ways, each of these figures presents the world as God's body. Jantzen promotes this idea against a dualistic view of God's relation to the world, suggesting it permits more convincing accounts of divine action, of divine awareness of worldly events, and of divine omnipresence.[9] Fox, endorsing the cosmic axis given by eastward celebration of the Eucharist, calls us to see the bread and all embodied life as "cosmological gifts" by which God becomes sacrificially intimate with the created order.[10] Keenan assimilates Buddhist categories, seeing Christ's eucharistic presence nurturing the whole desubstantialized created order and dissolved into it.[11]

Jantzen, Fox, and Keenan articulate important insights. Yet all three appear to overstate the distance that their intuitions require them to move from classic Christian doctrine. For example, Fox suggests that Christians need to develop a greater sense of immanentism from Native American worship.[12] However, Jantzen, Fox, and Kennan could all engage more closely with the historic Christian tradition. In the remainder of this chapter I shall do just this, and thereby map a possible path for them back into mainstream Christian theology and liturgy.

---

9. Grace M. Jantzen, *God's World, God's Body* (London: Darton, Longman and Todd, 1984), 69, 157.

10. Matthew Fox, *The Coming of the Cosmic Christ: The Healing of Mother Earth and the Birth of a Global Renaissance* (San Francisco, CA: Harper & Row, 1988), 211–15.

11. John P. Keenan, "A Mahāyāna Theology of the Real Presence of Christ in the Eucharist," *Buddhist-Christian Studies* 24 (2004): 89–100.

12. Fox, *Coming of the Cosmic Christ*, 225–27.

A perennial eucharistic paradox is addressed as early as the mid-third century by the Roman antipope and Stoic sympathizer Novatian. On the one hand, a recurring objection to Christ's bodily presence in the Eucharist is that Christ's power and action would thereby be restricted, due to being "contained," as it were, "within" matter. Set against this objection is the truth, expounded by Paul in Ephesians 1:23 and 4:10, that Christ is present everywhere and fills (*plero*) all things. In his treatise on the Trinity (240–250), Novatian presents the tension between these propositions and seeks their resolution.[13] Regarding divine presence, he writes, Scripture employs problematic anthropomorphisms. He accepts that God fills all things and that there is no thing in which he is not. Nevertheless, humans' capacity for perceiving God is, Novatian reasons, finite, which is why God is regarded as dwelling in specific locations.

The following century, another Latin theologian, Hilary of Poitiers, grappled with the same issues in his influential *De trinitate*. Like Novatian, Hilary recognized that although all things exist within God because of God's infinity, precisely because God is unlimited it is natural for humans to seek him in particular places.[14] The resulting paradox of divine presence is stated with stark clarity: God is "outside of all things and within all things; He comprises all things and is comprised by none."[15] Hilary states his thesis on divine presence in the world with extended eloquence. After expounding how God holds the entire heavens in his palm as his throne and the whole earth in his hand as his footstool, he writes that this is so

> in all these beginnings of created things God might be recognized as in them and outside of them, reaching beyond them and being found within them, that is, poured about [*circumfusus*] everything and permeating [*infusus*] everything, since what the palm and the hand grasp reveal the power of His external nature, and the throne and the footstool show that external things are subject to Him as the One who is within, since He who is within rests upon the things that are without. Thus, He Himself with His whole being

---

13. Novatian, *The Trinity* 6 (1–5), trans. Russell J. DeSimone (Washington, DC: Catholic Univ. of America Press, 1974), 35–36.

14. Hilary of Poitiers, *On the Trinity* 2 (6), trans. Stephen McKenna (Washington, DC: Catholic Univ. of America Press, 1968), 39–40.

15. Hilary, *On the Trinity* 3 (2), 66.

contains [*contineo*] all things that are within Him and outside of Him, nor is He, the infinite One, separated from all things nor are all things not present within Him who is infinite.[16]

For Hilary, the idea that God could not suffuse creation while at the same time remaining complete in himself was anthropomorphic. The term "Spirit of God" serves as a reminder, he avers, that being unlike a human, God does not remain in his own place within himself. God is not restricted to where he is, but is "present everywhere and is absent from nowhere."[17]

For an explicitly christological exposition we may turn to Theodore of Mopsuestia, who maintains that the task of containing and preserving the created order is necessarily human. Only humans, he argues, combine the material, mental, and spiritual capacities. These were primordially given to Adam, but after the Fall were assumed by Christ. A striking aspect of Theodore's exposition is his portrayal of the original creation as a single body. Drawing, like Novatian, on Ephesians, Theodore states that God made the universe as a body (*corpus*) "composed of many members from rational as well as sensible orders."[18] Similar language appears in his commentaries on other classic New Testament passages in which Christ exercises a cosmic role in the created order. With reference to Colossians 1:16, Theodore writes, "The first fruits . . . of our renovation, in whom all things are bonded (*connexio*) and reintegrated (*redintegro*), is Christ according to the flesh."[19]

Maximus the Confessor expounds these themes in demanding depth in his *Ambiguum* 41, in which he discusses how Christ progressively reunifies the fallen world. At the culmination of his ascent, the whole of the created order is interpenetrated (*perichoresas*) by God.[20] As for

16. Hilary, *On the Trinity* 1 (6), 7.

17. Hilary, *On the Trinity* 8 (24), 393.

18. Frederick G. McLeod, *Theodore of Mopsuestia* (London: Routledge, 2009), 121–22, on Eph 1:10. See also McLeod's comments at pp. 26–29 on similar imagery in the *Commentary on Genesis*, and Rowan A. Greer, *Theodore of Mopsuestia: Exegete and Theologian* (London: Faith, 1961), 67.

19. McLeod, *Theodore of Mopsuestia*, 124–25.

20. The same term is used to describe the interpenetration of the natures of Christ and the persons of the Trinity. See *Maximus the Confessor*, ed. Andrew Louth (London: Routledge, 1996), 213.

Theodore, it is also essential for Maximus that Christ accomplishes this reunification as a human who has entered fully into the material world. As already emphasized, the cosmic reunification of material things and spiritual things is naturally the task of all humans but due to sin can now be accomplished only by Christ. As Hans Urs von Balthasar puts it, the Chalcedonian formula "expands, for Maximus, into a fundamental law of metaphysics." In Balthasar's words, "the goal God sets for the world is now not simply dissolution in him alone but the fulfilment and preservation also of the created realm, 'without confusion (*asygchytos*),' in the Incarnation of his Son."[21] Maximus himself writes that God became man "in order to save lost man" by uniting "through Himself the natural fissures running through the general nature of the universe" and revealing the "universal pre-existing principles (*logoi*) of the parts," through which the "union (*henosis*) of the divided naturally comes about."[22] Christ thereby becomes the "universal union (*henotes*) of all things,"[23] restoring material things by bringing them back into right relation with spiritual things, and showing forth the spiritual principles by which this work of material restoration is achieved.

Maximus's fivefold cosmic hierarchy made its way westward into Latin theology in the ninth century thanks to the labors of his translator Eriugena. In his own *Periphyseon*, the Irish monk invokes Christ's moving words to his disciples in Matthew's gospel, said as he ascends from them into heaven: "I will be with you always." Eriugena states that this "sufficiently and clearly indicates that not only as the Word by which all things are fulfilled and which is above all things, but also according to the flesh which He raised from the dead and which He changed into God,

21. Hans Urs von Balthasar, *Cosmic Liturgy: The Universe according to Maximus the Confessor*, trans. Brian E. Daley (San Francisco, CA: Ignatius Press, 2003), 70, 153.

22. Maximos, Ambiguum 41, in *On Difficulties in the Church Fathers: The Ambigua*, trans. Nicholas Constas, 2 vols. (Cambridge, MA: Harvard Univ. Press, 2014), vol. 2, 108–11.

23. Maximos, Ambiguum 41, in *On Difficulties in the Church Fathers*, vol. 2, 110–11, echoing Eph 4:3 and 4:13. For Maximus's cosmology as fundamentally christological rather than Neoplatonic, Torstein T. Tollefsen, "Christocentric Cosmology," in *The Oxford Handbook of Maximus the Confessor*, ed. Pauline Allen and Bronwen Neil (Oxford: Oxford Univ. Press, 2015), 307–21.

He exists always and everywhere, though not circumscribed by place or time or any (other) means."[24] Eriugena restates this idea at greater length at the culmination of his massive text. Citing Hilary's *De trinitate*, he writes that after the resurrection Christ's flesh is everywhere, being omnipresent throughout space rather than limited within space.[25] This is because, Eriugena states, flesh has been transformed into the power and indestructibility of God's Spirit. Christ's presence in the Eucharist is thereby associated with his universal presence, with the possibility that universality implies circumscription explicitly excluded.

Eriugena's dependence on both Maximus and Hilary places him squarely within the christological trajectory of this chapter. Nevertheless, the eucharistic implications of his speculations remain implicit. However, his concerns were taken up again by Martin Luther, who had an intense awareness of Christ pervading the created order. In Scripture, the imagery of a crystal is used to represent this: the crystalline sea and river coming forth from the throne, the jeweled radiance of the Holy City descending from God, and the refreshing crystals of water (dew) envisioned by Jesus son of Sirach.[26] Such imagery excited the theological and liturgical imagination of Adam of Saint-Victor, who in a sequence for the octave of Christmas that alludes to Mary writes:

> If the crystal is moist
> and it is exposed to the sun
> it sparkles like a little fire.
> The crystal is not ruptured
> nor is the seal of her purity
> broken in the birth.[27]

Luther develops this incarnational imagery theologically, picturing a spark or flame appearing within a crystal and playing on word associations. Just as the spark or flame appears to be at the front of the crystal

---

24. Eriugena, *Periphyseon* 539b–c, trans. I. P. Sheldon-Williams and John J. O'Meara (Montreal: Bellarmin, 1987), 139. See Matt 28:20.

25. Eriugena, *Periphyseon* 991c–995b, 677–81.

26. Rev 4:6; 22:1; 21:11; Sir 43:22.

27. Adam of Saint-Victor, *Sequences*, ed. and trans. Juliet Mousseau (Paris: Peeters, 2013), 38–39.

(*Kristall*) when it is in fact at its center, he suggests, so Christ (*Christus*) sits in heaven, in one place at the center of the universe, yet is perceived throughout.[28] As for Maximus, Christ's presence in the world is grounded in the recognition of Christ's role as preserver, which entails that Christ is present in creation "both in its innermost and outermost aspects" and "in every creature in its innermost and outermost being, on all sides, through and through, below and above, before and behind, so that nothing can be more truly present and within all creatures."[29] In Luther, this doctrine is known as ubiquity. Paraphrasing the passage from Hilary previously discussed, he continues that "God in his essence is present everywhere, in and through the whole creation in all its parts and in all places, and so the world is full of God and he fills it all, yet he is not limited or circumscribed by it, but is at the same time beyond and above the whole creation."[30] Relating this exposition to the Eucharist, Luther adds that "in comparison with this it is a trivial matter that Christ's body and blood are at the same time in heaven and in the Supper." Following Hilary and his successors, Luther thereby approaches the question of how Christ is present in the Eucharist via a consideration of how he is present, through his incarnation, in the wider created order. Indeed, for Luther the principal issue is not how Christ might be present in the Eucharist, but how he could possibly *not* be present in the Eucharist given his wider presence.

Responding to Cartesian skepticism regarding the consistency and substantiality of the created order, the Lutheran thinker Gottfried Leibniz recognized the forgotten truth that the problem of how eucharistic substance is generated and preserved is inseparable from the problem of how

28. Martin Luther, "Confession concerning Christ's Supper" (1528), trans. Robert H. Fischer, in *Works*, 55 vols. (St Louis, MO: Concordia, 1955–86), vol. 37, 151–372 (224). For the crystal imagery, Martin Wendte, *Die Gabe und das Gestell: Luthers Metaphysik des Abendmahls im technischen Zeitalter* (Tübingen: Mohr Siebeck, 2013), 389–92; Niels Henrik Gregersen, "Natural Events as Crystals of God: Luther's Eucharistic Theology and the Question of Sacramentality," *Tro & Tanke* 5 (1995): 143–58.

29. Martin Luther, "That these words of Christ, 'This is my body,' etc., still stand firm against the fanatics" (1527), trans. Robert H. Fischer, in *Works*, vol. 37, 3–150, here 58.

30. Luther, "That these words," 59; Jörg Baur, "Ubiquität," in *Creator est creatura: Luthers Christologie als Lehre von der Idiomenkommunikation*, ed. Oswald Bayer and Benjamin Gleede (Berlin: de Gruyter, 2007), 186–301, here 196–220.

other substances are generated and preserved. In correspondence with the Jesuit Bartholomew des Bosses, Leibniz came to recognize that the doctrine of transubstantiation required him to modify his entire metaphysics. The key issue was to understand how simple, indivisible substances, which he termed monads, were combined to produce composite substances with their own consistency and substantiality. Using the suggestive example of bread, Leibniz states that this is "not a substance, but a being by aggregation, or a substantiated being resulting from innumerable monads through some added union."[31] However, he is not content to conceive the bread as a mere aggregate. Rather, Leibniz argues that it is a substance produced by the addition to the aggregation of an objective union beyond any apparent union that is given to the bread by perception. He writes, "Either bodies are mere phenomena, and so extension also will be only a phenomenon, and monads alone will be real, but with a union supplied by the operation of the perceiving soul on the phenomenon; or, if faith (*fides*) drives us to corporeal substances, this substance consists in that unifying reality, which adds something absolute (and therefore substantial), albeit impermanent, to the things to be unified."[32] Monads, Leibniz continues, are not constituents of the unifying reality. A body's true substantiality can only be granted from a source external to it. Only with such gifted substantiality may the transition be effected from the realm of phenomena into the realm of substance and thereby of true materiality.

Leibniz's "bond of substance" theory excited the interest of the French Roman Catholic lay philosopher Maurice Blondel, who is best known for his thesis on action.[33] At the Sorbonne in the 1890s, however, the state doctorate required a second thesis written in Latin, and this provided its topic.[34] Blondel writes that the "question raised by Leibniz and des Bosses concerning transubstantiation during the Eucharist leads us to

31. Leibniz, letter of January 1710, in *The Leibniz–Des Bosses Correspondence*, trans. Brandon C. Look and Donald Rutherford (New Haven, CT: Yale Univ. Press, 2007), 170–71.

32. Leibniz, letter of 15 February 1712, in ibid., 224–27.

33. Maurice Blondel, *Action: Essay on a Critique of Life and a Science of Practice*, trans. Oliva Blanchette (Notre Dame, IN: Univ. of Notre Dame Press, 1984).

34. Maurice Blondel, *De vinculo substantiali et de substantia composita apud Leibnitium* (Paris: Alcan, 1893); translated as *Le Lien substantiel et la substance composée d'après Leibniz*, trans. Claude Troisfontaines (Louvain: Nauwelaerts, 1972).

conceive of Christ, without detriment to the constituent monads, as the bond which makes substantiation possible, the vivifying agent for all creation: *vinculum perfectionis.*[35] Blondel later published a résumé of his thesis, in which he argues that neither Leibniz nor des Bosses (nor, it might be added, he himself) had appreciated the full significance of the *vinculum substantiale.* In fact, he now boldly maintains, the theory calls into question the whole of metaphysics.[36]

Blondel presents matter in Plotinian terms as indeterminate and passive and as awaiting its spiritual, forming principle. Despite matter's indeterminacy, he states, it nevertheless individuates, multiplies, opposes, and consolidates (*solidariser*) real beings in the world. In so doing, Blondel continues, it opens the possibility that a chimerical unity (*unité*) be transposed into a real union (*union*).[37] This assessment stands in sharp opposition to the opinion, widespread among metaphysicians as well as in the common mind, that matter is itself substantial. Matter, Blondel writes, admittedly exhibits a capacity for reality (*une capacité réele*) by receiving concrete and substantial reality from form. However, in addition to matter and form there must exist, he contends, a "bond [*un lien*] that unites them in a harmony, in an intelligible unity."[38] This bond effects a kind of resurrection, drawing a diffuse and disintegrating multiple into an enduring spiritualized yet physical whole. Moreover, acknowledging that to regard matter as itself substantial would be idolatrous and alluding to the opening versicle of the Roman Catholic Canon of the Mass, Blondel describes a "*sursum* of the universe" by which matter is vitalized.[39]

This chapter has sought to dismantle conceptual obstacles to a robust eucharistic theology, clearing the way for such a theology to be

---

35. Paper of 5 December 1919, in *Pierre Teilhard de Chardin—Maurice Blondel: Correspondence* (New York, NY: Herder & Herder, 1976), 23. For an overview, David Grumett, "The Eucharistic Cosmology of Teilhard de Chardin," *Theology* 110 (2007): 22–30.

36. Maurice Blondel, *Une énigme historique: le "vinculum substantiale" d'après Leibniz et l'ébauche d'un réalisme supérieur* (Paris: Beauchesne, 1930), 82–83, 131.

37. Maurice Blondel, *La Pensée*, 2 vols. (Paris: Alcan, 1934), vol. 1, 279–80; and generally J. Trouillard, "Pluralité spirituelle et unité normative selon Blondel," *Archives de philosophie* 62 (1961): 21–28.

38. Maurice Blondel, *L'Être et les êtres: essai d'ontologie concrète et intégrale* (Paris: Presses universitaires de France, 1963), 260–62.

39. Ibid., 263.

developed in interaction with liturgical practice. The specific mode of Christ's presence in the Eucharist has not been considered. Although this presence certainly needs to be viewed against the backdrop of Christ's cosmic presence in the wider created order, it cannot be regarded as a mere iteration of cosmic presence. At the least, liturgical eucharistic presence qualitatively intensifies general presence by explicitly framing it within the contexts of scriptural reading, the proclamation of the Word, liturgical action, and liturgical speech. Some of the other contributors to this volume consider these specific intensifications in greater detail.

CHAPTER ELEVEN

Fruit of the Earth, Work of Human Hands, Bread of Life

The Ordo Missae on Creation and the World

Joris Geldhof

The goal of this chapter is to present—that is, to interpret and explain—what the Ordo Missae currently in use in those segments of the Catholic Church where the Roman Rite is celebrated says about the grand Christian vision of the transformation of creation and thereby to contribute meaningfully to the overall topic of this volume. However, the decision to study this particular source, part of an authoritative liturgical book, the Missale Romanum, and therefore requiring a textual approach, needs to be well grounded, for it is neither evident nor usual to look at a *liturgical* text (of this kind) to develop *theological* thoughts.

In particular, I do not aim at confronting existing theological visions about creation and the cosmos with the rubrical and euchological material that is found in the Ordo Missae. Rather, I want to carefully examine how the material world is mentioned and imagined in the Ordo Missae, with the specific question in mind of what God is requested to do upon it and how its inhabitants are invited and incited to partake in these actions. In other words, it is my intention to stimulate theological reflection and discussion based on a thorough analysis of a central part of the *lex orandi* of the Eucharist.[1] Hence, it comes as no surprise that my approach is in

---

1. Inspiration for a theological approach to the Eucharist that prioritizes liturgical shape can be drawn from, among others, Cesare Giraudo, *In unum corpus: Traité*

line with the direction adopted by "liturgical theology," in particular the model developed by Alexander Schmemann, Aidan Kavanagh, and David Fagerberg,[2] as well as with the methodological reflections of Winfried Haunerland and Kevin Irwin that justify the use of euchological sources to develop theological insight.[3]

The Ordo Missae itself is a strange kind of text, a complex composition of prayers, rubrics, acclamations, formalized dialogues, etc. It constitutes the basic outline of the eucharistic celebration and contains all those elements that remain the same in every Eucharist. The document has a notoriously difficult history; noteworthy is Dom Bernard Botte and Christine Mohrmann's commentary and edition from 1953,[4] which was a great gift to the liturgical movement and useful preparation for the liturgical reforms after the Second Vatican Council. Coetus X of the *Consilium ad exsequendam constitutionem de sacra liturgia*, chaired by the renowned scholar and director of the Liturgisches Institut at Trier Johannes Wagner, carried out the reform of the "order of Mass."[5] Major changes were adopted, and while it is impossible to subsume all of them

---

mystagogique sur l'eucharistie, trans. Éric Iborra and Pierre-Marie Hombert (Paris: Cerf, 2014); John D. Laurance, *The Sacrament of the Eucharist*, Lex Orandi Series (Collegeville, MN: Liturgical Press, 2012); Martin Stuflesser, *Eucharistie: liturgische Feier und theologische Erschließung* (Regensburg: Friedrich Pustet, 2013); and, of course, Alexander Schmemann, *The Eucharist: Sacrament of the Kingdom*, trans. Paul Kachur (Crestwood, NY: St. Vladimir's Seminary Press, 1987).

2. For a concise presentation of this line of thinking, see Joris Geldhof, "Liturgy as Theological Norm: Getting Acquainted with 'Liturgical Theology'," *Neue Zeitschrift für systematische Theologie und Religionsphilosophie* 52 (2010): 155–76. And for a particularly representative study from this school, see David W. Fagerberg, *Consecrating the World: On Mundane Liturgical Theology* (Kettering, OH: Angelico Press, 2016).

3. Winfried Haunerland, *Die Eucharistie und ihre Wirkungen im Spiegel der Euchologie des Missale Romanum*, Liturgiewissenschaftliche Quellen und Forschungen 71 (Münster: Aschendorff, 1989); Kevin W. Irwin, *Context and Text: A Method for Liturgical Theology*, rev. ed. (Collegeville, MN: Liturgical Press, 2018).

4. Bernard Botte and Christine Mohrmann, *L'ordinaire de la messe: Texte critique, traduction et études* (Paris: Cerf, 1953).

5. For relevant historical background information to these intriguing post-conciliar developments, see Johannes Wagner, *Mein Weg zur Liturgiereform 1936–1986: Erinnerungen* (Freiburg, Basel, and Vienna: Herder, 1993), 78–85; Annibale Bugnini, *The Reform of the Liturgy 1948–1975*, trans. Matthew J. O'Connell (Collegeville, MN: Liturgical Press 1990), 337–59, 383–92.

under one principle, it is fair to say that the inclusion and "active participation" of the faithful was the overarching concern.[6]

Since the first edition of the new Ordo Missae in 1969—one year
prior to the publication of the entire Missale Romanum[7]—there have
been several editions, each characterized primarily by additions. For the
purposes of the present chapter I refer exclusively to the 2008 edition,
which is the slightly amended version of the *editio typica tertia*.[8] While
the third typical edition of the Roman Missal dates from 2002, there was
a need for an amended version only six years later, which, however, was
not identified as the fourth typical edition.

The 2008 Missale Romanum presently constitutes the official Latin
text of the Mass for translation into any vernacular language.[9] The English translation of the Missale Romanum, which was implemented from
Advent 2011, was one of the first and fairly controversial.[10] Since I will
be looking primarily at the Latin text, and only secondarily refer to the
English translation of the Ordo Missae,[11] I leave these controversies aside.

---

6. A particularly useful study that helps the reader understand the adaptations and
carefully maps the editorial process is Maurizio Barba, *La riforma conciliare dell'
"ordo missae." Il percorso storico-redazionale dei riti d'ingresso, di offertorio e di
communione*, Bibliotheca Ephemerides Liturgicae. Subsidia 120 (Rome: Edizioni
Liturgiche, 2008).

7. See Bugnini, *Reform of the Liturgy*, 383–85.

8. *Missale Romanum, editio typica tertia, reimpressio emendata* (Rome: Typis
Polyglottis Vaticanis, 2008), cited as MR. The Ordo Missae lies between the *proprium
de tempore* (temporal cycle) and the *proprium de sanctis* (sanctoral cycle), i.e., on
pages 501–662. The Ordo Missae is numbered in 146 paragraphs; I use the abbrevia-
tion OM plus the corresponding paragraph number when referring to it in the text.

9. In principle the guidelines for that translation work are given in *Liturgiam
authenticam*, the fifth instruction for the implementation of the liturgical reforms
after Vatican II, dating from 2001. The thrust of that document is that translations
should be as close to the Latin original as possible. Pope Francis recently gave more
liberty to bishops' conferences to oversee the translation of liturgical books into
vernacular languages. See his 2017 motu proprio *Magnum principium*.

10. Keith F. Pecklers, *The Genius of the Roman Rite: On the Reception and
Implementation of the New Missal* (Collegeville, MN: Liturgical Press, 2009);
Gerald O'Collins, *Lost in Translation: The English Language and the Catholic Mass*
(Collegeville, MN: Liturgical Press, 2017).

11. I refer to the English translation of the third typical edition of the Roman Missal, which was approved for use in the United States by the United States Conference
of Catholic Bishops and of which different editions are available.

Given the topic of this volume, I have chosen not to follow the structure of the Ordo Missae. Instead, I will first look at the introductory rites, the liturgy of the Word, and the concluding rites, three of the four major parts containing the celebration of the Eucharist in the Roman Rite.[12] We will see that the concept of the world does not play a significant role here, unlike in the part called *liturgia eucharistica*, with the liturgy of the Eucharist in a stricter sense. I will then address the rites that together constitute the preparation of the gifts, previously called "offertory,"[13] the rich euchology of the prefaces, and the eucharistic prayers.[14] In addition, I will consider the material objects mentioned in the Ordo Missae, such as incense and candles, in a concise separate section. The examination of all these components is guided by the central question of how creation, matter, and the world are imagined and what God and human beings do with them and in them. In the conclusion I draw together some general ideas and make suggestions for further theological debate.

1. The Introductory Rites, the Liturgy of the Word, and the Concluding Rites

The only explicit references to the concept of the earth and the world in the introductory rites of the Eucharist are found in the text of the Glo-

---

12. Usually, one distinguishes between four parts of the Eucharistic celebration—introductory rites, liturgy of the Word, liturgy of the Eucharist (more strictly speaking), and concluding rites—although the layout of the 2008 Missale Romanum allows for a fivefold subdivision, with a special mention of the Communion rites (between the liturgy of the Eucharist and the concluding rites). The greatest part of the text of the Ordo Missae concerns the liturgy of the Eucharist, which has the preparation of the gifts, the Eucharistic prayer including the prefaces, and the post-anaphoral rites as its constituent parts. For a comprehensive commentary, see Ed Foley, John F. Baldovin, Mary Collins, and Joanne M. Pierce, eds., *A Commentary on the Order of Mass of the Roman Missal* (Collegeville, MN: Liturgical Press, 2011).

13. For a detailed study that maps and interprets this significant shift, see Anne-Marie Petitjean, *De l'offertoire à la préparation des dons: Genèse et histoire d'une réforme*, Liturgiewissenschaftliche Quellen und Forschungen 104 (Münster: Aschendorff, 2016).

14. The 2008 Missale Romanum has the four Eucharistic prayers that were included in the first 1969 edition of the Ordo Missae and includes those added later, such as the two Eucharistic Prayers *pro reconciliatione* and the four versions of the prayer *pro variis necessitatibus*, in an appendix. I limit the discussion here to the four prayers of the Ordo Missae itself and leave aside the material in the appendix.

ria, traditionally known as the "angelic hymn," which was not originally meant for the Eucharist.[15] The hymn opens with the famous chiasmus *Gloria in excelsis* and *in terra pax* (OM 8), words that were taken from the second chapter of Luke's Gospel, where, in the context of the proclamation of Christ's birth to the shepherds, a choir of angels suddenly sings, "Glory to God in the highest heaven, and on earth peace among those whom he favors" (Luke 2:14, NRSV, used throughout).

The other compound which mentions the world is *peccata mundi*. The text of the Gloria, which twice repeats the phrase *qui tollis peccata mundi*, here evidently refers to the first chapter of John's Gospel (1:29), where this relative clause qualifies the "Lamb of God"; John the Baptist is speaking, pointing to Jesus.[16] The Gloria hymn integrated these intriguing words into a supplicatory act of prayer, prolonging the exalted titles for God and the firm expressions of praise for him.

The second passage in the Ordo Missae where we find a reference to the world is the Creed, which constitutes the end of the Liturgy of the Word. The 2008 Missale Romanum provides two options, the (longer) Nicene-Constantinopolitan Creed (OM 18) or else the shorter *symbolum apostolorum*, or Apostles' Creed (OM 19). It considers the former normative but allows bishops' conferences to select the latter instead.[17] The line with which we are most concerned opens both these creeds, with God, the almighty Father (*Patrem omnipotentem*), immediately characterized as the creator of heaven and earth.

Whereas the older Apostles' Creed says *creatorem caeli et terrae*, the younger Nicene-Constantinopolitan Creed has *factorem caeli et terrae*— a slight difference that English speakers may notice when they say or hear "creator" rather than "maker" of heaven and earth. The idea of the "maker" in the Nicene-Constantinopolitan text corresponds with what is then said of the Son, who is "consubstantial with the Father," through whom "all things were *made*" (*per quem omnia facta sunt*; OM 18, my emphasis). Moreover, the Nicene-Constantinopolitan text specifies the compound "heaven and earth" with *visibilium omnium et invisibilium*,

15. Josef Andreas Jungmann, *The Mass of the Roman Rite: Its Origins and Development*, 2 vols., trans. Francis A. Brunner (London: Burns & Oates, 1961), vol. 1, 346–59.

16. The "Lamb of God" is also venerated in chapter 5 of Revelation.

17. Interestingly, the 1969 Ordo Missae did not include the text of the Apostles' Creed.

"of all visible and invisible things." This specification underscores the universal dimension of God's being the creator of *everything*—a dimension that will occupy us further in this chapter. There is a clear sense that God's creation does not coincide with the physical or material world but goes infinitely beyond it. Thus the liturgy not only represents a premodern or a-scientific worldview but also offers food for thought.

Apart from the solemn blessings and prayers over the people at the end of the Eucharist, the concluding rites—even the three new alternatives for *ite, missa est*[18]—do not contain any direct reference to the world or creation. Although these benedictions are rich in biblical and spiritual imagery, allusions to creation are scarce. One is found in the blessing formula for Christmas (called the Nativity of the Lord), where the text says that God through his incarnation joined the earthly and celestial things (*qui per eius incarnationem terrena caelestibus sociavit*; MR, p. 607).[19] A second is found in the blessing for the celebration in which a church is dedicated, where the epithet for God is Lord of Heaven and Earth (*Dominus caeli et terrae*; MR, p. 614). A final reference is made in a funeral celebration where it is said that God in his ineffable goodness created the human being (*qui hominem ineffabili bonitate creavit*; MR, p. 615). These solemn blessing prayers are anything but common practice. Despite their beauty and depth, they are only rarely used.

2. The Preparation of the Gifts

One finds another set of blessing prayers in the context of the preparation of the gifts (*praeparatio donorum*), a term which the Ordo Missae does not use but which appears in the *Institutio Generalis Missalis Romani*.[20] The sequence of these rites, traditionally known as the *offertorium*, is as follows: first the altar is prepared and then, perhaps in a

18. They are *Ite, ad Evangelium Domini annuntiandum*; *Ite in pace, glorificando vita vestra Dominum*; and the simple *Ite in pace* (OM 144).

19. Since these blessing prayers are not part of the numbered paragraphs of the Ordo Missae, I give the page number from the Missale Romanum.

20. See *Institutio Generalis Missalis Romani* no. 72. For systematic commentary on this document, see Edward Foley, Nathan D. Mitchell, and Joanne M. Pierce, eds., *A Commentary on the General Instruction of the Roman Missal* (Collegeville, MN: Liturgical Press, 2007).

procession, gifts are brought—bread and wine of course, but also other gifts for supporting the church and the poor (OM 22)—then the priest says the blessing prayer over the bread. The corresponding blessing prayer over the wine is preceded by the rite of mixing a little water with the wine.[21] After the blessing prayer over the wine, the priest continues with a private prayer (*In spiritu humilitatis et in animo contrito*; OM 26), which can be interpreted as a remnant of the many *apologiae*, prayers that expressed the priest's unworthiness and sinfulness and at one time pervaded almost the entire celebration of the mass.[22] Then follows an optional incensing of the gifts, the altar cross, and the altar itself, after which the presiding priest and the other faithful can also be incensed. After the incensing rites come the washing of hands and the *Orate fratres* prayer, followed by a response by the congregation in which they express their desire that the sacrifice that is about to happen be beneficial to the church. The offertory rites finish with the second *oratio*, or presidential prayer of the Mass, the prayer over the offerings (*oratio super oblata*).[23]

21. It is peculiar that as commentators in Foley et al., *Commentary on the Order of Mass*, noted liturgists Michael Witczak and Patrick Regan talk about the "prayers of blessing over the chalice" instead of over the wine. Granted, there is no strict parallel in the terminology around bread-body of Christ versus wine/chalice-blood of Christ in the Eucharistic Prayers, but that is not the case in these blessing prayers. One observes a clear parallel between bread/fruit of the earth/bread of life and wine/fruit of the vine/spiritual drink. The accompanying rubrics, however, do show a minor imbalance in the parallel. Whereas OM 23 prescribes that the priest takes the paten with the bread (*sacerdos [. . .] accipit patenam cum pane*), OM 25 simply says that the priest takes the chalice (*sacerdos accipit calicem*). In this chalice, however, there is evidently wine, since the rubric in OM 24 stipulates that the deacon or the priest pours wine and a little water into the chalice (*infundit vinum et parum aquae in calicem*).

22. These developments are most probably connected with the origins of the private mass and seem to have had a predominantly Frankish stamp. See Jungmann, *The Mass of the Roman Rite*, vol. 2, 41–44, 46–52; but also vol. 1, 77–80. In this context, Hans Bernard Meyer speaks of a *Bedeutungswandel* in the rites of offering under the influence of Vatican II; see Hans-Bernard Meyer, *Eucharistie: Geschichte, Theologie, Pastoral*, Gottesdienst der Kirche: Handbuch der Liturgiewissenschaft 4 (Regensburg: Friedrich Pustet, 1989), 342.

23. The first one is the *collecta* or opening prayer, which finishes the opening rites (OM 9), and the third one is the prayer after communion. Together these three prayers co-constitute the individual mass forms or *proprium* (as distinct from the *ordinarium*).

We note in particular the parallel blessing prayers over the bread and over the wine (see Table 1). These prayers were not included in the Ordo Missae prior to the Second Vatican Council, and the reformers of the Missale Romanum found inspiration for them in the Jewish *berakot* prayers.[24] These were prayers that were said in the context of family and festive meals and expressed a profound gratitude to God for the goodness of creation.[25] The prayers begin with the same words of blessing God: *Benedictus es, Dominus, Deus universi* (OM nos. 23, 25). The current English version translates this solemn title as "Lord God of all creation," which is correct but not literal, for the concept of the entire universe (*universum*) is contained in the Latin original, not the more strictly theological concept of creation.

The text continues with an interesting use of two verbs in first-person plural, *accepimus* and *offerimus*. The idea is that nothing can be "given" to God that human beings have not previously "received" from his bounty. God can never be more God because of what human beings offer him; he must be conceived as beyond any representational logic. The aforementioned bounty is *largitas* in Latin, which the current English translation obscures somewhat by using the more general "goodness." This translation has the advantage of evoking a great deal through possible associations with the compound "good creation," but it has the disadvantage of losing the connotations of generosity and abundance.

The bread and wine are first to be received and then offered. There is another interesting duality in the text: this bread and wine are the result of a double process—they are "fruits" of the earth, or more specifically in the case of the wine the vineyard, as well as the result of human labor. Bread and wine are surely gifts of nature, but not without human hands working upon them, that is, their cultivation. Grain and grapes need to undergo a natural as well as a cultivational process for them to become

24. Christian Schramm and Nicole Stockhoff, "Segensgebete über Brot und Wein," in *Das Wort Gottes hören und den Tisch bereiten: die Liturgie mit biblischen Augen betrachten*, ed. Birgit Jeggle-Merz, Walter Kirschschläger, and Jörg Müller, Luzerner Biblisch-Liturgischer Kommentar zum Ordo Missae 2 (Stuttgart: Katholisches Bibelwerk, 2015), 79–95.

25. Enrico Mazza, *The Celebration of the Eucharist: The Origin of the Rite and the Development of its Interpretation*, trans. Matthew J. O'Connell (Collegeville, MN: Liturgical Press, 1999).

bread and wine. The underlying understanding of creation is that the world is the space in which nature can flourish and produce crops, but also the space where human interventions take place. The fundamental oneness of this space is an important given. Nature and cultivation do not coincide, but humanity is never and never can be detached from nature. Human cultivation is curiously interwoven with nature.

Moreover, there is a third parallel aspect that the blessing prayers make explicit: the bread and wine will become *panis vitae* (bread of life) and *potus spiritalis* (spiritual drink) respectively. These images are taken from the New Testament: Jesus twice calls himself the "bread of life" in John 6 (vv. 35 and 48) and "spiritual drink" is taken from Paul's first letter to the Corinthians (10:4). In both these scriptural passages, references are made to Old Testament practices and meanings related to food and drink and, more importantly, to God's saving intervention for his people. In this context, we note in particular Psalm 116, where we find the expression "cup of salvation" (v. 13). This concept resonates with other references to cup and chalice in the Bible,[26] most prominently again with the "cup of blessing" and "cup of the Lord" from First Corinthians (10:16, 21), and therefore with the core symbolic references of the Eucharist itself.

These rites of offering gifts of bread and wine are key to our investigation of the Ordo Missae and the way in which it imagines creation. Creation is considered a divine gift to humanity and consequently fundamentally good. Creation moreover brings forth fruits that share in that profound givenness and goodness. Human beings' attitude of gratitude, their call to praise and thank God always and everywhere or, in other words, their *being* Eucharistic,[27] contains an important degree of continuity. The rites of the preparation of the gifts imply a positive and welcoming attitude toward the created world. In negative terms, there cannot be an opposition, let alone a contradiction, between the work of creation and the work of salvation. Both constitute "orders" in which the human being is invited to participate. The guiding hypothesis of the following sections about the prefaces and the four Eucharistic prayers is that this line of thought can be corroborated by careful interpretations of these texts.

---

26. Schramm and Stockhoff, "Segensgebete über Brot und Wein," 87–89.
27. Schmemann, *The Eucharist*, passim.

Table 1: The blessing prayers over bread and wine (emphases added)

Blessing prayer over the bread (OM 23)	Blessing prayer over the wine (OM 25)
Benedictus es, Domine, Deus universi, quia de tua largitate accepimus *panem*, quem tibi offerimus, fructum *terrae* et operis manuum hominum: ex quo nobis fiet *panis vitae*. Benedictus Deus in saecula.	Benedictus es, Domine, Deus universi, quia de tua largitate accepimus *vinum*, quem tibi offerimus, fructum *vitis* et operis manuum hominum: ex quo nobis fiet *potus spiritalis*. Benedictus Deus in saecula.

3. The Prefaces

The 2008 Ordo Missae contains exactly fifty prefaces,[28] covering the entire cycle of the liturgical year including memorial feasts for different kinds of saints and masses for the deceased.[29] Prefaces consist of four components, of which the second and the fourth are of particular interest for this chapter: (1) the continuation of the introductory dialogue with which the Eucharistic prayer begins, (2) the presentation of the motive of thanksgiving, usually in an elevated style and with ample reference to the *mirabilia Dei*, (3) a formula that inserts the human motives for thanksgiving into the eternal praise of God by the angels and other inhabitants of heaven; there are sixteen variants of this component, (4) a final section that is the same for every preface: the Sanctus (including the Benedictus).[30]

28. This is a considerable increase when compared to the 1969 Ordo Missae, which had only twenty-two prefaces, seven more than the last "Tridentine" missal, dating from 1962. The growth in the number of prefaces is an interesting phenomenon for study of the vitality of the church's liturgy.

29. These prefaces are not the only ones in the Missale Romanum. Some feasts have their own specific preface, in which case it is part of the individual Mass form (an example in the temporal cycle is Pentecost, in the sanctoral cycle the Exaltation of the Cross). As a rule, however, the prefaces in the Ordo Missae can be used on more than one day or occasion.

30. The best available study of the Sanctus is still Bryan D. Spinks, *The Sanctus in the Eucharistic Prayer* (Cambridge: Cambridge Univ. Press, 1991).

The Sanctus itself is noteworthy for two reasons: it repeats the juxtaposition of heaven and earth that we also encountered in the creeds and it reaffirms the omnipresence and plenitude of glory that is extended both in heaven and on earth, to which the Gloria also alludes. For the liturgy, creation clearly includes heaven and does not coincide with the material world accessible to the senses. Telling in this context, moreover, is that the Latin text of the Sanctus, which is taken from Isaiah 6:3,[31] has the verb *sunt* in the indicative, not in the subjunctive, *sint*, suggesting not a devout wish but sheer reality.

Of the fifty prefaces, one demands our specific attention because it bears the title—and thus embraces the theme and theological program— *de creatione* (for the Latin text and English translation, see Table 2). It is the fifth out of eight prefaces for the Sundays in Ordinary Time (*per annum*). Each of the prefaces lays a particular accent, which is usually emphatically Christological. But this preface is a little different in this respect. The preface first addresses God the Father and refers to the foundations of the world as well as to the special position that the human being occupies in the order of creation. The text has the famous image of God (*imago Dei*) and expresses the idea of the subjection of the universe to the human being to be ruled. What exegetes and moral theologians sometimes tend to milden or contextualize is stated here in a straightforward manner: the task of humanity is to take the lead in creation. However, to take this preface as uncompromising religious justification of the violence humanity is exerting on the earth, in spite of its limited capacity and resources, would not do justice to the text as a whole.[32] The text suggests that the highest goal of the created order, in which the human being doubtlessly has a particular responsibility, is to praise God and to thank God. And the destruction of nature can under no circumstance be part of that.

---

31. Other passages where the fullness of God's glory on earth is expressed include Numbers 14:21, Psalm 72:19, Jeremiah 23:24, and Habakkuk 2:24; 3:3.

32. One can think here of Lynn White's well-known criticism that the creation story from Genesis is co-responsible for the damage done to the earth and for the environmental crisis because of the dominance of human beings over nature it endorses. According to White, this story had great influence on (Western) society and culture. See Lynn White Jr., "The Historical Roots of Our Ecological Crisis," *Science* 155 (1967): 1203–7.

Table 2: The preface *de creatione*

Praefatio V de dominicis "per annum" (OM 56)	Preface Five of the Sundays in Ordinary Time
De creatione	*Creation*
Qui omnia mundi elementa fecisti,	For you laid the foundations of the world
et vices disposuisti temporum variari;	and have arranged the changing of times and seasons;
hominem vero formasti ad imaginem tuam,	you formed man in your own image
et rerum ei subiecisti universa miracula,	and set humanity over the whole world in all its wonder,
ut vicario munere dominaretur omnibus quae creasti,	to rule in your name over all you have made
et in operum tuorum magnalibus iugiter te laudaret,	and forever praise you in your mighty works,
per Christum Dominum nostrum.	through Christ our Lord.

Two other prefaces, the second one for Christmas and the fourth one for Easter,[33] also deserve our attention, for they reflect the single idea, probably not coincidentally on these high days in the liturgical calendar, that Christ restores the entire creation. The words used in the two texts are *universum* and *integritas*. The Christmas preface expresses the hope and expectation that "he might restore unity to all creation," but in Latin one reads *ut [. . .] in integrum restitueret universa* (OM 36)—so, again, the universe, not "creation" per se. The paschal preface observes that "with the old order destroyed, a universe cast down is renewed, and integrity of life is restored to us in Christ" (*vetustate destructa, renovantur universa deiecta, et vitae nobis in Christo reparatur integritas*; OM 48).

The idea that creation is the place where everything will be regenerated through Christ and the paschal mystery is also present in other prefaces. Worth noting are the first three of the five "common prefaces," which can be used in Masses without a preface of their own or have no indicated link with the course of the liturgical year. They are relatively often used and very brief. The first common preface contains Pius X's renowned

---

33. There are three prefaces *De nativitate Domini* (OM 35–37) and five *Praefationes paschales* (OM 45–49).

motto *omnia restaurare (in Christo)* (OM 72) and alludes to the Christ hymn in the second chapter of Paul's letter to the Philippians: Christ was *in forma Dei* but emptied himself and "by the blood of his cross brought peace to all creation" (*per sanguinem crucis suae pacificavit universa*), after which he was elevated above everything (*exaltatus est super omnia*). The second common preface simply says that God created the human being out of goodness (*bonitate hominem condidisti*; OM 73) (see also the solemn blessing after a funeral mass), whereas the third preface sees a parallel between God's creation of the human race and God's benign initiative to reform it from within. Both have to do fundamentally with God's love (OM 74).[34]

Finally, the textual body of the prefaces reinforces the *universal* nature of creation, which is evident from expressions such as *totus mundus* (first preface of the Passion of the Lord; OM 43), *unus orbis* (second preface of the Most Holy Eucharist; OM 61), or *in omnes terrae fines* (second preface of the Blessed Virgin Mary; OM 63). All in all, however, one must conclude that creation is by no means a dominant theme in the fifty prefaces of the Ordo Missae. The incarnation and its many salvific effects, in other words soteriology, are much more dominant. This observation suggests that from a liturgical perspective creation needs to be seen primarily from the perspective of the mystery of redemption as condensed in the paschal event. As a corollary, the doxological calling of the human being is more important than the human being's situation in nature. It is, however, in the world that the Son of God appeared and through what happens in the world that humanity's ultimate reconciliation with God will be accomplished.

4. The Eucharistic Prayers

In a similar way, creation is not a dominant topic in any of the four Eucharistic Prayers. Two points about the first Eucharistic Prayer, the Roman Canon, should be noted. First, some of the semantics of the benediction prayers over bread and wine reoccur.[35] In the *Unde et memores*

---

34. The Latin text of this third common preface is *Qui per Filium dilectionis tuae, sicut conditor generis es humani, ita benignissimus reformator.*

35. From a historical perspective, the reverse is true: first there was the Roman Canon and only much later came the blessing prayers modeled after the Jewish *berakot* prayers.

part of the prayer, reference is made to "the holy Bread of eternal life" and "the Chalice of everlasting salvation" (*Panem sanctum vitae aeternae et Calicem salutis perpetuae*; OM 93). The language is slightly more lyric here, and it is the chalice, the container of the wine but not the wine itself, that is mentioned. Second, there is an echo of the universalism that we noticed earlier. It is applied to "the holy Catholic Church," in particular, with God asked "to grant her peace, to guard, unite and govern her throughout the whole world" (*toto orbe terrarum*; OM 8).

The second Eucharistic Prayer, which is an adaptation of the anaphora from the *Traditio apostolica*,[36] contains the same elements as the Roman Canon, although in a more modest fashion. In the anamnetic part of the prayer there is a simple mention of *panem vitae* and *calicem salutis*, as well as an entreaty for the church, which is dispersed all over the earth (*Ecclesiae tuae toto orbe diffusae*; OM 105).

The third and the fourth Eucharistic Prayers reflect a more developed understanding of creation and the world. After the Sanctus, the third Eucharistic Prayer starts with an acclamation of God's sanctity and immediately refers to the Son and the Holy Spirit. In this context the prayer explicitly recalls that God is the creator, but it does so in a doxological way. The prayer particularly says that it is justified that every creature praises God (*merito te laudat omnis a te condita creatura*) and that God, through the Son and the Spirit, vivifies and sanctifies everything (*vivificas et sanctificas universa*; OM 108). The world appears a second time quite prominently in the intercessions of the third Eucharistic Prayer. The request to God is that the sacrifice of the Eucharist promote the peace

36. For some background to the adaptation, see Bernard Botte, "The Short Anaphora," in *The New Liturgy: A Comprehensive Introduction to the New Liturgy as a Whole and to its New Calendar, Order of Mass, Eucharistic Prayers, the Roman Canon, Prefaces and the New Sunday Lectionary*, ed. Lancelot Sheppard (London: Darton, Longman & Todd, 1970), 194–99. Dom Bernard Botte, from the abbey of Keizersberg near Leuven, prepared a critical edition of this ancient liturgical document, published as one of the first books (vol. 11) in the famous *Sources chrétiennes* series and acknowledged as a major accomplishment of the liturgical movement. Today, however, many of the assumptions Botte took for granted are doubted and debated, but these scholarly discussions seem to have had no impact on the position of the second Eucharistic Prayer in the Ordo Missae. See Paul Bradshaw, Maxwell E. Johnson, and L. Edward Philips, *The Apostolic Tradition: A Commentary*, Hermeneia Series (Minneapolis, MN: Fortress Press, 2002).

and salvation of the whole world (*ad totius mundi pacem atque salutem*; OM 113). In the same passage, one also prays for the church, which is peregrinating "on earth" (*in terra*) and—just as in the first Eucharistic Prayer—this plea is connected with the figure of the pope.[37] His role is to establish and guarantee the unity of the church, wherever she is.

Most references to creation and the world, however, are to be found in the fourth Eucharistic Prayer, of which noted French liturgist Joseph Gelineau, SJ, observed in one of the earliest commentaries that it reflects a "cosmic sense."[38] Unlike for the first, second, and third Eucharistic Prayers, the preface of this prayer is fixed; the accompanying rubric clearly stipulates that it cannot be replaced by another. In that preface, one finds a striking evocation of God's goodness and his creation. God is addressed as the unique good one and the source of life who made everything such that his creatures may be replete with blessings (*qui unus bonus atque fons vitae cuncta fecisti, ut creaturas tuas benedictionibus adimpleres*; OM 116). The idea that creation as a whole can be filled with God's benediction no doubt reflects a powerful and inspiring theology of creation and resonates with what is affirmed in the Sanctus and the Gloria.

The fourth Eucharistic Prayer is noted above all, however, for its dense evocation of the history of salvation, which immediately follows the Sanctus. This evocation starts with creation (see Table 3 for the Latin original and the English translation). The text of this prayer is known for its countless biblical allusions, as evident in this excerpt. There are allusions to the creation story in Genesis 1, where it is said that God creates the human being after his likeness (Gen 1:26), but also to the Psalms (136:5) and Proverbs (3:19), where one finds the idea that God's motivation for creation is love and wisdom. As in the preface *de creatione*, one observes here the idea that the human being is entrusted with rule

37. We must remember that the structure of the first Eucharistic Prayer is significantly different from that of the other Eucharistic Prayers. For commentaries see Sheppard, *The New Liturgy*; Meyer, *Eucharistie*; Vincenzo Raffa, *Liturgia eucaristica: Mistagogia della Messa: dalla storia e dalla teologia alla pastorale pratica*, Bibliotheca Ephemerides Liturgicae. Subsidia 100 (Rome: Edizioni Liturgiche, 1998); Enrico Mazza, *The Eucharistic Prayers of the Roman Rite*, trans. Matthew J. O'Connell (Collegeville, MN: Liturgical Press, 2004).

38. Joseph Gelineau, "The Fourth Eucharistic Prayer," in Sheppard, *The New Liturgy*, 221.

over the earth, although the verb choice here (*imperare*) is different from
the one in that preface (*dominare*). Nevertheless, the fourth Eucharistic
Prayer reflects an open and overall positive attitude toward the world
that was typical of the Second Vatican Council. Notably, it was drafted
by one of the most intriguing figures of that era, the Italian Benedictine
monk Cipriano Vagaggini. Enrico Mazza comments:

> The object of praise is the greatness of God which manifests itself in his
> doing everything in wisdom and love. The logic of wisdom and love guides
> the creative activity of God, which therefore cannot fail to be perfect. The
> perfection is described concretely by speaking of human beings, who are
> defined as God's images. Because they are his images, dominion over the
> universe is entrusted to them, and they become his representatives in the
> world. But, human beings are not autonomous in their activity as caretak-
> ers of the universe; this activity is a service of God the creator and a form
> of worship of him. Consequently, when human beings rule creation, they
> render to God their own special obedience and service.[39]

In other words, one should not forget the doxological, eschatological,
and soteriological embedding of the words that are spoken.

Table 3: Excerpt from the fourth Eucharistic Prayer

Post-Sanctus of the fourth Eucharistic Prayer in Latin (OM 117)	Post-Sanctus of the fourth Eucharistic Prayer in English
Confitemur tibi, Pater sancte, quia magnus es et omnia opera tua in sapientia et caritate fecisti.	We give you praise, Father most holy, for you are great and you have fashioned all your works in wisdom and love.
Hominem ad tuam imaginem condidisti,	You formed man in your own image
eique commisisti mundi curam universi,	and entrusted the whole world to his care,
ut, tibi soli Creatori serviens, creaturis omnibus imperaret.	so that in serving you alone, the Creator, he might have dominion over all creatures.

39. Mazza, *The Eucharistic Prayers*, 164–65.

Other telling details in the fourth Eucharistic Prayer's attention to creation are that in the institution narrative the chalice is explicitly "filled with the fruit of the vine" (*calicem, ex genimine vitis repletum*; OM 120) and that the anamnesis expresses the hope that Christ's sacrifice "brings salvation to the whole world" (*toti mundo salutare*; OM 122), confirming the strong universalism of the Ordo Missae's euchology already noted. This observation is reinforced by the final praying content of the fourth Eucharistic Prayer, before the final doxology. Allusion is made to God's kingdom, where his children will eventually reside with Mary and the saints: "There, with the whole of creation, freed from the corruption of sin and death, may we glorify you through Christ our Lord, through whom you bestow on the world all that is good" (OM 122).[40] Mazza again:

> We find here the same theology that we saw at the beginning of this anaphora: the human person is priest for creation. Final salvation will bring the redemption of all that exists and the definitive epiphany of the kingdom; in the glory of the end-time, the aspiration of every creature will be satisfied as all together form a choir that sings for ever the praises of the father.[41]

5. Incense and Candles

As we seek to grasp the meaning of creation in the Ordo Missae, we can, indeed must, look to additional elements and, I suggest, especially at the material objects mentioned in the text. Because there is so much meaningful literature about them,[42] I will leave aside here the most obvious material objects, bread and wine,[43] and instead focus on two elements that only rarely receive the attention they deserve—candles and incense.

---

40. In Latin: *in regno tuo, ubi cum universa creatura, a corruptione peccati et mortis liberata, te glorificemus per Christum Dominum nostrum, per quem mundo bona cuncta largiris.*

41. Mazza, *The Eucharistic Prayers*, 189.

42. Ghislain Lafont, *Eucharistie: le repas et la parole* (Paris: Cerf, 2001); David Grumett, *Material Eucharist* (Oxford: Oxford Univ. Press, 2016).

43. The major passages where bread and wine are mentioned are in the offertory rites. Bread is mentioned in OM 22 and 23; wine in OM 22, 24, and 25, with the imbalance a result of the aforementioned rite of mixing water with wine. One also finds mentions of bread and wine—although, as indicated above, more often the chalice than the wine itself—in the context of the Eucharistic Prayers.

Candles are explicitly mentioned in the context of the reading of the Gospel (OM 15). A small procession is to travel from where the Gospel book is placed at the beginning of the eucharistic service to the item of furniture (preferably an ambo or lectern) from where the Gospel is proclaimed, by either a deacon or the priest himself. The accompanying rubrics make mention of candles that are to symbolize that the Word of God is the origin of light for one's mind and life. Of note is the phenomenological observation that candles, too, are both "fruit of the earth" and "work of human hands," requiring not only beeswax but also an artisanal production process.[44] Moreover, candles bring about a transformation of sorts: they offer themselves for light and once they are burnt, they exist only in the memory of those who thankfully received the light they gave or even were.

Something similar can be said about incense. It is a natural product, resin, upon which human hands have worked to obtain a wished-for result, in particular by drying and compressing the material. Incense likewise realizes a transformation in which the worshipers are deeply involved, for they can and should symbolically become incense themselves, through their prayers, so that they are—and not just have—an offering pleasing to God in and through Christ (see 2 Cor 2:15).[45]

The references to incense are found in the Ordo Missae in different contexts: during the entrance procession when the altar is incensed, the reading of the Gospel (again), and the preparation of the gifts (OM nos. 1, 15, 27). Not only the gifts themselves and the altar but also the presiding priest and the people can be incensed. In a thought-provoking essay about the relation between liturgy and contemporary culture, German cardinal Walter Kasper notes an intriguing connection here with what *Sacrosanctum concilium* taught about God's presence in the liturgy, namely, that it is not restricted to the eucharistic "species" but extended to other bearers of the same presence as well: the assembly of the faithful, the Gospel,

---

44. Stephen S. Wilbricht, " 'The Work of Bees and of Your Servants' Hands.' A 'New' Exultet with Ancient Cosmic Imagery," *Questions liturgiques / Studies in Liturgy* 93 (2012): 74–99.

45. For a richly documented work on incense, see Michael Pfeifer, *Der Weihrauch: Geschichte, Bedeutung, Verwendung* (Regensburg: Friedrich Pustet, 2018).

and the presider.[46] This broadened understanding of *praesentia* is made possible precisely by the material mediation of liturgical objects, which is not simply an intellectual exercise or an act of will.

6. Concluding Remarks

What can we conclude from this survey of the appearance of the terminology and theology of creation and the world in the Ordo Missae? I limit myself to three brief considerations.

First, the presence of creation vocabulary in the prefaces and in the Eucharistic Prayers is representative of the entire Ordo Missae (and probably also of the Missale Romanum as a whole). Creation is neither a dominant topic nor a primary concern; incarnation and salvation are much more important. However, creation is not as a result unimportant in the Ordo Missae. To the contrary, creation is a crucial underlying theological reality that at significant points surfaces in undeniable allusions as well as in explicit references throughout the Ordo Missae, including the rites constituting the preparation of the gifts, the prefaces, and the Eucharistic Prayers.

Second, it is appropriate to shed light on the vocabulary itself. It has become clear that the terminology around creation and the world is not straightforward. To the contrary, one notices a rich semantics of verbs and nouns. The act of creation is essentially expressed through three verbs: *creare*, *condere*, and *facere*. There is, moreover, consistency in the use of these verbs with God as the only actor. Albeit extremely rarely, God is correspondingly called *Creator* and *Conditor*.[47] For creation itself and the material world there are many nouns: *mundus*, *creatio*, *universum*, *orbis (terrarum)*, *terra*. Each in its own way and with its own accent

---

46. Walter Kasper, "Aspekte einer Theologie der Liturgie: Liturgie angesichts der Krise der Moderne—für eine neue liturgische Kultur," in *Die Liturgie der Kirche*, Walter Kasper Gesammelte Schriften 10 (Freiburg, Basel, and Vienna: Herder, 2010), 58, commenting on *Sacrosanctum concilium* no. 7.

47. The most common words used to address God are *Deus*, *Pater*, and *Dominus*. For a detailed analysis and commentary, see Joris Geldhof, "Le rapport à Dieu dans la liturgie: Une analyse de la dynamique théurgique dans l'Ordo Missae," *Recherches de science religieuse* 105 (2017): 207–22.

264 Theological-Liturgical Perspectives

adds to the overall picture of a rich and deep understanding of the world and its relation to God.

Third, and from a theological point of view, for the Ordo Missae creation is universal. It does not know geographical boundaries; creation is everywhere and anywhere. It is also universal in that it is all-inclusive: there is no human being or any other living creature that is not contained in it. Moreover, it is extended to the world of the dead, the unborn, and even the unseen, and to the inhabitants of heaven, to saints, angels, archangels, etc. Such inclusivity is highly significant in contemporary cultures where identity-focused and diversity-driven ideologies often tend to exclude one another. Perhaps the euchology of the Ordo Missae, as a premier carrier of the Christian faith, can be instrumental in criticizing mechanisms of exclusion and overcoming binaries.

This last idea is supported by one final facet of this investigation. Creation in the Ordo Missae seems not to be simply an ontological status one has or does not have. Being created is not a simple property next to other properties and even less a possession. Being created is something of the order of being and having at the same time, and thereby intrinsically related to mystery.[48] It is, however, above all something to *share*. Creation is what human beings participate in together, among themselves but also in a real connection to the entire world including every living creature and nature as a whole. It is within this constellation that the human being has a special vocation and a special responsibility, as it is within this constellation that the Christ event took place, with lasting effects on who and what and how we are, and who and what and how we are to become and have to become. Creation is the unshakable foundation for the universal transformation, the motor of which is salvation and the goal of which is deification. It is thanks to God and his creation that human persons can flourish, as the Psalmist exclaims:

---

48. One can think here of the inspiring existentialist philosophy of Gabriel Marcel and its possible connections with a Caselian understanding of mystery: see my essay Joris Geldhof, "Meandering in Mystery: Why Theology Today Would Benefit from Rediscovering the Work of Odo Casel," in *Mediating Mysteries, Understanding Liturgies: On Bridging the Gap Between Liturgy and Systematic Theology*, ed. Joris Geldhof, Bibliotheca Ephemeridum Theologicarum Lovaniensium 278 (Leuven, Paris, and Bristol: Peeters, 2015), 11–32.

From your lofty abode you water the mountains;
    the earth is satisfied with the fruit of your work.
You cause the grass to grow for the cattle,
    and plants for people to use,
to bring forth food from the earth,
    and wine to gladden the human heart,
oil to make the face shine,
    and bread to strengthen the human heart.

Psalm 104:13-15

CHAPTER TWELVE

Sacramental Theology after *Laudato Si'*

Kevin W. Irwin

In his ground-breaking encyclical *Laudato Si'* (On Care for Our Common Home), Pope Francis relies on his namesake Saint Francis of Assisi as well as on the Franciscan theological tradition and way of life as his paradigm and source.[1] *Laudato Si'*, published on Pentecost Sunday in 2015, has been identified as "the most important encyclical ever written in the history of the Catholic Church."[2] In what follows here, I ask what *Laudato Si'* has to say for sacramental theology in the future, highlighting five issues derived from the encyclical and noting ties with the Orthodox churches and common roots in Judaism.[3] The intention is to make contemporary and future sacramental theology *ecumenical* and the fruit of the kind of *dialogue* Pope Francis calls for in *Laudato Si'*. In addition, my premise is always to call for a sacramental theology that is based on, immersed in, and a consequence of the *celebration of the liturgy*.[4] The first three issues reflect where and how Pope Francis uses variations on

---

1. Pope Francis, encyclical letter, *Laudato Si'* (On Care for Our Common Home), 24 May 2015, http://w2.vatican.va/content/francesco/en/encyclicals/documents/papa-francesco_20150524_enciclica-laudato-si.html [henceforth cited as LS].

2. See Paul Crowley, "Editorial," *Theological Studies* 77, no. 2 (2016): 293.

3. See my own "Ecology," in *The Oxford Handbook of Ecumenical Studies*, ed. G. Wainwright and P. McPartlan (Oxford: Oxford Univ. Press, 2017), https://doi.org/10.1093/oxfordhb/9780199600847.013.23.

4. Among others, see my own *Context and Text: A Method for Liturgical Theology*, rev. ed. (Collegeville, MN: Liturgical Press, 2018).

the term "sacrament" itself in the encyclical; the final two issues derive from other parts of the encyclical.

1. A Sacramental Vision of the World

Roman Catholic theologians from Edward Schillebeeckx in 1952 to Karl Rahner, Otto Semmelroth, and others in the 1960s and 1970s worked to provide a way to appreciate the sacraments less as seven channels of grace and more as experiences always underpinned by both Christ and the church. The terms *Ursakrament* or *Grundsakrament* (original sacrament or foundational sacrament) were (and are) regularly used to describe these foundations for the sacraments, depending on the author.[5] The shift in understanding marked by these terms saw official endorsement in Vatican II's *Lumen Gentium*, which stated that the church in Christ is "like a sacrament."[6] A similar attempt to move beyond seven channels of grace has been endorsed in the *Catechism of the Catholic Church*, where sacraments are called (for the first time in the magisterium) "sacraments of initiation," "sacraments of vocation," and "sacraments of mission."[7]

5. See, among many others, the summary use of these terms in Raymond Vaillancourt, *Vers un renouveau de la théologie sacramentaire* (Montreal: Fides, 1978), translated by Matthew J. O'Connell as *Toward a Renewal of Sacramental Theology* (Collegeville, MN: Liturgical Press, 1979). At the same time, several theologians critiqued this equivocation of "Christ" and "church" as "sacrament," not least Edward Kilmartin, who asserted that "there is a world of difference" between these two: Edward J. Kilmartin, "A Modern Approach to the Word of God and Sacraments of Christ," in *The Sacraments: God's Love and Mercy Actualized*, ed. Francis A. Eigio (Villanova, PA: Villanova Univ. Press, 1979), 59–109.

6. Pope Paul VI, *Lumen Gentium* (Dogmatic Constitution on the Church), 21 November 1964, par. 1, http://www.vatican.va/archive/hist_councils/ii_vatican_council /documents/vat-ii_const_19641121_lumen-gentium_en.html.

7. *Catechism of the Catholic Church*, par. 1211, states, "Following this analogy, the *first chapter* will expound the three sacraments of Christian initiation; the *second*, the sacraments of healing; and the *third*, the sacraments at the service of communion and the mission of the faithful. This order, while not the only one possible, does allow one to see that the sacraments form an organic whole in which each particular sacrament has its own vital place. In this organic whole, the Eucharist occupies a unique place as the "Sacrament of sacraments": "all the other sacraments are ordered to it as to their end." *Catechism of the Catholic Church*, http://www.vatican.va/archive /ccc_css/archive/catechism/p2s2.htm.

However, as useful as these moves have been in theology and official teaching, one might offer the critique that emphasizing Christ and the church limits the broader, long-standing category of *sacramentality* on which all practice of liturgy and sacraments is based. Put differently, if we understand *sacramentality* as referring primarily to the church's (seven) sacraments, then we lose the rich basis for viewing the world as sacramental, a notion upheld certainly from Tertullian onward.[8] To celebrate sacraments is not to shun the world and all our fellow creatures. In raising them up in worship (rather than "using them"), we engage the world at a deep level of reality through which we experience nothing less than the living God. The first reference to "sacrament" in *Laudato Si'* is in paragraph four of the first section, in a quotation from Patriarch Bartholomew:

> As Christians, we are also called "to accept the world as a sacrament of communion, as a way of sharing with God and our neighbours on a global scale. It is our humble conviction that the divine and the human meet in the slightest detail in the seamless garment of God's creation, in the last speck of dust of our planet."[9]

Pope Francis reveals here both his concern about the environment and, through sacramental language, his passion for ecumenical progress through dialogue with the Orthodox tradition.

For reflection on sacraments, the Orthodox tradition offers rich insight from which Roman Catholics can learn. Since the early 1980s, the Orthodox Patriarchate in Istanbul has taken significant leadership in a variety of ways on ecology.[10] In 1989, for example, the Ecumenical Patriarch set aside a day of prayer for creation. Following his lead, in 2015

---

8. See my own *The Sacraments: Historical Foundations and Liturgical Theology* (New York, NY and Mahwah, NJ: Paulist Press, 2016), 45–48; Tertullian, *De Baptismo*, in *Tertullian's Homily on Baptism*, ed. and trans. Ernest Evans (London: SPCK, 1964); Tertullian, *On the Resurrection of the Flesh*, in *De resurrectione carnis liber: Tertullian's Treatise on the Resurrection*, ed. and trans. Ernst Evans (1960; repr., Eugene, OR: Wipf & Stock, 2016).

9. LS 4, citing Bartholomew's "Global Responsibility and Ecological Sustainability," Closing Remarks, Halki Summit I, Istanbul, 20 June 2012.

10. For a detailed account of these efforts, see the essay by Bert Groen in this volume.

Pope Francis designated 1 September as a Day of Prayer for the Care of Creation. And since the early 2000s, the Ecumenical Patriarch and the Pope have issued several joint statements on creation and ecology. On 25 May 2014, for example, Ecumenical Patriarch Bartholomew and Pope Francis issued a common declaration in Jerusalem, stating on the subjects of creation and the environment:

> It is our profound conviction that the future of the human family depends also on how we safeguard—both prudently and compassionately, with justice and fairness—the gift of creation that our Creator has entrusted to us. Therefore, we acknowledge in repentance the wrongful mistreatment of our planet, which is tantamount to sin before the eyes of God. We reaffirm our responsibility and obligation to foster a sense of humility and moderation so that all may feel the need to respect creation and to safeguard it with care. Together, we pledge our commitment to raising awareness about the stewardship of creation; we appeal to all people of goodwill to consider ways of living less wastefully and more frugally, manifesting less greed and more generosity for the protection of God's world and the benefit of His people.[11]

Orthodoxy's many ecological initiatives have clearly influenced Pope Francis, as can be seen throughout *Laudato Si'*. In a particularly rich paragraph he links environmental interconnectedness to the sacrament of the Eucharist:

> It is in the Eucharist that all that has been created finds its greatest exaltation. Grace, which tends to manifest itself tangibly, found unsurpassable expression when God himself became man and gave himself as food for his creatures. The Lord, in the culmination of the mystery of the Incarnation, chose to reach our intimate depths through a fragment of matter. He comes not from above, but from within, he comes that we might find him in this world of ours. In the Eucharist, fullness is already achieved; it is the living centre of the universe, the overflowing core of love and of inexhaustible life. Joined to the incarnate Son, present in the Eucharist, the whole cosmos gives thanks to God. Indeed the Eucharist is itself an

---

11. Common Declaration of Pope Francis and the Ecumenical Patriarch Bartholomew I, par. 6, 25 May 2014, http://w2.vatican.va/content/francesco /en/speeches/2014/may/documents/papa-francesco_20140525_terra-santa -dichiarazione-congiunta.html.

act of cosmic love: "Yes, cosmic! Because even when it is celebrated on the humble altar of a country church, the Eucharist is always in some way celebrated on the altar of the world." The Eucharist joins heaven and earth; it embraces and penetrates all creation. The world which came forth from God's hands returns to him in blessed and undivided adoration: in the bread of the Eucharist, "creation is projected towards divinization, towards the holy wedding feast, towards unification with the Creator himself." Thus, the Eucharist is also a source of light and motivation for our concerns for the environment, directing us to be stewards of all creation. (LS 236)

It is notable that Pope Francis uses the term "stewardship" only twice in *Laudato Si'*. In article 119 he cites the Federation of Asian Bishops' Conferences' text *On the Love of Creation*, stating, "our 'dominion' over the universe should be understood more properly in the sense of responsible stewardship," and he cites the concept a second time at the end of this section on the Eucharist. On every other occasion when "stewardship" might have been used, the pope refers to "care" for "our common home." Avoiding "stewardship" means avoiding any understanding that humans are to use nature or that creation requires humans to give voice to nature. A sacramental vision of life means that liturgy is contextualized as derived from the earth and human life and that liturgy returns us to respect and revere the earth and all that dwells on it in daily life.

2. Sabbath Rest, Restoration and Belonging

The second variation on the term "sacrament" in *Laudato Si'* is "sacramental signs," found in a subtitle in chapter six, "Ecological Education and Spirituality," for a subsection entitled "Sacramental Signs and the Celebration of Rest" (pars. 233–37). Here Francis links the Jewish Sabbath with the Christian experience of Sunday, a day on which Christians receive the Eucharist and, moreover, "a day which heals our relationships with God, with ourselves, with others and with the world" (par. 237). The requirement that the Sabbath be observed derives from the Old Testament and has remained a hallmark of Jewish practice up until today. That it begins at table in the evening with the lighting of candles and invocation "Lord, God of all creation" is poignant and rich for all Jews and Christians ritually, theologically, and spiritually.

The Sunday celebration of the Eucharist is meant to be framed by leisure—the kind of sacred leisure that the Sabbath prescriptions ensured.

To celebrate the Eucharist with and for each other is part and parcel of the kind of "human" ecology which popes have called for since Pope John Paul II. Integral ecology is forcefully argued by Pope Francis in *Laudato Si'* and constitutes a central contribution to a Catholic ecological vision.[12] For example, in article 237 of *Laudato Si'*, Francis asserts,

> On Sunday, our participation in the Eucharist has special importance. Sunday, like the Jewish Sabbath, is meant to be a day which heals our relationships with God, with ourselves, with others and with the world. Sunday is the day of the Resurrection, the "first day" of the new creation, whose first fruits are the Lord's risen humanity, the pledge of the final transfiguration of all created reality. It also proclaims "man's eternal rest in God". In this way, Christian spirituality incorporates the value of relaxation and festivity. We tend to demean contemplative rest as something unproductive and unnecessary, but this is to do away with the very thing which is most important about work: its meaning.

Yet even as we can assert these values, the fact that many of us live in a 24/7 culture of instant access anytime, anywhere needs to be evaluated. What is happening to us when handheld devices and continuous access to the internet become presumptions and assumptions about the way we live our lives? The language of paragraph 47 of *Laudato Si'* is forceful and compelling and invites us into a different way of living, with the internet held in check: we are to learn "to live wisely, to think deeply and to love generously." At the center here is the issue of our relationships with each other and with all in "our common home," relationships that are presumed, raised up, and, where necessary, set in proper order by the celebration of the liturgy.

In America, one congenital difficulty has been with jettisoning rugged individualism and individual freedoms in favor of the common good and of caring for one another just because we are each other. In the practice of sacraments, I see more than a creeping individualism in confirmation theologies and programs that emphasize making a "personal commitment to Jesus," in making "my mature act of faith," or when candidates

---

12. See my own *A Commentary on* Laudato Si'*: Examining the Background, Contributions, Implementation and Future of Pope Francis' Encyclical* (New York, NY and Mahwah, NJ: Paulist Press, 2016), 117–19.

"become adults in the faith."[13] This development is also seen in wedding and funeral planning, and it sometimes encroaches on the celebration of First Masses by newly ordained priests.

The celebration of the liturgy should express and deepen our commitment to belonging to a parish or other community, day in and day out. But what if when determining how and what we will experience, we work hard not to hear what we do not want to hear or not to celebrate with people who do not look like us or who are from different ethnic backgrounds? In choosing with whom they will worship, individuals might mitigate, or even bring to an end, their being part of each other if the "other" are the poor, the ostracized, or of different educational backgrounds or political persuasions. The church is and ought to be a mosaic of different colors, shapes, and sizes which together make up the Body of Christ. If we do not accept the immigrant, feed the poor, or work to assist the unemployed, have we been faithful to the Gospel of Christ preached by both Francis the pope and Francis the saint of Assisi? Have we been faithful to the Gospel described in the words of the fourth Eucharistic Prayer:

> To the poor he proclaimed the good news of salvation,
> to prisoners, freedom,
> and to the sorrowful of heart, joy.

3. Sacramental Mediation through Creation and the Incarnation

Near the end of *Laudato Si'*, in article 235, Pope Francis asserts,

> The Sacraments are a privileged way in which nature is taken up by God to become a means of mediating supernatural life. Through our worship of God, we are invited to embrace the world on a different plane. Water, oil, fire and colours are taken up in all their symbolic power and incorporated in our act of praise. The hand that blesses is an instrument of God's love and a reflection of the closeness of Jesus Christ, who came to accompany

13. See the brilliant analysis of the coopting of the sacrament of confirmation by both the individualist tendencies of American culture and by religious education and faith formation programs since Vatican II in Timothy R. Gabrielli, *Confirmation: How a Sacrament about God's Grace Became All about Us* (Collegeville, MN: Liturgical Press, 2013).

us on the journey of life. Water poured over the body of a child in Baptism is a sign of new life.

There is a primalness to Catholic worship that stands alongside the use of prayers that contain concepts, images, and metaphors about God and the human condition. If we lose, or eclipse, the primalness of liturgy, we cut ourselves loose from a mooring characteristic of the way we have always worshiped God—through fellow creatures and creation herself.[14]

Sacrosanctum Concilium (Constitution on the Sacred Liturgy) speaks of Christ as "the Word made flesh" and that "His humanity, united with the person of the Word, was the instrument of our salvation."[15] Here the constitution reiterates the famous phrase from Tertullian about the flesh being the hinge of salvation that Cipriano Vagaggini popularized in writing and teaching shortly after Vatican II.[16] To my way of thinking, bodily use and bodily expression have been given less emphasis than they should in the implementation and celebration of the reformed liturgy. (One explanation might be that the implementation of the vernacular liturgy required a major focus on the texts of the liturgy, both in their translation and for the execution of the reformed liturgy.) The corporality of the liturgy resonates well with classical sources that describe how gestures and postures function in the liturgy. The liturgy presumes the active engagement of the whole person—body, mind, heart, and will—through the senses. Especially because the sacramentality of creation is a major tenet of Roman Catholicism, the principle and doctrine of the sacramentality of creation are closely linked with the principle of the incarnation—that God is revealed through created means, including the

14. In light of the appeal of *Laudato Si'*, I am making an effort to avoid the objectification or reification of any aspect of creation or the symbols used in the liturgy. I am working to move from language using "things" to a language of relationship and relatedness. Hence the personal pronoun *herself* used here rather than *itself*.

15. Paul VI, *Sacrosanctum Concilium* (Constitution on the Sacred Liturgy), 4 December 1963, par. 5, http://www.vatican.va/archive/hist_councils/ii_vatican_council /documents/vat-ii_const_19631204_sacrosanctum-concilium_en.html.

16. Cipriano Vagaggini, *The Flesh, Instrument of Salvation: A Theology of the Human Body* (Staten Island, NY: Alba House, 1969), originally published as *"Caro Salutis est Cardo": Corporeità, eucaristia e liturgia* (1st ed., 1966; new ed., Arezzo: Edizioni Camaldoli, 2009). More recently, see Frank Senn, *Embodied Liturgy: Lessons in Christian Ritual* (Minneapolis, MN: Fortress Press, 2016).

human, and that salvation for the human race came through the incarnation of God's Son. The sacramentality of creation and the incarnation underscores the discoverability of God in human life and explains why created things are used both as a motivation and a means to praise and worship God.

Every celebration of the liturgy is an act of "mediated immediacy."[17] This phrase proposes that we experience God in the church's most privileged moments and manner through all that dwells in this world, through human beings and through rites and texts crafted by the church. One of the main values of the liturgy is that it invites us into a direct encounter and experience of God. It does so not by shunning the world, but by experiencing the elements of this earth as mediators of divine realities. At least two premises are operative here: that the ecclesiological foundation of the liturgy counters the individualism that plagues many in (Western) Catholicism today and that mediation through creation and "the work of human hands" is always christological. The prayers that we use to accompany creation and the result of human work articulate these meanings, always ending "through Christ our Lord."

The prayers in the Roman Rite do not address Jesus without a modifier or a modifying phrase. Catholics pray "through Christ our Lord" or address "Lord Jesus Christ who said . . ." All liturgy is mediated through, with, and in the risen and exalted Lord. It is not about the earthly Jesus. Christ's paschal dying and rising are the means for our union with God and our sanctification.

The triad of creation, incarnation, and mediation should be kept in mind as we articulate our understanding of the principles of sacramental theology as influenced by *Laudato Si'*, in order that sacraments can be appreciated in their theological depth.

4. The Interrelationship of All Creatures on This Good Earth

The God we believe in is a God who acts. We believe in the biblical God of the covenant, the God of creation, and the God of redemption. Ever since God invited human beings into covenant, all of us are related to God in and through that relationship and are related to one another

17. See my own "Liturgy as Mediated Immediacy: Sacramentality and Enacted Words," *Josephinum Journal of Theology* 19, no. 1 (2013): 129–40.

and every living creature as sharers in the covenant. The biblical phrase "the God of Abraham, the God of Isaac and the God of Jacob/Israel" is shorthand for the idea that God is a relational God and that we are related to each other and to all creatures on this good earth, as Pope Francis reminds us again and again in *Laudato Si'*, where this rich and recurring theme requires that we rethink and reimage how we understand plants, animals, and all other living things as companions.

In religious discussions of ecology, the covenant with Noah, his family, and the animals (Gen 9) is an important basis for debate about creation and the apparent inherent interrelationships.[18] Notably, the covenant with Noah has a prized place in liturgy. For example, the prayer to bless water at the Easter Vigil refers to:

Deus, qui regeneratiónis spéciem in ipsa dilúvii effusióne signásti, ut uníus eiusdémque eleménti mystério et finis esset vítiis et orígo virtútum	O God, who by the outpouring of the flood foreshadowed regeneration, so that from the mystery of one and the same element of water would come an end to vice and a beginning of virtue

Further, when the priest takes the bread and wine and places it on the altar at Mass, he says:

Benedíctus es, Dómine, Deus univérsi, quia de tua largitáte accépimus panem, quem tibi offérimus, fructum terræ et óperis mánuum hóminum: ex quo nobis fiet panis vitæ.	Blessed are you, Lord God of all creation, for through your goodness we have received the bread we offer you: fruit of the earth and work of human hands, it will become for us the bread of life.

18. Among other sources see "Faith Based Statements on Climate Change, June, 2012," https://citizensclimatelobby.org/files/images/Faith%20Based%20Statements%20PDF%20for%20printing.pdf.

. . . fructum vitis et óperis mánuum hóminum, ex quo nobis fiet potus spiritális. Benedictus Deus in saecula	. . . fruit of the vine and work of human hands, it will become our spiritual drink. Blessed be God for ever.

The acclaiming of the God of creation is supported the liturgy's frequent acclamation of what we might regard as "things" as "creatures." The rite for the blessing and sprinkling with holy water on Sundays begins with the priest saying these or similar words:

Dóminum Deum nostrum, fratres caríssimi, supplíciter deprecémur, ut *hanc creatúram aquæ* benedícere dignétur, super nos aspergéndam in nostri memóriam baptísmi. Ipse autem nos adiuváre dignétur, ut fidéles Spirítui, quem accépimus, maneámus.	Dear brethren (brothers and sisters), let us humbly beseech the Lord our God to bless this water he has created [or, *this creature water*], which will be sprinkled on us as a memorial of our Baptism. May he help us by his grace to remain faithful to the Spirit we have received.

In the same rite, when the priest adds salt to the water, he blesses it, saying:

Súpplices te rogámus, omnípotens Deus, ut *hanc creatúram salis* benedícere + tua pietáte dignéris, qui per Eliséum prophétam in aquam mitti eam iussísti, ut sanarétur sterílitas aquæ.	We humbly ask you, almighty God: be pleased in your faithful love to bless + this salt you have created, [or, *this creature salt*] for it was you who commanded the prophet Elisha to cast salt into water, that impure water might be purified.

Similarly, the blessing prayer for baptismal water at the Easter Vigil begins:

Deus, qui invisíbili poténtia	O God, who by invisible power
per sacramentórum signa mirábilem	accomplish a wondrous effect
operáris efféctum,	through sacramental signs
et *creatúram aquæ* multis modis	and who in many ways have
præparásti,	prepared water, your creation,
ut baptísmi grátiam demonstráret	[or, *your creature water*]
	to show forth the grace of Baptism

If Pope Francis calls us to appreciate the "interrelationship of all" and that we are fellow creatures on this common home, then we need to examine how the language we use reflects the working of liturgy and sacrament. Rhetoric that speaks of "using" "things" or "objects" in worship needs to be rethought and our conventional categories about sacraments reenvisioned. We should use rhetoric that acclaims, raises up, values, and reveres God's gifts to us in nature and as fellow beings on this earth. The opening words of *Laudato Si'*, from Saint Francis's Canticle of the Creatures, provide a meaningful example: "Praise be to you, my Lord". . . "praise to you, my Lord through our Sister, Mother Earth, who sustains and governs us." An immediate correlative is the singing of the Canticle of the Three from Daniel in the Liturgy of the Hours for Sunday Morning Prayer (Dan 3:57-88, 56).[19]

It is admittedly a herculean task first to rethink our relationships with fellow creatures on this earth in light of who we are in the celebration of the liturgy of the sacraments and then to recast our sacramental vocabulary so that it is truly sacramental. Nevertheless, the precedent set in the liturgy's phrases "creature water" and "creature salt" as indicated in the sacramental celebrations cited above should become a paradigm.

In addition to using words of relationship to refer to fellow creatures like water, when we appreciate that we cannot live without water, we recognize in the sacrament of baptism the sharing of a primal element needed to sustain human life. That water is life-giving and life-sustaining is central to any understanding and appreciation of what water baptism is and means. Catholic social teaching has asserted, and under Pope Francis has repeatedly reiterated, that everyone on the planet has a right to potable water. In *Laudato Si'* Francis argues,

---

19. See also the article in this volume by Anathea Portier-Young, on Daniel 3.

Fresh drinking water is an issue of primary importance . . . One particularly serious problem is the quality of water available to the poor. Every day, unsafe water results in many deaths and the spread of water-related diseases, including those caused by microorganisms and chemical substances . . . Even as the quality of available water is constantly diminishing, in some places there is a growing tendency, despite its scarcity, to privatize this resource, turning it into a commodity subject to the laws of the market. Yet access to safe drinkable water is a basic and universal human right. (LS 28–30)

5. "The Work of Human Hands"

Another aspect of valuing fellow creatures on our common home is our valuing of humans and human work. In the case of liturgy and the sacraments, we are concerned with how humans respect and revere their fellow creatures and their ingenuity and productivity. Manufactured goods such as bread, wine, and oil carry meaning about humanity on various levels, including that of human work. Pope Francis reminds us in *Laudato Si'* that humans are to "have dominion" over the earth (Gen 1:28), to "till it and keep it" (Gen 2:15). Then he deepens these assertions by saying in article 67:

> We are not God. The earth was here before us and it has been given to us. This allows us to respond to the charge that Judaeo-Christian thinking, on the basis of the Genesis account which grants man 'dominion' over the earth (cf. Gen 1:28), has encouraged the unbridled exploitation of nature by painting him as domineering and destructive by nature. This is not a correct interpretation of the Bible as understood by the Church.

Pope Francis asserts that "tilling" refers to cultivating, ploughing, or working, while "keeping" means caring, protecting, overseeing, and preserving. The suggestion is of a reciprocal relationship between human beings and nature: each community can take from the bounty of the earth what it needs for its subsistence, but it also has a duty to protect the earth and to ensure its fruitfulness for coming generations. That relationship is part of the theology that underlies our working with fellow creatures to manufacture bread and wine for the Eucharist. In effect, the processes of making bread and wine are paschal processes. Bread requires planting seeds, tilling the earth, harvesting the wheat, milling the grain, and baking. John 12:24 states that unless a grain of wheat falls and dies it remains a single grain; if the grain dies, it yields rich fruit. The case for the wine is similar: someone plants the vine and trims, waters and cultivates it, the grapes are harvested, crushed, and left to ferment—a paschal process. There is a rich theology of creation in reflecting on the "bread-ness" of the bread and the "wine-ness" of the wine consumed in the Eucharist. Their reality remains true even as we place them on the altar as gifts to be transformed into the gift beyond all telling—the paschal sacrifice of our Lord Jesus Christ.[20]

The presentation of these "works of human hands" also benefits the other eucharistic participants, including workers and donors.[21] In *Laudato Si'* the pope links a theology of ecology with food distribution, especially for the poor. In a poignant section of the encyclical the pope offers a piercing challenge, not to say condemnation, by asserting that "we know that approximately a third of all food produced is discarded, and 'whenever food is thrown out it is as if it were stolen from the table of the poor' " (LS 50). This reference to food brings us back to the celebration of the Eucharist where the presentation of the bread and wine on the altar as gifts represents the collecting (and distribution) of gifts for the poor. The first summary description of the way the early Christians celebrated the Eucharist comes from Justin Martyr in the middle of the second century, and he notes that the wealthy offer gifts for the poor at the time of the presentation of the eucharistic gifts.[22] The custom of having deacons collect and distribute these gifts continued to be attested in liturgical literature until the (permanent) diaconate faded during the Middle Ages from the practice of the Roman Church.

In addition to our concern for the immediate need of others for food and drink, we must recognize the impoverishment that the earth can experience as a result of unfair work practices. In addition to reiterating Catholic social teaching on receiving a "just wage,"[23] Pope Francis

20. This line of argument reflects the value which the Roman Rite has placed on (wheat) bread for the celebration of the Eucharist.

21. See Edward J. Kilmartin, "The Sacrifice of Thanksgiving and Social Justice," in *Liturgy and Social Justice*, ed. Mark Searle (Collegeville, MN: Liturgical Press, 1980), 53–71.

22. Justin Martyr, *The First Apology*, in *Justin Martyr: The First and Second Apologies*, trans. Leslie William Barnard, Ancient Christian Writers 56 (New York, NY and Mahwah, NJ: Paulist Press, 1997), especially chaps. 65 and 67.

23. One such example is found in relating the human work required for the symbols of the liturgy to just working conditions and a just wage. See, for example,

cites pollution, deforestation, and ecological imbalances that result from unjust practices. For example, he speaks in some detail about pollution in article 20 of *Laudato Si'*:

> Some forms of pollution are part of people's daily experience. Exposure to atmospheric pollutants produces a broad spectrum of health hazards, especially for the poor, and causes millions of premature deaths. People take sick, for example, from breathing high levels of smoke from fuels used in cooking or heating. There is also pollution that affects everyone, caused by transport, industrial fumes, substances which contribute to the acidification of soil and water, fertilizers, insecticides, fungicides, herbicides and agrotoxins in general.[24]

Pope Francis's emphasis here on pollution leads to his now often-used phrase "a throwaway culture." Here the pope combines a critique of unchecked free-market approaches to the economy that destroy this good earth with a challenge to us in light of our use and abuse of our fellow companions on the earth: plants, animals, fellow humans and the earth itself.

Conclusion

What can we say about the celebration of sacramental liturgy in response to these key issues from Pope Francis's encyclical? I wish to highlight three issues. First, sacramental liturgy substantiates the contemporary emphasis on the theology of creation and places it on a truly

---

Cardinal Peter Kodwo Appiah Turkson, "The Eucharist and Care for Creation," 2016, https://www.catholicculture.org/culture/library/view.cfm?recnum=11139, an address given at the Fifty-first International Eucharistic Congress, Philippines, 28 January 2016.

24. In LS 21 Pope Francis continues, "Account must also be taken of the pollution produced by residue, including dangerous waste present in different areas. Each year hundreds of millions of tons of waste are generated, much of it non-biodegradable, highly toxic and radioactive, from homes and businesses, from construction and demolition sites, from clinical, electronic and industrial sources. The earth, our home, is beginning to look more and more like an immense pile of filth. In many parts of the planet, the elderly lament that once beautiful landscapes are now covered with rubbish. Industrial waste and chemical products utilized in cities and agricultural areas can lead to bioaccumulation in the organisms of the local population, even when levels of toxins in those places are low."

theological foundation in stressing that the things of this earth used in liturgy are from God's goodness, as natural symbols of God's providence (water) or the result of human manufacture from what the earth has produced (bread, wine). These are not objects; they are means for us humans to articulate our faith in the triune God. Sacramental liturgy regularly provides a biblical and paschal prism through which we are to view creation and the world—biblical in that we see the world as created and sustained by the God of the covenant, God the Creator and Redeemer, and paschal in that we see all things in life from the perspective of Christ's paschal mystery. In an incarnational worldview, to see the world as sacramental means that even as we name the world's flaws, Christ's paschal victory makes us confident of its final perfection.

Second, sacramental liturgy prevents us from being pessimistic about the world and world events. By its very shape and structure, sacramental liturgy is a ritual experience that reflects an optimistic approach to human life. In the end, all will be well. In the meantime, we need sacramental liturgy to bring the world into focus and to provide perspective. Opportunities for experiences of hope abound in the celebration of sacraments— hope in the act of liturgy and hope derived from the act of liturgy, which enable us to deal with and face into human life. Among other examples in the eucharistic liturgy, the singing of the "Holy, Holy, Holy" acclamation is insightful and instructive. Every time Roman Catholics celebrate the Mass we acclaim "heaven and earth are full of your glory." In the earth, too, God's glory is seen and experienced.

Third, sacramental liturgy articulates our belief that we worship God by raising up this good earth, our fellow creatures, and "the work of human hands." It is therefore always both anthropological and cosmic; it articulates what we believe about the human person and the cosmos. Through sacramental liturgy human persons put their lives and the world itself into proper perspective. We raise up "daily and domestic things" in the liturgy, specifically in bathing at baptism and in dining during the Eucharist. Both of these sacramental signs emerge from creation and human productivity, and they allow us to reflect back on the goodness, generosity, and largesse of the God we worship. We raise up the daily and domestic in sacramental liturgy to order (what is sometimes) the chaos of human life and to set us in proper relation with the world and all who dwell in it.

Our task is to make sure we view liturgy as a deep and strong ritual expression of the fact that God lives among us prior to, within, and following upon sacramental engagement. The function of sacramental liturgy in its uniqueness is certainly about bringing to the world what we have experienced in the liturgy, but it is also about underscoring how what we do in liturgy derives from the world and everyday life. This liturgical ritualization helps us order our lives and our world once more in God's image and likeness. From the perspective of sacramentality, we can say that sacraments are less doors to the sacred than they are the experience of the sacred in and through human life, an experience shaped by the liturgical action of the sacraments.

Every time we take bread and wine in the act of "doing" the Eucharist and "dining" in and from it, we articulate the theology of the goodness of creation and our need for food to sustain us as the "pilgrim church on earth" until we are fed at the "Supper of the Lamb." In the meantime, the very taking, blessing, breaking, and sharing of bread and wine make the central theological statement about our place in the cosmos. All sacramental liturgy makes sense in the first place because in it we raise up goods from the earth, which action reminds us of our place in this world even as we yearn for it to pass away. All sacramental liturgy is like our anticipatory participation in the "supper of the Lamb" (Rev 19:4) in and through the Eucharist. When all is complete at last, when the Eucharist has become viaticum, when "sacraments shall cease" (in the words of Charles Wesley), then we will share in a "new heaven and a new earth" for all eternity (Rev 21:1). In the meantime, sacraments matter, words matter, and matter matters.

CHAPTER THIRTEEN

A Spring of Blessing

Creation and Sanctification in Byzantine Liturgy and Piety

Nicholas Denysenko

In the summer of 1993, with my brother and grandfather, I visited Kyiv, the capital of Ukraine and native homeland of my grandparents. Our apartment was a five-minute walk from St. Volodymyr Cathedral, the primatial cathedral for the Ukrainian Orthodox Church. We attended daily Vespers during our stay, and on 19 August we attended the Divine Liturgy for the feast of the Transfiguration. It is customary for Byzantine Rite Christians to bring fruit to the church for the Transfiguration feast, a tradition that coincides with the harvesting of produce, as the summer rains had met fertile soil to make sweet fruit.[1] I had only experienced this festal blessing in the United States and was amazed at the difference in Kyiv: the inside of the church was packed (on a working day!) with people, and it was impossible not to trip over the enormous baskets of fruit filled high. At the end of the liturgy, the presiding bishop emerged from the sanctuary bearing a large brush and escorted by subdeacons holding jars of water. He walked up and down the line, inside and outside the church, blessing the baskets of fruits and drenching the people with

---

1. *The Festal Menaion*, trans. Mother Mary and Kallistos Ware, intro. Georges Florovsky (South Canaan, PA: St. Tikhon's Seminary Press, 1990), 502–3. For a good translation of the blessing of fruits and similar blessings, see *The Divine Liturgy: An Anthology for Worship*, ed. Peter Galadza et al. (Ottawa: Metropolitan Andrey Sheptytsky Institute, 2004), 1116.

water. As he approached, the people pressed forward, and we were caught in a crowd of bodies, packed like sardines—they wanted the blessing, and we received a makeshift summer shower of holy water.

A crowd of human bodies pressed together to come close enough to the bishop for a holy sprinkling discloses humanity's desire to be touched by God. The desire for blessing through bodily touch is a recurring theme in popular religion, and the New Testament witnesses to it: the woman with the flow of blood comes to mind, as she makes her way through the crowd just to touch Jesus, who is in high demand. The people believe that God will touch them: the divine touch *makes everything whole*, and it happens in the materials of garments, water, oil, food, and drink.

The last century has witnessed to an outpouring of groundbreaking theological scholarship showing how God acts in liturgy to *make everything whole* with great reverence. The eucharistic revival is the fruit of generations of liturgical studies that reunited word with sacrament and showed that the extraordinary transformation occurring at liturgy is that of people partaking of God's gifts, and not limited to changing bread and wine to Christ's body and blood. The liturgical traditions of the Christian East are familiar with the divine grace formulary of the rite of ordination: God's grace heals that which is infirm, making the ordinand whole, and in the Byzantine liturgy, the assembly invokes God to impart the same divine grace at every Divine Liturgy: "that our God who loves mankind, having accepted them at His holy and celestial and mystical altar as an offering of spiritual fragrance, may in return send down upon us the divine grace and the gift of the Holy Spirit, let us pray."[2] This generation of liturgical scholars and students has inherited the fruits of those who showed how God has acted for the people and changed them through the liturgy: there is a symbiosis of theocentrism and anthropocentrism in the liturgy, with honor given to God as liturgy's initiator and its most active participant. It is one thing to claim that God has imparted divine grace and that participants have received it; it is another to substantiate the claim that communicants "have seen the true light" and have "received the heavenly spirit" and divine grace.[3] Liturgists have an opportunity

2. *The Liturgy of St. John Chrysostom*, priest edition (Brookline, MA: Holy Cross Orthodox Press, 2015), 61.

3. In the Byzantine Rite Divine Liturgy, the people sing a troparion after Communion and before the dismissal proclaiming, "we have seen the true light, we have received the heavenly Spirit," ibid., 79.

to enrich liturgical study and practice by reintroducing humankind's abandoned partner to the academic dialogue: creation.

The remainder of this essay presents examples of the active participation of creation in God's salvation of humankind through Byzantine liturgical texts and practices. I compare the liturgical ordo with the people's insatiable attraction to material stuff to call for the restoration of a muted Christian ministry during a time of crisis: to reflect on how humankind might account for its stewardship of the stuff God has given it when it stands before the awesome judgment seat of Christ.[4]

Divine Activity in Matter

The liturgical texts appointed to the services of the blessing of waters establish a pattern in which God uses water to save and sustain humankind, over and over again. The texts form a repetitive or ongoing anamnesis of the instrumentality of water in God's saving activity: an anamnesis that positions the assembly to invoke God to use water to save us again, at the blessing of baptismal waters and also at the blessing of waters on Theophany.

The Theophany blessing of waters celebrated in the Eastern tradition on 6 January has many texts mentioning God's use of water to save humankind, but the central prayer is the Great are You prayer.[5] A different version of this prayer is also used for the consecration of baptismal waters. The beginning of the prayer recalls how God called creation into being:

> Great are you, Lord, and marvelous are your works: no words suffice to praise of your wonders. For you by your own will have brought all things out of nothingness into being, by your power you hold together the creation, and by your providence you govern the world. Of four elements have you compounded the creation: with four seasons have you crowned the circuit of the year. All the spiritual powers tremble before you. The sun

4. See Peter Bouteneff, "Sacraments as the Mystery of Union: Elements of an Orthodox Sacramental Theology," in *The Gestures of God: Explorations in Sacramentality*, ed. Geoffrey Rowell and Christine Hall (New York, NY: Continuum, 2004), 91–108.

5. See Nicholas Denysenko, *The Blessing of Waters and Epiphany: The Eastern Liturgical Tradition*, foreword by Dominic Serra, Liturgy, Worship and Society Series (Burlington, VT: Ashgate, 2012), 83–101.

sings your praises; the moon glorifies you; the stars supplicate before you; the light obeys you; the deeps are afraid at your presence; the fountains are your servants; you have stretched out the heavens like a curtain; you have established the earth upon the waters; you have walled about the sea with sand; you have poured forth the air that living things may breathe. The angelic powers minister to you; the choirs of archangels worship you; the many-eyed cherubim and the six-winged seraphim, standing round about you and flying about you, hide their faces in fear of your unapproachable glory. You, the uncircumscribed God without beginning and beyond speech, have come upon earth, taking the form of a servant and being made in the likeness of man.[6]

An anamnesis is multifunctional, and one of those functions is to recreate a picture of the world God created for the assembly. The prayer is deeply theocentric, and from its beginning it is not humankind that worships God, but creation: the sun and moon praise and glorify God; the stars and lights worship obediently; the waters serve the Lord's will. God is in charge and creation is not a mere subject to be acted upon, but voluntarily surrenders itself to God in service to the divine will. The creatures have life and inhabit this world created by God. The prayer's thesis is that God is the master of creation, and creation executes God's will. Creation bears God's touch, it comes into contact with God because of the Incarnation: God comes into the world "in the likeness of man" and "in the form of a servant." The prayer does not hesitate to introduce the paradox of God's condescension from the outset: we already know that Paul said that Christ "did not consider it robbery" to be equal with God (Phil 2:6, NKJV). The prayer quotes Philippians 2:7 when it says that Christ took on the form of a servant and took on the likeness of man: this event took place in the same created world inhabited by people, the servant of all living with the creation that also serves God. The prayer mentions God's mercy for humankind, held captive "by the tyranny of the devil," with the incarnation of the Logos God's response to the divine dilemma. After recalling Christ's birth, the prayer then recalls his epiphany, noting again that creation joins in praising Christ when he appears: "At your epiphany the whole creation sang your praises. For you, our God, have appeared on earth and dwelt among men, you have sanctified the streams of the

---

6. Translation based on *The Festal Menaion*, trans. Mother Mary and Ware, 356–58.

Jordan, sending down from on high the most Holy Spirit, and you have broken the heads of the dragons hidden therein."[7]

The prayer's theological priority is to establish the godhead of Christ: Christ is in charge of the spirits in the waters, too—just as they trembled at the divine presence at creation, because God is the king, they trembled when Jesus entered the waters of the Jordan, as he "breaks the heads" of the dragons hidden within. This rich anamnesis of creation as the worshiper and servant of God recalled in the anamnesis carries over into the epiclesis:

> Therefore, king who loves humankind, come forward now as then through the descent of your Holy Spirit, and bless this water. And grant it the grace of redemption, the blessing of Jordan. Make it a spring of blessing, a gift of sanctification, a protection against disease, a destruction to demons, inaccessible to the adverse powers and filled with angelic strength: that all who draw from it and partake of it may have it for the cleansing of their soul and body, for the healing of their passions, for the sanctification of their homes, and for every purpose that is expedient.[8]

The key to the anamnesis is God's appointment of creation as God's servant: creation serves God in the blessing of waters by becoming a source of blessing, protection, redemption, healing, cleansing, and every good thing for humankind. The anamnesis stated that God entered the created realm to release humankind from the tyranny of the devil. Creation's service to God is to become that medium of encounter with the divine, so the human participant can be transformed when they touch creation since divine grace is given to humans through created matter. As in the original act of creation, created matter does not stand still: its service to God, its glorification of God takes place when it creates the space and the event through which humans encounter God.

The next section of the text from the Great are You prayer establishes the consistent service of creation to God's will throughout salvation history. This text is a series of doxologies that refer to acts through which God saved or sustained humankind. A selection of texts from this section of the prayer reads:[9]

7. Ibid., 356.
8. Ibid., 357.
9. Ibid.

> For you are our God, who has renewed through water and the Spirit our nature grown old through sin (John 3:5). You are our God who drowned sin through water [in the days of] Noah (Gen 7).
>
> You are our God, who in the days of Moses set free the Hebrew nation through the sea from the bondage of Pharaoh (Exod 14).
>
> You are our God who cleft the rock in the wilderness: the waters gushed out, the streams overflowed, and you satisfied your thirsty people (Exod 17, Ps 78).
>
> You are our God who by water and fire through Elijah brought back Israel from the error of Baal (2 Kgs 10:18-28).
>
> You are our God, who healed the bitter and barren waters by the salt of Elisha (2 Kgs 2:19-22).

The waters created by God rendered service in baptism by destroying the enemies of God's people, quenching human thirst, and revealing Baal as a false God (and therefore catalyzing Israel's return to the covenant). The oldest extant euchologion of the Byzantine tradition, *Barberini 336* (dating from the eighth century), contained petitions for the consecration of water that also referred to the blessing and multiplication of Jacob's flock of sheep through rod and water (Gen 30:25-43) and the promise of salvation by drawing from the water of salvation foretold by the Prophet Isaiah (Isa 12:4).[10] The references to these diverse biblical stories show that God's servant of creation acts every time God creates and renews covenant with God's chosen people. It is not enough to suggest that God employs created matter as an instrument: creation is an active and consistent participant in the salvation of humankind. Creation is a consistent and willing agent in the exchanges that occur when God forges covenant with humankind. The excerpts from the blessing of waters highlight the solemnity of the Theophany feast in the Eastern traditions. The baptismal features are evident to us, and these illustrate the way Theophany connects incarnation to Pascha. The sixth-century Syrian father Jacob of Serugh sets the stage for Jesus' baptism in the Jordan in a homily, by depicting a dialogue between Jesus and John the Baptist in which John does not understand the purpose of Jesus' baptism since he is fully divine and sinless.[11] Jesus explains that he descends into the water to recover

10. Denysenko, *The Blessing of Waters and Epiphany*, 104, 164.

11. Jacob of Sarug, *Jacob of Sarug's Homily on Epiphany*, ed. Thomas Kollamparampil (Piscataway, NJ: Gorgias Press, 2008), 26–30, nos. 181–201.

Adam, so that the image that has become faded might be cleansed, an image of the universal cleansing of humanity through Jesus' baptism:

> Our Lord says "I am not lacking but in one thing: the recovery of Adam who was lost from me is being sought by me. Allow me to descend to seek Adam, the fair image, and when I find him the whole of my desire shall be fulfilled. It became a great search for me in his case and on account of that I have come, and it would be a deficiency if I cannot find the lost one. The recovery of him, that alone is what is lacking with me: to regain Adam who was willing to perish at the hands of the evil one. In this recovery my desire will come to perfection, because Adam is needed by me to enter into his inheritance. Therefore, allow me to descend to cleanse the image that has become faded, lest it too would remain deficient, should you withhold me."

Jacob's reference to the entrance of Jesus into the Jordan echoes the epiclesis petitioning Christ to enter the water again, "now as then."[12] In this liturgical imagination, the Jordan is a portal to Hades—unpacking the layers of Theophany-Paschal connections would be a worthwhile pursuit, but for our purposes acknowledging that the Jordan provides passage for Jesus to descend into Hades is another instance of our thesis of water as God's servant. While the Byzantine tradition does not make this explicit connection between Theophany-Jordan and descent into Hades, an old Troparion appointed to the Third Antiphon of the Divine Liturgy from twelfth-century Constantinople speaks of the waters as becoming a furnace for the destruction of the sins of those who enter therein:

> The one who, as God, is cloaked in light, but was being bodily surrounded by water, was baptized by the Forerunner. He made the Jordan into a furnace and destroyed all the sins of those who received the bath of regeneration there. For Christ is truly the unapproachable light.[13]

This particular hymn, which is not used in the contemporary office, identifies Christ as the light of the world as its primary theme. Implicit

---

12. *The Festal Menaion*, trans. Mother Mary and Ware, 357.

13. *Codex Paris Greek 1590*, a twelfth-century manuscript constituting a synaxarion and Typikon representing Hagia Sophia, cited from Juan Mateos, ed., *Le Typikon de la grande église: ms Sainte-Croix no. 40, X siécle*, Orientalia Christiana Analecta 165, vol. 1 (Rome: Pontificium institutum orientalium studiorum, 1962), 180, n. 1.

in this hymn is the service of the Jordan, which becomes a furnace for those who are partaking of the water. Jacob's homily also refers to Christ as light and fire, saying that "the waters were inflamed by the lightning of flames because the Living Fire had come for baptism to be washed by them. It sets the ages on fire and casts its flame into the fountain and the glow from it kindled the river in holiness."[14] While the theme of Christ as light is not quite as prominent in the contemporary office, the transformation of the participants through Christ's entrance into the Jordan and the cooperation of the natural elements remains salient. The water's service leads to humankind's salvation, and the texts make bold claims on how God re-forms the people. One of the verses chanted from the prologue of the Great are You prayer makes this claim: "Today we have been released from our ancient lamentation, and as the new Israel we have found salvation." The euchologion *Codex Athens National Library 663* contains a notable variant of this verse from the prologue (highlighted with italics): "Today we have been released from our ancient lamentation, and as the new *Jerusalem* we have been saved *and we who are being deified are being clothed in the new vesture of incorruption.*"[15] There are dozens of examples from the liturgical texts that echo this assertion (e.g., "Today the Master hastens towards baptism that he may lift man up to the heights").

Many theologians have written about the paradox of water as a symbol of both life and death. The Theophany office and its baptismal parent depict the church's cosmic view of all the agents of interest present when God recreates humankind. Besides God, the human participants, and the natural elements, the office depicts the presence of evil spirits, whose interest is to retain their tyranny over the humans and prohibit them from entering into covenant with God. The end of the opening anamnetic section of the Great are You prayer mentions that Christ has broken the heads of the dragons in the water. The prayer petitions Christ to make the water "a destruction to demons, inaccessible to the adverse powers and filled with angelic strength." In other words, Christ's entrance into the water casts out all evil spirits, with the angels present to ensure that the only covenant forged in God's act is between God and the human participants. The language of casting and keeping out adversarial pow-

---

14. Jacob of Sarug, *Jacob of Sarug's Homily on Epiphany*, 46.

15. Panagiotis Trempelas, *Μικρόν Εὐχολόγιον, τόμος Β΄. Ἀκολουθίαι καὶ τάξεις ἁγιασμοῦ ὑδάτων, ἐγκαινίων, ὄρθρου καὶ ἑσπερινοῦ* (Athens: n.p., 1950), 41.

ers is even stronger in the blessing of baptismal waters. The epiclesis in this version of the Great are You prayer contains this passage: "let all those that conspire against your creature flee from it because I, Lord, have called upon your name, which is wondrous and glorious and fearful to adversaries."[16] At this point in the baptismal blessing of waters, the celebrant breathes on the water and traces the sign of the cross on it three times, saying, "let all adverse powers be crushed beneath the sign of the image of your cross." The next textual passage completes the act of casting out adversarial powers: "we pray to you, o God, that every aerial and obscure phantom may withdraw itself from us, and that no demon of darkness may conceal himself in this water." The nature of the water's service is similar for the two related blessings of waters: the water permits the entrance of angels and the light of Christ to cast and keep out evil spirits for both the forging of a new covenant (baptism) and its annual renewal (Theophany).

Have we transitioned from a theocentric liturgical office to one that is anthropocentric, one that focuses not on the glory of God, but solely on the glorification of the assembly? The service of creation assists in unveiling the meaning of what transpires in the Theophany blessing of waters: the glory of God is manifest in the re-creation of humankind, and Christ's descent into the waters of the Jordan removes the curse of broken communion and begins the process of re-creating humankind in God's image and likeness. The waters of the Jordan become the host for Christ, whom we know as the unapproachable light: the waters become the location for the washing God gives to humankind that "reboots" humanity (if you will) into God's holy people. Practically speaking, the fonts, water basins, jars, and other containers that are used for the ritual celebration of the blessing of waters become that space of the Jordan when Christ enters them, "now as then," to paraphrase our Great are You prayer. Just as the church confesses that Christ enters the waters today as he did in the past, the church confesses that the water remains God's faithful servant for God to perform the divine work of remaking humanity. The act of humanity's re-creation manifests the glory of God; it is therefore both anthropocentric and theocentric. The evidence presented to this point emphasizes the substantial participation of creation, especially water, in God's work of recreating humanity. Therefore, the divine act

16. See my adaptation of Archimandrite Ephrem Lash's translation in Denysenko, *The Blessing of Waters and Epiphany*, 205.

of recreating humanity also carries a geocentric quality. This geocentric quality has always been present; it deserves more attention in Orthodox Christian consciousness.

Liturgy and Creation: Other Sources

The Theophany blessing of waters contains abundant material that depicts a cosmos in which created matter is an essential partner in providing space for the encounter between God and humankind. Certainly, the Byzantine Rite contains several other offices that also promote these kinds of encounters. These include the so-called "Lesser" blessing of waters, the offices for blessing waters affixed to specific feasts (such as the finding of the cross on 1 August), and the numerous blessings of oils that also belong to the liturgy.[17] The use of the ritual oils supports the thesis of this paper, as the oils, like the water, are employed liturgically for the re-creation and restoration of the liturgical participant. The use of sanctified oil in the mystery of healing is well-known to us, especially given the renewed emphasis on the healing of body and soul, the imparting of divine forgiveness through the rite, and restoring the rite to all the people of God, an initiative that freed it from the stigma of preparation for death.[18] Two related examples from offices related to the Theophany water blessing are illustrative. Earlier, we heard how the water protected humans from evil spirits and adversarial powers in the two water blessings. Immediately before baptism, the celebrant blessed the oil of the catechumens as a "sign of reconciliation and of salvation from the flood" (referring to the olive branch from the Genesis narrative on Noah), and also to "perfect"

---

17. On the history and theology of the blessings of oil in the Byzantine tradition, see Paul Meyendorff, *The Anointing of the Sick*, Orthodox Liturgy Series 1 (Crestwood, NY: St. Vladimir's Seminary Press, 2009); Bert Groen, "Curative Holy Water and the Small Water Blessing in the Orthodox Church of Greece," in *Rites and Rituals of the Christian East: Proceedings of the Fourth International Congress of the Society of Oriental Liturgy, Lebanon, 10–15 July 2012*, ed. Bert Groen, Daniel Galadza, Nina Glibetic, and Gabriel Radle, Eastern Christian Studies 22 (Leuven: Peeters, 2014), 387–404.

18. See Meyendorff, *The Anointing of the Sick*, 64–70. For a detailed analysis, see Jean-Claude Larchet, *The Theology of Illness* (Crestwood, NY: St. Vladimir's Seminary Press, 2002), and Bruce Morrill, *Divine Worship and Human Healing: Liturgical Theology at the Margins of Life and Death* (Collegeville, MN: Liturgical Press, 2009).

those to be baptized.[19] The prayer asks God to bless the oil through the indwelling of the Holy Spirit so that through its anointing, the candidates for baptism would receive "a weapon of righteousness, renewal of soul and body, a driving away of every operation of the devil" and "for the removal of all evils of those who are anointed with it in faith." That the candidates are anointed all over with the oil of catechumens would seem to be enough, but before anointing the candidates, the rite calls for the water itself to receive the oil, as the celebrant pours the oil into the water three times (in the sign of the cross, of course), chanting "Alleluia!" three times. The addition of the oil provides yet another layer of protection from adversarial powers—the joined forces of the oil and water ensure that the font will become the place of a covenant forged between only God and the candidates for baptism. The blessing of waters and anointings with oil provide assurance of protection for those who are gathered. As to the inhabitants of this visible and invisible cosmos, the office clearly identifies the opponents of God who would like to claim or recapture covenantal tyranny over the participants. In other words, these offices are blunt in providing brief descriptions of those who are present and active in the cosmos: though unseen and bodiless, evil spirits and bodiless adversaries are quite real. In the cosmos where God, humankind, and creation share life together, God's opponents stake a claim to mastery over humankind. God does not use otherworldly matter to defeat these opponents, but calls upon the service of creation itself.

This review of the function of creation in the offices of water blessing and the blessing of the oil of catechumens leads us to a hypothesis on the necessity of created matter in the celebration of the mysteries. The examples explored here refer to the outcome of God's re-creation of humankind: the re-creation of a covenant between God and humanity. For the human participants, that covenant is quite tangible; it is not abstract or opaque but is experienced in the human sense of touch. Creation's function is to facilitate a real, human encounter between the human participants and God, one that is assured by the theophanies of salvation history. The gift of creation is to create an experience of relationship with God through the human senses. Creation makes this possible because of its obedience to God's divine command to serve: this is creation's gift to humankind, a matter to which we shall return shortly.

---

19. "Baptism," trans. Ephrem Lash, 3 November 2008, https://web.archive.org /web/20160305185715/http://anastasis.org.uk/baptism.htm.

Popular Religion and Creation

If we move outside of liturgy, or at least to its periphery, we can discover instances of popular religion that support this hypothesis on creation. Let us take, for example, this same Theophany water blessing we have already explored with some rigor. The liturgical scholar is drawn immediately to the rich texts of the offices, with some references to the ritual gestures. Were any one of us to examine the Theophany office without prior knowledge of it, I suspect that we would become fixated quite quickly on the Great are You prayer. For the general population, the highlight of the Theophany water blessings focuses on ritual actions. The people are drawn to the invitation to partake of the water; they stand in line to drink it, anoint themselves with it, and fill their jars to take home for the rest of the year. In most instances, people respond joyfully when the celebrant takes the water and blesses the whole church, drenching the walls, icons, and floors with the sanctified water. People ask the priest to bless them with this water, sometimes asking him to sprinkle them again and again. Many parishes have the office for the water blessing outdoors. In warmer climates, when the priest blesses the natural source of water (river, lake, reservoir, even the ocean) with a cross, it is customary for him to throw the cross into the water, often tied to a rope so it will not be lost, and for volunteers to jump into the water and swim to fetch the cross to bring it back.[20] In cold climates, people gather on the ice of a natural water source: they will often carve ornate crosses of ice and bless the open portions of the water, or they will hazard the frigid temperatures and arrange for volunteers to fetch the cross out of the cold water.[21]

Obviously, these images are dramatic; they are playful, fun, and have a certain entertainment value. But it is not blasphemous to insert this sense of play into the ritual: it is quite natural, because it is this sense of play and ritual on the periphery of liturgy that permeates the liturgy that expresses the people's strong desire to touch God through created matter.

20. For an assessment of gender issues in the traditional outdoor water blessing, see Joanna Theophilopoulos, "The Problem with Gendering Epiphany Celebrations," Public Orthodoxy, 4 January 2018, https://publicorthodoxy.org/2018/01/04/gendering-epiphany-celebrations/.

21. See, for example, Corey Flintoff, "In Russia, Epiphany Comes with a Shockingly Cold Swim," NPR, 20 January 2016, https://www.npr.org/sections/parallels/2016/01/20/463632705/in-russia-epiphany-comes-with-a-shockingly-cold-swim.

History testifies to this desire to obtain access to God through created matter. Antoninus, the sixth-century pilgrim to Jerusalem from Plaisance, mentions the Theophany water blessing with Alexandrians who poured aromatic substances into the blessed water and sprinkled their boats with it before departing home from their journey.[22] The development of the liturgical history of this office itself testifies to the people's recognition that touching the water brings them into covenant with God. Perhaps the strongest evidence of this is the appearance of a rite of communion with the water, evolving from the possibility of communing from Theophany water in the penitential *kanonaria* attributed to John the Faster of Constantinople in the sixth century through a rite of communion of the Theophany water found in several Slavonic euchologia of the sixteenth century.[23] These paraliturgical and liturgical developments substantiate water as a natural substance that serves God's will, this time through reconciliation as well as the forging and renewal of the baptismal covenant.

The Byzantine churches also witness to the phenomenon of wonderworking icons.[24] The theophanies that take place through wonderworking icons exemplify the tendency for the paraliturgical to enter the liturgical realm. When icons or other relics begin to stream myrrh, it is customary for the original event on which the icon was discovered (or when the holy figure depicted on the icon was manifest to a person or a local community) to become a new feast day in the liturgical year. The history of wonderworking icons tends to follow the path of the translation of relics from late antiquity, with the local becoming the universal, especially when an icon begins to travel and visit parishes in other cities and countries.[25] There are many such icons that have created feast days in the

22. Denysenko, *The Blessing of Waters and Epiphany*, 21.

23. See John the Faster, Patriarch, Ἀκολουθία καὶ τάξις ἐπὶ ἐξομολογούμενον, in *Clavis Patrum Graecorum*, 5 vols., ed. Maurice Geerard and F. Glorie (Turnhout, Brepols, 1974–87), 7559, PG 88, 1889–1919, and Λόγος πρὸς τὸν μέλλοντα ἐξαγορεῦσαι τὸν ἑαυτοῦ πνευματικὸν Πατέρα, PG 88, 1919–1937.

24. For background reading on wonderworking icons, see Bissera Pentcheva, *Icons and Power: The Mother of God in Byzantium* (University Park: Pennsylvania State Univ. Press, 2006); Vera Shevzov, "Icons, Miracles, and the Ecclesial Identity of Laity in Late Imperial Russian Orthodoxy," *Church History* 69, no 3 (2000): 610–31; Jim Forest, "Icons and Miracles: An Intensity of Faith," *Christianity and Crisis* 45, no 9 (1985): 201–5.

25. For a survey on the translation of relics and their wonderworking powers, see Paul F. Bradshaw and Maxwell Johnson, *The Origins of Feasts, Fasts, and Seasons in*

churches of the Byzantine Rite, and the point we take from this feast is the way wonderworking icons draw crowds. Again, it is tempting to dismiss this practice as an evangelical gimmick from a pastoral perspective, especially if there is controversy involved, as was the case when the belt of the Mother of God visited Moscow in 2011.[26] The festivities surrounding Mary's belt drew millions of people in a cold November in Moscow, and the international press reported how the patriarch and other clergy used the visitation of Mary's belt as an opportunity for people to receive healing of diseases or to conceive children after infertility ended. Copies of the belt were made and distributed, just as copies of icons and other famous relics are not only made, but even bought and sold. While one can criticize the political motivations and actions of the church officials (as I have done), we should pay attention to the reason people form crowds for a chance to venerate these holy relics and icons.[27] Surely, some of the people who lined up to kiss Mary's belt did indeed hope that the Queen of Heaven would bear their prayers to God's divine throne. There is no reason to doubt that a critical mass of people, upon hearing about the visitation of Mary's belt, took the opportunity to come near to experience an encounter with Mary by touching her relic. The veneration of these relics is intensified when they stream myrrh, as the myrrh itself is an even more tangible manifestation of divine favor through the person of the saint whose relic or icon the people have venerated. In other words, the saint permits the people to touch God, and in these instances, the myrrh offers another service to God.

Early Christianity (Collegeville, MN: Liturgical Press, 2011), 183–88. For a seminal essay on pilgrimage and the veneration of relics, see Pierre Maraval, "The Earliest Phase of Christian Pilgrimage in the Near East (before the 7th Century)," *Dumbarton Oaks Papers* 56 (2002): 63–74; for the theological rationale underpinning relic veneration, see Sergius Bulgakov, "On Holy Relics," in *Relics and Miracles: Two Theological Essays*, trans. Boris Jakim (Grand Rapids, MI: Eerdmans, 2011), 1–40.

26. On the visit of Mary's belt to Russia, see "Завершилось пребывание в России великой христианской святыни — ковчега с Поясом Пресвятой Богородицы," 28 November 2011, Moscow Patriarchate web site, http://www.patriarchia.ru/db/text/1787233.html.

27. See Nicholas Denysenko, "An Appeal to Mary: An Analysis of Pussy Riot's Punk Performance in Moscow," *Journal of the American Academy of Religion* 81, no. 4 (2013), 1061–92.

Our final example of the paraliturgical permeating the liturgical is when the people bring food into the church for blessing. People who have visited a Greek or Slavic church may be aware of the tradition of receiving antidoron, the leftover bread from the offerings for the eucharistic meal, immediately after Communion and again at the end of the liturgy (the Slavic tradition offers a nice bonus of "zapyvka"—a sip of unconsecrated wine to wash Communion down).[28] Distributing antidoron is the church's way of giving the people a snack, since they have fasted (presumably) from at least midnight of the previous eve, and it is also a way to extend hospitality to visitors who are not partaking of Communion. At Vigils, it is customary to include a blessing of wheat, wine, oil, and bread, and again, the bread and wine are consumed by the people, a vestige of sustenance for the post-vigil fast that would extend through the liturgy the following morning. There is also the venerable tradition of blessing *kolyva*, or buckwheat, for certain feast days and memorial offices of the dead.[29] But two other traditions are extraordinarily popular: the blessing of fruit on the Transfiguration feast on 6 August and the blessing of foods on Pascha.

The blessing of the baskets of food and drink on Pascha is similar to the Theophany tradition of diving into the water to fetch the cross: a trained liturgist would probably overlook this aspect of the liturgical celebration, especially since it takes place after the conclusion of the Divine Liturgy on Pascha. This blessing is preceded by the blessing of the *artos* that occurs during the liturgy, immediately before the dismissal.[30] Certainly, the people do not come for the blessing of *artos*; they are preoccupied with the blessing of baskets filled with meats, cheeses, eggs, alcohol, chocolate, whatever foods constitute their feasting following the conclusion of Lenten and Holy Week fasting. In the contemporary

28. Antidoron is also known as eulogia. For a definition, see *The Festal Menaion*, trans. Mother Mary and Ware, 544–45.

29. These traditions vary by region, as some Byzantine Rite people offer sweet breads and others a bottle of wine for the offices of the dead.

30. Artos is a special bread blessed during Paschaltide and distributed to the people, originating from the communal meal of the Constantinopolitan monastic tradition. The first liturgical reference to artos occurs in the twelfth-century Evergetis Typikon. For additional details, see the article "артос," 17 March 2010, http://www.pravenc.ru/text/392501.html.

church, the ritual setting of the blessing of food and drink takes place in church halls or outdoors (weather permitting). The rite begins with the paschal verses and the singing of the paschal troparion. The first prayer is for the blessing of paschal bread, followed by a prayer for the paschal lamb (and other meats) and for eggs, cheese, milk, and other foods:

> Holy Master, Father almighty, Eternal God! We beseech you to bless this bread with your holy blessing, that it would be for the salvation of souls, bodily health, and protection against all ailments and every adversarial offense for he who partakes of it—through our Lord Jesus Christ, who came down from heaven and gives life and salvation to the world, who reigns with you in the unity of the holy Spirit, now and ever and unto ages of ages.[31]

The prayer for the blessing of the bread reminds us of the thematic thread with which we are now familiar: in this case, the festive eating of the sweet bread is an act of renewing communion with God. Participating in this act of eating brings about the divine covenantal promise of protection from evil spirits, illnesses, and the salvation of souls. The second and third prayers continue this theme and add a new element by connecting the paschal meats to the sacrificial lambs offered to God by Abraham and Abel and to the fatted calf prepared by the father when his prodigal son returned. The prayer asks for God's blessing to enjoy these foods. The final blessing of cheese, eggs, milks, and other foods also asks for Christ's blessing to enjoy "these your graciously given gifts," calling upon Christ as "Master, Lord, our God who created everything."[32] The prayers of blessing capture the liturgical language of God as creator who received food offerings and bestows blessing in return in non-liturgical ritual spaces. While these prayers are not omitted for this short rite of blessing foods, they are not the featured highlights either. Many people annoy pastors by requesting that they bless the baskets of food at a time more convenient for the people, times that do not require them to attend the entire paschal liturgy. While one should not overlook the problem of limiting paschal liturgy to its manifestation in domestic celebration—the

---

31. I have opted to translate the Ukrainian text published in *Требник*, vol. 2 (Kyiv: Publishing Office of the Ukrainian Orthodox Church, Kyivan Patriarchate, 2013), 179. See also *The Divine Liturgy: An Anthology*, ed. Galadza et al., 113–15.
    32. See *Требник*, vol. 2, 181.

first post-paschal meal—one should also acknowledge the popular piety invested in desiring the blessing of Paschal foods and drink. The people's commitment to bringing their holiday food to the church to receive this blessing demonstrates their innate understanding that they can touch God through the act of eating and drinking a holiday meal. The prayers appointed for the short rite of blessing simply show us that the church acknowledges that the joy of savory, festive eating is a gift from God and that all of creation renders service to God in bringing humankind and God together, in joyful communion, even for the enjoyment of a holiday meal. Allow me to emphasize the influence of the domestic feast on the liturgical offices in this particular instance—the people's understanding that they are touching the divine becomes liturgized through the coalescing of this special office around the rather ordinary act of preparing savory foods for a family feast.

Conclusion

This snapshot from the Byzantine liturgical heritage and observance of popular piety demonstrates the church's understanding of cosmos. God is the master of all who acts to save, sustain, and deify humankind; creation provides the space and material for God to perform these saving acts, and humans understand innately that they can touch God through created matter. They also understand that God's opponents are present in this cosmos and compete with God for mastery over humankind. Creation performs the thankless service of casting out God's opponents and protecting human participants from harm. Creation's service in this dangerous universe is thankless: creation receives no glory and no accolades, but continuously gives of herself for the deification of humanity. God employs creation to recreate humanity; humans receive God through the service of creation, human acts that include both sacramental and ordinary eating and drinking. The ritual context reveals that humanity is the recipient of this gift, over and over again, and in the exhortations of the prayers and hymns we occasionally hear that creation joins humankind in falling down in worship before God.[33]

33. Of the many examples of creation thanking and worshipping God, the following sticheron appointed to Vespers on Christmas Eve stands out: "What shall we offer Thee, o Christ, who for our sakes hast appeared on earth as man? Every creature

The Byzantine tradition accentuates the glorification of God along with a high Christology, and it would seem trite to ask more from the liturgy. But theology truly makes its mark not only in texts and orderly ritual actions, but also when it is lived faithfully by its adherents. Missing from this beautiful process of gift exchange is reference to the gift offered by humankind to creation, in thanksgiving for its thankless service. Reverence for creation is implicit in the lived theology of the Byzantine tradition: I have attempted to explicate creation's service in this article. There is no doubt that the people respond to the liturgical theology revealing creation as God's faithful servant: were it not the case, they would not press forward in crowds to be touched by the sanctified water or bring their baskets of food to the church for another blessing. Acknowledgement is not service, and there is scant reference in the liturgical or theological repositories of Orthodoxy to the crisis endured by creation and the dangers threating its vitality, with the notable exception of the consistent appeals of Ecumenical Patriarch Bartholomew, in numerous speeches, appeals, public appearances, and homilies, to preserve and protect the natural environment.[34]

The time has arrived for the Byzantine churches to devote considerable energy to exhorting faithful to become servants of creation. The failure to offer service to creation is a denial of receiving God's gift, because ignoring creation and contributing to its decay and suffering will create new obstacles to touching God through the divine gift of creation. The Byzantine churches must exhort the faithful to become servants of creation as acts of thanksgiving for God's gift. This process begins by generating awareness of creation: first, by acknowledging its place as God's faithful servant, necessary and good creations of God in this cosmos, and

---

made by Thee offers Thee thanks. The angels offer Thee a hymn; the heavens a star; the Magi, gifts; the shepherds, their wonder; the earth, its cave; the wilderness, the manger; and we offer Thee a Virgin Mother. O pre-eternal god, have mercy upon us," in *The Festal Menaion*, trans. Mother Mary and Ware, 254.

34. Patriarch Bartholomew, *On Earth as It Is in Heaven: Ecological Vision and Initiatives of Ecumenical Patriarch Bartholomew*, ed. John Chryssavgis (New York, NY: Fordham Univ. Press, 2012). See also chapter 13 of the Basis of the Social Concept of the Russian Orthodox Church, which identifies the ecological crisis as requiring Christian intervention: https://mospat.ru/en/documents/social-concepts/ (accessed 17 August 2018).

second, by lamenting the damage done to creation on account of human ignorance, sin, and greed. One component of a campaign to generate such awareness would be to add special petitions for the protection, preservation, and care of creation to the liturgy in litanies, special prayers, and ritual acts. The offices examined here provide excellent building blocks for such an endeavor. The people are not likely to respond affirmatively to such exhortations without becoming aware of creation as God's faithful servant: acts of protecting, preserving, and cultivating creation can come only from an identity that God has appointed Christians to serve creation, just as creation serves God for humanity.

Enhancing the awareness of the goodness of creation in liturgical celebration and catechesis is a very modest step—it pales in comparison to the bold challenge issued by Pope Francis in *Laudato Si'* (On Care for Our Common Home).[35] But a step is just that: taking it leads the church to the next step, and a series of steps can be the beginnings of a foundation that results in a church culture that venerates creation as God's faithful servant. A first step toward awareness can also result in the realization that all of humanity has been consumed by the temptations of anthropocentrism, a crisis that threatens the well-being of humankind as well as creation (LS 115). The liturgical theology of the church has the capacity to do much good in repairing creation so it can render its service to God in the cosmos; it would also be a dignified way for the church to enact its thanksgiving to God.

35. Pope Francis, encyclical letter, *Laudato Si'* (On Care for our Common Home), 24 May 2015, http://w2.vatican.va/content/francesco/en/encyclicals/documents/papa-francesco_20150524_enciclica-laudato-si.html.

PART THREE

REFLECTIONS ON CONTEMPORARY PRACTICES

CHAPTER FOURTEEN

The First of September

Environmental Care and Creation Day

Bert Groen

Because of increasing environmental pollution, a drastic reduction of biodiversity, global warming, and climate change, ecology and care for the natural environment have become key factors for the quality of life, even for the continuation of existence, on our planet Earth.[1] The Conciliar Process for Justice, Peace, and the Integrity of Creation, which the World Council of Churches initiated during the 1980s, included reflection on sustainability and the preservation of God's gift par excellence—that is, creation. In a solid number of Christian denominations, the Conciliar Process resulted in growing awareness that our natural environment was being increasingly damaged, planetary life itself was threatened, and theological reflection on this danger was necessary. Besides a Forum on Religion and Ecology founded for academic research, education, and outreach—a worldwide network of individuals and organizations involved in ecological issues[2]—there were numerous other local and regional initiatives, both within churches and in society at large.

Several Orthodox and Oriental Orthodox churches also made their voices heard, especially in conferences and publications.[3] One of the

---

1. I wish to thank Stefanos Alexopoulos for several valuable remarks on this chapter.

2. See The Forum for Religion and Ecology at Yale, http://fore.research.yale.edu.

3. See, e.g., Gennadios Limouris, ed., *Justice, Peace and the Integrity of Creation: Insights from Orthodoxy* (Geneva: WCC Publications, 1990) as well as the references below, esp. in n. 8.

highlights was an ecological congress that took place in September 1988 on the island of Patmos, where according to tradition Saint John wrote his Revelation. The conference participants requested the Patriarchate of Constantinople, to whose jurisdiction Patmos adheres, to establish a fixed annual day dedicated to environmental protection. Responding to this request, the Holy Synod in Istanbul decided to designate 1 September, that is, the beginning of the new ecclesiastical year in the Byzantine Rite. The jurisdiction of the Ecumenical Patriarchate of Constantinople comprises Turkey, parts of Greece (especially Crete, the Dodecanese, and Mount Athos), as well as the Greeks in the diaspora in America, Australia, and Western and Central Europe. Other Orthodox churches, such as the Patriarchates of Alexandria, Antioch, Jerusalem, Russia, Romania, and Serbia, attribute an honorary primacy to Constantinople, not a juridical one. Hence, while Constantinople cannot impose its decisions on the other Orthodox churches, its initiatives are closely watched and may be adopted by sister churches as a result.

Magna Carta of Orthodox Environmental Care

In 1989, the Patriarch of Constantinople, Dimitrios (Papadopoulos, in office 1972–1991), issued a message that can be regarded as the Magna Carta of Orthodox care for the environment.[4] A first striking feature of this impressive statement is its concreteness. The message brings up "the merciless trampling and destruction of the natural environment caused by human beings," natural pollution, the extinction of many species of plant and animal life, and the greenhouse effect. It appeals to all faithful to respect and protect the natural environment and to governments and nations to take measures. Finally, it appoints 1 September as "environment day," on which prayers and supplications are to be offered to God, the maker of all, for creation. This is to be done with thankfulness for the gift of creation and with petitioning for the environment to be saved. The patriarchal declaration appeals not merely to Orthodox but to all Christians.

---

4. For the original Greek text see *Episkepsis* (Greek edition) no. 425 (15 September 1989): 2–3. For the English version, from which I quote here, see John Chryssavgis, ed., *Cosmic Grace, Humble Prayer: The Ecological Vision of the Green Patriarch Bartholomew I*, with a foreword by Metropolitan John (Zizioulas) of Pergamon (Grand Rapids, MI: Eerdmans, 2003), 37–39. I had no access to the 2009 revised edition.

A second striking feature of the text are the statements that humanity abuses its position; that humans are not the owners of creation, but its guardians and stewards; that "under the influence of extreme rationalism and self-centeredness," and of consumer society, humanity has lost a sense of the sacredness of creation, has left the eucharistic and ascetic attitude of the Orthodox Church, and rapes nature.

Finally, the text insists on the priestly office of humankind. Just as the Son of God incarnate, Jesus Christ, unceasingly leads the fallen creation back to the Father as a eucharistic offer and sacrifice, the church acts likewise in its Divine Liturgy (Eucharist), when it offers and refers creation to God in the shape of the material elements of bread and wine. Thus the church declares that as the steward of creation, humanity must lovingly cultivate creation and refer it to God with gratitude, respect, and reverence.[5]

Eucharistic, Liturgical, and Ascetic Ethos

Since 1989, the Patriarch of Constantinople has been issuing a similar message on the protection of the environment every year.[6] Patriarch Bartholomew (b. 1940 as Dimitrios Archontonis), who has been holding office since 1991, annually addresses care for the environment and protection of creation. Just like his predecessor, in his messages he emphasizes God's call to humans to be co-creators, *leitourgoi* (participants in the worship service), and stewards of creation. Human beings must energetically cooperate with God, be active enactors in an ongoing worship act. They are called to serve as kings, priests, and prophets, that is, "to reign, minister and teach in the vast expanse of creation, to study, serve and pray to transform what is corruptible into what is incorruptible."[7] Divine grace and personal willingness and human endeavor are interrelated. However, in spite of this call and responsibility, humankind ruthlessly exploits nature, is guilty of overconsumption, pollution, and excessive

---

5. For more extensive comments on this message see, e.g., Nicholas P. Constas, "Commentary on the Patriarchal Message on the Day of the Protection of the Environment," *Greek Orthodox Theological Review* 35 (1990): 179–94.

6. Exceptions are the years 1991, when Patriarch Dimitrios died, and 2000, when Orthodoxy focused on the commemoration of Jesus' birth two thousand years before.

7. Chryssavgis, *Cosmic Grace, Humble Prayer*, 48 (from the 1995 message); *Orthodoxia* 2 (1995): 393–94.

waste of energy, and might finally destroy itself. Such destructive behavior is suicidal and sinful. Hence, repentance and a return to eucharistic spirituality, giving thanks to the Creator for the beauty and goods of this world, as well as asceticism, are required.

In his 1994 message, for instance, the patriarch points to three principles manifesting Orthodox ethos: first, the eucharistic ethos, which means "using the natural resources with thankfulness," offering both them and ourselves back to God: "In the Eucharist, we return to God what is His own: namely, the bread and the wine. Representing the fruits of creation, the bread and wine are no longer imprisoned by a fallen world but are returned as liberated, purified from their fallen state, and capable of receiving the divine presence within themselves. At the same time, we pray for ourselves to be sanctified, because through sin we have fallen away and have betrayed our baptismal promise." Secondly, ascetic ethos is necessary. This involves fasting and spiritual works. They make people recognize that all things they take for granted are God's gifts for their needs, not to abuse and "waste simply because we have the ability to pay for them." Thirdly, the liturgical ethos "emphasizes community concern and sharing. We stand before God together; and we hold in common the earthly blessings that He has given to all creatures. Not to share our own wealth with the poor is theft from the poor and deprivation of their means of life; we possess not our own wealth but theirs, as one of the holy Fathers of the Church reminds us."[8] An ascetical attitude

8. Chryssavgis, *Cosmic Grace, Humble Prayer*, 45–47 (the imperative to share property and riches with the poor and outcast, because wealth does not belong to the affluent, is a recurrent subject in John Chrysostom's homilies). Various Orthodox theologians have taken up the gauntlet of the ecological challenge. See, e.g., John Chryssavgis and Bruce V. Foltz, eds., *Toward an Ecology of Transfiguration: Orthodox Christian Perspectives on Environment, Nature and Creation*, with a prefatory letter from Ecumenical Patriarch Bartholomew, foreword by Bill McKibben (New York, NY: Fordham Univ. Press, 2013); John Chryssavgis, *Beyond the Shattered Image: Orthodox Insights into the Environment* (Minneapolis, MN: Light and Life, 1999); Elizabeth Theokritoff, "From Sacramental Life to Sacramental Living: Heeding the Message of the Environmental Crisis," *Greek Orthodox Theological Review* 44 (1999): 505–24; Elizabeth Theokritoff, *Living in God's Creation: Orthodox Perspectives on Ecology*, Foundations 4 (Crestwood, NY: St Vladimir's Seminary Press, 2009); Elizabeth Theokritoff, "Ethics and Ecology as an Issue for Joint Dialogue and Work with other Christian Traditions," in *Orthodox Handbook*

remains essential: through self-restraint we can free ourselves from our self-centeredness, reduce our consumer behavior, and ensure that natural resources are also for others, especially for the poor and the developing nations.[9] Self-limitation in consuming food and natural resources as well as distinction between our wishes and our needs make us travel lightly. Fasting, in particular, facilitates moderation, mercifulness, and sharing with others.[10]

In addition to references to worship, liturgical theology, and asceticism, Patriarch Bartholomew addresses the subject of ecclesial iconography. In a 1997 homily on beauty and nature, for example, he preaches that icons express the world's sacredness and are a mirror of eternity. In icons, material resources like wood, eggs, and paints are transfigured and enable sacramental encounter and experiencing the living God.[11] Ideally (my addition), the church embodies and sanctifies the entire world, whereas the created world's vocation is to become the church. According to the patriarch, "Icons break down the wall of separation between the sacred and the profane . . . between earth and heaven . . . All things are sacramental when seen in the light of God."[12] Because not only humans—cf. Genesis 1:26 (Septuagint): *kat' eikona 'ēmeteran* ("according to our image")—but all creatures, the entire creation, are icons of God, God can and should be contemplated through this iconographic lens.[13]

---

on Ecumenism: Resources for Theological Education, ed. Pantelis Kalaitzidis et al. (Oxford: Regnum Books International, 2014), 667–71; Stanley S. Harakas, " 'The Earth is the Lord's': Orthodox Theology and the Environment," *Greek Orthodox Theological Review* 44 (1999): 149–62.

9. Cf. Chryssavgis, *Cosmic Grace, Humble Prayer*, 219–20, 304–5. See also the written interview with Bartholomew, Ecumenical Patriarch, " 'Everything that Breathes Praises God,' " *Reflections: A Magazine of Theological and Ethical Inquiry from Yale Divinity School*, spring 2007 (special issue on "God's Green Earth"), where he expresses himself in the same vein.

10. John Chryssavgis, ed., *On Earth as in Heaven: Ecological Vision and Initiatives of Ecumenical Patriarch Bartholomew* (New York, NY: Fordham Univ. Press, 2012), 97–98, 125–26, 132–35, 182, 200–4, 213–14, 222–23.

11. Ibid., 152–53, 208.

12. Chryssavgis, *Cosmic Grace, Humble Prayer*, 215–17.

13. Chryssavgis, *On Earth as in Heaven*, 95–100. Cf. Chryssavgis, *Cosmic Grace, Humble Prayer*, 22–33.

Pan-Orthodox Follow-Up

These and similar accents and appeals resound in many other messages and statements of Patriarch Bartholomew. Not only on 1 September, but also on other occasions such as World Water Day (22 March) and Earth Day (22 April), he appeals to the world community to attend to environmental degradation in general and to pollution of the oceans and the unfair distribution of worldwide access to clean water in particular.[14] The patriarch speaks likewise on the occasion of conferences about climate change and water quality. The tone of these succinct appeals is often compelling: time is running out if no adequate measures are taken to stop environmental decay, and humanity must absolutely assume its God-given responsibility regarding nature and creation.

Several heads of other Orthodox churches, such as the Patriarchate of Antioch, the Church of Greece, and the Church of Cyprus, have followed suit, also publishing messages on 1 September about the increasing degradation of the environment and the necessity of stewardship of creation. In July 2015, the Patriarchate of Moscow decided to adopt a day for the preservation of creation, but to celebrate it on a moveable day, that is, the first Sunday of September. The Russian Holy Synod argued that in that way overlap with other services in the same period, when the new academic year also begins, could be avoided.

Concurrently various Pan-Orthodox gatherings have addressed this burning issue.[15] During a 1992 synaxis (meeting and liturgical assembly) of the heads of all Orthodox churches in Istanbul, the primates underscored in their message the negative aspects of human domination over the environment and the "careless and self-indulgent use of material creation by humanity, with the help of scientific and technological progress." The assembly participants invited all Orthodox to dedicate the first day of September to prayer for the preservation of God's creation and "to adopt the attitude to nature found in the Eucharist and the ascetic tradition of

---

14. See, e.g., Patriarch Bartholomew's 2015 messages in the *Greek Orthodox Theological Review* 60 (2015): 164–65, 183–84.

15. For succinct surveys see Chryssavgis, *Cosmic Grace, Humble Prayer*, 5–14; Chryssavgis, *On Earth as in Heaven*, 4–15; Kevin W. Irwin, *A Commentary on Laudato Si': Examining the Background, Contributions, Implementation, and Future of Pope Francis's Encyclical* (New York, NY and Mahwah, NJ: Paulist Press, 2016), 59–71. Cf. the personal impressions in John Grim and Mary Evelyn Tucker, *Ecology and Religion* (Washington, DC: Island Press, 2014), 91, 96–108, 165–68.

the Church."[16] And in 2008, the primates reaffirmed the significance of 1 September and recommended the introduction of environmental issues in sermons, catechesis, and pastoral action.[17]

In addition, the Great and Holy Council convened in June 2016 in the Orthodox Academy of Crete denounced sinful human behavior like greed and egotism. It stated that the Creator's property is in dire need of protection and that humankind should repent, act in a responsible way, and practice asceticism, because not only the present but also future generations are entitled to employ the natural goods. Humanity is called to doxologically offer creation to the Creator and cultivate a eucharistic relationship with the natural environment.[18]

So far the Patriarchate of Constantinople has organized nine international ecological congresses and seminars. They were interdisciplinary—theology, economy, law, business administration, ethics, politics, and journalism were represented—and took place in regions whose ecosystems are severely threatened, such as the Black Sea, Amazon, Danube, Mississippi, Aegean, and the Arctic. During these conferences, often co-organized with other organizations, such as the World Wide Fund for Nature (WWF),[19] the "Green Patriarch," as he is nicknamed, has repeatedly pointed to the interrelatedness of prayer to the Creator and safeguarding his handiwork; of care for the poor and marginalized and sound economy; and of God's gift, environmental care, and conversion of human hearts.

Worship Services on the First of September

As we noted, in the Byzantine tradition 1 September is also the first day of the new church year, the first day of the *indiction*.[20] In the Eastern

16. Chryssavgis, *Cosmic Grace, Humble Prayer*, 85–90, here 86 and 90.

17. "Message of the Primates of the Orthodox Churches," *Greek Orthodox Theological Review* 53 (2008): 305–12, here 311.

18. "The Mission of the Orthodox Church in Today's World," § F 10; "Encyclical," § 11, 13–4, at Official Documents of the Holy and Great Council of the Orthodox Church, https://www.holycouncil.org/documents.

19. In 1998, in his capacity as WWF president, Prince Philip, duke of Edinburgh, proposed to Patriarch Dimitrios the appointment of a special day of celebration and reflection on the world's natural inheritance.

20. The Latin word *indictio* originally meant imposing a duty or tax, then it meant a fiscal year, and later a cycle of fifteen years as well as the *-th* year of a certain indiction cycle. Between 452 and 459, Roman authority decreed that its beginning

Roman Empire, the new fiscal year began on that day—the farmers had harvested their fields, and the authorities could calculate the required taxes. In church, on the same day, Saint Symeon the Stylite (d. 459), his mother, the Old Testament saint Joshua, son of Nun, and a good many other, less well-known saints are commemorated.[21] For centuries, hymns about the new beginning and the annual cycle, as well as chants about the pillar saint who spent thirty-seven years on a small platform on top of a column near Aleppo, Syria, have characterized that day. Now that an additional accent has been added to the day, the composition of new worship texts has been necessary. Therefore, the Holy Synod of Constantinople commissioned Fr. Gerasimos Mikragiannanitēs (d. 1991) to write a specific service. Fr. Gerasimos was by then well-known for his numerous hymns for the services of newly proclaimed saints.[22] He completed his assignment quickly and his "Holy Service for the Protection of the Natural Environment"[23] was chanted in the cathedral at the Phanar for the first time in 1989. It was later re-edited and entitled "Supplicatory Service to our Humankind-Loving God and Savior, Jesus Christ, for the Protection of our Environment and the Well-Being of the Whole Creation."[24]

As for the Church of Greece, the Metropolitan of Patra, Nicodemos (Ballêndras/Vallindhrás, d. 2008, in office 1974–2005), who had also composed numerous services,[25] drew up a new worship formulary. In January 1992, the Holy Synod in Athens approved this service, which

---

be on 1 September. For more, see Panagiōtēs I. Skaltsēs, *"Eis kairous kai eniautous"*: *ʾĒ Indiktos ʾōs aparchē eniausios kai heortē tēs oikologias* ["For times and seasons": The indiction as annual beginning and festival of ecology] (Thessalonica: Kyriakidēs, 2017), 21–65.

21. *Mēnaion tou Septembriou*, 6th ed. (Athens: Apostolikē Diakonia, 2003), 7–19. See also the 2018 liturgical directory, http://www.ec-patr.org/gr/typikon /2018/2018-09-01.htm.

22. Mōysēs [Athos monk Moses], *Mega Gerontiko enaretōn ʾagioreitōn tou eikostou aiōnos* [Great elders book of virtuous Athos monks from the twentieth century], vol. 3: *1984–2000* (Thessalonica: Mygdonia, 2011), 1315–23.

23. *ʾIera akolouthia dia tēn prostasian tou physikou periballontos.*

24. *Akolouthia ʾiketērios pros ton philanthrōpon Theon kai Sōtēra ʾēmōn Iēsoun Christon ʾyper tou periballontos ʾēmas stoicheiou kai eustatheias pasēs tēs ktiseōs* (Thessalonica: Organization Cultural Capital of Europe, 1997).

25. Cf. *Diptycha tēs Ekklēsias tēs ʾEllados 1996* (Athens: Apostolikē Diakonia, 1995), 687.

the Apostolic Diakonia, responsible for the edition of official liturgical books, published a year later.[26] Whereas the worship service Fr. Gerasimos compiled is fairly well-known, the one Metropolitan Nicodemos wrote is far less so, and I will therefore sketch the structure of the latter. It contains a short introduction on the ecological problem (pp. 7–8) and chants for Vespers—in the Byzantine Rite, a new day begins at sunset, so in this case in the evening of 31 August —the morning service, and the Divine Liturgy (pp. 9–22). Finally, one finds the musical notation of some stanzas (pp. 23–29). The text consists mainly of the proper parts (*proprium*), assuming that the fixed parts (*ordinarium*) are well-known.[27]

Because 1 September is also the beginning of the church year and Symeon the Stylite, Joshua, and other saints are commemorated, our service not only deals with environmental care, but also frequently refers to the other feasts. The *apolytikion*, the specific chant for the feast of the day, for example, sings the praises of the Creator, who established times and seasons, and petitions God to bless the crown of the year and to preserve and save the nation—according to the Greek original, "the emperors and your city"—and us.[28] On other days, too, the Byzantine Rite sings of creation. Every Vesper service, for instance, begins with the recitation of Psalm 103, which magnifies the Lord's creation.[29]

Another possibility is that one uses the regular 1 September formulary, which concentrates on the *indiction* and the aforementioned saints, and intersperses it with various hymns from the protection of creation service. Normally, the *Typicon*, a kind of liturgical directory that lays down for each period and situation which hymns and other worship elements should be used, would also make provision for this. Yet, this provision is not self-

26. *'Iera akolouthia 'yper prostasias tou periballontos* (Athens: Apostolikē Diakonia, 1993).

27. The fixed parts are indicated only in several places. The complete texts of the parts concerned can be found in the *Great Book of Hours* (*'Ōrologion to Mega*) and the *'Ieratikon*. In the *Great Eight Tones Book / Supplicatory Book* (*Oktōēchos 'ē Megalē* and *Paraklētikē* respectively), one finds the usual variable chants of Vespers and Matins.

28. *'Ōrologion to Mega*, 7th ed. (Athens: Apostolikē Diakonia, 1977), 199; *Mēnaion tou Septembriou*, 10. The *Mēnaion* is the service book for the choir and the lector with the proper parts of a certain month, here September.

29. *'Ōrologion to Mega*, 146–48.

evident at all. The revised *Typicon* which Fr. Konstantinos Papagiannes (Papayannis, d. 2014) drew up, for instance, is outstanding, but in its provisions for 1 September it makes no reference whatsoever regarding the creation festival.[30] And although the Church of Greece officially furthers the creation day, any reference to that event is lacking under the 1 September heading in its annual worship directory, and there is also no indication of the hymns to be sung on that account.[31] The same goes for the current service book for the month of September, which seems not to know the feast day in question.[32] By contrast, the yearly directory of the Patriarchate of Constantinople, in its 1 September section, explicitly mentions that this important day—the patriarch has to attend—is also dedicated to the protection of the natural environment. However, it provides only a small selection from the hymns on safeguarding the ecosystem. The reason is that the *troparia* (short hymns) and other worship elements about the beginning of the new ecclesiastical church year and the Marian icon venerated in the patriarchal cathedral must also be accounted for. So, given the plethora of hymns for the divergent events on 1 September, only a few chants of each feast can be sung.[33]

Related to this issue is the question of the reception of the service formularies concerned. Where are they used in the Greek Orthodox world? In many dioceses, parishes, and monasteries, or only in a few? And if they are used, to what extent? The important question of reception requires further research.

Liturgical Language

The linguistic form Fr. Gerasimos and Metropolitan Nicodemos employ is a much older form of Greek than the contemporary vernacular. The foreword of the service Metropolitan Nicodemos drew up is written in an archaizing form of Greek that used to be the official language of

30. Kōnstantinos Papagiannēs, ed., *Systēma Typikou tōn ʾierōn akolouthiōn tou ʾolou eniautou* [Foundation of a typicon of the holy services of the entire year] (Athens: Apostolikē Diakonia, 2006), 143–47.

31. *Diptycha tēs Ekklēsias tēs ʾEllados: Kanonarion-Epetēris 2018* (Athens: Apostolikē Diakonia, 2017), 281–82.

32. *Mēnaion tou Septembriou*, 7–19.

33. *ʾĒmerologion tou Oikoumenikou Patriarcheiou etous 2013*, 369–79 and, as for the 2018 liturgical directory, http://www.ec-patr.org/gr/typikon/2018/2018-09-01.htm.

the Greek state and was only replaced in 1976 with the actual people's language, the *dēmotikē / dimotiki*.[34] Both Nicodemos's and Gerasimos's services themselves are in Ancient Greek. For biblical references and paraphrases, they rely on the original texts of the Septuagint and New Testament, namely, the version used in the Greek liturgical books.

For many of the faithful, however, these ancient language forms, though related to their mother tongues, are hardly intelligible. This applies especially to many psalm texts, readings from the Pauline corpus, and numerous hymns. It is less true of the gospels, whose simple language forms are still partly intelligible. Although in present-day Greek Orthodoxy in America the liturgy is usually celebrated in English, in Greece and Cyprus nearly all bishops, several theologians and clergymen, and also some learned laypeople are *against* the celebration of the liturgy in the vernacular. For the Holy Synod of the Church of Greece, for example, among the essential arguments are that the Septuagint is the normative version of the Old Testament; that the New Testament itself was written in Greek; that the great church fathers, hymnographers, and the seven ecumenical councils made use of this language; and that in the Byzantine hymns, text and melody are interdependent, so that the text cannot be altered without rendering it incompatible with the melody. Moreover, according to the opponents of adopting the vernacular in the liturgy, it is very difficult to translate specific grammatical and syntactical phenomena and, therefore, people who do not understand these arduous linguistic phenomena must learn more about them, or use a grammar, manual, or dictionary. All in all, in their opinion, translation into Modern Greek would mean "unfaithfulness" to holy tradition and the original biblical texts. Others point to additional reasons, such as the "difficulty of this endeavor" and the "fear of polarizing reactions."[35] So it comes as no surprise that even new liturgical formularies, such as the ones for

34. Peter Mackridge, *Language and National Identity in Greece, 1766–1976* (Oxford: Oxford Univ. Press, 2009); Geoffrey Horrocks, *Greek: A History of the Language and Its Speakers* (London and New York, NY: Longman, 1997), 332–65; Margaret Alexiou, *After Antiquity: Greek Language, Myth, and Metaphor* (Ithaca, NY: Cornell Univ. Press, 2002), 31–42.

35. See my "Liturgical Language and Vernacular Tongues in Eastern Christianity," in *Sanctifying Texts, Transforming Rituals: Encounters in Liturgical Studies—Essays in Honour of Gerard A.M. Rouwhorst*, ed. Paul van Geest, Marcel Poorthuis, and Els Rose, Brill's Studies in Catholic Theology 5 (Leiden: Brill, 2017), 407–24, here 412–17.

environmental care, are still composed in the old liturgical language. Metropolitan Nicodemos and Fr. Gerasimos's use of ancient linguistic forms for their services is in line with the policy of the hierarchy. The question of whether the congregation understands the contents of the hymns and prayers is another issue. In the diaspora the situation is different: the service Fr. Gerasimos compiled can be celebrated in English, French, or German,[36] and Nicodemos's compilation in French or Dutch.[37]

An observation on gender-related language is in order here. In many an Orthodox worship formulary and statement on environmental decay, one reads words like "rape," "abuse," and the like. This applies also to Pope Francis's *Laudato Si'* (see below). On the one hand, these are strong expressions, sending a clear message about what serious kind of damage humans are inflicting on this planet. On the other, according to some critics, this may evoke images of male dominance and submission of and discrimination against women, as well as—especially for victims of harassment and sexual violence—painful memories.[38]

Sacred Music

Sacred singing has great value and gives wings to the verbal statements on creation and the Creator. In the Byzantine Rite, there exists

36. Printed English translations that contain only Vespers are: (1) "Vespers for the Protection of the Environment," trans. S. Kezios (Northridge, CA: Narthex Press, 2001), (2) "Office of Vespers for the Preservation of Creation," trans. Ephrem Lash, in *Orthodoxy and Ecology: Resource Book*, ed. Alexander Belopopsky and Dimitri Oikonomou (Białystok: Syndesmos, 1996), Annex 1, pp. 3–17. The full service, that is, Vespers, Matins, and Eucharist, can be found in Chryssavgis and Foltz, *Toward an Ecology of Transfiguration*, 379–97. Its title, however, announces merely the evening service: "Vespers for the Environment: September 1 (or the First Sunday in September)", translated by Archimandrite Ephrem Lash. While the Bible readings are nearly identical with those of the Greek revised version, the acrostichon of the canon now goes "O Christ Savior, keep us safe." I possess also copies of Fr. Gerasimos's full service in German and French translations. I owe thanks to Metropolitan Elpidophoros Lambriniadis (Patriarchate of Constantinople), who sent me these copies.

37. The French version was published in 1994 at the Orthodox St. Nicholas Monastery in La Dalmérie, France.

38. Cf. Irwin, *A Commentary on* Laudato Si', 241–42. I wonder whether the fact that in Greek "creation" (*ktisis*), "nature" (*physis*), and "earth" (*gē*) are female words is relevant here.

an enormous variety of ways, styles, and schools of chanting. In the Greek tradition, generally speaking, one hears Byzantine plainchant hymnody with rich melismas, intervals, and characteristics that tend to strike Western ears as "oriental." In Greece, those in attendance hardly sing along with the choir, but leave the performance of the hymns to the skilled cantors. Nearly all choirs there remain exclusively male, but in quite a few Greek Orthodox parishes in Western Europe and North America the choirs are mixed.[39]

In their hymns, Fr. Gerasimos and Metropolitan Nicodemos on the one hand extol the beauty of creation as a treasure which humanity should guard. On the other hand, both compilers denounce the abusive behavior of humans who sinfully destroy the environment, and they call them to repentance and thankfulness for God's gift. An essential part of the service is the canon sung during Matins. This is a group of nine series of stanzas, each series being called "ode." They go together with the biblical canticles (also called "odes"). These are the chants of joy sung by Moses and the Israelites, Hannah, Isaiah, Jonah, Habakkuk, the Three Youths in the furnace, and Mary (Exod 15:1-19; Deut 32:1-43;1 Sam 2:1-10; Hab 3:1-19; Isa 26:9-20; Jonah 2:3-10; Dan 3:26-56, 57-88; Luke 1:46-55, 68-79—because of its harsh contents, the second canticle is mostly omitted). The *acrostichon*, a hallmark of most canons, runs in Metropolitan Nicodemos's canon: "Save the world, O governor of the world; poem of Nicodemos," whereas in Fr. Gerasimos's poem it says: "May you Christ Savior preserve us; from Gerasimos." The odes that the Metropolitan of Patra composed sing the praises of creation and admonish humanity not to taste the fruits from the forbidden tree of knowledge, but to keep God's commandments and attend carefully to nature. God nurtures all creatures, so let us rejoice in God's goodness. We should not pollute the air, earth, and water, but purify ourselves. Anyone who destroys nature rebels against its maker. The stanzas that accompany the Lauds (Pss 148–150) sung at the end of Matins also commend the beauty of the cosmos, stars, heavens, birds, sea, and animal and plant life. They ask concurrently for protection and salvation.

---

39. From the cornucopia of fine literature I refer here only to Kenneth Levy and Christian Troelsgård, "Byzantine Chant," in *The New Grove Dictionary of Music and Musicians* 4 (2001): 734–56; and Dimitri Giannelos, *La musique byzantine: le chant ecclésiastique, sa notation et sa pratique actuelle* (Paris: L'Harmattan, 1996).

Regarding the structure of the service that the Metropolitan of Patra composed, most *troparia* are *prosomoia*, that is, they have to follow the melody, meter, and rhythm of other *troparia* serving as examples. In that way, the odes of the canon have been composed according to the model of *irmi / heirmoi*.

Throughout his hymnody, Metropolitan Nicodemos refers to Scripture. Favorite passages are, inter alia, Genesis 1–3 (creation of the universe and the fall of Adam and Eve) and psalms that praise the impressive cosmos, such as Psalms 8, 32, 103, and 148, also Isaiah 6 (God on his throne with the seraphs, the prophet's vocation, and the people's stubbornness), and Daniel 3 (the song of praise by the three youths), the latter text specific to the Septuagint.[40] In addition to the Scripture-inspired hymns, the Metropolitan provides three lessons for Vespers: Isaiah 61:1-10a (the prophet proclaims the year of the Lord's favor), a section from Leviticus 26 (vv. 3-12, 14-17, 19-20, 22, 33, 23-24a: if Israel obeys God's commandments it will prosper, if it disobeys it will be punished and suffer), and Proverbs 9:1-11 (wisdom invites everyone, those listening to her will live longer). The first two readings belong to the extant 1 September evening service, and the third lesson has been borrowed from the Vespers of the festival of the Birth of the Mother of God on 8 September. The Scripture verses sung during the three antiphons at the beginning of the Eucharist are again from Daniel 3 (vv. 52-53, 56-63, 82-87 but whereas in v. 83 the critical edition speaks of "Israel," our service here says "new Israel," namely the church). The lessons during the Eucharist are the regular ones for the beginning of the new church year: 1 Timothy 2:1-7 (on the apostle's appeal that supplications be made for everyone and that God desires all to be saved) and Luke 4:16-22 (Jesus reading Isaiah's proclamation of the year of the Lord's favor and telling the congregation in Nazareth that "this scripture is now fulfilled in your hearing").

The Bible readings which Fr. Gerasimos offers for Vespers are partly different: besides the common Leviticus 26, the two other lessons are now Isaiah 63:15–64:5a, 8-9 (petition to our Father, the Lord, to return to the people) and Jeremiah 2:1-12 (the Lord's accusation of apostasy). In the revised version of this service, two readings have been changed: Genesis 1:1-19 and Genesis 1:20–2:2 (creation narrative), the Isaiah

---

40. For the Bible texts, the editions of the Patriarchate of Constantinople are used. In many places, these vary from the critical edition. On the Septuagint version of the three youths in the furnace, see Anathea Portier-Young's chapter in this volume.

lesson remaining identical. During Matins, Luke 18:2-8 (need to pray always: the unjust judge and the persistent widow) is read. The lessons for the Eucharist are again 1 Timothy 2:1-7 and Luke 4:16-22, an alternative gospel reading being Mark 13:24-31 (Second Coming in a universe that falls apart, lesson from the fig tree).

The First of September: An Ecumenical Feast

The designation of 1 September as creation day is an Orthodox initiative, but it has also become an "ecology day" or "creation day" in several other denominations. In 2002, the Central Committee of the World Council of Churches urged the member churches to observe 1 September as a day of prayer for the environment and its sustainability. Earlier, the *Charta Oecumenica*, which the Conference of European Churches and the (Roman Catholic) Council of Bishops' Conferences of Europe jointly signed in 2001, urged the churches in Europe to introduce an ecumenical day of prayer for the preservation of creation.[41] This initiative went even further, because the Third European Ecumenical Assembly, held in September 2007 in Sibiu, Romania, recommended that the entire period from 1 September to 4 October (on the latter date see below) be "dedicated to prayer for the protection of creation and the promotion of sustainable lifestyles that reverse our contribution to climate change."[42]

Several Roman Catholic Bishops' Conferences have also separately advised following the Orthodox example. Italian Catholicism, for instance, has been observing that day since 2005. In addition, on 10 August 2015, Pope Francis urged that the entire Catholic Church join Orthodoxy in this respect and adopt 1 September as a World Day of Prayer for Creation. Although in the Roman Rite that day is not the beginning of a new ecclesiastical year (it begins with Advent), 1 September marks the end of summer vacations, a new working year, a novel academic year, with meetings and worship services related to that fresh start, and therefore the world day of prayer need not be an isolated event. Significant are also the common statements of Patriarch Bartholomew and the Roman pontiffs

41. See "Charta Oecumenica: Guidelines for the Growing Cooperation among the Churches in Europe," no. 9, 22 April 2001, https://www.ceceurope.org/wp-content/uploads/2015/07/ChartaOecumenica.pdf.

42. "Message": Recommendation no. 10. See *Greek Orthodox Theological Review* 52 (2007): 315–21, here 321.

John Paul II, Benedict XVI, and Francis on creation and ecology. In his apostolic letter *Orientale Lumen* (1995), John Paul II had pointed to the eucharistic potential of the created world: matter is adopted in the liturgy, humans praise God by way of material elements, and transfiguration of all is intended.[43] Furthermore, on 1 September 2017, the Phanar and the Vatican issued their common statement on the Day of Prayer for the Care of Creation, in which they censured the deterioration of the planet, invited "all people of good will" to pray for, and look after, the environment, and appealed to those in positions of power and responsibility to "support the consensus of the world for the healing of our wounded planet."[44] Both the Phanar and the Vatican were also involved in the Paris agreement on climate change (November/December 2015).

To crown it all, in May 2015, Pope Francis published his encyclical letter *Laudato Si': On Care for Our Common Home*.[45] This comprehensive encyclical, an invitation to dialogue with every person on this planet, concretely names the manifestations of environmental degradation, examines its human roots, and outlines key aspects of a Christian theology of creation, "integral ecology." It provides guidelines for awareness and action and emphasizes ecological formation and spirituality. Concurrently, it reflects on the sacraments, especially the Eucharist, as effective ways to incorporate the material world into the spiritual one and to unite them with one another (nos. 233–37). The lengthy papal reflection ends with two prayers: "A prayer for our earth" and "a Christian prayer in union with creation" (no. 246). It deserves mention that Pope Francis refers positively to Patriarch Bartholomew's appeals to repent for the sins against nature, attend to the ethical and spiritual roots of environmental decay, and change human behavior (nos. 7–9) and also that the pope appreciates the beauty and divine transfiguration of matter in Eastern

43. *Apostolic Letter* Orientale Lumen *of the Supreme Pontiff John Paul II to the Bishops, Clergy and Faithful to Mark the Centenary of* Orientalium Dignitas *of Pope Leo XIII* (Vatican City: Libreria Editrice Vaticana, 1995), no. 11.

44. See Holy See Press Office, Summary of Bulletin, "Joint Message of Pope Francis and the Ecumentical Patriarch Bartholomew for the World Day of Prayer for Creation, 01.09.2017," https://press.vatican.va/content/salastampa/en/bollettino /pubblico/2017/09/01/170901a.html.

45. *On Care for Our Common Home, Laudato Si': The Encyclical of Pope Francis on the Environment*, with commentary by Sean McDonagh (Maryknoll, NY: Orbis Books, 2016). Cf. Kevin W. Irwin's chapter in this volume.

Christian spirituality (no. 235). On top of this, a foremost theologian and hierarch of the Patriarchate of Constantinople, Metropolitan John Zizioulas, assesses the encyclical most positively. Speaking on behalf of his church, he underscores the theological significance of ecology, the spiritual dimension of the ecological problem, and the ecumenical value of Pope Francis's document.[46] Various other Orthodox church leaders and theologians spoke in the same vein.[47]

Besides 1 September, 4 October, the feast of Saint Francis of Assisi, also serves in many places as a feast day that focuses on nature and creation. The title and a high number of statements in *Laudato Si'* explicitly refer to the saint. It is easy to understand why the *Poverello*, a friend of birds, animals, and flora and fauna as well as a champion of justice for the poor and outcast and a classic example of internal harmony, has become a patron saint of creation, environmental care, biodiversity, and a sober human lifestyle. Against this background, Assisi has become the venue for several international and interdenominational meetings on creation and environmental care.

A good many member churches of the Anglican Communion and also Methodist, Lutheran, Presbyterian, and other Protestant churches now observe a Season of Creation,[48] a Time for Creation, when they pray and care for the environment (1 September–4 October). In several places, this is done together with the Orthodox and Catholics. Special liturgical resources are available, online prayer services are celebrated, awareness of environmental degradation is raised, and networks of "green churches" take practical steps regarding refuse and energy use in order to meet this huge challenge.

Environmental decay has become a key issue in both ecumenical and interreligious dialogue. As for ecumenism, I have already mentioned the Conciliar Process for Justice, Peace, and the Integrity of Creation. In a similar way, the Social Mission Statement of the Ecumenical Council of Churches in Austria, to which all major denominations adhere, discusses the need for responsibility, sustainability, eco-justice, and new economic

---

46. Elder Metropolitan John (Zizioulas) of Pergamon, "A Comment on Pope Francis' Encyclical *Laudato Si'*," *Greek Orthodox Theological Review* 60 (2015): 184–91.

47. See, e.g., "La recezione ecumenica della *Laudato Si'*," *Studi Ecumenici* 34 (2016): 27–162, here 97–149.

48. Season of Creation, http://seasonofcreation.org.

concepts (quality of life instead of quantity) in view of the exploitation of nature. Besides a good many recommendations to corporations, society at large, the member churches, and every Christian, "the Churches intend to cultivate a spirituality of creation anchored in prayer and liturgy" and they promote 1 September as a day of responsibility for creation in order to strengthen awareness.[49] Furthermore, in Germany, at the initiative of the Cooperative Body of Christian Churches, all major denominations now concentrate on creation and environmental care on the first Friday of September, or (if that proves to be impossible) any day in the period between 1 September and 4 October.[50] The first Friday of September has been selected by analogy with the first Friday of March, when the Women's World Day of Prayer is celebrated.

So it is quite common nowadays that in diverse interdenominational meetings, as well as in encounters with Judaism, Islam, and so forth, ecology is on the agenda.[51] Common reflection and action with respect to environmental decay and care are not only urgent in order to respond to the huge challenge of adequate concern for our habitat and God's handiwork, but they also foster interdenominational and interreligious cooperation and deepen mutual relationships. In a time of multifaceted communication and globalization, on the one hand, and increasing tension, on the other, this "collateral advantage" is of high significance.

For many centuries, Orthodoxy, Catholicism, and other confessions have been petitioning God not only to bless seeds, harvests, grapes, animals, and so forth, but also to deliver humankind from natural calamities of all kinds, such as earthquakes, storms, extreme drought, and floods. The *Euchologion*, for example, contains a host of such orations and services.[52] Currently, however, Christians are praying for creation to be safeguarded from further human negative intervention and destruction.

---

49. *Social Mission Statement* (Vienna: Ecumenical Council of Churches in Austria, 2006), nos. 285–308. Title of the original German 2003 version: *Sozialwort*.

50. Cf. the presentations in *Una Sancta* 65 (2010): 81–136.

51. See, e.g., *Faith-Based Statements on Climate Change* (Coronado, CA: Citizens Lobby, 2015); *Islamochristiana* 43 (2017): 43–147.

52. The *Euchologion* is a service book for the clergy that contains the texts and rubrics for the Liturgy of the Hours, the sacraments, and the funeral and other services, as well as blessings of all kinds and exorcisms. As for the prayer texts in question see, e.g., Skaltsēs, *"Eis kairous kai eniautous,"* 69–134, 168–79, 185–201. Cf. Nicholas Denysenko's chapter in this volume.

"Liturgy First"

After we have studied the aforementioned messages and worship services, a major observation is in order. The documents in question demonstrate the primary significance of the liturgy. In many churches, perhaps even more in the Eastern traditions, worship celebrations are the apogee of ecclesiastical life and spirituality. Led by the Holy Spirit, the faithful represent the mystery of the covenant between the eternal Three-Personed One and the people of God. God's everlasting covenant with Israel culminates in the paschal mystery—that is, the life, passion, death, and resurrection of Jesus Christ, as well as the gift of the Holy Spirit and the expectation of the Second Coming. More than Western Christian theologians, Eastern theologians use liturgy as the point of departure for their reflections. The *lex orandi* and the *lex credendi* are entwined: the way Christians pray and celebrate defines their faith, and their faith constitutes their worship.

This applies also to the subject of this chapter: the messages and worship texts I have discussed lay emphasis on liturgy as a major source of ecological theology. Worshiping the Triune God in prayer and ritual is not an illustration of ecological theology but its point of departure and its basis. Good ecological theology is doxological, a "cosmic Eucharist."[53] It knows also that God is always greater than any human effort, experience, and verbal approach. Therefore, it is interwoven with hymnody praising God as the source of life and, at the same time, the horizon that can never be grasped. All in all, good theologians know that at the end of the day, there is silence. Doxological ecological theology is an unfinished and infinite history of thought and spiritual search. It aims at moving toward God and tries to address and pronounce God's mystery, not to fathom and penetrate it, but to praise it and understand it as mystery.

Interconnectedness of Reflection and Action

Yet some critical questions must also be asked when we study the documents mentioned here. To what extent do they contribute not merely to reflection but also to action regarding ecology and environmental crisis? Do they stimulate Greek Orthodox, other Orthodox, and non-Orthodox Christians to relate to nature in a less self-centered and more "priestly"

53. Theokritoff, "Ethics and Ecology," 670.

way? Do they really boost the eucharistic, liturgical, and ascetic ethos? Can they push Christians and others into behavior as guardians and stewards instead of owners, even plunderers, of nature? As the Orthodox theologian Elizabeth Theokritoff observes critically: "There is little point in talking eloquently about the 'eucharistic ethos' of the Church without examining minutely and honestly how far such an ethos is reflected in the whole way we live, as church communities and as members of the Church."[54]

Hence, a major concern is the question of the reception and aftereffects of the worship services, in other words, the question of whether the interrelatedness of theory and practice works. There is a risk, a temptation that such a host of statements remains on a merely theoretical level. Spiritual contemplation, *theōria*, is a key characteristic of Orthodox theology. On the one hand, spirituality and prayer are essential and indispensable. On the other, sometimes *theōria* is esteemed to such an extent that it is at the cost of practical involvement, like taking a public stand against various concrete cases of environmental pollution, in the everyday reality of church and society. In addition, laying emphasis on cultic enactments and seeing the world primarily through the prism of the celebration of the liturgy certainly entails bright sides, including self-restraint and living in gratitude, but at the same time may veil the urgent problem of tackling concrete social needs. Patriarch Bartholomew underscores the interconnectedness of theological reflection and practical action, as his numerous initiatives in writing, preaching, and acting so far have demonstrated.

Asceticism

Spiritual landmarks recurring in the aforementioned patriarchal messages, such as asceticism and sanctification of one's own life—through the phases of purification, illumination, and deification (unification with God)—are pivotal. These hallmarks are meant not merely for monks and nuns but for all believers. Certainly, the emphasis on asceticism is a feature of the Orthodox tradition. For instance, Archpriest Georgios Metallinos, professor emeritus of theology in the University of Athens, calls asceticism an essential characteristic of Christian worship.[55] Liturgy

---

54. See Theokritoff, "From Sacramental Life to Sacramental Living," 522.

55. Georgios D. Metallinos, *Ē theologikē martyria tēs ekklēsiastikēs latreias* [The theological witness of the ecclesiastical liturgy] (Athens: Grēgorēs, 1995), 185–92.

constitutes the entrance to life in Christ, to deification and sanctification, but only the ascetic way gives access to that entry. Asceticism enables all faithful to acquire pure hearts, although, according to Metallinos, monasticism is the best and most authentic way in Christianity. Metropolitan Emilianos Timiadis (d. 2008), an open-minded hierarch of the Ecumenical Patriarchate, also thinks that asceticism is seminal for any genuine Christian spirituality. In his perspective, living an ascetic life consists of self-discipline, endurance, and struggle with sins like consumerism and hedonism.[56] The objective of asceticism is not to kill our desires, because that would also harm our spiritual life, but to orient them toward God. For Orthodox theologian Elizabeth Theokritoff, too, asceticism possesses a positive meaning: purifying our observations, creating balance, and strengthening the relationships between humans, nature, and community.[57]

Yet for many people asceticism has the negative connotation of denial of bodily pleasure and dualism, that is to say, of a constant battle between the material and the spiritual dimensions. That connotation is not totally unfounded, because in the long monastic ascetic tradition, the struggle with corporality, sexuality, and lust has not been a rare phenomenon. In the monastic tradition, the Greek word *askēsis*, which literally means "exercise," "training," "workout," stands for spiritual training, discipline, and the right way of life with a view to ascension to God and thus salvation of one's own soul, that of others, even that of the world.[58] In ecological spirituality, asceticism means moderation and self-restraint instead of uncontrolled consumerism and waste culture, hence liberty

56. Emilianos Timiadis, *Towards Authentic Christian Spirituality: Orthodox Pastoral Reflections*, ed. Markos Nickolas (Brookline, MA: Holy Cross, 1998), 73–100.

57. Elizabeth Theokritoff, "Embodied Word and New Creation: Some Modern Orthodox Insights Concerning the Material World," in *Abba, The Tradition of Orthodoxy in the West—Festschrift for Bishop Kallistos (Ware) of Diokleia*, ed. John Behr, Andrew Louth, and Dimitri Conomos (Crestwood, NY: St Vladimir's Seminary Press, 2003), 221–38, here 234–38.

58. It is impossible to do justice here to the numerous connotations and contexts of asceticism in diverse cultures and religions, but see, for example, Vincent L. Wimbush and Richard Valantasis, eds., *Asceticism* (Oxford: Oxford Univ. Press, 1998); and Alice-Mary Talbot, "Asceticism," in *The Oxford Dictionary of Byzantium* 1, ed. Alexander P. Kazhdan and others (New York, NY and Oxford: Oxford Univ. Press, 1991), 203–4.

from greed and compulsion.[59] Sometimes, however, the emphasis on asceticism promotes an introvert attitude to life and a high degree of passivity. Certainly, the danger of concealing urgent practical issues in an impenetrable cloud of introvert spirituality is not an exclusively Orthodox problem. It is a challenge for any religious denomination. *Theōria* must be coupled with *praxis*, action. The entanglement of *lex orandi* and *lex credendi* must be joined with *lex vivendi / lex agendi*. The way Christians pray and celebrate does not alone define their faith, but these two "laws" determine the way of living and acting, and, vice versa, the right way of living and doing things lays down the correct way of worshiping and believing.[60] Orthodoxy and orthopraxy are interrelated, the latter being no less important than the former. Hence, liturgical and ecological theology should not be isolated from other essential aspects of Christian life, especially *diakonia.*

Of utmost importance here is the "liturgical triangle," an expression that the French Catholic sacramental theologian and liturgist Louis-Marie Chauvet coined.[61] That term points to the close connection between, first, the word of God, read and heard in Scripture; secondly, God's word celebrated in the entire worship service; and, thirdly, God's word lived out in active charity, social care, and the commitment to fight poverty, injustice, and environmental pollution. These three forms of responding to the word of God are inseparably interrelated.[62] If they are detached from one another, ecological theology risks becoming only navel-gazing.

---

59. Cf. Chryssavgis, *Cosmic Grace, Humble Prayer*, 30–33.

60. See, e.g., Winfried Haunerland, "Liturgie als *lex vivendi?*," *Orthodoxes Forum* 28 (2014): 37–41; Martin Stuflesser and Stephan Winter, eds., *"Ahme nach, was du vollziehst . . .": Positionsbestimmungen zum Verhältnis von Liturgie und Ethik*, Studien zur Pastoralliturgie 22 (Regensburg: Pustet, 2009).

61. Louis-Marie Chauvet, *Du symbolique au symbole: Essai sur les sacrements*, Rites et symbols 9 (Paris: Cerf, 1979), 81–122.

62. See also Basilius J. Groen, "The Alliance between Liturgy and Diakonia as Witness of the Church: Theological Foundation and Several Examples," in *La liturgie comme témoin de l'Église: LVIIe Semaine d'Études Liturgiques, Institut Saint-Serge, Paris, 28 juin-1 juillet 2010*, ed. André Lossky and Manlio Sodi, Monumenta studia instrumenta liturgica 66 (Rome: Libreria Editrice Vaticana, 2012), 239–55. Irwin's study *A Commentary on* Laudato Si' is a fine concrete example of the "liturgical triangle."

Sacramentality

Essential to all abovementioned messages and other ecclesial documents is the sacramental aspect. The liturgy utilizes material elements, such as bread, wine, oil, water, and fire, in order to transfigure them, make them transparent for God's love and commitment to his covenant. Iconographers employ colors, drawings, wood, mosaic stones, or other matter to symbolize God's liberation of and reconciliation with fallen humankind. So, divine metamorphosis of matter presupposes that the entire material world is taken seriously. God's activity and energy take place in cooperation with receiving and thanksgiving "priestly" humans. Hence, in the sacramental celebration, heavenly and earthly worship blend, angelic song and human adoration are coupled.

An essential characteristic of Christian worship is assembling in order to hear and experience the biblical words of liberation and reconciliation, partake of the bread and cup of life, celebrate the Body and Blood of Christ, and become these eucharistic offerings themselves, as living sacrifices (see Rom 12:1-2). Essentially everything belongs to God; the act of human offering is only giving back what has always been God's property. Consequently, the participants' eucharistic offerings are not their property, but are God's own. As Byzantine Rite eucharistic prayers put it, "We offer to you yours from your own, everywhere and for everything."[63] It is crucial that this is connected with the other parts of the "liturgical triangle."

However, in Western societies, including traditionally Orthodox regions in southeastern and eastern Europe, rapid processes of de-churching, de-traditionalization, and individualization are currently taking place. Many people eschew involvement with institutional religion. They may believe in God without belonging to any denomination or be "spiritual, but not religious." They experience transcendence and mysticism, the encounter with the Eternal One outside the traditional churches and their worship services. Hence, in the field of religious rites, the church is losing its monopoly; in the market of rites, it has become only one of the providers and has to cope with a lot of competition there. Instead of being ubiquitous established centers, the churches increasingly resemble

63. *'Ieratikon*, 7th ed. (Athens: Apostolikē Diakonia, 2009), 132 (Liturgy of John Chrysostom), 172 (Liturgy of Basil the Great), 343 § 5 (linguistic comment).

monuments, even ruins, of faded glory and power. In a terrain unfamiliar to them, they have to re-contextualize without giving in to the temptation to flee into a supposedly great past and isolate themselves from society and other religious and non-religious groups. Their challenge is to find new ways, inter alia in the digital world and new social media, to present their pressing and topical message on ecological involvement and its sacramental dimensions. Do the "nones," "somes," and "dones" think and feel that ecological liturgy, spirituality, and theology are relevant for them?[64]

A related problem concerns the possibility for the assembly to experience what I just called the blending of heavenly and earthly worship, of angelic song and human adoration. According to the prominent Orthodox theologian Andrew Louth, regrettably the Protestant Reformation has destroyed sacramental ontology. Western Christianity, including Catholicism, is no longer able to experience that the church, actually the entire world, is sacramental. In his opinion, only Orthodoxy enables its believers to share in this sacramental vision.[65] Although he touches an important subject, it seems to me that he does not do justice to the diversity of Western Christianity, where in many places and in manners of all kinds, people experience that the world mirrors God's wonderful presence and is replete with references to the Godhead.[66]

Epilogue

We have seen that 1 September is now being celebrated in various churches. In a way, the day has become an ecumenical creation festival. Ecological theology serves all denominations, indeed all humanity. It has

64. Irwin, *A Commentary on* Laudato Si', 243–45.

65. See Andrew Louth, "Orthodox Reflections on the Reformation and Its Legacy," *One in Christ* 51 (2017): 314–33.

66. For Catholic sacramental theology, see e.g., Mathai Kadavil, *The World as Sacrament: Sacramentality of Creation from the Perspectives of Leonardo Boff, Alexander Schmemann and Saint Ephrem*, Textes et Études Liturgiques / Studies in Liturgy 20 (Leuven: Peeters, 2005); Kekong Bisong and Mathai Kadavil, eds., *Celebrating the Sacramental World: Essays in Honor of Emeritus Professor Lambert J. Leijssen*, Textes et Études Liturgiques / Studies in Liturgy 24 (Leuven: Peeters, 2010); Kevin W. Irwin, *The Sacraments: Historical Perspectives and Liturgical Theology* (New York, NY and Mahwah NJ: Paulist Press, 2016).

definitely been a step forward that, in the choir of environmental care singers, Orthodoxy wants to unite its voice with the Catholic, Anglican, and Protestant parts and that it mostly does not insist on singing high solos. At the same time, Western Christians involved in responding to the environmental crisis should be open-minded toward the Orthodox approach. Are they willing to temper Western activism, haste, utilitarianism, and humanity's dominance over (the remains of) nature in favor of abstinence, *apatheia*—not apathy, but superseding one's own passions, such as anger and greed—and *eucharistia*, dependence on and harmony with creation, of which they are part? Ideally, human autonomy, activity, and creative urge, on the one hand, and awareness of our dependence on nature and its Creator, on the other, go together.

According to some traditionalist groups, ecological liturgical theology is an illegitimate innovation, mere activism, and not God-oriented thought and worship. My reading of the evidence, however, demonstrates that this reproach is not correct. In addition, tradition is a dynamic process. As an appropriate adage puts it, tradition "does not consist in the veneration of burnt ashes, but in passing on the flame."[67]

67. Ascribed to the English statesman and Catholic martyr Sir Thomas More (1478–1535), as well as to some other historic protagonists of intellectual and artistic life.

CHAPTER FIFTEEN

Troubled Waters, Troubling Initiation Rites

Mary E. McGann

At the heart of Christian sacramental practice is a water rite through which believers are "born again," in and through the initiatory waters. The profound ecological symbolism of this rite is self-evident. Water is the birthplace of life on Earth, the matrix of all living. Water carries in its flow the history of planet Earth, the story of evolutionary emergence. The finite and fragile waters that we use today and that grace our sacramental rites reach back to the formation of our common home, where they helped to form and cool the planet, and, as part of God's creative energies at work in planetary formation, engaged in the great birthing of life itself.[1]

The Hebrew Scriptures speak of water's cooperation with God throughout salvation history. "God does not work alone," writes Linda Gibler, "but creates the world through the medium of water."[2] The significance of this cooperation is dramatically told in stories of the Garden of Eden, the great Flood, the Red Sea crossing, and the desert thirst of the Hebrew people. And in an image that is very timely today, prophetic voices hold out the promise of a rehydration of arid and desert places

---

1. Images taken from Linda Gibler, *From the Beginning to Baptism: Scientific and Sacred Stories of Water, Oil, and Fire* (Collegeville, MN: Liturgical Press, 2010), 3–19.

2. Ibid., 13.

as integral to a "redeemed Creation."[3] Isaiah 35 sings of this watery re-demption: "For waters shall break forth in the wilderness and streams in the desert: the burning sand shall become a pool, and the thirsty ground springs of water" (Isa 35:6b-7a, NRSV, used throughout). Second Isaiah likewise holds out a similar promise for those marginalized by oppression: "When the poor and needy seek water, and there is none, and their tongue is parched with thirst, I the Lord will answer them . . . I will open rivers on the bare heights, and fountains in the midst of the valleys; I will make the wilderness a pool of water, and the dry land springs of water" (Isa 41:17-19).[4]

Water permeates the Gospel narratives as well, especially John, where Jesus identifies himself to the Samaritan woman as living water, welling up in believers as life and new birth (4:8-30). Water flows through the New Testament accounts, offering manifold images of God's action in the world: as creation and new life (Rev 22:1-22); as sign of God's blessing and grace (John 2:1-11); as place of Jesus' teaching the crowds and his disciples (Mark 4:1-4); as medium of healing (John 5:1-5); and as metaphor for entrance into the life of the Spirit (John 3:5-8).

The narrative of Jesus' baptism in the Jordan, recounted in the Gospel of Mark (1:9-11), reverberates with stories from the Hebrew Scriptures: the Spirit hovering over Jesus and over the waters echoing the creation accounts (Gen 1:2); his entrance into the Jordan reflecting the passage of Israelites into the Promised Land (Josh 3:14-17); the Spirit imaged as dove, reminiscent of a dove's promise of dry land and new life to Noah in the ark (Gen 8:10-11); and the outpouring of the Spirit in Jesus' glorification imaged as blood and water flowing from his wounded side (John 19:33-34).

The earliest references to baptism, such as the *Didache* (ca. 70–160), instruct those engaging in the rite to baptize in running water, preferably cold, and assumedly in a natural watercourse such as a local river.[5] Other sources, such as the *Canons of Hippolytus* and the *Testamentum Domini* invite participants to rise early and "sanctify the water, water from a river," so that the initiatory waters will be "pure and flowing."[6] All these

---

3. See Ched Meyers, "Prophetic Visions of Redemption as Rehydration: A Call to Watershed Discipleship," *Anglican Theological Review* 100, no. 1 (2018): 61–77.

4. For additional examples see ibid.

5. Gibler, *From the Beginning*, 24–28, including what follows.

6. *The Apostolic Tradition: A Commentary,* ed. Paul F. Bradshaw et al., Hermeneia (Minneapolis, MN: Fortress, 2002), 113.

instances suggest an early Christian assumption that clean, living water was a "connection to the larger fullness of life considered intrinsic to the sacrament itself."[7] Moreover, these waters did not need further blessing. Only in the fourth century do we find a discussion of blessing the water, a custom that became stronger in subsequent centuries. As Gibler points out, blessings grew in length "as the amounts of water used in baptism became smaller" and as the "living water" of the earliest communities was replaced with waters stored in indoor cisterns.[8]

The positive and restorative images of water threaded through the Scriptures, and the assumption of natural watercourses as holy presence in instructions on baptism in the earliest centuries, are in marked contrast to the troubled state of Earth's waters today. Due in large measure to human activity, water insecurity, food shortages, polluted water sources, and changes in climate that create flooding and severe droughts plague every part of the planet. In the face of such challenges, can Christians responsibly engage in rites of initiation that center on the symbolic expressiveness of water without acknowledging the ecological catastrophes that contextualize these very waters? Moreover, can the Christian practice of baptismal immersion and rebirth contribute to the healing, restoration, and regeneration of this precious resource?[9]

These are questions for us to ponder well into the future, and that I will engage in a preliminary way in this essay. I begin by sketching five critical dimensions of the global crises that surround and impact water, then propose a framework for the practice, teaching, and theologizing about Christian initiation that is at once ecological, sacramental, and ethical.

Troubled Waters: A Global Crisis

Today, access or lack of access to clean, fresh water is a map of global inequality. According to the United Nations, 2.1 billion people lack access to safely managed drinking water and 4.5 billion people lack safely

---

7. Lisa E. Dahill, "Rewilding Christian Spirituality: Outdoor Sacraments and the Life of the World," in *Eco-Reformation: Grace and Hope for a Planet in Peril*, ed. Lisa E. Dahill and James B. Martin-Schramm (Eugene, OR: Cascade Books, 2016), 183.

8. Gibler, *From the Beginning*, 28.

9. See also Meyers, "Prophetic Visions," 61.

managed sanitation.[10] Women and girls in communities with severe short-ages are water bearers, walking miles each day to gather a few precious drops, often from contaminated sources. "Every day, unsafe water results in many deaths," writes Pope Francis in *Laudato Si'*, "and the spread of water related diseases, including those caused by microorganisms and chemical substances. Dysentery and cholera, linked to inadequate hygiene and water supplies, are a significant cause of suffering and infant mortality."[11] Indeed, more than 340,000 children under five die annually from diarrheal diseases—almost a thousand children a day. Moreover, clean water has become a sign of privilege, a right based on personal or communal economic status. "Our world has a grave social debt towards the poor who lack access to drinking water," continues Pope Francis, "because they are denied the right to a life consistent with their inalienable dignity" (LS 30).

Second, global thirst has reached epic proportions. Water use worldwide is increasing twice as fast as population growth. In the last fifty years, water use has tripled, due in large part to an increased standard of living and economic development.[12] Overconsumption of water is especially evident in countries like the United States, which carries the largest international water footprint. Compare the citizens in drought-stricken Cape Town, South Africa, who are restricted to 13.2 gallons of water a day, to Americans, who consume up to 100 gallons daily.[13] This overconsumption is creating risks at home as well: the US government claimed in 2008 that thirty-six states across the country will face water shortages in the near future.[14]

---

10. UN Water, Water Scarcity, http://www.unwater.org/water-facts/scarcity/ (accessed 13 March 2018).

11. Pope Francis, encyclical letter, *Laudato Si'* (On Care for Our Common Home), 24 May 2015, http://w2.vatican.va/content/francesco/en/encyclicals/documents/papa-francesco_20150524_enciclica-laudato-si.html [henceforth LS], 29.

12. Christiana Zenner, *Just Water: Theology, Ethics, and Fresh Water Crises*, rev. ed. (Maryknoll, NY: Orbis, 2018), 32.

13. Brian Pellot, Religion News Service, "As Cape Town's Water Crisis Nears 'Day Zero,' Faith Groups Spring into Action," *National Catholic Reporter* (7 February 2018).

14. David Gutierrez, "At least 36 U.S. States Face Water Shortage," *Natural News* (31 March 2008). See also Bill McKibben, *Eaarth: Making a Life on a Tough New Planet* (New York, NY: St. Martin's Griffin, 2011), 156.

The simple truth is that on a finite planet there are no more rivers to discover and no hidden lakes or fresh water streams to exploit. Urgent action must be taken to conserve and protect sources of fresh water, not only for human consumption but also to maintain the immense variety of marine life that feeds much of the world's population and to provide for the diverse species that depend on these water sources for habitat (LS 37, 40).

Third, climate chaos and water disruption are deeply entwined. As dry places become dryer and wet places wetter, progressive droughts and extreme flooding are more and more evident. The Horn of Africa has experienced four of its severest droughts ever in the last two decades, pushing millions of the world's poorest to the edge of survival.[15] In the United States, 1996 saw the worst drought of the century, destroying millions of acres of wheat in Kansas and Oklahoma, while reducing wheat reserves to the lowest level in fifty years.[16] Aridity and desertification of the land are affecting the whole planet, but not uniformly. The United Nations recently estimated that 180 million people will be living with absolute water scarcity by 2025, while two-thirds of the world population could face significant water-stress.[17]

Loss of a reliable climate and increasingly erratic weather patterns raise issues of food security for Earth's poorest communities. The growing wave of climate refugees from Central America seeking refuge in the United States is driven by a simple chain of events: "no water, no crops, no harvest, no food!"[18] Central America is ground zero for climate change in the Americas. With very dry seasons forecast for the future of the region, causing water to disappear and crops to fail, people will seek life and sustenance in other places. This pattern is reflected all over the globe, with refugees arriving uninvited at ports on every continent. In many cases, there are few if any legal or social frameworks for dealing with climate refugees.[19]

15. Somini Sengupta, "In Horn of Africa, Drought is the New Normal," *New York Times* (12 March 2018), A1.

16. Vandana Shiva, *Water Wars: Privatization, Pollution, and Profit* (Cambridge, MA: South End Press, 2002), 40.

17. Zenner, *Just Water*, 43.

18. Todd Miller, "Walls Rising against Tide of Refugees," *San Francisco Chronicle* (21 January 2018). Material in this paragraph from this source.

19. Regarding the lack of legal frameworks in the United States, see ibid.

Fourth, industrial agriculture is dehydrating the planet and poisoning many of its waterways with chemical runoff from fertilizers and pesticides. Corporate agribusiness drains 70 percent of the world's fresh water supplies while producing only 40 percent of its food,[20] and this at great cost to the Earth and its poorest communities. Industrial agriculture depends on intensive irrigation. Water is often drawn from underground aquifers—those ancient reservoirs beneath Earth's surface that are the most precious sources of drinking water.[21] Depleted aquifers can take upward of 10,000 years to refill.[22] In the central valley of California, the "salad bowl" for much of the nation, the water table has fallen by fifty feet and the valley floor is sinking as the resident aquifers are depleted.[23] In addition, food produced by this industrial system consumes unsustainable amounts of water: producing a pound of beef requires some 1,800 gallons of water, while some 2,650 gallons are needed to grow a pound of coffee. Radical shifts in agriculture must take place if water is to be protected for the future well-being of the Earth and all her inhabitants. Moreover, writes Pope Francis in *Laudato Si'*, "the control of water by large multinational businesses"—which today control a major part of global production and distribution—"may become a major source of conflict" as the century ahead unfolds (LS 31).

Fifth, today's troubled waters represent a profound spiritual and moral crisis. Questions of how water is to be valued and protected are critical; challenges of inequality, injustice, and unsustainability affecting the whole Earth community must be addressed in light of the future of the planet. Christiana Zenner, writing in *Just Water*, notes that over the past few decades, a debate has been raging about whether water should be seen as "a commodity or as a human right."[24]

20. Zenner, *Just Water*, 33. See also McKibben, *Eaarth*, 155.

21. Bobby Magill, "Large Aquifers Discovered under California's Drought-Stricken Central Valley," Climate Central, 28 June 2016, https://weather.com/science/environment/news/california-aquifers-discovered.

22. Zenner, *Just Water*, 37. Sea-level rise, fueled by warming temperatures, is leading to seawater intrusion into aquifers, causing salination of water supplies. This situation is found in the Patasco aquifer beneath much of the state of Maryland, as well as the coastal aquifer beneath Gaza and Israel. See ibid., 171.

23. See Magill, "Large Aquifers," for additional information.

24. Zenner, *Just Water*, 59.

A commodity is something that can be owned, bought and sold for profit, and traded in the market economy. As commodity, water is extracted from nature, hiding from view the complex relationships that constitute its identity, including the ecological and social cost of its extraction. Bottled water is an obvious example of such commodification. Mined from local water supplies, purchased by corporations for a pittance, packaged in fossil-fuel-laden bottles that are rarely reused or recycled, and resold at great profit,[25] bottled water often leaves local populations without essential resources.[26] Fiji water, for example, is flown nearly seven thousand miles to the United States, and sold here for some $4 a liter. Yet, the people of Fiji are suffering a severe water shortage. A third of all Fijians lack clean drinking water.[27]

In contrast to water as commodity, valuing it as a human right sees it as something due all people regardless of their ability to pay. Water as a human right suggests that social equity is far more important than profit; that water is a public good, part of a "global commons" that requires shared responsibility for its health and well-being.[28]

Put simply, the right to clean water is the right to live,[29] a right to life.[30] Many of our churches have taken a stand, claiming that the value of water lies not in its economic worth but as "an essential, finite, and irreplaceable element of human and ecosystemic existence."[31] "Access to safe drinkable water is a basic and universal right," notes *Laudato Si'*, "since it is essential to human survival, and as such, is a condition for

25. The Nestlé corporation has been pumping water from the public lands of San Bernadino national forest for years, paying almost nothing for that privilege, and despite court cases against it, is being protected by the National Park Service. See Peter H. Gleick, *Bottled and Sold: The Story behind Our Obsession with Bottled Water* (Washington, DC: Island Press, 2011).

26. Bottled water, it is to be noted, is some two thousand times more expensive than tap water and twenty times less regulated for contamination.

27. See "Fiji Water Leaves Fiji without Water," TapThat, 18 September 2012, https://tapthatunsw.wordpress.com/2012/09/18/fiji-water-leaves-fiji-without-water.

28. Zenner, *Just Water*, 59. See also John Hart, *Sacramental Commons: Christian Ecological Ethics* (Latham, MD: Rowman & Littlefield, 2006), 59–95.

29. Image used by Maude Barlow, in *Blue Future: Protecting Water for People and the Planet Forever* (New York, NY: The New Press, 2013), 19.

30. Zenner, *Just Water*, 68–85.

31. Ibid., 51.

the exercise of all other human rights" (LS 30). The United Nations has likewise claimed that the right to clean, accessible water is a fundamental right, supported by international law.[32]

One of the challenges today is that the language of rights, as developed in Western thought, is most often focused on the rights of individuals rather than rights of communities. Gary Chamberlain points out that new legal documents, such as an amendment to the constitution of Uruguay and recent statements from the United Nations, underscore "the communal nature of natural resources such as water and air."[33] "Rights are the basic necessities"—the minimal conditions—that "enable all to live in accord with their God-given dignity and to participate in social decision-making."[34]

Beyond its value to humans, water has a dignity, beauty, and value in itself, and its availability is predicated on respect, care, and mutuality. Water has a "right to be," a "right to its own flourishing . . . and well-being," writes Chamberlain. Current assaults on water—the poisoning of water with pesticides, the fouling of water with waste products, the toxification of water through hydraulic fracturing—undermine its integrity and cry out for continued ethical response.[35] Moreover, seeing water as a universal right must include the needs of all Earth's living creatures who depend on water to quench thirst and to provide habitat—thus extending understandings of rights to embrace the entire biotic community.[36] In all of this, one principle is foundational: water's health is always primary. All other health, including human health, is derivative.

---

32. See Barlow, *Blue Future*, 20–32.

33. Gary Chamberlain, *Troubled Waters: Religion, Ethics, and the Global Water Crisis* (New York, NY: Rowman & Littlefield, 2008), 136.

34. James Nash, *Loving Nature: Ecological Integrity and Christian Responsibility* (Nashville, TN: Abington, 1991), 168, as quoted in Chamberlain, *Troubled Waters*, 136.

35. Issues of water justice, including justice for the waters themselves, have been the primary focus of numberless groups in the US and elsewhere. These issues are addressed in "Universal Declaration of the Rights of Mother Earth," drafted at the World People's Conference on Climate Change and the Rights of Mother Earth, Cochabamba, Bolivia, 22 April 2010. The document was later presented to the United Nations for adoption.

36. Chamberlain, *Troubled Waters*, 136, with reference to the work of James Nash and John Cobb.

New Sacramental Frontiers and Frameworks

In light of what we have just seen, Christians stand today at a sacramental frontier, a new moment in the practice of the rites of initiation. It is my contention that these rites, as well as teaching and theologizing about them, require a new framework, an integrated vision, at once ecological, sacramental, and ethical—a vision that perceives a community gathered around the font as an interdependent species in the larger tapestry of life, part of the planetary web of creatures and elements through which courses the sacred energy of life itself.[37]

Such an integrated vision would involve at least three critical dimensions: first, a truthful ecological vision of human identity within the web of life; second, an expansive sacramental vision of God's redemptive grace in rites of initiation and beyond; and third, a clear ethical vision of baptismal responsibility for Earth's precious waters. In what follows I will sketch some starting points for each of these perspectives.

Towards a Truthful Ecological Vision of Human Identity within the Web of Life

Louis-Marie Chauvet, in his extensive work *Symbol and Sacrament*, asserts that water, used sacramentally, speaks of the foundational identity of the baptized as members of the planetary web of life. As sacramental symbol, he claims, water becomes "a metaphor of [human] existence . . . [conveying] intimations of our indissoluble marriage to the Earth, our original existential condition of *being-in-the-world*."[38]

As a metaphor of our own webbed existence, baptismal waters remind humans that we are water creatures, born of amniotic waters, composed of water, with three billion years of watery energy coursing through our veins, essentially related to all other species in the web of life, and thriving only in interdependence and mutuality.[39] Moreover, the experience

---

37. Cynthia Moe-Lobeda, *Resisting Structural Evil: Love as Ecological-Economic Vocation* (Minneapolis, MN: Fortress, 2013), 105.

38. Louis-Marie Chauvet, *Symbol and Sacrament: A Sacramental Reinterpretation of Christian Existence* (Collegeville, MN: Liturgical Press, 1995), 356. Italics in the original.

39. Larry Rasmussen, *Earth-Honoring Faith: Religious Ethics in a New Key* (New York, NY: Oxford Univ. Press, 2013), 260–63, 274. Some 70 percent of the human body is composed of water.

of fluidity and flowingness, felt in our own bodies as a source of life and well-being, invites reflection on our thirst for water as a thirst for God—as Psalm 42 suggests—and our desire for God as deeply related to the fullness of earthly life and flourishing.[40]

In and through baptismal waters, this foundational earthly identity is inexorably joined with a Christian's new identity in Christ, the Christ who in his "deep incarnation" embraced the waters of the Earth in all their beauty and suffering and in his resurrection claimed them as part of God's redemptive future.[41] In coming into the world, Christ entered not only human existence but also the "whole interconnected world of fleshly life,"[42] uniting himself with the "biological world of living creatures and organisms in the web of life."[43] In Christ, writes Neil Darragh, "God became an earth creature,"[44] entering "evolving creation in a radically new way," embracing all forms of life in their suffering and limitation, and revealing God's redemptive presence to all creatures that face destruction, decay, or defilement.[45] From this perspective, baptismal identity in the incarnate Christ corroborates, deepens, expands, and strengthens the earthly identity of the baptized—their call to co-responsibility as protectors of the Earth-commons and as servants of the web-of-planetary-good.[46]

Christ teaches his followers the proper role of those called in his name, which is not to reengineer creation for human benefit—a pattern so evident in the use of water today, as already seen—but to inhabit rightly their

40. See Mary C. Grey, *Sacred Longings: Ecofeminist Theology and Globalization* (London: SCM Press, 2003), 92.

41. This section draws on Mary McGann, "Committed to Earth's Waters for Life," in *Drenched in Grace*, ed. Lizette Larson Miller and Walter Knowles (Eugene, OR: Pickwick Publications, 2013), 182–85. The term "deep incarnation" was introduced by Niels Henrich Gregersen.

42. Denis Edwards, *Ecology at the Heart of Faith* (Maryknoll, NY: Orbis, 2006), 58.

43. Ibid., summarizing the work of Australian theologian Duncan Reid.

44. Neil Darragh, *At Home in the Earth*, 124, as quoted in Edwards, *Ecology*, 58.

45. Edwards, *Ecology*, 59, summarizing Gregersen, "The Cross of Christ in an Evolutionary World," *Dialog: A Journal of Theology* 40 (2001): 205.

46. Image taken from Rasmussen, *Earth-Honoring Faith*, 261.

place and responsibilities in the community of Earth, serving and preserving the intrinsic value of nature, and especially its precious waters.[47]

Moreover, rites of initiation celebrated with abundant flowing water invite communities to encounter the divine economy of creation—in which the orders, the patterns, and the sources of life that compose our planetary existence are recognized as God-given and inviolable, demanding that the human community live with restraint and respect in its use of created goods,[48] and with humility regarding its place in the complex ecosystems of the world. Celebrating this divine economy in rites of initiation acknowledges that God is "with us, for us, and within all creation."[49] Waters are cherished as precious gift and sacred trust, recognized as having intrinsic value, and claimed as sacramental—as an integral part of a world that is "full of the life of a God whose nature is known in Christ and the Spirit."[50] Moreover, they are part of a sacramental universe, described by John Hart as "creation infused with the vision, love, creative presence, and active power of the transcendent-immanent Spirit."[51]

Clearly, this divine economy is in marked contrast to a consumerist economy, with its demands for resource extraction and profit; its preoccupation with growth at the expense of Earth's limits; its poisoning of resources essential to life; its concerns for the bottom line, rather than for

47. Ched Meyers, "Toward Watershed Ecclesiology: Theological, Hermeneutic, and Practical Reflections," in *Watershed Discipleship: Reinhabiting Bioregional Faith and Practice* (Eugene, OR: Cascade, 2016), 204–5.

48. See Norman Wirzba, *Food and Faith* (Cambridge: Cambridge Univ. Press, 2011), 90. Mary Grey uses a similar image, "God's gift economy." See Mary C. Grey, "Troubled Waters: Becoming Ecologically Awakened to the Sacred, and the Implications for How We Live," in *Ecological Awareness: Exploring Religion, Ethics and Aesthetics*, ed. Sigurd Bergmann and Heather Eaton (Münster: Lit Verlag, 2011), 46–47.

49. Image of the triune God, taken from Therese DeLisio, "Stretching the Sacramental Imagination in Sacramental Theology, Liturgy and Life: A Trinitarian Proposal for a Cosmologically Conscious Age" (Ph.D. Dissertation, Union Theological Seminary, New York, 2007), 13.

50. Rowan Williams, "Foreword," in *The Gestures of God: Explorations in Sacramentality*, ed. Geoffrey Rowell and Christine Hall (New York, NY: Continuum, 2004), xiii.

51. Hart, *Sacramental Commons*, 61.

the well-being of the Earth and her inhabitants. In the divine economy evoked by sacramental waters, destruction or desecration of water is an affront to divine presence, to the Spirit of God dwelling in all creatures as divine animator.[52]

For this vision of a divine economy of creation to come alive sacramentally, it must be threaded through the sounds, prayers, songs and gestures of the entire sacramental event—evoking awareness of the beauty and sacredness of all Earth's waters. Moreover, throughout the processes that surround the initiatory event, the shaping of a community's imagination might take place through reflection on stories and experiences of water, and prayer with biblical images of water, thirst, and restoration of desert places. Communities must likewise be called to remember the rivers and streams that once flowed abundantly and have now been silenced or desecrated; to express prophetic lament for the waters that have disappeared, been desecrated or destroyed; and to acknowledge the glory of God that will never be expressed because of what has been lost.[53]

In a unique way, the proposal of Lisa Dahill to restore the ancient church practice of baptizing initiates outdoors, in the fresh, flowing waters of a local watershed, might heighten awareness of a community's graced and fragile relationship with sacramental waters.[54] This practice would corroborate the truthful ecological vision we have just explored, connecting communities physically, spiritually, and in vulnerable ways with the "living waters" of a local river or stream and enabling them to pray with and for these waters. Such baptismal vision and practice affirm the sacredness of earthly waters as God-bestowed, Earth-caressed, and filled with the swarming life of God's creation. Moreover, it would underscore the importance of a baptismal discipleship that cares for local

---

52. Heather Murray Elkins asks these related and vexing questions: "What happens when a natural symbol, water, source of sacramental identity, turns toxic? Can we convert this natural symbol back to its source through our narratives of baptism? If we could follow the stream from font or pool back to its place of origin through an act of liturgy, would it 'altar' our economic and social choices?" See Heather Murray Elkins, *Worshiping Women: Re-forming God's People for Praise* (Nashville: Abingdon, 1994), 43.

53. Grey, "Troubled Waters," 53.

54. See Dahill, "Rewilding Christian Spirituality," 182–85 for her proposal and the challenges it might entail.

waters in such a way that they are fit for baptismal practice—a focus we will return to later in this essay.

Towards an Expansive Sacramental Vision of God's Redemptive Grace

In her recent book *Creation and the Cross*, Elizabeth Johnson raises a timely question: "How in our day can we understand cosmic redemption?"[55] Invoking images of a "groaning creation waiting to be set free," as described by Paul in Romans 8, Johnson continues, "At a time of advancing ecological devastation, what would it mean to rediscover this biblical sense of the natural world groaning, hoping, waiting for liberation?"[56] "What would it mean for the churches' understanding, practice, and prayer to open the core Christian belief in salvation to include all created beings?" And how, we might add, would such understandings of cosmic redemption impact and shape an expansive vision of God's redeeming grace in sacraments of initiation?

Johnson grounds her understandings of cosmic redemption in the integral relationship between divine creation and redemption, identifying them as two dimensions of the one mystery of God's self-bestowing love, and traces the development of this interrelationship through the biblical narrative of both testaments. Focusing first on the biblical message of Second Isaiah, she summarizes the prophet's message: Have hope! "The Holy One who powerfully creates the world, marking off the heavens and weighing the mountains . . . this same holy God is coming to save you."[57] Second Isaiah repeatedly images God as "your Redeemer," announcing that this very God, who is likewise Creator of heaven and Earth, is about to create "something new" (Isa 43:14): a return of the people from exile and a liberation of God's people estranged from their homeland. Pouring out divine energy in a new moment of creation, God's redemptive activity will overflow into the larger earthly community of life: "The rough path will be made straight, streams will flow in the dry

---

55. Elizabeth A. Johnson, *Creation and the Cross: The Mercy of God for a Planet in Peril* (Maryknoll, NY: Orbis, 2018), xi.

56. Pope Francis likewise underscores the importance of creation's "groaning in travail" by opening his encyclical *Laudato Si'* with a reference to Paul's words in Romans 8:22, see LS 2.

57. Johnson, *Creation and the Cross*, 33.

land, and the wilderness will bloom."[58] And as the people of Israel return to their homeland, healed, forgiven, redeemed, and restored, "the rest of creation will take notice and rejoice: 'the mountains and the hills before you shall burst into song; and all the trees of the field shall clap their hands' ([Isa] 55:12)."[59]

" 'Jesus brought no new concept of God,' Brevard Childs argues, but demonstrated in action and in a new setting God's redemptive will for the world."[60] New Testament authors writing about Jesus took Jewish creation faith for granted, assuming that "the God whom Jesus revealed and embodied as self-expressing Word is none other than the God of Israel"—Creator and Redeemer. Throughout his life and ministry, and especially in his paschal death and resurrection, Jesus revealed a God who "enters into the darkest trials of human suffering, death and near-despair."[61] In his anguished death, Jesus discloses divine solidarity with all creatures of the flesh, with the whole of biotic life, whom he first embraced in his deep incarnation and whom he now accompanies in the groans of their suffering.[62]

Imaging Christ's paschal mystery as his "deep cross and resurrection," Johnson asserts that Jesus' death places him in company with all creatures of the flesh, revealing divine solidarity with all who are perishing and disclosing that the Creator of all flesh is "silently present with creatures in their pain and dying." In rising from the dead, Christ "has opened the door to a redemptive metamorphosis of all creation."[63] As "first fruits of an abundant harvest," the risen Christ is "reborn as a child of the earth, radiantly transfigured" and pledging future life and the fullness of redemption not only for the human species but for all species whom he has already embraced in deep love.[64] "In Christ's resurrection," preached Ambrose of Milan in the fourth century, "the earth itself arose."[65]

Pope Francis echoes these perspectives in *Laudato Si'*, noting that in his earthly life, Jesus cherished the natural world with an attention full

58. Ibid., 47.
59. Ibid., 50.
60. Ibid., 63.
61. Ibid., 187.
62. Ibid., 188.
63. Ibid., 192.
64. Ibid., 190.
65. Quoted in ibid, 190.

of fondness and wonder. Now risen from the dead, Christ is intimately present to each creature, "holding it to himself," "surrounding it with his affection," "imbuing it with his radiant presence," and directing all creatures "towards fullness as their end" (LS 96–100). "Eternal life," Francis concludes, "will be a shared experience of awe, in which each creature, resplendently transfigured, will take its rightful place" (LS 243). "The coming final transformation of history will be the salvation of everything," writes Johnson, "including the groaning community of life, brought into communion with the love of God."[66]

In the waters of initiation, the action of this creating-redeeming God-in-Christ is dynamically present, enabling those who enter them to be identified with Christ's redemptive death and resurrection and his solidarity with the groaning creation in its yearning for restoration. Immersed in Christ's paschal mystery, those baptized are summoned to carry in their own bodies the dangerous memory of the cross of Christ, a memory that challenges "all complacency before the suffering of others."[67] The death of Christ, writes Niels Gregersen, is "an icon of God's redemptive co-suffering with all sentient life as well as with the victims of social competition."[68] To enter baptismal waters is to be plunged with Christ into the wound of the world, lived out in the suffering bodies of creatures of manifold species and carried on the troubled waters of the Earth. To embrace this watery dying and rising is to be invited to carry in one's body the thirst that consumes so many of Earth's poor and marginalized for the waters of life. Christ's death embodies divine solidarity with all who are perishing, writes Johnson, and his accompanying them in their affliction.[69]

At the same time, the resurrection of Christ offers a dynamic vision of hope for the suffering world—a promise of new creation already realized in the risen Christ and a hope of restoration and future glory, when "God will be all in all" (1 Cor 15:28). The ritual of Christian baptism, writes Robin Jensen, "has cosmic significance and benefit that transcends person and place." Initiation rites recall "the moment when all Creation

66. Ibid., 193.
67. Edwards, *Ecology*, 106.
68. Quoted in ibid., 105.
69. See Johnson, *Creation and the Cross*, 106–12, where Johnson posits a "theology of accompaniment" that engages a "double solidarity" that includes Jesus' solidarity with all who suffer and God's solidarity with Jesus, accompanying him through his anguish.

began and foreshadows the unending moment when all Creation will be transformed."[70] Joined to the risen Christ, those baptized are likewise joined with all creation in anticipation of the full revelation of this new creation. "The Risen Christ has already planted in the material world"— indeed, in its troubled waters—"a seed of definitive transformation," by which creation as a whole is "projected toward divinization," towards unification with the divine Creator (LS 235, 236).

How, then, can these images of the groaning creation and of the hope for cosmic redemption held out by the risen Christ be reflected in the songs, prayers, blessings, and gestures used when communities engage in rites of initiation? Can the injustices and suffering that surrounds the Earth's troubled waters today be heard and seen in local baptismal practice—the voices of God's people and species who are in anguish because they are denied their rightful share of this precious resource? And how might the spatial-aesthetic environment of the rites reflect the healing and restoration of God's creation promised in the risen Christ and brought about in part through the ethical response of initiating communities? Robin Jensen points out that images of a new creation were extensively symbolized in the art that permeated some of the earliest baptisteries: rich nature imagery, including "birds, animals, flowers, fruit-bearing trees, fish, flowing rivers and splashing fountains" all imaging a "joyous cosmic renewal at the dawn of the eighth day."[71] Surrounding a contemporary community with such imagery would invite it to view the baptismal font, or the living waters of a local river used for initiation, as a "fountain of life" flowing out to cleanse and revivify the whole world.[72]

Towards a Clear Ethical Vision of Baptismal Responsibility for Earth's Precious Waters

Immersion in Christian initiatory waters comes with an ethical imperative. As with all Christian sacramental practice, writes Chauvet, initiation acknowledges that creation is a gift that can only be fully received through a return gift. In sacramental action, he posits, "human creativity [is] charged with bringing the universe into conformity with the creator's

---

70. Robin Jensen, *Baptismal Imagery in Early Christianity* (Grand Rapids, MI: Baker Academic, 2012), 177.

71. Ibid., 213.

72. Ibid., 192.

gift; commissioned with rendering it habitable by all, culturally and economically." Christian initiation "presents the world as something one may not use in an arbitrary manner" but must make "a world for all, not just for the privileged."[73] Chauvet concludes, "Grace is given as a task to be accomplished."[74]

A community's ethical response to initiatory waters must begin with profound respect for the gift of water, recognizing that as part of the same web of life, human actions are continuously impacting water, either positively or negatively. In welcoming the gift of sacramental waters, communities are invited to become agents of change on behalf of Earth's waters, especially the waters of their own place, their own local watershed, from which their sacramental waters are drawn.

Although the challenges facing water today are global in scope, writes Zenner, there is no universal solution to water scarcity or desecration.[75] Rather, water issues must be addressed locally and regionally—within each community's watershed. "We need a new ethos around water," adds Gary Chamberlain. "We must shift from technological, large-scale hard approaches to water issues to more communitarian, democratic, local, small-scale and technologically soft movements based on valuing, respecting, and reverencing water, not just for our immediate benefits, but also for the future of the globe."[76] Hence a turn to each community's watershed.

Watersheds are natural formations described by Brock Dolman as "basins of relations," places of ecosystemic interdependence, in which every living organism is interconnected and dependent on the health of the whole.[77] A community can turn to its local watershed as a place of

73. Chauvet, *Symbol and Sacrament*, 358.

74. Ibid., 440.

75. Zenner, *Just Water*, 50.

76. Chamberlain, *Troubled Waters*, 4, 7. This approach is likewise underscored by the United Nations' 2006 *World Water Development Report 2,* which encourages locally-based participatory management systems; see http://www.unwater.org/publications /water-shared-responsibility/. "The key issue in the 'unfair' sharing of water globally," writes Chamberlain, "revolves around the management systems that tend to use global markets and international corporations in ways that end up increasing the gap between the water wealthy and the water poor" (*Troubled Waters*, 135).

77. Brock Dolman, *Basins of Relations: A Citizen's Guide to Protecting and Restoring Our Watershed* (Occidental, CA: Water Institute, 2008), http://www .oaecwater.org. See discussion in Meyers, "Prophetic Visions," 72.

baptismal discipleship,[78] discovering there the myriad relationships—social, natural, and inter-species—that affect the health and well-being of water in this their place, and becoming advocates on water's behalf. A community's efforts to "learn its watershed," coming to know it more intimately, are essential. Through observation and direct experience, they begin to confront the reality of degraded water firsthand, to discern the sometimes conflicting demands for water by various stakeholders, and to recognize the needs of the multispecies inhabitants of the watershed.

Based on this knowledge and in conjunction with other concerned groups, they can shape a hydro-social vision of what healing and restoration are needed. Ethical principles drawn from Christian faith traditions, including justice, the common good, and a preferential option for the poorest and most endangered, can impel the process.[79] Practices of restorative justice can enable a community to focus on all who have been negatively impacted by issues of water in this watershed: indigenous communities, for example, who might have suffered in the past; groups marginalized and suffering in the present; and generations who will be affected in the future.

A focus on ecological principles such as sustainability, with its unique local and regional challenges, is essential as well. Subsidiarity is likewise critical—involving those most impacted by decisions about water access and management to be engaged in the process. While local church communities will not be making these decisions directly, they can play a critical role in representing what they have learned from their own engagement in the watershed to decision-making bodies.

In all of this, watershed discipleship will be felt most keenly in personal, familial, and communal choices regarding water conservation—such as minimizing home usage, recycling grey water, collecting rainwater—and restoring local waterways. How wonderful if communities participating in the restoration of a river or stream were to engage

---

78. See Dahill, "Rewilding Christian Spirituality," 187, for discussion of outdoor baptism and local concern for the health of the watershed. Meyers's term "watershed discipleship" is complementary to my image of "baptismal discipleship"; see Meyers, *Watershed Discipleship*, 1–25.

79. For an exploration of these ethical principles in light of Roman Catholic social teaching, see Zenner, *Just Water*, 68–85, and Chamberlain, *Troubled Waters*, 131–53. Maude Barlow likewise offers similar ethical principles in *Blue Future*.

these waters for their sacramental immersion, with the restored river now experienced as "baptismal river"—holy and calling out for reverence and love.

Only as communities come to know and love their own places, to reinhabit their own watersheds, knowing them as places of the Spirit's life-giving presence—and perhaps even places of baptismal rites—will they have the energy needed to defend and restore them; to take up their baptismal vocation, in the words of *Laudato Si'*, to be "protectors of God's handiwork" (LS 217); to stand in solidarity with communities around the globe who are defending their own watersheds, in such places as Standing Rock, South Dakota; Kerala, southern India; Flint, Michigan; or the Niger Delta, Nigeria; and to work together in networks of care to restore Earth's precious waters as a sacramental commons, intended for all.[80]

80. Hart, *Sacramental Commons*, 61–96.

CHAPTER SIXTEEN

Wisdom's Buried Treasure

Ecological Cosmology in Funeral Rites

Benjamin M. Stewart

A cartoon from the *New Yorker* depicts a Wild West gunslinger snarling a warning to his opponent as they prepare to duel. "Say your prayers, liturgies, tefillah, daily salat, sacred mantra, ritual incantation, or the secular affirmation of your choice, varmint!"[1] The joke parodies the dilemma of proliferating ritual options in the face of death. That same dilemma provokes this essay. What is at stake among the expanding options for death ritual? Does it matter *how* or *that* we ritualize our return to the earth? What is at issue for cosmology? Among the diverse possibilities for ritualizing death, this chapter proposes that there is buried treasure in the Wisdom tradition's approach to mortality. I make this argument in three sections that attend respectively to Scripture, liturgy, and the natural burial movement.

Negation: The Dominant Scholarly Frame

Scholars often characterize the Wisdom literature's approach to mortality in negative terms, focusing on its deficiencies, negations, and contradictions. For example, Lawrence Boadt summarizes mortality in the Wisdom tradition as death "without power or possessions . . . without memory, joy, or voice to praise God . . . In Sheol there will be no

---

1. Joe Dator, "A Wild West Duel," *New Yorker* (11 January 2016), 41.

happiness."[2] Similarly, Robert Davidson describes a "chill negativity" and "bleak destructiveness" in the sapiential approach to death, summarizing the entire tradition in negative terms: "on the whole, the Psalms and the wisdom literature share an approach to death which regards death as the final disintegration of all meaningful life, and a descent into the darkness and weakness of Sheol."[3]

Other scholars accent the diversity within the tradition. Gerhard von Rad's classic *Wisdom in Israel* describes death as "ambivalent," depicted sometimes as "bitter," while at other times as "good."[4] James Crenshaw portrays some writings as being marked by "ambiguity" and some as "wholly negative."[5] Likewise, Leo Perdue emphasizes the diverse, if largely negative, approaches of the tradition.[6] Roland Murphy describes the corpus's perspective as "paradoxical" and "bleak and murky."[7] Even scholars employing an ecological hermeneutic can implicitly denigrate the dust motif by accenting instead the vegetative growth from dust, even describing it as a form of "continued living" and "permanence of existence," implying that dissolution into dust itself remains essentially objectionable.[8]

2. Lawrence Boadt, "The Scriptures on Death and Dying," in *Rites of Death and Dying*, ed. Anthony F. Sherman (Collegeville, MN: Liturgical Press, 1988), 15.

3. Robert Davidson, *Wisdom and Worship* (London: SCM Press, 1990), 90, 97.

4. Von Rad writes that the corpus is "not greatly concerned with ultimate mortality" (Gerhard von Rad, *Wisdom in Israel* [Nashville, TN: Abingdon Press, 1972], 304–5).

5. James L. Crenshaw, "The Shadow of Death in Qoheleth," in *Urgent Advice and Probing Questions: Collected Writings on Old Testament Wisdom* (Macon, GA: Mercer, 1995), 573–85, here at 585.

6. Death appears briefly in short sections on the theme of "artistry" (the human person shaped from the dust) and the "breath of God" (on which creation depends for life) in Leo Perdue, *Wisdom and Creation: The Theology of Wisdom Literature* (Nashville, TN: Abingdon Press, 1994), 334. Also see Perdue's later iteration of the work: *Wisdom Literature: A Theological History* (Louisville, KY: Westminster John Knox Press, 2007).

7. Ronald E. Murphy, "Death and Afterlife in the Wisdom Tradition," in *Judaism in Late Antiquity*, vol. 4: *Death, Life-after-Death, Resurrection and the World-to-Come in the Judaisms of Antiquity*, ed. Jacob Neusner and Alan Avery-Peck (Boston, MA: Brill, 1996), 101–16, here at 102–3.

8. Marie Turner describes bodies in Ecclesiastes returning to the "Eternal Earth" while their breath returns to the eternal God within the "permanence of existence of all Earth's creatures" (Marie Turner, *Ecclesiastes: An Earth Bible Commentary: Qoheleth's Eternal Earth* [New York, NY: Bloomsbury, 2018], 118). In this ecologi-

Dust Wisdom: A Name and a Conceptual Frame

While it is important to call attention to the negations, contradictions, and silences that characterize Wisdom literature's approach to death, this focus has consistently overlooked the affirmative foundation on which the negations and contradictions logically depend. This essay argues that the logic of mortality in Wisdom literature is neither inscrutable nor incoherent but first of all ecological. Further, while it is certainly characterized by some profound negations and contradictions, the tradition is founded on universal affirmations, that is, on categorical claims that can ground a cosmology.

It is helpful to give this topic a name. Rather than awkwardly referring to "the Wisdom tradition's approach to mortality" or "the conception of death in the sapiential literature," I refer to this body of thought as the "dust wisdom tradition."[9] The theme is centered in the books of the Wisdom corpus and yet is also found more broadly throughout Scripture. There are important questions not addressed here regarding the diverse cultural and historical influences on biblical Wisdom motifs. Instead this chapter makes a case for discerning a coherent logic in the scriptural sapiential tradition. Thus, I am sketching a model by which the logic of dust wisdom can be understood, schematized, and liturgically enacted. The foundation of this model comprises three main motifs: the measure of a lifespan, the universality of death, and the return to the dust.

Creaturely Lifespan

First, the dust wisdom tradition offers metaphors for creaturely lifespan that foreground the transience of earthly life. The tradition deploys metaphors of passing natural phenomena to create simple, arresting images of the relative transience of life for all earthly creatures. Life is like "a passing shadow" (Ps 144:4, NRSV, used throughout), and "all flesh is like grass" (1 Pet 2:23). Life dissipates "like the traces of a cloud" and

---

cal reading of Ecclesiastes, human personhood dissipating into the dust is implicitly portrayed as a "negative" reading of the text, while a "positive" reading has humans "living" forever. Death here remains fundamentally negative.

9. I introduce this term in Benjamin M. Stewart, "All Flesh Is Grass: Natural Burial as Embodiment of Wisdom Literature's Mortality Tradition," *Proceedings of the North American Academy of Liturgy* (2017), 153–63, https://issuu.com /naal-proceedings/docs/17-naal_proceedings2017_fnlweb.

is "scattered like mist" (Wis 2:4). Life is like a single day, a "watch in the night," and a dream (Ps 90:3-5). "Surely everyone stands as a mere breath" (Ps 39:5b). "Our years come to an end like a sigh" (Ps 90:9b). The Hebrew *hebel*, usually translated "vanity" especially in Qoheloth ("all is vanity"), refers in its most basic sense to a breath or sigh. Among the images of transience *sigh* seems paradigmatic because of its frequent use and evocation of the final breath. How shall we understand the span of human life? The dust wisdom tradition offers a set of metaphors drawn from transient earthly phenomena: shadow, dream, mist, season, day, grass, sigh, breath.

The Universal Claims of Dust Wisdom

Second, the word *all* sounds like a drum through the dust wisdom literature. Death comes to all. Sirach counsels "remember that we must all die" (Sir 8:7). Death is "the house appointed for all the living" (Job 30:23), for "all flesh" (1 Pet 2:23). It is the "way of all the earth" (Josh 23:14). Even when *all* is not grammatically explicit, it is implied in categorical assertions about the inevitability of death for members of broad classes: humans, animals, flesh, plants, creatures. Before addressing the contradictions within the literature, we are faced with these perfectly consistent universal assertions to which—as the texts emphasize—there are no exceptions. Even the metaphors for the transience of life—that our lifespan is like a breath or a passing shadow—imply a sort of universality. They push every moment of life into adjacency with death, as close as our breath.

Toward the Dust

Third, in death all creatures share a common destination: the dust. There are no open questions about the end of this journey. This claim is paired with a related assertion that is sometimes implied and sometimes explicit: our going down to the dust is a return to the dust from which we were first formed. This tradition asserts a universal destination for all creatures and a universal origin for all creatures: the earth, the soil. The common ground across diverse Wisdom traditions is that we are the common ground, dust.

This is a remarkable set of assertions describing a common creaturely life and death. "There is for all one entrance into life, and one way out" (Wis 7:6), for "the fate of humans and the fate of animals is the same; as one dies, so dies the other. They all have the same breath . . . All go to one place; all are from the dust, and all turn to dust again" (Eccl 3:19-20). The dust wisdom tradition offers a foundational assertion that humans return to and are part of the earth in common membership with all other creatures. In this tradition death is a uniquely clear vantage point from which to behold our common creaturely citizenship.

Thus I am arguing that there is a foundational logic to dust wisdom: after a *lifespan measured by other transient natural phenomena* (a breath, season, grass that flourishes and then fades, passing shadow, mist burned away by the sun) *all plant and animal creatures* (a massive, categorical affirmative claim that places humans in a pan-species solidarity and class identity, and necessarily brings the entire earth and its history in view) *die and return to the dust* from which they were formed. I describe this tripartite scheme as the *ground* of dust wisdom.

Contemplative, Conversant, Fruitful

A pause here is in order for a few reasons. First, these categorical assertions about life and death are designed for contemplation. In the Wisdom tradition, the full (biological) stop of human death is meant to bring living humans to a full (reflective) stop. The Psalmist prays, "so teach us to number our days that we may commit our hearts to wisdom" (Ps 90:12). Second, the claims of dust wisdom are assertions made against possible cosmological claims to the contrary. Dust wisdom's universal claims invite us to scan the landscape for observable data and ask about possible exceptions: is it true that there are no exceptions, that all creatures return to the dust, and that human lives, in the wider cosmic story, are like a day, a passing shadow, a breath? One popular-scientific way of considering this claim proposes if all the past history of life on earth were compressed to the previous hour, meaning that the oceans had hosted life for the equivalent of an hour, then fish have only been swimming in the oceans for the equivalent of the past eight minutes, primates emerged just one minute ago, and modern humans only in the last less-than-half-second. This is a prosaic acknowledgment that "surely everyone stands as a mere breath" (Ps 39:5) and illustrates why the dust wisdom tradition can be especially fruitful ground for contemporary Christian cosmology. Partly because of the inductive method of its authors, it is meaningfully conversant with the cosmological insights of the scientific and ecological age. Third, this categorical claim—that after a lifespan that passes like a breath all of us die and return to the dust—evokes some kind of response, perhaps emotional, existential, repentant, or defensive. Certainly we see this in the Wisdom texts: authors and characters respond with heart and mind, with diverse and even contradictory responses to being addressed by a sure future as the dust of the earth. I am calling these responses the *fruit* of dust wisdom.

The Fruit of Dust Wisdom

Distinguishing between the ground and the fruit of dust wisdom is one way of making sense of the diversity and contradictions within the dust tradition. The ground of dust wisdom—the universal claim that after a lifespan that passes like a breath all of us die and return to the dust—is a major premise that provokes and inspires a diversity of conclusions. We might say that the ground of dust wisdom is so fertile that it produces bountiful and diverse fruits. This is a very different perspective from a "chill negativity" and "descent into meaninglessness." Rather than negation or incoherence there is within this body of thought a (primary) ecological observation that is fertile ground for a (secondary) diversity of reflective fruit that emerges from that ground. Having established the ground, what sorts of diverse fruits can we discover sprouting from it? The following section offers some examples, calling attention to their diversity.

Wisdom and Agnosticism

The injunction to seek wisdom in the face of mortality is familiar: "our years come to an end like a sigh . . . Teach us to count our days, that we may gain a wise heart" (Ps 90:9, 12). Qoheleth, however, suggests a more agnostic approach. Considering the transience of life and the certainty of death, Qoheleth writes that "what happens to the fool will happen to me also; why then have I been so very wise? . . . this also is vanity" (Eccl 2:15). One can almost hear the sigh, *hebel,* of agnosticism. "Who knows what is good for mortals while they live the few days of their life?" (Eccl 6:12).

Riches and Power

A number of texts relate to riches and power. Some warn against one potential fruit of dust wisdom: a turn to hedonism that says, "life is short, so, *carpe diem*, live it up." Such logic leads to gross injustice, says the book of Wisdom.

> [the ungodly say]: Our allotted time is the passing of a shadow, and there is no return from our death . . . therefore let us enjoy the good things that exist . . . let us take our fill of costly wine and perfumes . . . Everywhere let us leave signs of our enjoyment, because this is our portion and this is our lot. Let us oppress the righteous poor man; let us not spare the widow . . . let our might be our law of right, for what is weak proves itself to be useless. (Wis 2:5, 7, 9-11)

The book of James comes to the same ethical conclusion, but not because the powerful see life as short. Instead, in James the rich mistakenly assume life will simply go on without a check on their consumption:

> Come now, you who say, "Today or tomorrow we will go to such and such a town and spend a year there, doing business and making money." Yet you do not even know what tomorrow will bring. What is your life? For you are a mist that appears for a little while and then vanishes . . . Come now, you rich people, weep and wail for the miseries that are coming to you. Your riches have rotted, and your clothes are moth-eaten. Your gold and silver have rusted, and their rust will be evidence against you, and it will eat your flesh like fire. (Jas 3:13-14, 5:1-5)

Sometimes today dust-to-dust cosmology is associated with a shallow bourgeois spirituality, bearing the blandest of fruits. In this passage, however, James is growing habaneros in the garden of dust wisdom: "it will eat your flesh like fire."

In the two passages above, the rich are indicted for their hoarding of luxuries in light of the shortness of life. However, the fleeting nature of life leads Qoheleth to offer a different counsel for those whose life is full of difficulty. If this short life offers some luxury, Qoheleth writes, "it is exquisitely fine to eat and drink and find enjoyment in all the toil with which one toils under the sun the few days of life that God has given."[10] In other words, Qoheleth says something like "this is all we've got in this hard life, so raise a glass while you can."

---

10. Translated in William P. Brown, *Wisdom's Wonder: Character, Creation, and Crisis in the Bible's Wisdom Literature* (Grand Rapids, MI: Eerdmans, 2014), 168.

Fruits of Contemplation

How do we contemplate what some describe as our cruel fate of going down to the dust? Psalm 139 may be a surprising fruit of dust wisdom. Quite the opposite of a cold or stoic view, the psalmist mystically blends the perspective of a divine mother with an artist whose comforting presence extends even to *sheol*: "you knit me together in my mother's womb. I praise you, for I am fearfully and wonderfully made . . . My frame was not hidden from you, when I was being made in secret, intricately woven together in the depths of the earth" (Ps 139:8, 13-15). A similar motif in Psalm 103 portrays divine remembrance of the dust as generating compassion for humanity: "As a father has compassion for his children, so you have compassion for those who fear you . . . For you know well how we are formed; you remember that we are but dust" (Ps 103:13-14). In these instances, contemplation of the dust nature of humanity yields fruits of wonder and compassion.

Eternity Contrasted with Mortality

Another fruit of dust wisdom contrasts the transient nature of mortal lives with the eternal nature of God and God's word. Psalm 90 uses images of the formation of the earth and the human return to dust for perspective in contemplating the eternal nature of God: "before the mountains were brought forth, or ever you had formed the earth and the world, from everlasting to everlasting you are God. You turn us back to dust, and say, 'Turn back, you mortals.' For a thousand years in your sight are like yesterday when it is past, or like a watch in the night" (Ps 90:2-4). Similar cross-testamental imagery of creaturely mortality pivots to the eternal word of God: "The grass withers, the flower falls, but the word of the Lord endures forever" (1 Pet 1:24-25 citing Isa 40:6-8). Even the vague gestures toward human immortality in the Wisdom of Solomon are founded on divine righteousness in contrast to the mortal children of earth (Wis 7:1), "for righteousness is immortal" (Wis 1:15).

Justice, Reconciliation, and Peace

Dust wisdom can bear the fruit of reconciliation and peace. "Remember the end of your life, and set enmity aside" (Sir 28:6a). The universal return to dust inspires striking reflections on equality: "no king has had a different beginning of existence; there is for all one entrance into life, and one way out" (Wis 1:5-6). Qoheleth's assertion of a cross-species equality in death may still be challenging for some to contemplate today: "humans have no advantage over the animals . . . They all have the same breath" (Eccl 3:19-20, 12:7).

Job, however, protests equality in death as a mockery of justice. One dies in prosperity and one dies bitter, "never having tasted of good. They lie down alike in the dust, and the worms cover them" (Job 21:23-26). In this case the motif of equality in death is critiqued as shallow and is evidence of unremedied injustice in life.

Divine Agency

Psalm 104 ascribes divine agency to the ecological cycle of death and life: "when you take away their breath, they die and return to their dust. You send forth your Spirit and they are created; and so you renew the face of the earth" (Ps 104:29-30).[11] This may be the most notable example in Scripture of the dust of death being imaged as fertile.

While many texts do not speculate about the reasons why all creatures return to the dust, some texts suggest that the return is at God's direction, including as punishment for sin. For parts of the tradition, the sense is that everyone is bound for the dust but one may join forces with the ways of death and therefore arrive to the dust more quickly. For example, Sirach observes "to all creatures, human and animal, but to sinners seven times more, come death and bloodshed and strife and sword" (Sir 40:8-9). Similarly, the imagery of Proverbs can suggest a landscape marked by two paths: paths of life on the land, where there is life for the righteous, and paths down to death in *sheol*, where there is early death for the unrighteous. The level path on the land treads narrowly above *sheol*, the place of the dead, into which paths of wickedness lead. In this metaphorical system, gravity and age will eventually draw all down to *sheol*, but sin hastens the journey.[12]

11. Together with John 12:24, these images are notable for ascribing divine agency to creaturely death and life in ecological terms. I am grateful to colleagues Eunyung Lim and Esther Menn for encouraging me to pursue these images of fecundity in death.

12. See Richard W. Medina, "Life and Death Viewed as Physical and Lived Spaces: Some Preliminary Thoughts from Proverbs," *Zeitschrift für die alttestamentliche Wissenschaft* 122, no. 2 (2010): 199–211.

Thus far this essay has posited a logical foundation to the Wisdom tradition's engagement with death: after a lifespan measured by other transient natural phenomena, all plant and animal creatures die and return to the dust. Further, from this ground emerges the fruit of diverse pieties, moral-ethical reflections, and existential dispositions. This understanding of dust wisdom is distinct for the logical center it proposes as well as the order and fecundity it discerns in the sapiential corpus. The following section examines liturgy. When dust wisdom is used as a lens, what comes into focus in an assessment of the liturgical tradition?

Dust Wisdom in Christian Liturgy

In a turn to liturgy one could examine prayers, hymns, and rites from across the church's repertoire. This essay, however, focuses on two of the most condensed liturgical expressions of dust wisdom: Ash Wednesday and the funeral rite.

Ash Wednesday

In the Ash Wednesday rite, generally celebrated only in Western churches, the living are individually addressed with archetypal words of dust wisdom and have ashes applied to their heads. Ash Wednesday's origins are in a rite that segregated out a group of penitents on account of what was identified as their particularly egregious sinfulness.[13] Over time, Ash Wednesday has increasingly come to address the entire assembly (rather than only a few penitents) in contemplation of the dust of mortality (rather than only sinfulness). A recent opening prayer for Ash Wednesday includes no penitential themes at all but instead focuses largely on mortality in dust wisdom terms. It takes a compassionate view of human bodies and uses the creation-from-dust anthropology as a premise from which to name the original purpose of the human creature: "Out of your love and mercy you breathed into dust the breath of life, creating us to serve you and our neighbor. Call forth our prayers and acts of kindness, and strengthen us to face our mortality with con-

---

13. Thomas Talley traces the origins of Ash Wednesday to fifth-century Turin (as a day for the exclusion of penitents), with clear evidence for the imposition of ashes on this day emerging only in the tenth century in the Romano-Germanic Pontifical and then only for penitents. See Thomas J. Talley, *The Origins of the Liturgical Year* (Collegeville, MN: Liturgical Press, 1991), 223–24.

fidence in the mercy of your Son."[14] In terms of scriptural dust wisdom, however, the prayer is inaccurate. The purpose named in this prayer ("to serve you and our neighbors") is not actually the purpose described in Genesis 2. Instead, the dust creature is created to "till and keep" or "serve and protect" the garden.[15] What if the Ash Wednesday prayer faithfully reflected this motif? The slight change would be remarkable: "Out of your love and mercy you breathed into dust the breath of life, *creating us to serve and protect the garden of your earth.*" Such a simple adaptation, besides attending more carefully to scriptural nuance, rightly links the dust with the earth's fecundity and places the vocation of earth-keeping at the center of the anthropology of today's penitential dust rite.

Psalm 51 has typically been the primary psalm appointed for Ash Wednesday ("surely I was a sinner from my birth"), but some rites now also include Psalm 103, with its dust wisdom and penitential themes. This shift evokes a different emphasis regarding the divine perspective on human birth. In Psalm 103 God's compassion is for humans because they are born from the dust, not, as in Psalm 51, only in spite of a sinful birth. The Ash Wednesday rite is increasing its accent on dust wisdom and seems to inspire wonder and growing popular demand for its encounter with the ground of mortality.

Committal

The most prominent dust wisdom motif in Western funeral texts is at the committal, when the body is lowered into the ground in a ritualized embodiment of the ground of dust wisdom. Some reference to Genesis 3:19 is typically appointed to be spoken: "In sure and certain hope of the resurrection to eternal life through our Lord Jesus Christ, we commend to almighty God [name], and we commit her/his body to the ground: earth to earth, ashes to ashes, dust to dust. The Lord bless her/him and keep her/him." Notice that just before the most central ritual embodiment of dust wisdom, this text inserts a preface that responds in advance to the word of dust wisdom: "in sure and certain hope of the resurrection." In the logic of the model advanced in this essay, resurrection motifs are certainly a fruit of the ground of dust wisdom. However, the resurrection

---

14. Evangelical Lutheran Church in America, *Evangelical Lutheran Worship: Leader's Desk Edition* (Minneapolis, MN: Augsburg Fortress, 2006), 615.

15. The NRSV translation is "till and keep." Some scholars, especially those employing an ecological hermeneutic, translate ʾ*abad*, serve, and *shamar*, protect.

text in this committal can be read as a caveat and even as a prophylactic—qualifying the core assertion of dust wisdom by allowing the return to earth only temporary, partial status. The "sure and certain hope" doubly asserts the inviolability of the caveat and is preemptively inserted before the invocation of dust wisdom, suppressing the force of the word about the dust (which is to say, in this model, suppressing its fecundity). This is not an insignificant occasion for a caveat. The committal is a rare, emphatic (note the three-fold repetition), and archetypal evocation of dust wisdom, spoken at the very moment at which the body is returned to the earth. What is said here matters.

I have wondered if this way of naming resurrection is like a black walnut tree. Black walnut trees are prolifically fruitful partly because their fruit, leaves, and roots produce chemicals that suppress the growth of other plants such that other black walnut trees can grow but many other plants cannot. In other words, black walnuts suppress the diversity around them. Are some ways of naming resurrection like a black walnut tree in the garden of dust wisdom? If the most evocative articulation of dust wisdom is always preempted by a "sure and certain" caveat even as the body is returned to the dust, is such a caveat like planting a black walnut tree in the center of the funeral rite? Does that make for a pungent resurrection fruit but not much diversity among the other fruits of dust wisdom? Black walnuts bear prolific fruit, but gardeners know that without being contained these trees will suppress the fruitfulness of others and take over the garden. Perhaps there could be options to use the strong "sure and certain" words elsewhere in the rite, in more contained and less central places.

A common Orthodox committal offers a contrasting model. The committal similarly invokes Genesis 3 as the body is prepared to be lowered into the grave and sprinkled with earth, but the dialog with dust wisdom here is remarkable. Rather than inserting a caveat about future resurrection, the text asserts another universal claim about the dust: "The earth is the Lord's, and the fullness thereof; the world and all that dwell therein. You are dust, and to dust you shall return."[16] The return to dust is not qualified or reversed in this committal text. Instead, the dust itself—including the body being lowered into the grave—is poetically portrayed as part of the earth, resting within a vast, divinely held cosmos.

---

16. For this translation, see Greek Orthodox Archdiocese of America, "Liturgical Texts of the Orthodox Church: Funeral Service," https://www.goarch.org /-/funeral-service.

Another Orthodox text at the committal gaining wider ecumenical usage has a more apparent resurrection motif that nevertheless does not subvert the universal return to dust. Instead, it subverts a liturgical expectation: instead of a dirge, the Easter song is sung by the dust creatures at the grave: "All of us go down to the dust, yet even at the grave we make our song: alleluia, alleluia, alleluia."[17]

A committal text from the Byzantine Rite addresses the earth itself, announcing the return of an earth creature to its mother: "Open wide, O earth, and receive the body formed from you by the hand of God, again returning to you as to its mother. What has been made in the divine image, the Creator has already reclaimed. O Earth, receive this body as your own."[18] Some other Byzantine rites turn the maternal imagery toward resurrection, speaking of returning the dead "to the womb of the earth from which they are to be born again."[19]

The above examples demonstrate the possibility of fertile dust wisdom imagery at the committal. However, it is increasingly the norm that there is no public ritual of return to the earth at all in American funeral practice. As Thomas Long's *Accompany Them with Singing: The Christian Funeral* aptly diagnoses, many have given up the practice of accompanying the dead all the way to the earth, partly because there is no body or remains at the funeral to accompany given the rise of memorial services. As Long memorably writes, the dead are increasingly banned from their own funerals.[20] In order to have a meaningful discussion about employing the language of dust wisdom at the committal, churches will

17. Adapted from Orthodox rites attributed to Saint Theophanes, hymnographer. The text here is now used widely and is found in the Episcopal Church's *Book of Common Prayer* (New York: Seabury Press, 1979), 499, and in the *Book of Common Worship* prepared by the Office of Theology and Worship for the Presbyterian Church (U.S.A), (Louisville, KY: Westminster John Knox, 2018), 797.

18. *Office of Christian Burial according to the Byzantine Rite* (Pittsburgh, PA: Byzantine Seminary Press, 1975). In a common Orthodox motif, the divine image of God is described as having already departed the body. If one substitutes "breath" for "divine image," one can see a parallel to dust wisdom: "the dust returns to the earth as it was, and the breath returns to God who gave it" (Eccl 12:7).

19. Armenian order, cited in Geoffrey Rowell, *The Liturgy of Christian Burial: An Introductory Survey of the Historical Development of Christian Burial Rites* (London: S.P.C.K., 1977), 39.

20. Thomas G. Long, *Accompany Them with Singing: The Christian Funeral* (Louisville, KY: Westminster John Knox Press, 2009), 75.

first need to welcome the bodies and remains of the beloved dead back to the funeral liturgy and invite the funeral assembly outside again to gather around the earthen grave.

Eastern Funeral Hymns

Our focus now turns from the grave to the songs. The dust wisdom motifs of the Eastern Rite become even more diverse in the funeral hymns, most of which are traditionally set as part of the liturgy. These are remarkable texts showcasing a wide range of sapiential imagery. There is significant debate within the Eastern churches about these hymns. They are considered by some to be "desolate" and "negative" in the same way some biblical scholars regard the biblical Wisdom corpus on mortality. Alexander Schmemann writes with colorful exasperation about a liturgical reference that evokes decomposition, "we are suddenly no longer with the saints but with the worms!"[21] A more balanced overview is found in Stelyios Muksuris's paper "Revisiting the Orthodox Funeral Service: Resurrecting a Positive Thematology in the Rite for the Dead."[22] The section below offers five examples of the fruits of dust wisdom from some of the hymns.

Near the end of the funeral rite, the choir sings a hymn as members of the assembly offer a final kiss to the deceased. Beginning by speaking honestly about the return to the earth and the vanities of life, the rite offers a community's compassion: "Departed from the bosom of his/her kin . . . he/she hastens to burial, no longer remembering vanity, nor yet the flesh which is often sore distressed. Where are now his/her kindred and comrades? Now is come the hour of partings."[23] The Wisdom motifs are designed to evoke the fruit of compassion for the deceased, literally

---

21. Alexander Schmemann, *The Liturgy of Death: Four Previously Unpublished Talks* (Yonkers, NY: St. Vladimir's Seminary Press, 2016), 77. The text draws on Job 21:26.

22. Stelyios S. Muksuris, "Revisiting the Orthodox Funeral Service: Resurrecting a Positive Thematology in the Rite for the Dead," paper presented at the International Conference on Liturgical Renewal, Hellenic College and Holy Cross Greek Orthodox School of Theology, Brookline, MA, 15 March 2013. Another significant overview is Elena Velkovska, "Funeral Rites according to the Byzantine Liturgical Sources," *Dumbarton Oaks Papers* 55 (2001): 21–51.

23. Stikhera of the Last Kiss, in Greek Orthodox Archdiocese of America, "Liturgical Texts of the Orthodox Church," www.goarch.org/-/funeral-service.

moving members of the assembly toward the body to offer the ritual final kiss.

Some *troparia* interspersed with the Beatitudes use the remarkable tradition of hymn stanzas sung *in persona defuncti*, in the voice of the deceased, in one case taking the form of a wry scold. The deceased addresses the mourners: "Human beings, why so greatly affected on my account, why this vain agitation? . . . Death brings rest to all. Listen to Job as he says: 'Death is humanity's rest.'"[24] This liturgical tradition allows the voice of the dead to sing the dust wisdom of Job as an address to be received as reassurance by the mourners. The universal nature of death is turned toward imagery of Sabbath rest and is intended to bear the fruit of comfort.

While the imagery of dust wisdom is found throughout the hymn, a few images of Christian resurrection are also included in a hymn attributed to Saint John of Damascus set within many orthodox funeral rites. The imagery in this stanza moves from the language of dust wisdom into metaphors of trumpet, earthquakes, and tents for dwelling: "Like a blossom that wastes away, and like a dream that passes and is gone, so is every mortal into dust resolved; but again, when the trumpet sounds its call, as though at a quaking of the earth, all the dead shall arise and go forth to meet you, O Christ our God," concluding with a prayer that Christ would "appoint a place in the tents of your saints." In this ten-stanza hymn, resurrection imagery is one fruit among other images of salvation in death.[25]

Two stanzas of the hymn announce in sapiential terms the destruction of wealth and status in death: "our wealth is with us no longer . . . all these things are vanished clean away . . . Where is now our gold, and our silver? . . . the surging crowd of domestics and their busy cries? All is dust, all is ashes, all is shadow." Another stanza sings of a rather humorous social disorientation in the community of the dead: "I saw the bones which of flesh were naked; and I said, 'Which indeed is he that

24. English translation in Alexis Kniazeff, "The Death of a Priest according to the Slavic Trebnik," in *Temple of the Holy Spirit: Sickness and Death of the Christian in the Liturgy: The Twenty-First Liturgical Conference Saint-Serge*, ed. Matthew J. O'Connell (New York, NY: Pueblo, 1983), 65–94, here at 86.

25. Funeral hymn attributed to Saint John of Damascus. See, for example, Greek Orthodox Archdiocese of America, "Liturgical Texts of the Orthodox Church," https://www.goarch.org/-/funeral-service.

is king? Or which is soldier? Which is the wealthy, which the needy? Which the righteous, or which the sinner?' "[26]

Thus, in a brief review of the orthodox funeral hymn stanzas it is apparent that the hymns bear diverse sapiential fruit, including the fruit of resurrection growing alongside others. While there is understandable concern today in Orthodox communities about how some of the imagery of the hymns can be received in contemporary funerals, Muksuris, as noted above, advocates supplementing these hymns with more imagery of baptism, resurrection, and paschal mystery. This is a laudable proposal. Yet this essay underscores the unique and fecund character of the dust wisdom patterns appearing in these Orthodox hymns, even if some of the language no longer neatly fits contemporary contexts. The hymns showcase images of resurrection beyond triumphalist Western imagery. Perhaps the problematic stanzas ("the worms" that troubled Fr. Schmemann) can be excised while new stanzas are interleaved. Images of bodies returning to a fruitful earth as a prayer for earth's healing and well-being might be explored. Texts such as Psalm 104, John 12:24, and recent Orthodox ecotheology are promising sources for imagery.

Natural Burial as Embodiment of Dust Wisdom

Thus far I have shown that dust wisdom is a fertile tradition that bears diverse fruit but survives only precariously in text and ritual action in most present-day Christian funeral rites. This essay has shown some observable embodiments of the dust wisdom tradition at Ash Wednesday, committal rites, and orthodox funeral hymns. The final section demonstrates how the emerging natural burial movement offers a powerful but incomplete encounter with what I have called the ground of dust wisdom. As expected of a dust wisdom tradition, its practitioners find this ground to be fruitful.

What is the natural burial movement? It has arisen in response to funeral practices that have become increasingly removed from the earth's natural cycles of death and life. It is most often defined by three characteristics: (1) no chemically toxic embalming fluids, (2) a biodegradable burial vessel (e.g., a wooden coffin, a woven basket, a shroud, a biode-

26. Ibid.

gradable urn), and (3) the earth to which the body is returned is not a vault or a niche but living earth, with a particularly compelling example being conservation burial, in which the legal protections of a cemetery are leveraged for the conservation of land from development so that the burial ground is also a nature sanctuary. In other words, the place for the dead becomes a place of diverse, flourishing life.

Foregrounding the Ground

Suzanne Kelly, in *Greening Death: Reclaiming Burial Practices and Restoring Our Tie to the Earth*, describes the current North American dominant culture's deathway as devoted to eradicating what I have called the ground of dust wisdom. Kelly claims that "distancing the dead body from its own decomposition and eradicating the ecological value of its reintegration into the cycles of nature," has "radically exclude[d]" the corpse from human community and its rightful biodiverse home. Currently dominant deathways "homogenize" the dead body "through uniformity and mechanization," and have effectively "created a prohibition on returning the dead body to the elements."[27] The central aim of the natural burial movement is to place the return to dust in the foreground. In other words, the central motif of dust wisdom—a body returning to the earth—is physically and ritually re-centered in the natural burial movement.

It is interesting to think of the natural burial movement as in this way a liturgical renewal movement. The ecclesial liturgical renewal movement centered in twentieth-century reforms recovered the strength and prominence of physical liturgical signs: real bread at the Eucharist, ample water used in baptism, the exchange of peace as a physical, embodied act. But in the same era the embodied symbols at the funeral have largely declined in church ritual, especially the central things of bodies and earth. Where the church has failed to renew its ritual, the natural burial movement emerged. In other words, the natural burial movement seems to be about the liturgical renewal of the funeral: recovering the centrality of the body and the earth, and ritually embodying their foundational bond at the uniquely vivid occasion of burial.

27. Suzanne Kelly, *Greening Death: Reclaiming Burial Practices and Restoring Our Tie to the Earth* (Lanham, MD: Rowman & Littlefield, 2015), 53–56.

The ground of the dust wisdom tradition is probably linguistically referenced most succinctly in some form of the phrase "dust to dust, earth to earth, ashes to ashes." The phrase is both scriptural and liturgical. Some form of that phrase normally appears in most literature about the natural burial movement. It is one of the most common ways that the movement is introduced in pamphlets, videos, and web sites. Within burial rituals themselves, even in spiritual-but-not-religious and secular natural burials, the phrase evokes a sort of sacramentality as it is invoked over the body or at the scattering of cremated remains.

One often hears natural burial advocates express the hope that in death they can "return directly and naturally to the earth from which we came." In statements like this, one may hear an affirmative case being made for the value of what I have identified as the ground of dust wisdom. However, this hope as an *individual choice* is something quite different from the *universal assertion* of dust wisdom that humans and animals all share the same fate. The absence of choice is essential to the scriptural dust wisdom tradition. Thus, considering and choosing natural burial can be a practice of postmodern, capitalist identity construction by which individuals engage consumer options to curate a sense of self and a public identity.[28] While this cultural phenomenon ostensibly puts the individual consumer in charge of identity construction, those involved with natural burial regularly report their surprise at how the land—the burial ground in its living personhood—subverts their expectations and exerts an agency of its own, sometimes with disconcerting force, as described below. Thus, in the natural burial movement there are complicated patterns related to the universality of the dust wisdom claims. Sometimes natural burial advocates speak universally or normatively about the natural return to dust: it is the way of all plant, animal, and human life. At other times, however, natural burial is framed as a consumer choice or the expression of a quirky personality. Yet the ground resists being domesticated into such patterns of identity construction. In natural burial the earth actively reclaims some of the force by which human life is experienced as contingent.

I have seen little evidence of natural burial advocates describing the human lifespan with sapiential images of transience (lives are like pass-

28. See Suzanne Kelly, "Dead Bodies that Matter: Toward a New Ecology of Human Death in American Culture." *Journal of American Culture* 35, no. 1 (2012): 47–48.

ing shadows, a mist, grass that withers, a sigh). This theme seems for contemporary people to be relatively separable from and even unrelated to the practice of natural burial. Yet there is ample evidence of those participating in natural burial developing an appreciation over time, after the burial, for the natural and seasonal cycles of death, decay, and growth. These cycles are sometimes described by the grieving as teachers: they reveal to them over time how human life is caught up in the transient cycles of all plant and animal life. This pattern will be noted below as one of the fruits of natural burial.

The Fruit of Natural Burial

What sort of "fruit" does natural burial bear? Below I briefly highlight five patterns of reflection that emerge from the ground of natural burial. Note that these twenty-first-century refections are relatively unique to the contemporary natural burial movement, yet, remarkably, they are structured by the same logic that we have identified at the heart of the ancient sapiential tradition.

"Giving something back"—body as gift

In natural burial the return of the body to the dust can be understood as a gift.[29] While the conceptual frame of giving at the time of death is likely familiar to many in terms of estate gifts and inheritances coming to expression in legal documents, currency, and property, in conservation burial the gift is focused precisely at the body as it returns to the earth. As it begins to nourish and protect the earth into which it is returned, the body itself is the gift. Edward Abbey's characteristically gruff description of death and burial articulates the sense of the body as gift that nourishes many other forms of life. At the moment of death "we should get the hell out of the way, with our bodies decently planted in the earth to nourish other forms of life—weeds, flowers, shrubs, trees, which support other forms of life, which support the ongoing human pageant—the lives of our

---

29. See Douglas Davies and Hannah Rumble, *Natural Burial: Traditional-Secular Spiritualities and Funeral Innovation* (New York, NY: Continuum, 2012), and Hannah Jane Rumble, " 'Giving Something Back': A Case Study of Woodland Burial and Human Experience at Barton Glebe" (PhD thesis, Durham University, 2010), http://etheses.dur.ac.uk/679/.

children. That seems good enough to me."[30] Practitioners often express the gift in terms of reciprocity. The body is gratefully reciprocating in response to a lifetime of air, clean water, meals, beloved vistas, familiar landscapes, and trees climbed in childhood.[31]

Toward Paradise

Second, practitioners of natural burial keenly understand that the creaturely return to the earth in death is part of what makes the earth flourish with life. Thus, especially with reference to conservation burial grounds people speak of their deaths as being part of the healing of the earth. Some burial grounds are founded not in already-idyllic settings but in deforested areas or other wounded landscapes into which people are buried as part of a project to restore a woodland or prairie that may take decades or a century. There is a sort of faith in a long-term paradise that exists beyond the sight of those who entrust their bodies to this hope. Douglas Davies wonders if this future orientation may be seen as a new quest for a form of eternal life that he labels "ecological immortality."[32]

Blessed Simplicity

Third, everything that goes to the earth with the deceased in natural burial must normally be biodegradable, able to return to dust. There is no vault, artificial turf, or metal-armored coffin. Rather, the burial might include a raw earthen grave with the soil mounded up beside it, a simple wooden coffin made by hand, or perhaps pine boughs in the grave to receive a body wrapped in a shroud. The return to dust creates a space where anti-consumerism and concern for economic justice intersect. Jane, pre-registered to be buried at a conservation burial ground, relates the ecological simplicity of the burial vessel to her concern for economic

---

30. Quoted in Jack Loeffler, *Headed Upstream: Interviews with Iconoclasts* (Santa Fe, NM: Sunstone Press, 2019), 18.

31. See the section on natural burial as gift-giving in Kelly, *Greening Death*, 71–73. Indigenous/traditional earth spiritualities are often built much more elaborately on systems of reciprocity, including at death. See Vine Deloria, "Death and Religion," in *God Is Red: A Native View of Religion* (Golden, CO: Grosset & Dunlap, 1994), 165–84.

32. See "Ecology, Death and Hope," chap. 4 of Douglas James Davies, *A Brief History of Death* (Malden, MA: Blackwell Publishers, 2005).

justice: "I would never want one of those big, brass-handle things. It doesn't disintegrate and I think that's important . . . I hate all that! I don't mind giving money if I have it, but what do people with no money do? It's just horrendous that for some people they have to think about all that [money] before they die."[33]

Interspecies Liturgical Participation

Fourth, the event of human burial creates a uniquely powerful ritual space and a porous ritual boundary. It is where the dead descend and "go down to the dust." Everything inside the ritual space has the potential to take on heightened significance. American funeral homes, churches, and cemeteries rightly control the elements within their ritual spaces, but a natural burial ground is alive with other actors. Those who attend natural burials frequently remark on the appearance of things like cottonwood seeds floating in the air, a dragonfly, thunderstorm, toad, or wild strawberries[34] and describe these appearances as significant to them. One minister active in the natural burial movement described a moment at a burial to which participants attributed spiritual significance:

> At that moment, when we put the body in the grave, there was a gasp and the people, we all looked up, and there was a hawk, a three-foot raptor with a three-foot wingspan, big ol' hawk just circling right above the grave and it just circled right into the heavens.[35]

While the appearance of a hawk might be interesting at any time, its appearance within the epistemically charged ritual space of a burial has the potential to inspire significant meaning and wonder. Some perceive these non-human creatures as bearing witness to the death or burial, and it is

33. Quoted in Rumble, "Giving Something Back," 179.

34. Teresa Berger, "Wild Strawberries on a Mother's Grave," in *Fragments of Real Presence: Liturgical Traditions in the Hands of Women* (New York, NY: Crossroad, 2005), 103–4.

35. Charles Morris, interviewed by Joe Sehee and Shari Wolf, in "Catholicism and Judaism in Green Burial," podcast, *The Green Burial Radio Program*, http://funeralradio.com/greenburial/religion-and-green-burial/ (accessed 27 December 2013).

common for mourners to describe the creature's appearance as offering some form of reassurance to them.

Seasons and Cycles

Fifth, during late fall through winter the landscape of natural burial grounds can for some be so bleak and strongly marked by the imagery of death as to be repellent. Hannah Rumble writes, "A field or newly planted woodland can be extremely barren when exposed by the seasonality of the landscape. For bereaved visitors to these landscapes, it is sometimes too much to bear in their grief and it feels heartless and disrespectful to bury the person they are mourning in a landscape that suggests the deceased has been abandoned or isolated by the living."[36]

This is an example of the ground exerting its agency, sometimes uncomfortably. Unable to see signs of life on such a landscape, this encounter with the ground of dust wisdom might push some toward the more resigned or stoic responses of the sapiential tradition. But one fruit that frequently emerges from natural burial grounds over time is an increasing appreciation for seasons and for the natural cycles of death, decay, and renewal. Mary, describing her husband's grave, reflected on her experience over time: "I went there last November and it was covered with all these bramble things, and I thought: well, it's not what I wanted! But I think my views are gradually changing so that I can see that the seasons are part of life and death; and they're illustrated at [the burial ground] in a beautiful way."[37] After a premature and difficult death for her son, one woman reflects on the transition of her own anger and grief through years of observable ecological change: "My son was just 22 years. He loved life. I cried and screamed after the funeral that I didn't want to hug a f***ing tree. I felt very angry, still do, but I do like seeing the tree taller now and representing beauty and life and I hope when his daughter, now 6 years old, one day stands beside the thick trunk of this tree, she

---

36. Rumble, "Giving Something Back," 126.

37. Ibid., 136. A related category of experience that might be considered an additional fruit of natural burial is the encounter with the disrupted earth of the grave. Participants commonly remark on the raw appearance of the grave, sometimes using metaphors of wounds and violence. The shock of the disruption sometimes evokes reflection on the emotional disruption of death as well as the need for human participation in the healing of the wounded earth.

will receive some pleasure and comfort from touching it."[38] The initial shock of burying loved ones in wild or barren landscapes may in fact be the beginning of a cycle of healing, with archetypal symbols of new life unfolding naturally over time. Thus, one of the fruits of burying in a natural burial ground is that the raw immediate grief of the participants, perhaps while they are yet unaware, is being integrated into longer natural cycles: the turning of seasons and years, patterns of decay and growth. This phenomenon may be especially powerful in the presence of trees that grow larger and over longer periods of time than the more transient humans who are buried among them.

Conclusions

This essay has proposed an orienting center to the theme of mortality in the sapiential tradition: after a lifespan measured by transient earthly phenomena, all plant and animal creatures die and return to the dust from which they were formed. This ground of dust wisdom produces the fruit of diverse pieties, moral-ethical reflections, and existential dispositions. The model proposed here highlights the fertility and comprehensibility of the dust wisdom tradition, showing it to be fruitful ground for Christian cosmologies.

This essay has argued that in the construction of ecological cosmology, a fruitful, perhaps foundational, ritual consideration is the return of our bodies to the earth from which they were formed—both *how* we do it and *that* we do it at all. I have argued that what I have called dust wisdom is a buried treasure, including in the sense that it has been hidden lately. A review of Ash Wednesday, the committal rite, and the Eastern funeral hymns demonstrated that the motifs of dust wisdom occupy significant but precarious places in the ritual repertoire of the church. The model of dust wisdom proposed here shows itself to be useful in evaluating potential reforms for funeral rites.

Finally, the natural burial movement can be understood as a sort of liturgical renewal movement demonstrating to the church that a new-old approach to death can bear abundant fruit. Especially the practice of conservation burial offers images of the healing and restoration of earth

---

38. Quoted in Andrew Clayden and Katie Dixon, "Woodland Burial: Memorial Arboretum versus Natural Native Woodland?" *Mortality* 12, no. 3 (2007): 257.

that are conversant with some of the earliest strata of Christian tradition. In Christ's death, to use the language of early Christian liturgy, the flaming sword guarding paradise has been quenched and sheathed, and the path to Eden has been opened again. This path of wisdom leading back to the garden—scientists, environmentalists, health-care professionals, biologists, and theologians tell us—is once again being urgently sought by the creatures of earth.

CHAPTER SEVENTEEN

Liturgical Free Association with *Symbiopsychotaxiplasm*: Take One

Gerald C. Liu

What do we mean when we say "liturgical tradition"? If we imagine, for example, the varieties of ritual formalism found in eucharistic liturgies across Catholic, Orthodox, and Protestant traditions, those resemble fourth-century Roman court practices more than they resemble what Jesus and the disciples did.[1] They are inventions formed over time that diverge with incredible range from originary mealtime worship patterns. Table worship and other sacramental practices also constitute only particular expressions of what might be described as liturgical tradition. Liturgical tradition pulses within all kinds of practices and continues to change. As Robert Taft writes, liturgy, as a tradition within history, can "only be understood in motion, just as the only way to understand a top is to spin it."[2] The following pages revolve around *Symbiopsychotaxiplasm*, the first feature-length, avant-garde film with an African American writer, director, producer, and protagonist, as an unprecedented cinematic vanishing point for envisioning how wide liturgical tradition can still be, especially with respect to ecology and cosmology, as it continues to evolve and move into the future.

1. Robert Knapp, *The Dawn of Christianity: People and Gods in a Time of Magic and Miracles* (Cambridge, MA: Harvard Univ. Press, 2017), 227.
2. Robert Taft, *Beyond East & West: Problems in Liturgical Understanding* (Washington, DC: Pastoral Press, 1984), 154.

In his essay "The Rule as Liturgical Text," Giorgio Agamben helpfully reminds his readers that *leitourgia* first meant "public tribute or service for the people."[3] The term belonged to the "political lexicon" and described services that well-to-do citizens performed for the polis, such as organizing public games or staging a chorus for a city festival. Agamben pulls from the *Politics*, where Aristotle cautions democracies "from taking on expensive but useless liturgies [public services], such as leading choruses, officiating at torch races, and other similar things" to illustrate the genealogy he wants to foreground.[4] What should not be missed in Agamben's partial quotation from Aristotle is a fuller statement from Aristotle suggesting that liturgy was, on the one hand, in its earliest expressions a civic responsibility appointed to the wealthy and, on the other hand, a chore that raised questions as to whether performing a liturgy was worth the financial inconvenience.

Aristotle's warning begins with an overall appeal to spare the well-to-do (the εὐπόρων φείδεσθαι) from the hassle of financing and performing liturgy, in order to keep them from losing money. And it concludes with final advice for the wealthy class of a *demokratias* that even if they are willing to participate in liturgies, they should be spared from doing so. "In democracies, the well-off should be spared, not only by not having their possessions redivided, but not even their incomes, which in some regimes happens unnoticed; it is better to prevent them from taking on expensive but useless public services [*leitourgia*]."[5] Aristotle appears to address an aversion palpable among the cultural elites to having to perform liturgies at all, especially if the public expense of doing so outweighed the personal and private benefit.

In fact, Athenians used to hide their wealth in order to avoid doing liturgies. Calum Carmichael notes that liturgical responsibilities were assigned by magistrates, who recommended the number and type of liturgies annually. The magistrates asked wealthy citizens to volunteer to facilitate liturgies in order to generate state revenue and benefit the public. Any liturgies without volunteers would be assigned to the wealthy

3. Giorgio Agamben, "The Rule as Liturgical Text (3.1)," in *The Omnibus Homo Sacer* (Palo Alto, CA: Stanford Univ. Press, 2017), 956.

4. See *Aristotle's Politics,* trans. Carnes Lord (Chicago, IL: Chicago Univ. Press, 2016), 151.

5. Ibid.

who had not yet offered their services. The incentives of prestige and reputation often sufficed to compel the well-off to lend a hand. Yet Carmichael contends that as the private benefit for the wealthy seemed to be outweighed by the expense of facilitating a liturgy for public munificence, wealthy Athenians began to conceal their visible wealth in order to outmaneuver being asked to perform a liturgy.[6] Aristotle and wealthy Athenians had a hard time seeing what was in it for them.

Symbiopsychotaxiplasm, crafted by Bill Greaves, constitutes one divergent expression of public liturgy in the ancient Hellenistic sense of the word. The film does not resemble a Greek chorus (although later this chapter discusses how chorus-like devices feature in the film, as critic Amy Taubin notes). Nor does it fulfill a civic duty. Yet it does offer public benefit in an inverse way. Greaves assumes the role of a privileged creator of cinematic art even though he is associated with an underprivileged and denigrated class. Due to his blackness Greaves did not hold the kind of social standing that a member of the Athenian elite would have possessed. Yet the blackness of Greaves subverts the viewing sensibilities of late twentieth-century American publics by outlining a new horizon of cinematic ingenuity within the racialized landscape of post–Civil Rights America. *Symbiopsychotaxiplasm* manages to claim new artistic space in spite of failing to win critical acclaim during its release. Greaves's groundbreaking content warrants liturgical study, especially if liturgy consists of material aesthetics that set conditions for transformational encounters with God's meaning and purpose, which are shared by humans even and especially when reality may seem far from holiness and also politically myopic.[7]

In 1968, when Greaves shot *Symbiopsychotaxiplasm*, he had just been appointed executive producer of the National Educational Television public-affairs series *Black Journal*, then the only national television series dealing with African American life. (His appointment resulted from a staff walkout protesting white control of the show.) Greaves also ran his own documentary-film production company and was a member

6. Calum M. Carmichael, "Public Munificence for Private Benefit: Liturgies in Classical Athens," *Economic Inquiry* 35, no. 2 (1997): 262.

7. For a sweeping empirical study with evidence suggesting that the material content of worship is the arts, see Mark Chaves, *Congregations in America* (Cambridge, MA: Harvard Univ. Press, 2004), 166–80.

of the Actors Studio, a New York collective formed in 1947 for artists to forge deeper connections between their work. There he participated as a director, actor, and teacher.

Greaves started acting in the 1940s, first on Broadway and then on-screen for films made specifically for the black post-war audience. He experienced success, especially for a black male actor of the time. Yet increasingly he became frustrated with what he called the "political problems of the African American in America" and found "America to be very oppressive."[8] In an interview included in the Criterion Collection transfer of *Symbiopsychotaxiplasm: Take One* and a sequel entitled *Symbiopsychotaxiplasm: Take 2½,* Greaves shared that "it was a very difficult environment for a young, and reasonably intelligent person of color . . . to pursue a productive career" and that most opportunities were "Uncle Tom" roles.[9] With uncaricatured roles in short supply for black actors, he decided that he wanted to be a director. After studies with avant-garde filmmaker Hans Richter and documentarian Louis de Rochemont in New York, he moved to Canada to work for the National Film Board because he could not see a way of breaking through the racist culture of the United States.

Greaves washed floors and windows and took other menial jobs assisting the film faculty to support himself. Eventually, a Canadian documentary he made in 1959 entitled *Emergency Ward* distinguished him. The United Nations hired Greaves in the 1960s to make a film about global airline flight, which allowed him to move back to the United States and form William Greaves Productions. Then the US Information Agency hired him to make several films on the civil rights movement. One of his most notable films, *Still a Brother: Inside the Negro Middle Class*, dealt with the conflict within the black community between integrationists and militants. It aired a few weeks before Greaves took the helm of *Black Journal* and started working on *Symbiopsychotaxiplasm.* While almost three decades would pass before the multilayered, simultaneous, documentary-within-a-documentary style of *Symbiopsychotaxiplasm* would even begin to attract critical praise, later films from Greaves such

---

8. William Greaves, "Discovering William Greaves," *Symbiopsychotaxiplasm: Two Takes by William Greaves* (New York, NY: Criterion Collection, 2006) [8:58–9:05].

9. Ibid. [9:11–9:29].

as the 1974 *From these Roots*, which relied strictly upon the framing of photographs, heavily influenced lauded documentarians such as Ken Burns.

Symbiopsychotaxiplasm came to fruition after Manuel Melamed, a former film student of Greaves's, asked him why he was not making feature films. Melamed stated, "You know how to make movies."[10] Though Greaves had taken the lead at *Black Journal,* he still did not have the personal capital that would enable him to pursue a feature-length project. Melamed offered to cover the costs, and when Greaves asked what kind of a film Melamed wanted him to make, Melamed responded that he would back whatever Greaves had in mind.

The title *Symbiopsychotaxiplasm* comes from "symbiotaxiplasm," a term coined by social scientist Arthur Bentley, who co-wrote *Knowing and the Known* with John Dewey.[11] In his *Inquiry into Inquiries: Essays for Social Theory*, Bentley borrows a term from physiologist Michael A. Lane: "symbiotaxiosis," a word with Greek roots that describes a way of understanding life together.[12] *Symbios* or *syn* (together) and *bios* (life) suggest life in common. *Taxis* can be rendered "arrangement" or "ordering," and *osis* as "action." Symbiotaxiosis can therefore be understood as describing a comprehensive way of delving into the togetherness of life and its associated actions. Bentley changed the term to "symbiotaxiplasm" to pivot it more toward the texturedness of human life, what he calls "the mass of men (or, alternatively, any associated animals)," and its overlapping relations between bodies and environment.[13] Greaves added "psycho" to incorporate a psychological dimension.[14] The ornery

10. Ibid. [36:58].

11. Arthur Bentley and John Dewey, *Knowing and the Known* (Boston, MA: Beacon Press, 1960).

12. Arthur Bentley, *Inquiry into Inquiries: Essays in Social Theory* (Boston, MA: Beacon Press, 1954).

13. Ibid., 12, where Bentley writes, "A symbiotaxium would be any society. Symbiotaxiplasm, or more simply taxioplasm, would be the mass of men (or, alternatively, any associated animals) and assimilated things which forms the society, regarded as matter. Symbiotaxis would be the social process or function, regarded as such."

14. See also Scott MacDonald, "The Country in the City: Central Park in Jonas Mekas's *Walden* and William Greaves's *Symbiopsychotaxiplasm: Take One*," *Journal of American Studies* 31, no. 3 (1997): 352, n. 19.

title *Symbiopsychotaxiplasm* captures the cinematic milieu that Greaves creates as he puts cast and crew together in a satirical, panoramic, and meandering documentation of absurd screen-test acting during a few days in Central Park. Greaves explained the film as follows:

> It's an attempt on my part to play around with the various concepts that were floating around the world of philosophy, mysticism, theatrical film-making, and so on. There were other crazy ideas that I had developed as an actor at the Actor's Studio and teaching acting, and so on and so forth. I was interested in what it would look like if you took a group of highly intelligent people and subject them to this complete revolt against the traditions of Hollywood filmmaking. I couldn't answer the question unless I subjected myself and these people to this. We'll see what it looks like.[15]

On the surface, *Symbiopsychotaxiplasm* is a screen test under the guise of the working title "Over the Cliff," where a couple fights in Central Park about marriage, pregnancy, and purported homosexuality.

The film was shot with three 16mm cameras. The first was trained on the actors. The second filmed the crew filming the scene. The third recorded actors, crew, onlookers, and anything interesting happening in the park. Greaves himself sometimes had a fourth camera. The film opens with a couple fighting. The woman yells at her male partner, stating, "You don't want marriage! You don't want children! You just want the gay world, Freddy! G-A-Y!" Interrupting the absurd and acerbic dialogue is a piercing feedback sine wave from a boom mic recording the scene and aleatory noises from the park that include traffic passing by.[16] The image also cuts to interspersed scenes of ordinary park visitors, who are not extras in the film, staring with bewilderment at the unusual assortment of multiple cameras recording both the abrasive lovers' quarrel and the crew filming the scene. The voice of Greaves cuts into the mix. The camera then shifts to Greaves, who is standing with headphones on, as he asks to hear the feedback looping sound, "Let me hear this sound."[17] With his hands cupping over-the-ear headphones, he looks confused and says with disgust, "That's dreadful. This is terrible," two statements that

15. Greaves, "Discovering William Greaves" [38:13–39:00].
16. *Symbiopsychotaxiplasm* (dir. Greaves, 1968, 2001) [3:47–3:53].
17. Ibid. [4:16].

probably sum up the response of most viewers upon first seeing *Symbio-psychotaxiplasm.* Then theme music plays, with the feedback sine wave still cresting over the audio mix like a theremin on the loose covering everything else with its frequency, and the film's title appears on screen: "Take One Ltd Productions presents *Symbiopsychotaxiplasm Take One.*"[18]

Though the dialogue is severe and unbelievable, it stands out as a satiric anticipation of counterpublics and social change related to the civil rights, reproductive rights, and gay rights movements galvanizing the late Sixties, without naming any of those countercultural movements. Martin Luther King Jr. was assassinated on 4 April 1968. Second-wave feminism was cresting after the publication of Betty Friedan's *The Feminine Mystique* (1963). The Stonewall Riots would occur in 1969. The National Black Feminist Movement would form in 1973. A decade after the making of *Symbiopsychotaxiplasm*, the National Coalition of Black Lesbians and Gays would be established. *Symbiopsychotaxiplasm* explores with sophistication the kaleidoscopic contingent connections between hidden directorial motives and acted and actual human behavior, set against the backdrop of an American political landscape undergoing upheaval and an urban ecology knit to social transformations occurring throughout the nation but oblivious to them.

Greaves presents the film as socially aware by means of bizarre indirection, indirection paradoxically punctuated by his role as a conspicuous but unremarkable and seemingly disorganized black writer, producer, director, and protagonist surrounded by a befuddled and frustrated multicultural cast and crew. Greaves attends to his experiment with uncanny nonchalance. Weaving his passive directorial style with confused acting and candid dialogue from cast and crew yields an extreme, panoramic portrait of cinematic self-reflexivity that confounds the casual observer. Yet it still raises questions about authorship, authority, individual agency, cooperative resistance, race, class, fiction, reality, and even American despair and populist hope, questions that open up vistas for liturgical imagination about the cosmos and creation.

In the director's notes on the film, Greaves calls *Symbiopsychotaxiplasm* a "fragment of the Godhead which is made up of other Godhead fragments." He declares that it is "jazz." "It is improvisation," he writes.

---

18. Ibid. [4:30, 4:51–5:12].

"It is an exploration into the future of cinema art." There is Pentecost-sounding language when he notes that "the film is about *fire. Life Fire which is all around us.*" He declares, "The film is free association," and states,

> This film will tell itself. This film is about us, about the cast, crew and onlookers, about us all as part of nature, and nature has its *own* story to tell. Our problem, or rather my problem, is to get out of nature's way and let nature tell her story. That's what a good director is—a person who gets his ego out of his own way, he is at best a collaborator and servant of nature . . . but who, paradoxically, firmly controls the conditions of spontaneity, theatricality, and drama on the set.[19]

Greaves's notes seem lost upon his cast and crew.

In between cuts of the excruciating dialogue between the screen-test actors is behind-the-scenes footage of the film crew, who share their dissatisfaction like an "angst-ridden chorus that voices the audience's objections," to borrow critic Amy Taubin's words.[20] In several scenes, male crew members criticize the film as proceeding with a superfluous concept, that Greaves "doesn't know how to direct," that the script is "bad writing," that "Bill is a bad actor," and that the entire production is all banal.[21] Soundman Jonathan Gordon perhaps puts it best:

> Here is an open-ended film with no plot that we can see, with no end that we can see, and an action that we can't follow. We're all intelligent people. The obvious thing is to fill in the blanks, to create for each of our own selves a film that we understand. And if we try to think about the reasoning of the director for allowing us the opportunity to do this, giving us the circumstances that enable us to be able to sit here, we can only conclude from last night, that he wanted it like this.[22]

19. William Greaves, "Production Notes," in *Symbiopsychotaxiplasm: Two Takes by William Greaves*, dir. William Greaves (1968, 2001), underlining as in the original.

20. Amy Taubin, "Still No Answers," in *Symbiopsychotaxiplasm: Two Takes by William Greaves*.

21. *Symbiopsychotaxiplasm* (dir. Greaves, 1968, 2001) [22:59, 37:36, 39:12]. Bob Rosen would go on to work on classics like *The Crow* and *Porky's Revenge*, and also became dean of the UCLA School of Theater, Film and Television.

22. Ibid. [19:57].

The seeming lack of direction that frustrates Gordon and his male com-
patriots is understood, however, as unusual creative vision by women
present in the room, such as camera assistant Maria Zeheri and boom
mic operator Nicky Kaplan.

Zeheri states that while it may seem as if Greaves does not know
what he is doing, "this is what he wants."[23] Challenging crew leaders
such as Gordon and production manager Rosen by asking them if they
have read the concept for the film, apparently made available by Greaves
before the shooting began, she interprets the multiple takes of the same
dialogue as an ongoing experiment adhering to the concept for the film.
For Zeheri, the multiple takes will acquire coherence and artistic purpose
in the editing room, where Greaves could edit and assemble the footage
in "300 ways."[24] Gordon states that he has not read the concept. Rosen
states that he has read it, but that "the concept doesn't help you at all."[25]
Kaplan, who admits that she has not read the concept, reflects upon the
entire affair as exploring multiple levels of reality, even "supra levels
of reality," and comments, "It may be the biggest put on of all time."[26]
One might wonder if the behind-the-scenes moments of lament from the
crew are a ruse, appearing accidental and operating as a foil to bolster
the ingenious randomness of the film and the director's intent. Yet as
recently as 2011, Rosen vehemently denied that any of the secret conversations were acting.[27] Film critic Geo Ong notes that the insights of the
women are quickly dismissed by Gordon, Rosen, and others. For Ong,
the views expressed by the women become legitimate only later, when
the "white males" come around to see the filming as Zeheri and Kaplan
do.[28] Perhaps Ong is correct. Yet even though the voices of the female
crew members are overwhelmed by male complaining, their thoughts

23. Ibid. [51:46].
24. Ibid. [53:14].
25. Ibid. [53:26].
26. Ibid. [54:09–54:29].
27. Akiva Gottlieb, " 'Just Another Word for Jazz': The Signifying Auteur in
William Greaves's Symbiopsychotaxiplasm: Take One," *Black Journal* 5, no. 1
(2013): 179–80 and note 43.
28. Geo Ong, " 'Don't Take Me Seriously': Symbiopsychotaxiplasm's Multiple Levels of Reality," Urchin Movement, 21 December 2015, http://www.urchinmovement
.com/2015/12/21/dont-take-me-seriously-symbiopsychotaxiplasms-levels-of-reality/.

name what Greaves is undertaking—a radicalized form of cinéma vérité or observational documentary that exposes something of what is real within a nonsensical production. Instead of seeing Gordon and Rosen as white males overriding the observations of the women, one could instead view them as foils who ultimately cannot deny the lines of interpretation from Zeheri and Kaplan.

Fifteen minutes before the film's end, Greaves confirms the hunches of the women as he sits with the crew on a patch of grass to clear the air. He discloses that he is most interested in the ability of the crew and actors to improve upon the film, to revolt against him, the representative of the "establishment," in a positive way, by pushing to the surface something new that is better than the film that is currently sinking into chaos. The outside huddle forms a striking contrast with the secret utility-room crew discussions. Greaves states, "This screen test, which we are supposed, uh, supposed to be shooting, is, um unsatisfactory. You've read the concept? I assume that you've read the concept." Gordon says, "I haven't read the concept." Greaves gently replies, "Oh, well you should read the concept." Rosen responds, "Well, talk . . ." as he rotates his hand from the wrist toward Greaves.[29] Greaves explains:

> The screentest proves to be unsatisfactory from the standpoint of the actors and the director. And then what happens is that the director and the actors undertake to improvise something better than that which is, has been written, you know, in the screen test. This sort of palace revolt, [chuckling after sensing some skepticism from the facial expressions of the crew] you know. No, no, which is taking place, uh, uh, is not dissimilar to the sort of revolution that is taking place, let's say, in America today. In terms of the fact that, uh, in the sense that I represent the establishment. You know. And, uh, and I've been trying to get you to do certain things which you've in a sense become disenchanted with. You know. Now, your, your problem is to come up with creative suggestions which would make this into a better production than uh, we now have.[30]

Rosen interjects, "I don't understand that at all." Greaves retorts:

29. *Symbiopsychotaxiplasm* (dir. Greaves, 1968, 2001) [59:00–59:16].
30. Ibid. [59:15–1:00:10].

It doesn't, it doesn't, it doesn't matter whether or not you don't understand it. The important thing is that we surface from this production experience with something that is entirely exciting and creative as a result of our collective efforts. As a result of Marsha's efforts, as a result of Audrey, uh, Sly Motell, you, Jonathan, you, Bob, Roland, Mitchell, Nicky, Frank, Baker, Barbara, Linden. It's important that as a result of the totality of all of these efforts, we, uh, arrive at a creative piece of cinematic experience.[31]

Greaves discloses a political ambition within his chaotic film, to compel his cast and crew to mutiny for something better. He hopes that their frustrations with the apparent disorganized, directionless, and absurd tenor of the filmmaking will mobilize them to rebel against him with cooperative counter-filmmaking, which they do to a certain degree. Greaves hoped for a collective resistance. Naming every crew member in the huddle, he calls them into a collective responsibility to make a more meaningful film with him, or even in spite of him.

To put it in a doxological register, Greaves sets conditions for redemption to break in. In *Symbiopsychotaxiplasm*, the possibility is humanistic. Yet it is no less liturgical if liturgy is conceived according to its ancient humanistic and Hellenistic roots. Central Park is not a polis and the cast and crew are not wealthy participants in a *demokratias*. Greaves does, however, explore how to produce a different kind of citizenship within his location-based improvisational filming, one of collective resistance that is capable of serving future viewing publics by redirecting an unintelligible situation into a better film.

The experiment fails. Cast and crew do not advance beyond behind-the-scenes lament. *Symbiopsychotaxiplasm* fell into obscurity for almost two generations. In 2015, in the *New Yorker* article "The Daring, Original, and Overlooked Symbiopsychotaxiplasm: Take One," critic Richard Brody describes the film as "one of the greatest movies about filmmaking ever made, and one that would have spoken to young independent filmmakers of the time. It's a vision of filmmaking that didn't get seen when it could have made a decisive difference for a new generation."[32] The

31. Ibid. [1:00:12–1:00:50].

32. Richard Brody, "The Daring, Original, and Overlooked Symbiopsychotaxiplasm: Take One," *New Yorker*, 5 February 2015, https://www.newyorker.com /culture/richard-brody/daring-original-overlooked-symbiopsychotaxiplasm-take-one.

limitations of the film and its subsequent rediscovery are also useful as points of reference to reconsider the horizons of liturgical tradition theologically understood. What would it entail to craft and practice liturgy that serves the public with higher-definition theological rigor and imagination, capable of piercing through the indifference and chaos of human life with radiant reflections of divine light, even if it means undertaking liturgical experiments that do not seem to yield ecclesial fruit immediately?

In *Sacramental Poetics at the Dawn of Secularism*, Regina Schwartz suggests that "when the Reformers gave up transubstantiation, they gave up on a doctrine that infuses all materiality, spirituality, and signification with the presence of God."[33] Sustaining and modulating her specific polemic against the Reformers and even its particular location in eucharistic thought, the redefinition of liturgy that included cutting loose the anchoring Hellenistic meaning has resulted in a stunted understanding of where liturgy itself or models for liturgy can be found.

It may be too much to say that *Symbiopsychotaxiplasm* is infused with divine presence. But it may not be too much of a stretch to see it as liturgy and as liturgically profound, in both social and theological registers. Broadly speaking, the disturbing screen-test dialogue, the disgruntled conversations from film and sound crew members, the anti-establishment hopes from Greaves, and his recurring and anchoring presence onscreen as an unassuming black director and protagonist within a multicultural cast at a time when there were no black directors of feature-length films provoke liturgically minded viewers to rethink questions about human identity and diversity, sexuality and partnership, the indifference of urban life, what constitutes notable art, and what it takes to realize a sense of vocation. It is remarkable how the bricolage of moral themes indicated in *Symbiopsychotaxiplasm* continues to appear within the fabric of interweaving social questions regarding acceptance, belonging, and togetherness. The telos of the film—to spark resistance from cast and crew to overcome Greaves as "the establishment"—remains astonishingly timely. Brody calls it "a crucial work of late-sixties politics in action,"

---

33. Regina Schwartz, *Sacramental Poetics at the Dawn of Secularism: When God Left the World* (Palo Alto, CA: Stanford Univ Press, 2008), 12.

and its political wattage still shocks and electrifies.[34] And yet, even the ethical concerns and the call for rebellion in *Symbiopsychotaxiplasm* are undone near the film's end when a homeless man by the name of Victor Butkowski interrupts filming with stream-of-conscious statements of hopelessness.

Explaining why he sleeps "in the bushes" for shelter, Butkowski states that he and many others have "given up."[35] When Greaves asks him, "Why are you giving up?" Butkowski responds that he cannot fight "politicians" or "money," explaining, "Cause I don't have money."[36] Butkowski points to how much Rockefeller spent on his last campaign. He states that perhaps "years ago" or "centuries ago" it was possible to "fight that, but not today," and reflects, "Even with words you can't fight."[37] Half a century later, Butkowski's sentiments still sound on point.

Rosen then asks Butkowski, "What about love, man?" Butkowski replies that love "is a feeling of the penis of the cunt, that's what love is." Greaves seeks to exit the conversation after that "searching thought." Butkowski then backtracks and re-describes love as a "feeling of a desire of one for the other." The scene eventually concludes with a cordial but awkward exchange of goodbyes.[38] If Butkowski's sense of hopelessness and his distorted understanding of love still resonate today, how might practitioners of liturgy draw attention to despair like his and find better rituals to bring renewal to lives like his?

Film critic Akiva Gottlieb believes that the exchange with Butkowski is staged, because the camera captures a production hand giving Butkowski a few dollars and Rosen asking him to sign a waiver. Authentic or not, Gottlieb sees Butkowski's entrance as an illuminating transition, "no matter how enlightened and socially progressive the film crew might be, they are still alienated from another level of reality."[39] Compounded by ignoring the proximate needs of someone like Butkowski, the rebellious undertone of *Symbiopsychotaxiplasm* also seems pale considering

---

34. Brody, "The Daring, Original, and Overlooked Symbiopsychotaxiplasm: Take One."

35. *Symbiopsychotaxiplasm* (dir. Greaves, 1968, 2001) [1:05:18].

36. Ibid. [1:10:43].

37. Ibid. [1:10:54–1:11:03].

38. Ibid. [1:11:27–1:11:35].

39. Gottlieb, " 'Just Another Word for Jazz'," 177.

the political climate of 1968. Yet Gottlieb sees that overarching self-absorption as a deeper expression of Greaves's hope a countermovement will be sparked by the film's dynamics. If the film itself is oblivious to what matters, what will the audience do?

Gottlieb also notes that even the title, *Symbiopsychotaxiplasm: Take One*, is provisional and the film "ends with the promise of *Take Two*."[40] Greaves converted 130,000 feet of 16mm film (five hours worth), originally conceived as five movies, into what is now known as *Take One*. *Symbiopsychotaxiplasm* is a project that assumes evolution and improvement into the future. The sine wave intruding into the opening of the movie also returns at the film's end, and the final image is a close-up of actress Audrey Heningham, an African American female lead who will take center stage thirty-five years later in *Symbiopsychotaxiplasm: Take 2½*.

The question of audience responsibility with respect to a film seemingly oblivious to the customs and etiquette of professional filmmaking and disregarding of cultural sensitivities related to the dynamics of human sexuality, race, and class could be reformulated to address the disconnect between some forms of liturgical ceremony and the responsibility of its participants. In *Under the Gaze of the Bible*, Jean-Louis Chrétien writes that "Christian wisdom does not consist in applying rules, nor in confronting what happens with the lessons of a manual, but in making our existence as disengaged, as ductile as possible, so that it tends to be nothing but an Aeolian harp on which the Spirit can improvise, according to the needs of the moment and the exigencies of such an encounter." He goes on to say that "this suppleness is all-important, having nothing to do with compromise" but being rather a practical disposition that is crucial for bearing witness to the measureless humility and excessive love of God.[41] I do not have precise advice for liturgically minded viewers of *Symbiopsychotaxiplasm*. I do want to suggest, however, that the situational and reverse-psychology approach of Greaves may be a fruitful model for re-imagining the paleness of liturgical expressions in so

40. *Take 2½* eventually appeared in 2005, after *Take One* had been rediscovered by actor Steve Buscemi and redistributed as a result of efforts by Buscemi and director Steven Soderbergh.

41. Jean-Louis Chrétien, *Under the Gaze of the Bible*, trans. John Marson Dunaway (New York, NY: Fordham Univ. Press, 2015), 42.

many churches today and developing the suppleness that Chrétien sees as so critical for effective witness to divine humility and the love of God.

What if experiences of underwhelming liturgy were reconceived as moments of apophatic urging from God to transform what seems so disappointing? At the time of this writing, the United Methodist Church, of which I am an ordained minister, has celebrated its 50th anniversary. The half-century birthday of the denomination arrives on the heels of the 500th anniversary of the Reformation a year earlier, the 400th anniversary of the first Church of England parish in colonial America, the 230th anniversary of the American Methodist Episcopal Church, the 115th anniversary of the arrival of Korean Methodists, and it coincides with the 110th anniversary of the Church of the Nazarene. All of those selected and related traditions are now declining in the United States. The US population of United Methodists is half of what it was when the denomination formed half a century ago. While many factors have contributed to such ecclesial withering, including perhaps a recent church-wide vote against full inclusion of LGBTQIA+ neighbors, uninspiring liturgy cannot be dismissed from the list of possibilities.[42] Instead of merely lamenting or complaining about routine and institutionalized forms of worship that seem staid and benefit neither the interior nor the social witness of the congregations in which they are found, what actions could liturgical participants collectively produce to brighten the light of Christ in the world?

Liturgy that dissatisfies should rouse its "audience" or assembly toward collective courage capable of initiating liturgical renewal, not as a movement that leads to vital institutional reform but rather as a

---

42. Sociologist Mark Chaves is reserved about whether innovations in worship are capable of stemming the tide of church decline. For example, of the trend of increased informality in worship and its relationship to decline in worship involvement, Chaves writes that it is "neither here nor there regarding decline" (Mark Chaves, *American Religion: Contemporary Trends*, 2nd ed. [Princeton, NJ: Princeton Univ. Press, 2017], 34). But he does see the arts as a principal activity of congregational worship and a locus for understanding what congregations actually do and as a promising activity for grasping and perhaps strengthening their cultural reach. He writes, "Although many might wish it were otherwise, congregations facilitate art, and perhaps, on occasion, even beauty, more commonly and more intensively than they pursue either charity or justice" (Mark Chaves, *Congregations in America* [Cambridge, MA: Harvard Univ. Press, 2004], 201).

spontaneous situational take-over of liturgical proceedings within sanctuaries and other sacred environments that aim to rescue discrete moments from contributing to a generally withering enterprise.[43] How can participants of liturgy form diffuse cooperatives to improve upon worship practices underway, even if it means being ahead of the times? How can liturgical participants deepen imaginings of how to plan and lead practices of worship able to speak to current human predicaments, ones that more often go un-filmed but are just as strange and seemingly unintelligible as *Symbiopsychotaxiplasm*, such as the multiple dimensions and expressions of implicit bias, the prejudice of the minoritized, a persistently naïve understanding of human diversity by those in power (including the powerful who have heterogeneous identities), the dependence of "successful" ministry and theological education upon late capitalism, imprecise understandings of mental health, the deception of high-functioning addiction, the idolatry of family and nation and other invisible individual and community insecurities, the meanness of the elderly, genetic engineering that will continue to redefine terms such as "human" and "creator," and the uncanny neglect of a calling as basic as loving our enemies, especially within communities of faith?

I will not venture to provide answers here. The kind of renewal I am suggesting requires collective contemplation and a collective effort. The only problem is that in many congregations, the available "cast and crew" is often short on time, and also older and tired.[44] Reforming liturgy requires a capable collective.

Still, undertaking the creative work of converting collective frustration into more fruitful liturgy follows the liturgical tradition of public benefit that has resulted from liturgical performance historically. While Cecilia Gaposchkin, in *Invisible Weapons,* convincingly shows how liturgy shaped warfare such as crusading, and crusading fashioned prayers, historian Alden Moshammer persuasively suggests how the Nativity date calculated by fifth- and sixth-century monk Dionysius Exiguus, in

---

43. "Dissatisfy" here describes something like a feeling that the practices are without clear social benefit as a witness of divine love and grace.

44. The Pew Research Centre reports that the majority of Americans who attend weekly religious services are older than sixty-five. See Pew Research Center: Religion & Public Life, "Age Distribution," http://www.pewforum.org/religious-landscape-study/age-distribution/ (accessed 10 October 2018).

consultation with works by Julius Africanus, Panodorus of Alexandria, and the Armenian churches, led to the computation of shared celebrations of Easter and the advent of Common Era time, or *Anno Domini Nostri Jesu Christi*, and its BC and BCE corollaries.[45] In other words, liturgical ingenuity permanently changed the way we publicly mark time. In my home tradition, even though John Wesley sought to reform the Church of England as an Anglican priest and remained one until his death, disenchantment from laity with the ceremonial structure and nature of Anglican worship in large part led to the formation of Methodism in the United States and the United Kingdom. It may be too much to describe the Methodist movement as one of liturgical innovation, yet liturgical frustration certainly contributed to the drive for a new kind of church.

Liturgy has continued to benefit the public in sweeping ways since the time of Aristotle. It has become a responsibility shared by more than the wealthy. Recognizing the panoramic evolution of liturgical tradition, and the artistic merits of a film like *Symbiopsychotaxiplasm,* a portrait of revolution that did not happen, we might find ourselves open and brave enough to defy the status quo as Greaves did, or even improve rebellion like his, but with convictions rooted in faith instead of film. With savvy and subversion, we might even go so far as to spin liturgies with intolerable discomfort and absurdity. Then, parishioners and interested publics might revolt and do more than complain. They might demand and enact love of God and love of neighbor more radical than anything we have ever known or seen.

45. M. Cecilia Gaposchkin, *Invisible Weapons: Liturgy and the Making of Crusade Ideology* (Ithaca, NY: Cornell Univ. Press, 2017); Alden Moshammer, *The Easter Computus and the Origins of the Christian Era* (Oxford: Oxford Univ. Press, 2008).

List of Contributors

Teresa Berger is Professor of Liturgical Studies at the Yale Institute of Sacred Music and Yale Divinity School, where she also holds an appointment as the Thomas E. Golden Jr. Professor of Catholic Theology. Her most recent publication is @ *Worship: Liturgical Practices in Digital Worlds* (Routledge, 2018).

M. Jennifer Bloxam is the Herbert H. Lehman Professor of Music at Williams College and a past president of the Society for Christian Scholarship in Music. Her most recent publication is "Cantus and Cantus Firmi: Solving Puzzles in Three Fifteenth-Century Annunciation Masses," in the *Journal of the Alamire Foundation* 10 (2018).

Nicholas Denysenko is Emil and Elfriede Jochum Professor and Chair at Valparaiso University. His most recent publication is *The Orthodox Church in Ukraine: A Century of Separation* (Northern Illinois Univ. Press, 2018).

Margot E. Fassler is Keough-Hesburgh Professor of Music History and Liturgy at the University of Notre Dame, where she also directs the Program in Sacred Music. She is Tangeman Professor of Music History, Emerita, at Yale University. Fassler co-authored, with Jeffrey Hamburger, Eva Schlotheuber, and Susan Marti, *Liturgical Life and Latin Learning at Paradies bei Soest, 1300–1425*, 2 vols. (Aschendorff, 2016). Her book *Cosmos and Creation in Hildegard's Scivias* will be published by the State University of New York Press.

Joris Geldhof is Professor of Liturgical Studies and Sacramental Theology at the Faculty of Theology and Religious Studies of the Catholic

University of Leuven, Belgium. He is the editor of *Questions Liturgiques/ Studies in Liturgy* and was elected President of Societas Liturgica for 2017–2019. His most recent publication is *Liturgy and Secularism: Beyond the Divide* (Liturgical Press, 2018).

Bert Groen is Professor Emeritus of Liturgical Studies at the University of Graz, Austria, where he also held the UNESCO Chair for Intercultural and Interreligious Dialog in Southeast Europe. His most recent two books deal with the strained relations between the Greek writer Nikos Kazantzakis and the Orthodox tradition.

David Grumett is Senior Lecturer in Theology and Ethics in the University of Edinburgh, United Kingdom, and author of *Material Eucharist* (Oxford University Press, 2016).

Felicity Harley-McGowan is a Lecturer in Art History at Yale Divinity School. She is currently preparing a monograph on the origins of crucifixion iconography in late antiquity. Her most recent book publication is *Ernst Kitzinger and the Making of Medieval Art History*, a collection of essays edited with Henry Maguire and published in 2017 by the Warburg Institute.

Kevin W. Irwin is a Catholic priest of the archdiocese of New York who has taught at The Catholic University of America since 1985, where he also served as Dean of the School of Theology and Religious Studies. His most recent publication is the revision of *Context and Text: A Method for Liturgical Theology* (Liturgical Press, 2018).

Peter Jeffery holds the Michael P. Grace II Chair in Medieval Studies at the University of Notre Dame and is Scheide Professor of Music History Emeritus at Princeton University. A Benedictine Oblate of St. John's Abbey, Collegeville, Minnesota, he has many publications about Gregorian chant and the liturgical musics of Eastern Christianity.

Gerald C. Liu is Assistant Professor of Worship and Preaching at Princeton Theological School and an ordained United Methodist Elder of the Mississippi Annual Conference. His most recent publication is *Music and the Generosity of God* (Palgrave, 2017).

Mary E. McGann is Adjunct Associate Professor of Liturgical Studies at the Jesuit School of Theology, Berkeley, and a member of the Core Doctoral Faculty of the Graduate Theological Union. Her book *The Meal That Reconnects: Eucharistic Eating and the Global Food Crisis* is forthcoming from Liturgical Press.

Andrew McGowan is Dean of the Berkeley Divinity School and McFaddin Professor of Anglican Studies at Yale. He is author of *Ancient Christian Worship* (Baker, 2014).

Anathea Portier-Young is Associate Professor of Old Testament at Duke Divinity School. She recently co-edited the volume *Scripture and Justice: Catholic and Ecumenical Essays* (Lexington, 2018). Her current research focuses on embodiment in Old Testament prophetic literature.

Nathan J. Ristuccia teaches Latin at Rockbridge Academy and is the author of *Christianization and Commonwealth in Early Medieval Europe: A Ritual Interpretation* (Oxford, 2018).

Benjamin M. Stewart is Gordon A. Braatz Associate Professor of Worship and Director of Advanced Studies at the Lutheran School of Theology at Chicago. He is author of *A Watered Garden: Christian Worship and Earth's Ecology* (Augsburg Fortress, 2011).

Duco Vollebregt is a doctoral researcher of the Research Foundation – Flanders (FWO) at the Faculty of Theology and Religious Studies of the Catholic University of Leuven, Belgium. His research focuses on the symbolic and ritual use of night and light during the Easter Vigil, particularly in the sacramentaries of a variety of Latin liturgical traditions of the early Middle Ages.

Rowan Williams is the Master of Magdalene College Cambridge in the United Kingdom. He is the former Archbishop of Canterbury, and a distinguished author and poet. His most recent publication is *Christ the Heart of Creation* (Bloomsbury, 2018).

Index